A POPULAR GUIDE TO
GOVERNMENT PUBLICATIONS

A POPULAR GUIDE TO GOVERNMENT PUBLICATIONS

Compiled by W. Philip Leidy

FOURTH EDITION

COLUMBIA UNIVERSITY PRESS

New York   1976

Library of Congress Cataloging in Publication Data

Leidy, William Philip.
  A popular guide to government publications.

  1. United States—Government publications—Bibliography.   I.   Title.
Z1223.Z7L4   1976   [J83]   015'.73   76–17803
ISBN 0–231–04019–9

Columbia University Press
New York   Guildford, Surrey

Copyright 1953 © 1963, 1968, 1976 Columbia University Press
Fourth Edition 1976
Printed in the United States of America

To Carper W. Buckley,
former Superintendent of Documents

INTRODUCTION

THE FOURTH EDITION OF *A Popular Guide to Government Publications* contains several thousand titles selected from materials issued by various agencies of the United States government between 1967 and 1975. In the case of series or of titles that have perennial interest these dates have been exceeded in both directions. Series have been carried through the July, 1975, issue of the *Monthly Catalog of Government Publications*, which remains the source on which any study of government documents must be based. Some older titles, for example those of the Smithsonian Institution, have been carried along because they have secure and lasting interest. In the case of some multivolume works one or more numbers have gone out of print. They are not cited in the entry. A listing may include, for instance, numbers 1, 3, 4, 6, etc., without explanation in the entry.

It is probably safe to assume that about 100,000 publications appeared in the *Monthly Catalog* between the dates assigned for this edition. Of that total, a great number were produced in self-eliminating editions that were soon exhausted; some others are not mentioned here because their appeal was limited to special, normally small, groups of readers; still others were strictly topical, so that after a short time they became out of date. Among the groups of publications too specialized for any popular guide may be cited the translations issued by the Joint Publications Research Service—although occasionally even here something has popular appeal; something, say, that describes the activities or attitudes of a foreign power on a topical subject. A vast number of the publications of the National Aeronautics and Space Administration and the publications of the Engineers Corps of the Army are highly technical and limited in appeal. (Again, the compiler once saw a study by the Engineer Corps dealing with flood plain conditions in Bryan County, Georgia, that looked as though it might be interesting.) One more instance: the publications of the Tariff Commission. One cannot cozily curl up with something titled "Footwear for Men, Kosa Shoe Co., Inc., Auburn, Maine." And so on.

Usually, in the past, a single issue of the *Monthly Catalog* contained between 200 and 250 titles that might interest an average reader or an average public library. Hence the compiler probably scanned some 15,000 titles to come up with this edition. The compiler actually went through a far greater total of government publications. From the impressive total, he chose those that make up this edition.

In the years since the third edition of this *Guide* appeared, there have been some notable developments in government printing. For one thing, there appears to be a wider use of color, with a resulting improvement of format. This assertion is made with some reservation, because government printing has for many years been of a high order indeed. But it remains the compiler's impression that the documents are more "decorative" than they used to be.

For another thing, there seems to be an increasing use of series; this fact (if it is a fact) has made the citation of titles easier for the compiler. But a word of caution is in order:

series may have wide subject coverage. Use of the detailed and analytic Index is indicated.

For evidence of the expansion of subjects in government printing, the reader is referred to the Contents, where he may see many new subject headings. Among these are pollution, mental health, mental retardation, civil rights, consumer guides. None of these areas is entirely new to government departments and agencies; but it is certainly true that the number of works dealing with them has swelled greatly in the last decade.

If the reader, through this work, becomes more familiar with the range and quality of government publications, the compiler will consider his time in preparing this *Guide* well-spent.

ACKNOWLEDGMENTS

I AM GRATEFUL to Mr. John D. Moore, Editor in Chief of Columbia University Press, and to Mrs. Dorothy M. Swart for their patience and their help at every stage in the selection and arranging of titles in the book. I want also to express my appreciation to Donald M. Quaid of the Government Printing Office, and to T. Bedford Jeffries and his associates at the GPO, Patricia Cabbell, Diana Floyd, Sandra Owens, and Annie Vaughan. Others who have helped me in this work are Miss Mary F. Chapman, Special Research Technician, Inquiries Section of the GPO; Mr. Ronald A. Beaudrie, Head Reference Librarian, Dowling College; in the Department of Agriculture, Mr. James L. Judd, Assistant Chief, Inquiries and Distribution Section, and Mr. Frank Caflisch, now retired; and in the Department of Health, Education, and Welfare, Miss Phyllis E. Cromwell, Technical Information Specialist, National Health Planning Information Center. Special thanks are due also to Mrs. Juanita Hilgarth, for her thoughtful and exhaustive help in 1972–73. In West Islip the author is much indebted to Mr. Albert Tumbiolo and Mr. Edward B. Krapf, who good-naturedly drove him all over Suffolk County, Long Island, on the chase for Government documents.

CONTENTS

HOW TO USE THIS BOOK

THE FIRST THING TO DO in making use of this *Guide* is to look over the Contents, for the publications described herein are arranged under 119 topics. The sequence of listing publications under each heading or subheading is strictly alphabetical by title. If you do not find the subject or title that interests you under what appears to you to be the appropriate heading, turn to the Index, which is detailed and analytic.

Titles are cited as they appear on the title page of the publications, or in the *Monthly Catalog of Government Publications,* issued by the Government Printing Office. The usual bibliographic information follows citation of title: author, where known; issuing office; year of publication, where known; number of pages; note of illustrations, if any; and stock number.

When you request a title from the Government Printing Office give the title of the publication and its stock number. The stock number is particularly important in ordering a title available from the Office since it identifies your title exactly (no two different works have the same stock number).* When you cite the stock number of your title, you save the GPO a

* Some titles may carry a stock number although they are obtainable directly from an agency or department other than the GPO: This indicates that if the agency cannot fulfill an order from its limited supply, the item can be purchased from the GPO.

great deal of work. To learn the price and whether the item you want is currently available write to:

> Superintendent of Documents
> U.S. Government Printing Office
> Washington, D.C. 20402

The GPO is very much overworked in some seasons and may not reply immediately, but do not give up; government publications are worth a bit of waiting.

It is now common to see on the indices of publications issued by various agencies of the government the warning statement that prices cited are subject to change without notice. Changes in price are so frequent that it is not feasible to list them in this *Guide*. Despite the increases, government publications are still great bargains when compared to similar materials produced by commercial publishers. And, as of now, the GPO makes no charge for postage on books ordered.

It is also possible to buy certain government publications other than by writing to the Government Printing Office or to the government agencies. The GPO operates bookstores in nineteen cities where the most popular government publications are stocked. See Appendix B for a list of these.

Many publications of the GPO may be found in libraries, particularly in those designated as "depository" libraries. Depository libraries have copies of all government publications they wish to request for their collections. In many states there is a *regional* depository library that has a complete collection of government publications. A list of the depository libraries is presented in Appendix C. Finally, the addresses of departments and agencies from which material may be obtained free or purchased directly are listed in Appendix A.

A POPULAR GUIDE TO
GOVERNMENT PUBLICATIONS

AGING

Basic Concepts of Aging; a Programmed Manual. T. A. Rich and A. S. Gilmore. Admin. on Aging, 1972. 148 p. il. 017-062-00072-7
Detailed guide, intended for practical help to those working in gerontology. "The subject matter delves into most of the major aspects of the field . . . , hence, the user will be able to acquire a broad knowledge of the older population and the processes, problems, and challenges of aging." Unusual in format: facts and figures, and then a series of self-tests.

Development of the Rodent as a Model System of Aging. Vol. 1. D. C. Gibson, ed. Natl. Inst. of Child Health and Human Develop. [1972]. 92 p. il. 017-046-00010-1
It was learned some time ago that certain rodents age in ways closely related to human aging. Here it is suggested that closer work with such animals may clear up many of the puzzling problems of why we age at all—and how.

Employment Problems of Older Workers. R. L. Stein and others. Bur. of Labor Standards, Bull. 1721 (1971). 46 p. 029-001-00704-3
Prepared for the White House Conference on Aging. Eleven chapters include discussion of such factors as work experience, mobility, discrimination. Some programs of the Labor Department are outlined, and there are statistical tables.

Facts and Figures on Older Americans. Admin. on Aging, 1972–1973. Free from the Admin.
Seven numbers of this series were published. Some issues are punched for notebook entry. The issues cited are notable for valuable statistics about the older population. The compiler has not annotated all of the issues; general tone is covered in nos. 1 and 2.

1. Measuring Adequacy of Income. H. B. Brotman. 1972. 6 p.
   How an adequate income is estimated; for the aged, the standard of living in "quantifiable terms." Some statistics on what the income *actually* is.
2. Older Population Revisited; First Results of the 1970 Census. H. Brotman. 1972. 9 p.
   Statistics show, among other things, that those over 65 increased in numbers more rapidly than the remaining population in the decade 1960–70. And those over 75 increased more rapidly than those 65-74!
4. Federal Outlays in Aging, Fiscal Years 1967–72. H. B. Brotman. 1972. 9 p.
5. An Overview. H. B. Brotman. 1972. 10 p.
6. State Trends, 1950–70. H. B. Brotman and B. S. Williams. [1973]. [24] p. il.
7. Income and Poverty in 1972—Advance Report. H. B. Brotman and B. S. Williams. [1973]. 10 p.

Fitness Challenge in Later Years; an Exercise Program for Older Americans. Admin. on Aging [1968]; repr. 1972. 28 p. il.

                                                    017-062-00009-3
Prepared by the President's Council on Physical Fitness and Sports and the Administration on Aging, this engaging booklet bristles with ideas for making the latter part of one's life active and happy. Includes exercises for keeping fit.

Handle Yourself with Care; Accident Prevention for Older Americans. [D. J. Lewis]. Admin. on Aging [1969]. [20] p. il.

                                                    017-062-00011-5
How the elderly can avoid accidents by exercising simple precautions.

Human Aging. I: Biological and Behavioral Study. J. E. Birren and others, eds. Natl. Inst. of Mental Health, 1971. 320 p. Purchase from the Inst.
Fifteen major chapters and one summary. The entire study is most

highly recommended. The papers deal with physiological, mental, sensory effects; psychiatric, social . . .

Human Aging. II: an Eleven Year Followup; Biochemical and Behavioral Study. S. Granick and R. D. Patterson, eds. Natl. Inst. of Mental Health, 1971; repr. 1974. 144 p. Purchase from the Inst.
Ten percent of our population are 65 and over, and of these only about 5 percent live in institutions. This study is concerned with a *positive* approach to the utilization of the abilities of the remaining 95 percent of our aging.

Legal Problems Affecting Older Americans; a Working Paper. The Senate, 1970. 60 p.   052-070-00788-5
Prepared for the Special Committee on Aging. ". . . identification of legal issues affecting the elderly poor and the development of solutions," including housing and health care.

Let's End Isolation. Admin. on Aging [1971]. 46 p. il.
                                                017-062-00041-7
The American elderly are often neglected in a way that puzzles those from other cultures. This is an appeal to remember what the older American has contributed to us, and to make him a more active member of society.

More Words on Aging . . . Supplement May, 1971. Admin. on Aging, 1971. 107 p.   017-062-00040-9
". . . a bibliography of selected 1968–70 references." Several hundred included.

Multiple Hazards of Age and Race; the Situation of Aged Blacks in the United States. The Senate, Special Comm. on Aging, Senate Rept. on Public Bills 92-450 (1971). 63 p. Free from the Senate Document Room.   052-070-01174-2

New Facts about Older Americans. Admin. on Aging [1973]. [12] p. il.   017-062-00081-6

With each advancing year, we learn more and more that age does not necessarily mean crippling and complete curtailment.

Nutrition and Aging; a Selected Annotated Bibliography, 1964–72.
M. D. Simko and K. Colitz, eds. Admin. on Aging, 1973. [42] p.

017-062-00080-8

The nature of aging; nutritional statistics; metabolism and nutritional research; meal-delivery systems.

Nutrition and the Elderly: Hearings before the Select Committee on Nutrition and Human Needs. The Senate, 1973–74. 2 parts.
A study of the nutritional needs of the "nation's 20 million elderly. . . . A first step in ending the cycle of malnutrition and isolation that has led far too often to costly and unnecessary institutionalization." The Administration's attitude on certain Congressional suggestions is examined. Separate parts are these (with the year of the inquiry indicated in each case):

1. Feeding the Elderly. 1973. 164 p.   052-070-01969-7
2. Elderly Americans' Nutritional Needs. 1974. [165-338] p.
052-070-02331-7

Older Americans: Special Handling Required. M. B. Tiven. Dept. of Housing and Urban Develop., 1971. 118 p. Free from the Dept.
Report of the National Council on Aging. A "result of the many requirements for basic information on the problems of older people. It identifies and discusses crucial issues . . . in all areas of life." A very fine book.

Partnership for Older Americans. Admin. on Aging [1973]. [19] p. il.
017-062-00075-1
Our aging population as an active part of our life; helping them make the contribution that only experience and age can provide.

Problems of the Aging. House of Representatives [1972]. 6 parts. Free from the House Document Room.
A study of the Government Operations Committee. Very thorough

work, containing many articles and data on every aspect of the problems of aging. Difficult to read, unfortunately, because of the small type. In addition, be warned that discussion is extremely detailed. But every serious student of aging, and every library, should have this group. It is exactly the sort of document that never gets the full attention it deserves. The single parts are as follows:

1. 453 p. il.
2. [455-637] p. il.
3. [639-826] p. il.
4. [827-1016] p.
5. [1017-1628] p. il.
6. [1629-1852] p.

Research on the Mental Health of the Aging. T. E. Andersen. Natl. Inst. of Mental Health, 1972. 74 p.   017-024-00251-8
Very thorough bibliographic guide (annotated) to the literature in four broad areas.

Space Benefits and Older Citizens. Natl. Aeron. and Space Admin. [1972]. [6] p. il. Free from the Admin.
Benefits from research in medicine, fire safety, building construction, and other fields that have applications to the problems of old age.

Transportation and the Aging; Selected Issues, Based on the Proceedings of an Interdisciplinary Workshop on Transportation of the Aging, Washington, D.C., May 24–26, 1970. E. J. Cantill and others, eds. Admin. on Aging [1971]. 208 p. il.   017-062-00042-5
". . . the first systematic effort to accumulate a body of information on the later phases of life and [to] analyze the nation's twenty million Americans over 65." Twenty-five essays on the questions involved, and suggested means of dealing with some of them.

Words on Aging; a Bibliography of Selected, Annotated References. D. M. Jones, comp. Admin. on Aging [1970]. 190 p.
                                                017-062-00036-1
Includes hundreds of titles on the processes and economic aspects of

aging; health and medical care; social relationships and adjustment; and services available. Many of the citations are briefly annotated.

COMMUNITY SERVICES, INCLUDING INSTITUTIONAL CARE

Community Planning for the Elderly. M. Powell and T. O. Byerts, eds. Dept. of Housing and Urban Develop., 1973. 59 p. Free from the Dept.

Guidelines for a Telephone Reassurance Service. V. Rogers. Admin. on Aging [1974]. 23 p.   017-062-00043-3
A report by the Institute of Gerontology, University of Michigan, in conjunction with Wayne State University, Ann Arbor.

Information and Referral Services; Reaching Out. M. Cushing and N. Long. Admin. on Aging, 1973. 49 p. Free from the Admin.
                    017-062-00087-5
How outreach workers can work in a community to establish useful services—"to offer community services to the people who need them." Primarily for the trained worker; certainly, however, of great value to all who wish to band together to help the aged. Suggested programs and approaches.

Institutional Long-Term Care and Alternatives; American University Report. F. Atelsek and others. Med. Serv. Admin., 1972. 2 parts. Free from the Admin.
"From first to last a program . . . cooperative . . . in both spirit and accomplishment." A project such as this is for the professional man and attendant, but of interest to the layman also. Status quo and improvements are discussed in detail. Many practical examples and programs are cited.

　1. Current Activities. 204 p.
　2. Proposals for Long-Term Care Alternatives. [198] p.

Management of Housing for the Elderly. Dept. of Housing and Urban Develop., Guide HM G 7460.3 [1972]. [76] p. il. Free from the Dept.
How to make the elderly feel at home in strange surroundings where, so often, things serve only to remind them that they *are* elderly.

Mental Health; Principles and Training Techniques in Nursing Home Care; Materials Developed for National Conference, Bridging Continuing Education and Mental Health in Long-Term Institutional Care for the Elderly. Natl. Inst. of Mental Health [1972]. 95 p.
017-024-00276-3
Examines mental health techniques and principles in caring for the aged in institutions.

Social Work Guide for Long-Term Care Facilities. E. M. Brody and others. Natl. Inst. of Mental Health [1974]. 216 p.
017-024-00323-9
The "overall goal is to improve services to institutionalized older people and their families: through the use of social work knowledge and skill." The types of services, and implementing them for individuals, groups, and organizations.

To Find the Way to Opportunities and Services for Older Americans. Admin. on Aging, 1975. 46 p.   017-062-00091-3
Every senior citizen and/or his spouse should own a copy of this. In general terms, it discusses benefits for older Americans in many areas—income and pensions, health, housing, nutrition, transportation, and so on. The booklet tells how to go about getting results, with advice to "go to the top" when necessary. Although there is no detailed directory, there is general advice on *where* to go for help in voluntary and governmental agencies.

Working with Older People; a Guide to Practice. Public Health Serv. and Community Health Serv., 1972. 4 vols. il.
Thorough study of the problems of the aging. (By the year 2000

there will be about 22,000,000 older persons in the United States.) The citation of these volumes is something of a bibliographic nightmare; the editor of only one volume is cited, and apparently the entire work was done in cooperation with the Projects Division of the Gerontological Society. The first volume appeared in 1969; but the entire set was revised and reissued in 1972.

2. Biological, Psychological, and Sociological Aspects of Aging ..." 1972. 51 p.   017-026-00003-8
"Prepared from materials developed by the Projects Division, Gerontological Society," and "devoted to the basic sciences most directly related to the process of aging and the aged individual."

3. Aging Person: Needs and Services. 90 p.   017-026-00009-7
". . . deals with many facets of social welfare as these relate to the health status of the aged."

4. Clinical Aspects of Aging. A. B. Chinn, ed. 388 p.

017-026-00011-9
". . . is written by specialists for the general practitioner, and is composed of three sections: diseases and disorders . . . ; clinical procedures . . . ; and aspects of special interest to allied health professions."

AGRICULTURE

In the third edition of this *Guide,* the compiler remarked on the difficulty of proper placement of Department of Agriculture publications because there are so many of them. The situation has not radically improved. The heading "Agriculture" as such is surely almost meaningless. Below, therefore, are cited only the most general works on the subject. For specific areas, the reader is referred to the index.

Agriculture USA. Dept. of Agr., 1974. [14] p. il. Free from the Dept.
"American agriculture has advanced more in the past 50 years than

in all the prior years in our history." We now have, however, fewer than three million farms. This booklet is a brief recital of their contributions to every aspect of our lives.

Agriculture in the United States and the Soviet Union. F. Pope, Jr., and others. Economic Research Serv., Foreign Agr. Econ. Rept. 92 (1973). 16 p. il. Free from the Serv.
Comparative tables show "acreage, yields, and production of grain, output of other agricultural crops, livestock numbers, livestock product output, selected agricultural inputs, and agricultural trade of the two countries."

Background on U.S. Agriculture. Dept. of Agr., Leaflet 491 (1972). Folder.   001-000-02462-1
Facts and figures in easy dosage.

Communities of Tomorrow; Agriculture/2000. Dept. of Agr. [1967]. 32 p. il. Free from the Dept.
"For too many years too many have crowded themselves into central cities. . . . As a result, our metropolitan areas have more people and problems than they can cope with. At the same time, many villages, towns, and their surrounding countryside are being drained of people and economic vigor." A new solution is found here: a community of towns that will combine rural and urban advantages. Lovely photos explain the plan.

Contours of Change; Yearbook of Agriculture, 1970. Dept. of Agr., 1970. 366 p. il.   001-000-01053-1
The "relevance" of rural America to our hopes and aspirations. The "Agricultural Revolution" (21 essays); "Country and City—One Nation" (16 essays); "New Role in World Agriculture" (14 essays); "A Look into the Future" (8 essays). A landmark, even in an extraordinary series.

Look of Our Land; Airphoto Atlas of Rural United States: East and South. S. Baker and H. W. Dill, Jr. Dept. of Agr., Agr. Handbook 406 (1971). 99 p. il.   001-000-01279-7

This, and the following three titles, shows our land as seen from the air.

Look of Our Land; Airphoto Atlas of Rural United States: Far West. S. Baker and H. W. Dill, Jr. Dept. of Agr., Agr. Handbook 372 [1970]. 48 p. il.   001-000-00755-6

Look of Our Land; Airphoto Atlas of Rural United States: Mountains and Deserts. S. Baker and H. W. Dill, Jr. Dept. of Agr., Agr. Handbook 409 (1971). 68 p. il.   001-000-01332-7

Look of Our Land; Airphoto Atlas of Rural United States: Plains and Prairies. S. Baker and H. W. Dill, Jr. Dept. of Agr., Agr. Handbook 419 (1971). 84 p. il.   001-000-01473-1

Our 31,000 Largest Farms. R. Nikolitch. Dept. of Agr., Agr. Econ. Rept. 175 (1970). 64 p. il.   001-019-00094-5
These are the largest farms in the agricultural economy. Even so, they form a surprisingly small percentage of our total land used for agricultural purposes.

ALCOHOL AND ALCOHOLISM

There have been, within the last three or four years, a great number of studies of the problem of alcoholism; the recent rise in adolescent drinking has emphasized the urgency of understanding the problem and its solution.

Alcohol and Alcoholism: Problems, Programs and Progress. Natl. Inst. of Mental Health, 1972. 42 p.   017-024-00240-2
Exceptionally perceptive study of alcoholism in the context of the "Age of Escape." Origins of alcoholism; diagnosis, treatment; how the federal programs help.

Alcohol and the Criminal Justice System; Challenge and Response. H. Erskine. Dept. of Justice, 1972. 30 p. Free from the Dept.

An attempt to "bring together information that might be useful to criminal justice personnel in planning programs and research in alcohol abuse."

Alcohol and Drugs; an Annotated Bibliography. Natl. Inst. of Mental Health, 1972. [32] p. Purchase from the Inst.
Listing primarily dealing with the question: alcoholism and drug addiction—one problem or two? Forty-six papers abstracted in detail.

Alcohol and Health; First Special Report to the U.S. Congress . . . from the Secretary of Health, Education, and Welfare. S. S. Rosenberg and others, eds. Natl. Inst. of Mental Health [1971]. 121 p. il.
017-024-00193-7
Eight chapters deal with ethanol (the basic substance in alcoholic beverages); extent and patterns of use and abuse of alcohol; alcohol and the central nervous system; alcohol-related illnesses; theories as to cause, treatment; legal questions involved; research needs, and future directions such research may take.

Alcoholism Treatment & Rehabilitation; Selected Abstracts. Natl. Inst. of Mental Health, 1972. 292 p.   017-024-00239-9
"For use of personnel directly engaged in treatment, rehabilitation research, program planning, administration . . ." Coverage is worldwide, and earlier bibliographies have been used as substitutes for earlier citations, so that the total number of articles and other sources can be kept within reasonable limits. Books, articles, monographs—438 abstracts altogether.

Comprehensive Community Services for Alcoholics; Williamsburg Papers . . . Natl. Inst. of Mental Health, 1970. 68 p.
017-024-00051-5
The papers deal with community health approach to the problem, and the principles of data collection and retrieval.

Drinking Driver and the Courts. Natl. Highway Traffic Safety Admin.. [1973?] [12] p. il. Free from the Admin.
About one half of our auto crash fatalities and *two thirds* of homicides are alcohol-related.

Drinking Driver and the Police. Natl. Highway Traffic Safety Admin. [1973?]. [7] p. il. Free from the Admin.
"The car has become more deadly than the gun."

First Aid for the Drunken Driver Begins in Your Office. Natl. Highway Traffic Safety Admin. [1973]. 11 p. il. Free from the Admin. The problem drinker; some methods of testing the degree of his inebriety; how to develop helpful programs.

National Alcohol Countermeasures Program; New Steps for Combating Drunken Driving: Research; State and Community Action Programs; Alcohol Safety Action Projects. Dept. of Transportation, 1974. [12] p. il. Free from the Dept.
Some very general guidelines for developing effective activities.

National Institute on Alcohol Abuse and Alcoholism. Natl. Inst. on Alcohol Abuse and Alcoholism [1972]. 11 p. il. Free from the Inst. Its work, its research, and its hopes for the future.

Occupational Alcoholism: Some Problems and Some Solutions. Natl. Inst. of Mental Health [1973]. 15 p. Free from the Inst.
                                                        017-024-00278-0
Valuable to the alcoholic and to the clinician.

Problem Drinker and You. Natl. Highway Traffic Safety Admin., 1974. [14] p. Free from the Admin.
Such a drinker is a danger not only to himself, but to you and yours. This booklet gives you some sound advice.

Proceedings of the 2nd Annual Alcoholism Conference of the National Institute on Alcohol Abuse and Alcoholism . . . M. E. Chafetz, ed. Natl. Inst. of Mental Health [1973]. 247 p. il.   017-024-00341-7
The second annual meeting dealt with "psychological and social factors in drinking, treatment, and treatment evaluation." Essentially, the report is in two parts: the "psychological factors" deal with adolescent drinking and behavior; alcohol and human motivation; interpersonal and social contacts. The second part ("treatment")

deals with criteria of treatment evaluation and the treatment procedures. Some 20 lectures.

Proceedings of the Third Annual Alcoholism Conference of the National Institute on Alcohol Abuse and Alcoholism. M. E. Chafetz, ed. Natl. Inst. of Mental Health, 1974. 312 p. Purchase from the Inst. "Alcoholism: a Multilevel Problem; Treatment, Origin, and Management" was the subject of this conference, held in June, 1972. There are 23 papers on: psychological aspects; biomedical aspects; sociological implications; inheritance factors; treatment; planning the program; treatment for the individual and in the community; specialized problems and resources.

Recent Advances in Studies of Alcoholism; an Interdisciplinary Symposium . . . N. K. Mello and J. H. Mendelson, eds. Natl. Inst. of Mental Health [1971]. 920 p. il.   017-024-00143-1
The Symposium was held in June, 1970. The report consists of more than 30 papers, which treat advances in the biological, physiological, and rehabilitation aspects of alcohol research. They discuss, also, new techniques of treatment. It is emphasized that the last few years have seen a dramatic increase in the scope and depth of work on this problem.

A Selected Guide to Audio-visual Materials on Alcohol and Alcoholism. Natl. Clearinghouse on Alcohol Information, 1974. [36] p. il.
                    017-024-00376-0

Thinking about Drinking. Children's Bur. and Natl. Inst. of Mental Health [1968]. 31 p.   017-024-00187-2
"Prepared for young persons as a basis for discussions of attitudes about drinking. It reflects the latest findings on alcohol research." The handsome little booklet gives friendly advice to the teenager on drinking, including discussions of its personal and social effects. Nineteen questions are listed; you are supposed to answer "true" or "false" about yourself, and thus determine your real feelings about drinking.

Treating Alcoholism: the Illness, the Symptoms, the Treatment. Natl. Inst. on Alcohol Abuse and Alcoholism, 1974. 16 p. Free from the Inst. 017-024-00396-4
A broad, nontechnical treatment of every aspect of alcoholism and what may be done about it.

Young Americans, Drinking, Driving, Dying. Natl. Highway Traffic Safety Admin., n.d. [9] p. il. Free from the Admin.

ANTHROPOLOGY AND ARCHAEOLOGY

It is difficult for the nonanthropologist to be sure of the placement of a number of titles in this edition of this *Guide*. For aid in distinguishing anthropology as a study, the compiler has turned to the *Reader's Digest Great Encyclopedic Dictionary* (1967). Here the definition of "anthropology" runs: (1) "The science treating of the physical, social, material, and cultural development of man, his origin, evolution, geographic distribution, ethnology, and communal forms. (2) The detailed study of the customs, beliefs, folkways, etc., of an ethnic group, especially on a comparative basis."

Anthropological Papers. Natl. Park Serv., 1971–72.
Only two numbers have appeared so far, both interesting and informative.

1. Introduction to Middle Missouri Archeology. D. J. Lehmer. 1971. 206 p. il. 024-005-00238-3
   The story goes back to about 6000 B.C. (early hunting complexes), through foraging complexes (500 B.C. to about A.D. 1720); then horse tribes. Photos of sites, artifacts, etc. Very fine.
2. Like-a-Fishhook Village and Fort Berthold Garrison Reservoir, North Dakota. G. H. Smith. 1972. 196 p. il. 024-005-00237-5
   Occupied by tribes of Indians before some of the site became an American fort. Its history is thus doubly interesting. Drawings and photographs very fine.

Archeological Research Series. Natl. Park Serv., [1951]–74.
This series—one of the most interesting of National Park Service's
groups—is unfortunately out of print, with the exception of No. 10.
In common with all the other titles in the series, this is expertly—
and most readably—written, and beautifully illustrated. Archeological techniques are discussed in detail; evidence is studiously ap-
praised. This thoroughness need emphatically not discourage any
reader—particularly one who might be interested in looking into a
field possibly new to him. (Prior to No. 10, the series was published under this title. No. 10 is properly "Publications in Archeology.")

   10. Ruins Stabilization in the Southwestern United States. R. von
      S. Richert and R. G. Vivian. 1974. 158 p.   024-005-00534-0

Bibliography of Weather and Archeology. J. F. Griffiths and M. J.
Griffiths. Environ. Sci. Serv. Admin., ESSA Tech. Mem. EDSTM-9
(1969). 72 p. Purchase from the Admin.

Canyon de Chelly; the Story of Its Ruins and People. Z. A. Bradley.
Natl. Park Serv., 1973. 57 p. il.   024-005-00508-8
History of the aborigines who inhabited the site (and the ruins).
Beautiful book.

Civilizational Process. D. Ribeira; B. J. Meggers, tr. Smithsonian
Inst. 201 p. il. Purchase from the Inst.
Foreword by B. J. Meggers. "A study of the dynamics of cultural
change utilizing both historical and anthropological data. Considers
archaic societies; regional civilization; world civilizations; and universal civilization."

Comparison of the Formative Cultures in the Americas. J. A. Ford.
Smithsonian Inst. 211 p. Purchase from the Inst.   047-001-00090-1
"Did man create his culture out of innate capabilities responding to
needs and desires? Or is culture a superorganic phenomenon that
has evolved according to its own laws, with man's role that of a more

or less fortunate inheritor, depending on the time and place in which he chanced to live? These questions pose the basis for this important anthropological study . . ."

Design for Scientific Conservation of Antiquities. R. M. Organ. Smithsonian Inst. 497 p. il. Purchase from the Inst.
"A detailed manual describing how to design and equip a conservation unit and how to authenticate and preserve antiquities. Concerned primarily with the conservation of archeological objects, much of the information is equally relevant to graphic art."

Horse in Blackfoot Indian Culture. J. C. Ewers. Smithsonian Inst., 1955. 358 p. il. Purchase from the Inst.
"A detailed analysis of the impact of the horse on Plains Indian culture, particularly on the Blackfoot—a nomadic, buffalo-hunting tribe—with comparative data on the horse complex of other Plains cultures."

John Wesley Powell and the Anthropology of Canyon County. D. W. Fowler and others. Geol. Survey, Prof. Paper 670 (1969). 30 p. il.
024-001-00845-9
"John Wesley Powell's anthropological fieldwork, archeology of Canyon County, and extracts from Powell's notes on the origins, customs, practices, and beliefs of Indians of that area."

Man and Beast; Comparative Social Behavior. J. F. Eisenberg and W. S. Dillon, eds. Smithsonian Inst. 364 p. il. Purchase from the Inst.
". . . discussions relating to these four areas: the biological bases for social behavior; the basic mechanisms of social behavior in man and animals; man's uniqueness; man's control of himself. Prominent sociologists, anthropologists, and behaviorists . . . are contributors."

Mohave Ethnopsychiatry: the Psychic Disturbances of an Indian Tribe. G. Devereux. Smithsonian Inst. 586 p. il. Purchase from the Inst.
". . . describes the types of abnormal behavior found in a primitive

culture . . . from the point of view of both anthropology and psycho-
analysis, and suggests how this behavior may be understood in terms
of modern psychiatric development."

National Park Service Archeological Program. Natl. Park Serv.
[1969]. 10 p. il. Free from the Serv.
Explanation of the Service's four-part program to recover and preserve archeological remains.

North Alaskan Eskimo; a Study in Ecology and Society. R. F. Spencer. Smithsonian Inst. 477 p. il. Purchase from the Inst.
"A full and detailed account of the culture of the North Alaskan
Eskimo, with major emphasis on ways in which two different modes
of earning a livelihood—caribou hunting by inland peoples and whal-
ing by coastal Eskimos—represent ecological adaptations within the
framework of a common Eskimo culture."

People of Lerna: Analysis of a Prehistoric Aegean Population. J. L.
Angel. Smithsonian Inst. 160 p. il. Purchase from the Inst.
"A comprehensive, multi-disciplinary investigation of the people of
the Aegean island of Lerna from early neolithic to Roman times.
From a study of skeletal remains, Dr. Angel reconstructs racial
origin, physical characteristics, physical and social changes . . ."

Peoples and Cultures of Ancient Peru. L. G. Lumbreras; B. J.
Meggers, tr. Smithsonian Inst., 1974. 272 p. il. Purchase from the
Inst.
"A comprehensive survey of the peoples and cultures of the Andean
area extending from 21,000 B.C. to A.D. 1532. Maps, drawings, and
photographs show the location and characteristics of all the sites,
regional cultures, and empires discussed."

Preservation of Historical and Archeological Data; Hearings . . .
House of Representatives, 1972. 113 p. Free from the Comm.
Before the Subcommittee on National Parks and Recreation of the
House Committee on Interior and Insular Affairs.

Roots of Mankind. J. Napier. Smithsonian Inst. 231 p. il. Purchase from the Inst.

"A major review of the evolution of the primates. Concerned primarily with anatomical and paleontological evidence . . . directed to the nonspecialist reader."

ART

American Artist and Water Reclamation. Bur. of Reclamation [1973]. 73 p. il.   024-003-00080-9

Reproductions of the works in the collection of the Bureau of Reclamation. Some of the reproductions are colored, but they are not framable.

American Printmaking; the First 150 Years. W. J. Shadwell. Smithsonian Inst. 180 p. il. Purchase from the Inst.

"Early American prints from the years 1670 through 1820 are described and illustrated. Among the subjects included are portraits of prominent personalities, plans of towns, views of Revolutionary War battles, and political broadsides and cartoons."

Apes and Angels; the Irishman in Victorian Caricature. L. P. Curtis, Jr. Smithsonian Inst. 140 p. il. Purchase from the Inst.

". . . shows how the popular Victorian stereotypes of the Irishman in British political cartoons changed from a coarse but amusing peasant to a menacing anthropoid ape after the 1860's. The author traces this simianization of Irish facial features to popular scientific theories about physiognomy and the Darwinian debate about the origins of man . . ."

Application of Nuclear Technology to Art Identification Problems; 1st Annual Report. B. Keisch. Atomic Energy Comm., Research and Develop. Rept. NYO-3953-1 (1969). 48 p. il. Purchase from the Nuclear Regulatory Comm.

No amount of annotation can possibly convey the excitement of this and the following three titles. They are the story of how techniques resulting from nuclear science have been applied to every type of art object from pottery to statuary and what has been revealed. The illustrations carry some of what the awe of the first work must have been. The techniques have been used both to authenticate and to debunk works of art.

—— Report 2. Atomic Energy Comm., Research and Develop. Rept. NYO-3953-2 [1970]. 48 p. il. Purchase from the Nuclear Regulatory Comm.
—— 3rd Annual Rept. B. Keisch and H. H. Miller. Atomic Energy Comm., Research and Develop. Rept. NYO-3953-3 (1971). 52 p. il. Purchase from the Nuclear Regulatory Comm.
—— Final Report. B. Keisch and H. H. Miller. Atomic Energy Comm., Research and Develop. Rept. COO-3034-2 (1972). 89 p. il. Purchase from the Nuclear Regulatory Comm.

Archipenko; International Visionary. D. H. Karshan. Smithsonian Inst. 116 p. il. Purchase from the Inst.
"Reproductions of Archipenko's works are integrated with illustrations which document many important events in the artist's life. These are accompanied by a biographical commentary and presented in chronological order."

Art of Organic Forms. P. C. Ritterbush. Smithsonian Inst. 149 p. il. Purchase from the Inst.
"In this provocative, perceptive synthesis, the author examines the subtle relationship among Romantic esthetic ideas, biological discovery in the nineteenth century, and abstract art of the twentieth century. The idea of organic form is shown to be a powerful influence on the work of philosophers, artists, poets, and biologists over the past 150 years."

Chicago School of Architecture; Plan for Preserving Significant Remnant of America's Architectural Heritage. H. C. Miller. Natl. Park Serv., 1972. 38 p. il.   024-005-00498-0
From this Midwest city came a tremendous nineteenth- and twentieth-century impetus toward a new architecture. There is now

under way an attempt to preserve some of the more daring examples of such architects as Frank Lloyd Wright.

Dedication of the Bust of Constantino Brumidi, "Michelangelo of the United States Capitol." House of Representatives, 1968. 32 p. il. Purchase from the House Document Room.
Beautiful illustrations; although hardly Michelangelo.

Design and Color in Islamic Architecture: Afghanistan, Iran, Turkey. S. P. Seherr-Thoss. Smithsonian Inst. 321 p. il. Purchase from the Inst.
"A photographic study of the use of pattern and color in the architecture of the Iranian and Anatolian plateaux over the past 700 years."

Do It the Hard Way; Rube Goldberg and Modern Times. Natl. Museum [1970]. 32 p. il. Purchase from the Museum.
Hilarious remembrance of things past.

English Yellow Glazed Earthenware. J. J. Miller II. Smithsonian Inst., 1974. 192 p. il. Purchase from the Inst.
"Based on the Leon Collection in the Smithsonian, this study discusses what yellow glaze is, types of decorations used, and the various forms into which it was made in the late 18th and early 19th centuries."

Graphic Art of Mary Cassatt. A. D. Breeskin. Smithsonian Inst., 1967. 112 p. il. Purchase from the Inst.
One of America's finest artists, noted for her lovely portraits of mothers and children. Beautiful book.

H. Lyman Sayen. A. D. Breeskin. Natl. Collection of Fine Arts, 1974. 34 p. il.   047-003-00008-3

How to Look at Works of Art: the Search for Line. L. A. Bingham. Natl. Gallery of Art, 1949. 40 p. il. Purchase from the Gallery.
The first (and only surviving member) of the Gallery's *Handbooks*.

Some of the basic features of great (or other, for that matter) art, with particular emphasis on line and composition.

Lee Gatch, 1902–68. A. D. Breeskin. Natl. Gallery of Art, 1971. 64 p. il. Purchase from the Gallery.

Lilly Martin Spencer, 1822–1902; Joys of Sentiment. Natl. Collection of Fine Arts, 1973. 254 p. il. 047-003-00018-1

Masterpieces of Sculpture from the National Gallery of Art. Natl. Gallery of Art, 1949. 184 p. Purchase from the Gallery.
Many full-page gravure illustrations of 56 important pieces executed by artists, 1200–1900. Fine commentary by Charles Seymour, Jr.

New Dimensions for the Arts, 1971–72. Natl. Endowment for the Arts [1973]. 135 p. il. 036-000-00012-1
How the Government is aiding the arts. Important for the information it gives on locating the right source for your art project.

Paintings and Sculpture from the Samuel H. Kress Collection. Natl. Gallery of Art, 1959. 468 p. il. Purchase from the Gallery.
Foreword by John Walker. Six color plates and 433 pages of halftone illustrations, covering this collection of Italian, Spanish, Flemish, German, Dutch, and French paintings (and 79 pieces of European sculpture).

Performing Arts in 19th-Century America; Supplement to Traveling Exhibit. Library of Cong., 1972. [28] p. il. Free from the Library.
A charming, and amusing booklet, which stands quite adequately on its own merit, if only for its illustrations.

Prospects for the Past; a Study of Notable Architecture in Sheboygan Renewal Area—1972 . . . Dept. of Housing and Urban Develop., 1973. 73 p. il. 023-000-00218-3
Lovely photographs and drawings of past and preserved glories of the nineteenth century in Sheboygan, Wis.; and recommendations for saving what is architecturally worth saving.

Report and Studies in the History of Art. Natl. Gallery of Art [1969]. 235 p. il.   047-004-00001-2
Contains 10 scholarly studies, as well as a general report for the year.

Sculptures at Hoover Dam. Bur. of Reclamation, 1968. 20 p. il. Free from the Bur.
A part of this beautiful booklet is by the sculptor himself, Oskar J. W. Hansen. As he points out, the Hoover dam "represents the building genius of America in the same sense as the Pyramids represent that of ancient Egypt, the Acropolis that of classical Greece, the Colosseum that of Imperial Rome . . ."

A Standard of Excellence; Andrew W. Mellon Founds the National Gallery of Art at Washington, D.C. D. E. Finley. Smithsonian Inst. 200 p. il. Purchase from the Inst.
"This personal recollection by the National Gallery of Art's first Director tells of financier-businessman Mellon's efforts to establish a national gallery that would attract great art gifts. The growth of the collections, the planning for the magnificent building, and the Gallery's development through the early years make this an important historical document, as well as a revealing portrait of one of this country's great benefactors."

Sublimations of Leonardo da Vinci; with a Translation of the Codex Trivulzianus. R. S. Stites. Smithsonian Inst. 432 p. il. Purchase from the Inst.
P. B. Castiglione co-translated the *Codex*. "A major interpretation of Leonardo . . . utilizing both aesthetic evidence from his art, and psychoanalytic argument based principally on the word lists in Leonardo's *Codex Trivulzianus*. Including the first English translation of the *Codex*, this work advances Dr. Stites' original thesis that the word lists were an ingenious attempt at self-psychoanalysis."

Swiss Drawings; Masterpieces of Five Centuries. W. Hugelshofer. Smithsonian Inst., 1967. 176 p. il. Purchase from the Inst.

Catalog of an exhibition of drawings by 38 Swiss artists spanning five centuries from Holbein to Giacometti.

Track and Road; the American Trotting Horse. P. C. Welsh. Smithsonian Inst., 1967. 174 p. il. Purchase from the Inst.

"A visual record, 1820 to 1900, from the Harry T. Peters *America on Stone* Lithography Collection. A history of trotting as a sport in Victorian America, illustrated with lithographs depicting trotting horses."

Trade Goods; Study of Indian Chintz in the Collection of the Cooper-Hewitt Museum of Decorative Arts and Design. A. B. Beer. Smithsonian Inst., 1970. 133 p. il.   047-000-00095-5

The Museum is one of many parts of the Smithsonian. This beautifully illustrated book tells how the chintzes were made, how they formed articles of trade, and how they make up a most interesting chapter in the history of the decorative arts.

PUBLICATIONS OF THE FREER GALLERY OF ART

Publications of the Freer Gallery in Washington, D.C., are *not* publications of the Government Printing Office, and they must be ordered from the Freer Gallery of Art, Smithsonian Institution.

Note that the Gallery cites the weight of its publications. Postage and handling charges: under 2 pounds, 50¢; 2-5 pounds, 75¢; 6-10 pounds, $1.25. Foreign, first class, air mail, and special handling are extra. Payment in checks, money orders, and postal orders must be made payable to the Freer Gallery of Art.

The above information and most of the annotations of the Freer titles are taken from the 1973 Catalogue of Publications of the Gallery.

In one of the loveliest buildings in Washington, D.C., the Freer Gallery specializes in Eastern art. For art lovers: not to have visited the Gallery is to have led a truncated artistic existence.

Since the publication of the 1973 Catalogue, several of the Freer

titles have gone out of print. Two of these the compiler has nonethe-
less included, since they are worth seeing, whatever museum the
reader has to visit to see them.

Ancient Glass in the Freer Gallery of Art. R. Ettinghausen. 1962.
44 p. 99 figures; 2 in color. 1 lb.
". . . illustrations show examples of Ancient Egyptian, Roman,
Christian, and Chinese glass. There is an introduction, a description
of the object following each plate, and a bibliography."

Ars Orientalis; the Arts of Islam and the Near East. 1959–73.
Described as a "journal." The entire group is by experts, and they
are all sumptuously bound and illustrated. The numbers remaining
in print contain essays in German, French, and English on all phases
of Eastern art. (Brush up on your foreign languages. The group is
worth it.)

   III. 1959. 263 p. 137 collotype plates. 6 lbs.
   IV. 1961. 462 p. 151 collotype plates and text illustrations. 8 lbs.
    V. 1963. 354 p. 206 collotype plates and text illustrations. 7 lbs.
   VI. 1966. 247 p.   97 plates and text illustrations. 5 lbs.
  VII. 1968. 178 p.   81 plates and text illustrations. 4 lbs.
 VIII. 1970. 267 p. 130 plates and text illustrations. 6 lbs.
   IX. 1973. 156 p. 116 plates and text illustrations. 4 lbs.

Ceramics from the World of Islam. E. Atil. 1973. [230] p. 178 il.;
20 in color. 3 lbs.
Third in a series of exhibitions organized to celebrate the opening of
the Gallery. The 101 pieces in the exhibition "were executed in Iran,
Iraq, Syria, Egypt, Turkey, and Spain between the 6th and 19th
centuries. . . . they represent the diverse techniques, styles, and
regional development of the art of Islamic pottery." Available also
as a slide set and catalog.

Eugene and Agnes E. Meyer Memorial Exhibition. 1971. 77 p. 32
plates. 1 lb.
". . . a memorial exhibition for Eugene and Agnes E. Meyer. . . .

Thirty-six Chinese and Japanese objects included in the exhibit were selected . . ." Each object is illustrated and discussed.

Freer Gallery of Art. 1967. 16 p. il. 1 lb.
". . . a brief history of the Gallery, a biography of the founder, Charles L. Freer, a description of the collections, and an account of the research and service activities of the staff."

Freer Gallery of Art. 2 vols. 1971.
". . . a selection of Chinese and Japanese objects from the collection . . ." Each volume contains large plates in both color and black and white. Materials selected range from porcelains, jade, cloisonné, gold, silver, and bronze ritual vessels to paintings and Buddhist sculpture.

    I. China. 184 p. 131 plates. 6 lbs.
    II. Japan. 184 p. 128 plates. 6 lbs.

Hokusai; Paintings and Drawings in the Freer Gallery of Art. H. P. Stern. 1960. 38 p. 36 il. 1 lb.
". . . selected works by Hokusai (1760–1849) . . ." There is a "short account of Hokusai's life, and illustrations of some of his works . . ." Like practically every Freer title in this section, the titles cited were prepared for anniversaries of one kind or another.

Medieval Near Eastern Ceramics in the Freer Gallery of Art. H. Ettinghausen. 1960. 38 p. 40 figures. 1 lb.
Includes an introduction to ceramic art of the Islamic world, and illustrates and describes 34 major pieces from Iraq, Iran, Egypt, and Syria.

Occasional Papers. 1951–71.

Papers presumably issued *occasionally* by the Freer Gallery; some are "Occasional Papers" of the Smithsonian Institution. All cited here are purchasable from the Freer Gallery and all are superb.

Vol. I. 1951–67.

2. Paintings, Pastels, Drawings, Prints, and Copper Plates by and Attributed to American and European Artists, Together with a List of Original Whistleriana in the Freer Gallery . . ." 153 p. 30 plates. 2 lbs.

Artists are listed alphabetically, with their works.

4. James McNeill Whistler; a Biographical Outline Illustrated from the Collections of the Freer Gallery of Art. B. A. Stubbs. 29 p. 28 plates. (Repr. 1963.) 1 lb.

". . . concise and factual outline, illustrated by examples of Whistler's work in the Freer Gallery. Especially important is the information obtained from the more than 270 Whistler letters in the collection."

5. A Royal Head from Ancient Egypt. G. Steindorff. 1951. 30 p. 29 plates. 1 lb.

"On the basis of comparative analysis the author tentatively dates the carved diorite head of a youthful king wearing the crown of Upper Egypt in Dynasty VI."

Vol II. 1955–[1970].

1. Fourteenth-Century Blue-and-White; a Group of Chinese Porcelains in the Topkapu Sarayi Muzesi, Istanbul. J. A. Pope. [1970]. 85 p. 40 plates. 1 lb.

"Mostly assembled by the Ottoman Sultans in the 16th to the 18th century . . ." Dr. Pope "records the history of the Freer collections, discusses the characteristics of early blue-and-white wares, and identifies and describes the floral, faunal and miscellaneous motives in the decoration of these wares."

2. Abstracts of Technical Studies in Art and Archeology, 1943–1952. R. J. Gettens and B. M. Usilton, comps. 1955. 408 p. 2 lbs.

". . . 1,399 individual entries are abstracts of articles from international art, technical, fine arts, and archaeological journals and museum publications. . . . They deal mostly with artifacts and their materials, and range in approach from popular to highly technical."

Vol. III. 1958–67.

1. Lohans and a Bridge to Heaven, by Wen Fong. 1958. 64 p. 18 collotype plates. 1 lb.

"A detailed study of two Chinese hanging scrolls . . . part of a famous Sung Dynasty set of 100 scrolls depicting the Five Hundred Lohans . . ."

2. Calligraphers and Painters; a Treatise by Qadi Ahmad, Son of Mir-Munshi; Translated from the Persian by V. Minorsky. 1959. 223 p. 8 collotypes. 2 lbs.

"The Treatise was composed in 1596/7, about ten years after the *Manaqab i-Hunerveran* of Mustafa 'Ali Hashhadi. The two works clearly draw on the same general tradition. Qadi Ahmad used two other sources: a verse epistle on "Writing and the Ways of Teaching It," completed in 1514 . . . and an anthology of about 1530 by Sam Mirza, son of Shah Isma'il I, who had been an early patron of the father of Qadi Ahman. . . . The bibliographical references are particularly rich; and there is an index arranged under authors, geography, terms and persons."

3. Li Ti (a Study of the Chinese Painter Li Ti). R. Edwards. 1967. 50 p. 30 plates. 1 lb.

"Li Ti, a member of the Southern Sung Painting Academy at Hangchou, was active in the late 12th century."

Vol. IV. 1971.

1. Two Early Chinese Bronze Weapons with Meteoritic Iron Blades. R. J. Gettens and others. 1971. 77 p. 29 figures. 2 lbs.

". . . two metal weapons acquired by the Freer Gallery in 1934 . . . said to have been found in 1931 in Honan Province and believed to date from the early Chou Dynasty. . . . of interest . . . for the combination of two different metals, one common at the time of manufacture and the other presumably unknown in China; evidence that the two metals were joined by the casting-on method, a well-known technique of the Bronze Age in China, and evidence that the iron in both weapons is of meteoritic origin."

Oriental Studies. 1949–70.

Some of the titles cited exceed the time limits set for the fourth
edition of this *Guide*—but what a feeble excuse for not including
exquisite books describing wonderful art!

4. Shiraz Painting in the Sixteenth Century. G. D. Guest. 1949.
   70 p. 50 plates. 4 lbs.
   "The main part of the work deals with the miniatures contained
   in a manuscript of Nizami's *Khamsa,* which was written by the
   scribe Murshid al-Shirazi and finished in 955 H (A.D. 1548)."
5. Field of Stones. R. Edwards. 1962. 131 plates. 4 lbs.
   ". . . the cultural background against which the celebrated Ming
   dynasty painter Shen Chou (1427–1509), traditionally considered the founder of the Wu school, lived and worked." His
   work is organized into: early (before 1471); middle (1471–90);
   and late (1491–1509).
6. Armenian Manuscripts in the Freer Gallery of Art. S. der Ner-
   sessian. 1963. 131 p. 108 plates. 5 lbs.
   ". . . six Four Gospels manuscripts, a Psalter, and a Hymnal.
   Each manuscript is treated in detail and against the background
   of comparable manuscripts in other collections." The full Armenian text is given, as well as an otherwise unknown interpretation of the Canon Tables found in one of the manuscripts.
7. Freer Chinese Bronzes, Vol. I. J. A. Pope and others. 1967.
   638 p. 116 plates; 8 in color. 9 lbs.
   ". . . 122 Chinese ritual bronzes . . ."
——Vol. II. R. J. Gettens. 1969. 277 p. Figures (some in color), including numerous X-rays. 5 lbs.
   ". . . the results of the laboratory research, on which the Technical Observations in Vol. I were based, are combined and summarized in the form of separate essays on various aspects . . .
   of ancient bronzes. Among these are chemical composition,
   fabrication, metal structure, and corrosion products. Special emphasis is placed on X-ray examination, which reveals much new
   information on structure, assembly, and ancient and modern
   repairs."

8. Freer Indian Sculptures. A. Lippe. 1970. 54 p. 55 plates. 3 lbs. ". . . presents a detailed study of the small group of Indian sculptures, both Hindu and Buddhist, in the Freer Gallery. Each image is studied from the point of view of style and iconography as essential elements in the ultimate spiritual impact. Illustrations show related monuments in Western collections and from India."

Turkish Art of the Ottoman Period. E. Atil. 1973. 84 p. 25 color il. 1 lb.
"A select galaxy of Turkish objects. . . . Ottoman art, which reveals Eastern and Western features during its formative years, evolved as a unique and independent tradition by the 16th century. The manuscripts, bookbindings, illuminations, miniatures, pottery, tile, and jade on display represent both the early years and the classical period of this highly creative and original culture." Dr. Esin Atil is curator of Near Eastern Art in the Freer. "Each of the 25 objects in the exhibition is discussed in detail and reproduced in full color."

Ukiyo-e Painting. H. P. Stern. 1973. 319 p. 171 il.; 20 in color. Out of print.
". . . a comprehensive selection of ukiyo-e painting . . . fascinating genre paintings which represent the popular art of Japan, cover a span dating from the early seventeenth into the late nineteenth century. In ukiyo-e the people and pleasures of Edo period Japan are depicted." This title is available as a slide set and catalog. A word needs to be added about the full-color reproductions of any book from Freer: they are magnificent.

Whistler Peacock Room. 1972. 22 p. Color frontispiece and 8 plates. 1 lb.
". . . containing a brief description and history of the Peacock Room decorated by James McNeill Whistler. A discussion of the "Princess from the Land of Porcelain." There is also a selected bibliography.

REPRODUCTIONS

The American Soldier [Full Color Reproductions]. Army Dept.,
1964–69.
"To dramatize the story of the United States Army from 1781 to
1969, the Office of the Chief of Military History has issued a series
of 30 full-color reproductions showing the American fighting man at
various periods in the Nation's past. H. Charles McBarron, dean of
American military artists, is creator of the series. Legends describing
the paintings are included in each set." For some of the compiler's
comments, see the U.S. Air Force Lithography Series below.

> 1. 1964. 10 lithographs 9″ × 12.5″.   008-020-00226-7
> 2. 1965. 10 lithographs 9″ × 12.5″.   008-020-00227-5
> 3. 1969. 10 lithographs 9″ × 12.5″.   008-020-00225-9

**Angelo Rizzuto's New York: "In Little Old New York, by Anthony
Angel."** [Angel Rizzuto]. Library of Cong., 1972. [53] p. il. Free
from the Library.
More than 50 captivating photographs of a captivating city. The
photos are in themselves superb, and they capture so many phases of
life in "the city." Rizzuto's photographs, left to the Library of Congress, may number as many as 60,000. He died in 1967.

Boston Massacre, 1770; Engraved by Paul Revere. Library of Cong.,
Facsimile 4 [1970]. 4 p. il. Purchase from the Library.
Not quite Rembrandt; but spirited.

**Gutenberg Bible; First Page of Genesis from the Library of Congress
Copy in Facsimile.** Library of Cong., Facs. 2a (1962; repr. 1972).
[2] p. Purchase from the Library.
Reduced reproduction of two pages in the first great book printed in
the Western world (1450–55). There is a fascinating page of explanation; and the Latin text reproduced is lovely (if puzzling to
the non-pro).

Old Navy . . . Prints and Watercolors Reproduced from the Collection of Franklin Delano Roosevelt at Hyde Park. Natl. Archives and Records Serv. [1970]. Portfolios, 2 vols.
President Roosevelt was a notable naval historian. The two portfolios cited here are very fine and the prints suitable for framing. Vol. 1 has 10 prints 11" x 14" or 14" × 11"; vol. 2 has 10 more of the same size. The first volume contains paintings and drawings of our Navy up to 1815; the second carries us from 1816 to 1860.

Symbol of Our Nation (Bald Eagle). U.S. Fish and Wildlife Serv. [1966]. [4] p. il.   024-010-00002-3
Reproduction of a large colored painting by Bob Hines; suitable for framing.

U.S. Air Force Lithography Series. Dept. of the Air Force, 1968–74. A series of colored lithographs that "illustrates the many aspects of Air Force activities." The prints vary in size, but all are suitable for framing. They would (like all Army, Air Force, and Navy lithograph sets) make wonderful decorations for high school libraries, for private libraries and, especially, for boys' rooms. They are, of course, entirely worth keeping in their original portfolio form (each set comes in an envelope). The compiler cannot sufficiently iterate the very high quality of a great deal of combat art represented in these reproductions: many were made, of course, right at the scene. Set number 1 is now out of print.

2. 1968. 12 lithographs, each 17" × 22" or 22" × 17".
008-070-00276-1
3. 1968. 12 lithographs, each 17" × 22" or 22" × 17".
008-070-00277-9
4. 1968. 12 lithographs, each 17" × 22" or 22" × 17".
008-070-00278-7
5. 1969. 12 lithographs, each 17" × 22" or 22" × 17".
008-070-00279-5
6. 1969. 12 lithographs, each 17" × 22" or 22" × 17".
008 070-00280-9

7. 1969. 12 lithographs, each 17" × 22" or 22" × 17".
008-070-00281-7

8. 1969. 12 lithographs, each 17" × 22" or 22" × 17".
008-070-00282-5

9. 1969. 12 lithographs, each 17" × 22" or 22" × 17".
008-070-00283-3

10. 1969. 12 lithographs, each 8" × 10" or 10" × 8".
008-070-00274-4

11. 1970. 12 lithographs, each 17" × 22" or 22" × 17".
008-070-00289-2

12. 1970. 12 lithographs, each 17" × 22" or 22" × 17".
008-070-00274-4

13. 1970. 12 lithographs, each 17" × 22" or 22" × 17".
008-070-00284-1

14. 1970. 12 lithographs, each 8" × 10" or 10" × 8".
008-070-00290-6

15. 1971. 12 lithographs, each 17" × 22" or 22" × 17".
008-070-00303-1

16. 1971. 12 lithographs, each 8" × 10" or 10" × 8".
008-070-00308-2

17. 1971. 12 lithographs, each 9" × 12" or 12" × 9".
008-070-00309-1

22. 1974. 12 lithographs, each 17" × 22" or 22" × 17".
008-070-00345-7

Water and the West. Bur. of Reclamation, 1971.   024-003-00073-6
Full-color reproductions of 12 paintings commissioned for the Bureau's art collection; 16" × 20", and suitable for framing. Commentary and biographical notes of the artists included.

Wildlife Portrait Series. Bur. of Sport Fisheries and Wildlife [1969].
024-010-00190-9
Ten colored plates 14" × 17", suitable for framing. Reproductions of paintings by Bob Hines, justly famous for his wildlife art.

Wildlife Portraits; Series 2. [Bob Hines]. Bur. of Sport Fisheries and Wildlife, 1971. 10 plates.   024-010-00277-8
The color reproductions by the famous wildlife painter are 17" × 24".

ASTRONAUTICS AND SPACE SCIENCES

For the Benefit of All Mankind; a Survey of the Practical Returns from Space Investment; Report of the Committee on Science and Astronautics, House of Representatives, 92nd Congress, 1st Sess., 1971. P. P. Dickinson, comp. 81 p. Free from the House Document Room.   052-071-00332-1
"America's space program can and does stand on its own feet, justified in its own right as an heroic manifestation of all the evolutionary progress of mankind toward a higher and better life."

Remote Sensing Platforms. A. P. Colvocoresses. Geol. Survey, Circ. 693 (1974). 75 p. il. Free from the Survey.
"Typical vehicles which carry remote sensors into the atmosphere or beyond into space [are] described and illustrated, and their performance characteristics are listed." Very clear statement; should be popular even with interested school students.

Space, Environmental Vantage Point. Natl. Oceanic and Atmos. Admin., 1971. [37] p. il.   003-017-00259-4
Story of the satellites that have helped us to learn and (at least in some senses) describe "man's physical world—the interacting composite of earth, sun, and atmosphere, of oceans, and oceanic life. . . . Man has needed an environmental vantage point. He has found one in the cold vacuum of space."

Space Program Benefits; Hearings . . . The Senate, 1970. 379 p. il. Free from the Comm.
Expert testimony before the Senate Committee on Aeronautical and Space Sciences. Deals with impact on society, technology, meteorology, communications, management, the Government's science program, information-flow process. Examples are cited, and an analysis of future possibilities follows.

Steps to the Moon. Geol. Survey [1970]. 35 p. il.   024-001-00232-9
Immensely interesting and informative booklet, with excellent illus-

trations (drawings and photographs): story of how man has finally walked on the moon. "Man has crossed the threshold of space, and the technology he has developed to reach and explain the moon can be applied to the exploration of the more distant planets. Man now has within his grasp the capability to study in greater depth the entire solar system and thereby gain a better understanding of his home—the earth." (How many of us can stand this knowledge?)

Toward a Better Tomorrow with Aeronautical and Space Technology. The Senate, 1973. 199 p. il. 052-070-01959-0
Prepared for the Committee on Aeronautical and Space Sciences. Every aspect of the subject is covered, from industrial applications to medical applications. Thrilling book.

Vanguard; a History. C. McL. Green and M. Lomask. Smithsonian Inst. 309 p. il. Purchase from the Inst.
"A record of the origin, course of development, and results of the first American earth satellite."

NASA PUBLICATIONS

Apollo. R. E. Chappell. EP-100 (1974). Copyright by the Natl. Geo. Soc. [65] p. il. 033-000-00553-9
Stunning illustrations (in color, largely), tell the story of the various Apollo flights and their precedessors from the birth of NASA in October, 1958, to the early 1970s. Excellent text explains anything the pictures do not.

Current Knowledge of Other Planets. 1958–68. Special Publications. "Technological advances in the last decade have made it feasible to consider launching spacecraft to all the planets. . . . To maximize the returns from ambitious planetary missions, however, it is important that we continually examine all information available. For this reason the preparation of a series of handbooks was undertaken . . ." (The quoted material is by Dr. Oran W. Nicks, of NASA.) The group on the planets is most extraordinary; the full and detailed annotation that each of them deserves is not possible here. Each one contains a glossary and gives scores of references in addition to new technical data.

3029. Handbook of the Physical Properties of the Planet Venus. L. R. Koenig and others. 1967. 132 p. il.   033-000-00227-1
The planet nearest to the earth.

3031. Handbook of the Physical Properties of the Planet Jupiter. C. M. Michaux and others. 1967. 142 p. il.   033-000-00229-8
The largest planet in the solar system.

4202. Vanguard—a History. C. L. Green and M. Lomask. 1970. [309] p. il. Purchase from NASA.   033-000-00364-1
Preface by Charles A. Lindbergh. The "origins, course of development, and results of the first American satellite program . . . in easy language."

4401. NASA Sounding Rockets, 1958–68; a Historical Summary. W. R. Corliss. 1971. 158 p. il.   033-000-00414-1
"A first attempt at sketching the evolution and history . . ." Appendices give detailed tables of types, dates, performance, etc.

5045. Contamination Control Principles. H. D. Sivinski and others. 1967. 55 p. il. Purchase from NASA.
". . . a basic model contamination control in pharmaceutical, electronic, and other industries where ultracleanliness is important. This is a guidebook for managers, foremen, and technicians." Needs updating.

E[ducational] P[ublications]. 1968–73.
". . . designed to meet the needs of educators, students and the public. They present and explain goals and projects, and the advances in science and technology made by the National Aeronautics and Space Administration." (From "NASA Educational Publications," August, 1973.) In arranging the *EP*-group, the compiler has followed the three suggested divisions in this 1973 publication. He has also used a good many of that index's annotations. It should be noted that the index does not cite dates; the compiler has, therefore, been at particular pains to check and recheck his own dates for the series titles.

44. Space Resources for the High School Industrial Arts Resource Units. 1967. 178 p. il. 033-000-00145-2

The first of four curriculum guides developed by NASA. "Industrial arts has been defined as the study of tools, materials, processes, products, occupations, and related problems of America's industrial society. As such, the profession of industrial arts teaching necessarily concerns itself with those societal developments which have relevance to its area of study. America's space program is such a development." The actual use of this document is discussed here in more detail than in the other three of these guides.

46. Medical Benefits from Space Research. [1968]. 16 p. il.

033-000-00147-9

Contributions from improved techniques and applications of X-ray technology to the field of neurology. (NASA has published a great deal on "technology transfer.")

48. Aerospace Bibliography; 6th ed. 1972 [1973]. 116 p.

033-000-00460-5

". . . elementary and secondary school teachers and general adult readers" are the audiences appealed to here. The listing is an updated bibliography of books, references, periodicals and other educational materials related to space flight and space science. Very fine. Almost all citations are annotated.

50. Space Resources for Teachers: Biology, Including Suggestions for Classroom Activities and Laboratory Experiments. T. E. Lee and others. 1969. 236 p. il. 033-000-00149-5

". . . the purpose of this publication is to bring the high school biology teacher, and thus the student, into focus with respect to scientific advances in space biology. Biological research in the field of space sciences progresses so rapidly that printed material soon is outdated. . . . Each chapter introduces the teacher, and through him, the student, to a major topic of significance relative to the space effort today." It should be borne in mind that this group of *Educational Publications* are curriculum guides; and of a very high order indeed. They are intended to help the science teacher plan difficult lessons, prepare the experiments necessary to illustrate or prove them, and help the student draw the proper implications from results obtained.

57. Man in Space. D. A. Anderton. 1968 [1969]. 30 p. il.

033-000-00155-0

". . . from pre-Sputnik days . . . to the preparation for a manned lunar landing and return."

66. Apollo 8: Man Around the Moon. [1968]. 24 p. il.

033-000-00157-6

The feats of astronauts Borman, Lovell, and Anders are reported in full, with wonderful colored photographs.

68. Code Name Spider: Flight of Apollo 9. 1969. [17] p. il.

033-000-00158-4

Beautiful description of the craft, including a cross section and the customary color photographs.

71. "In This Decade . . .": Mission to the Moon. [1969]. 46 p. il.

033-000-00160-6

This "pre-launch" booklet describes the complex steps leading to a manned lunar landing. The many and varied areas of research and development conducted by NASA are illustrated.

73. First Lunar Landing as Told by the Astronauts. [1970]. 24 p. il.

033-000-00162-2

Astronauts Aldrin, Armstrong, and Collins in a postflight conference.

76. Apollo 13: "Houston, We've Got a Problem." [1970]. 26 p. il.

033-000-00165-7

Failure of an oxygen tank some 200,000 miles out, and how the problem was solved.

84. Satellites at Work. [In communications, meteorology, geodesy, navigation, air traffic control, and earth resources technology.] W. R. Corliss. [1971]. 28 p. il. 033-000-00405-2

Sufficient annotation to this booklet is the full title thereof.

85. Aeronautics. D. A. Anderton. [1971]. 24 p. il.

033-000-00325-1

One of the group "Space in the Seventies," which the compiler has not tried to indicate separately here. "The state of the art in NASA's aeronautical research program is summarized and is followed by a discussion of ongoing projects, including quieter aircraft and engines, sonic boom, vertical and short take-offs, trailing vortex, runway safety, general aviation, and operation beyond the speed of sound.

87. Space Resources for Teachers: Chemistry, Including Suggestions for Classroom Activities and Laboratory Experiments. 1971. 228 p. il.   033-000-00362-5
"This publication is composed of 10 units, each based on an area of space science and technology in which chemistry plays an important role. Each resource unit can be used independently of the others, and materials can be selected from within a unit. The materials range in difficulty from the junior high level of understanding to those that will appeal to the advanced student seeking challenging research activities. Thus, a chemistry instructor can choose materials of appropriate depth and breadth for his particular teaching situation."

90. Two Over Mars; Mariner VI and Mariner VII, Feb.–Aug., 1969. J. H. Wilson. [1971]. 40 p. il.   033-000-00351-0
". . . integrated introduction, in narrative form, technically valid but not burdened with detail . . ."

91. Apollo 14; Science at Fra Mauro. W. Froehlich. [1971]. 48 p. il.   033-000-00347-1
The story of man's third landing on the moon.

95. On the Moon with Apollo 16; Guidebook to Descartes Region. G. Simmons. 1972. 90 p. il.   033-000-00421-4
A "pre-launch" guidebook to Descartes Region. The plan for exploration of Descartes Region is described, with explanations of the scientific experiments.

96. Space Shuttle. [1972]. 8 p. il.   033-000-00459-1
A picture book that illustrates the spacecraft and its missions in full-color paintings by Robert McCall. The economy and versatility of the space shuttle program are clearly shown.

97. Apollo 16 at Descartes. W. Froehlich. [1972]. 32 p. il.

                                                         033-000-00449-4
The flight of Apollo 16 to Descartes Region of the moon shows how well scientists and engineers can work together to get the most out of lunar exploration. Illustrated in full color.

101. On the Moon with Apollo 17; Guidebook to Taurus-Littrow. G. Simmons. 1972. 111 p. il.   033-000-00470-2

The mission that took Apollo 17 astronauts to the Taurus-
Littrow region of the moon. Written by a most distinguished
scientist.

106. Information for Teachers, Including Classroom Activities; Skylab Study Project. [1972]. 40 p. il.   033-000-00477-0
Brief description of the Skylab Program and the NSTA-NASA
Skylab Student Project; including experiment selection process
for flight, experiment performance and summaries of each of
the 25 national winning student experiments. Includes related
classroom activities.

Skylab Experiments
Of this most interesting and informative group, seven have so far
been issued. The group is described as a "series of documents
[meant] to apprise the educational community" of the experiments
conducted on Skylab, and of the results obtained from these experiments. Purpose of the group is to inform high school teachers about
the scientific investigations, and to enable them to evaluate the educational benefits the program can provide. "Readers are asked to
evaluate [these] investigations in terms of the scientific subjects
taught in secondary schools." Most of the group contain excellent
glossaries and bibliographies; they are all illustrated with precise
and very good drawings. (In the listing below, full titles—with the
exception of Volume 1—have been abbreviated.) All of the titles
were prepared with the cooperation of the University of Colorado.

110. Skylab Experiments. Vol. 1. Physical Science, Solar Astronomy;
Information for Teachers, Including Suggestions on Relevance
to School Curricula. 1973. 63 p. il.   033-000-00510-5
"Basic subject of this volume is the solar astronomy program
conducted on Skylab. In addition to descriptions of the individual experiments and the principles involved in their performance, a brief description is included of the Sun and of the
energy characteristics associated with each zone."

111. —— Vol. 2. Remote Sensing of Earth Resources . . . 1973. 83
p. il.   033-000-00512-1
A discussion of the multitudinous benefits that result from
such an experiment as Skylab. In a secondary sense, this in-

formation can have an important relation to school curricula planning, particularly where there may be an information time lag of months and years. It is the intention of the Skylab program to attempt to reduce this time lag, by timely presentation—in magnificent format!—of information generated by Skylab discoveries. This is a most thought-provoking work. Covers the broad area of earth resources in which Skylab experiments will be performed.

112. —— Vol. 3. Materials Science . . . 1973. 49 p. il.

033-000-00528-8

". . . materials science and technology investigations . . ."

113. —— Vol. 4. Life Sciences . . . 1973. 89 p. il. 033-000-00527-0
"Covers a broad spectrum of scientific investigations . . . that have been designed to improve man's understanding of himself and his physiological functions and needs . . ." Sections on mineral and hormonal balance; hematology and immunology; cardiovascular status; energy expenditures; neurophysiology.

114. —— Vol. 5. Astronomy and Space Physics . . . 1973. 74 p. il.

033-000-00529-6

"Considers four categories of space research": (1) phenomena in the solar system; (2) stellar and energetic particles; (3) stellar and galactic astronomy; (4) self-induced environment surrounding the Skylab spacecraft.

115. —— Vol. 6. Mechanics . . . 1973. 27 p. il.   033-000-00530-0
Sections on mobility aids, mass-measurement devices, space fluid/crew disturbances.

116. —— Vol. 7. Living and Working in Space . . . 1973. 39 p. il.

033-000-00531-8

Human engineering; performance in a weightless environment; living in space.

Most Asked Questions about Space and Aeronautics. 1973. [7] p. Free from NASA.

Twenty-three good questions; twenty-three good answers. Why do we explore space? What benefits have we received? How does an astronaut go to the bathroom in space?

NASA Ames Research Center. [16] p. il. Purchase from NASA, Ames Research Center.

What goes on in one of NASA's field laboratories.

NASA and Energy. EP-121 [1974]. 15 p. il. 033-000-00567-9
NASA's role in finding and developing new resources.

NASA: National Aeronautics and Space Administration. [1971]. 12 p. il. 033-000-00462-1
How NASA is organized; its work; some of its accomplishments.

Profitable New Aerospace Technology with Potential Industrial Application; Testing Methods, and Techniques of Quality Control and Non-destructive Testing. Small Bus. Admin. and Natl. Aeron. and Space Admin. 28 p. il. Purchase from NASA.
An explanation of techniques developed by NASA in areas of physical inspection and internal flow detection that might be of use to industry. (For any ideas discussed here, neither the Small Business Administration nor NASA anticipates any patent claims.)

Space Benefits and Older Citizens. [1972]. [8] p. il. Free from NASA.
Brief account of what space research has done for older people; for example, how it has contributed to the solutions of certain illnesses of age.

Space Benefits: Safety. [1972]. [7]. p. Free from NASA.
Our "homes and working environments . . . automobiles, roads and bridges, and travel have all benefited from the same aerospace research that enabled men to journey to the moon." And the research —and the good results—go on.

Space Benefits Today and Tomorrow. [7] p. il. Purchase from NASA.
Benefits in communications; weather; navigation; astronomy; earth resources; oceanographic research. NASA works with the Department of Agriculture and with the Geological Survey to survey lands, improve crops, identify wildlife, and so on.

SPECIAL PUBLICATIONS
167. Significant Achievements in Space Science 1967. 1969. 558 p.

There are earlier reviews for 1966 and 1965. For purposes of the present *Guide* these are not cited; it should be added, also, that there is a review of the years 1958–64 available. For details on these, the reader is again referred to the excellent "NASA Special Publications Currently Available, Fall 1969" from which so many of the annotations in this section are taken. Unfortunately, this valuable, annotated guide has not been carried forward.

168. Exploring Space with a Camera. E. M. Cortwright, ed. 1968. 214 p. il.   033-000-00207-6
"From tens of thousands of pictures taken during the first 10 years of space exploration . . . the most historic and striking." Captions are by outstanding authorities and are so arranged "as to trace the sequence of developments." The moon and Mars are covered. A superb book.

179. Book of Mars. S. Glasstone. 1968. 315 p.   033-000-00211-4
". . . reviews centuries of studies of the red planet, explains its place in the solar system, and sets forth clearly what is known about its atmosphere, clouds, haze, and surface. [Glasstone] turns then to the theories concerning the origin of life, the formation of prebiological materials, and the possibility of finding life on Mars." A publication that justly won an important award as one of the Government's outstanding publications of the year.

242. Guide to Lunar Orbiter Photographs. T. P. Hansen. 1970. 125 p. il.   033-000-00326-9
". . . information on the location and coverage of each photograph." Not for the casual reader; highly technical.

246. Lunar Photographs from Apollos 8, 10, and 11. R. G. Musgrove, comp. 1971. 119 p. il.   033-000-00352-8
". . . information on the location and coverage of each photograph." Superb, of course; but see comment on previous entry.

249. Cosmic Gamma Rays. F. W. Stecker. 1971. 243 p. il.
                                                        033-000-00338-2

250. This Island Earth. O. W. Nicks, ed. 1970. 182 p.
                                                        033-000-00321-8
". . . concerned with our home planet, [taken] in perspective

with its neighbors." This magnificent book of colored photographs does just that, too: makes us modest.

263. Mariners 6 and 7 Pictures of Mars. S. A. Collins. 1971. 159 p. il. 033-000-00367-6

267. Physical Studies of Minor Planets. T. Gehrels, ed. 1971. 687 p. il. Purchase from NASA.

"The understanding of the origin and evolution of the solar system is one of the major scientific goals of space research. The important data in this respect are the physical and chemical properties of the solar system. Bodies of the size of the moon and planets have necessarily undergone substantial evolution in the last 4.5 billion years, and these evolutionary processes have altered much of the initial record of their formation." The publication is divided into three parts: Observation (23 essays); Origin of Asteroids (26 essays); and Possible Space Missions and future work (20 essays). This is obviously an immensely valuable work.

272. Apollo 14; Preliminary Science Report. 1971. 305 p. il.

033-000-00376-5

"Third manned lunar landing . . . outstanding characteristic of this landing when Antares came down to the rolling foothills of Fra Mauro, was the exceptionally rich harvest in lunar science that the mission achieved." Includes discussion of preliminary geologic investigations of the lunar landing site; soil mechanics experiments; passive and active seismic experiments, and many, many more subjects.

315. Apollo 16; Preliminary Science Report. 1972. il.

033-000-00481-8

"The Apollo 16 astronauts observed, and scientists studying material they collected have subsequently deduced, that this landing site differed surprisingly from earlier explorations." This is a profound study of the tests made on the flight—similar to those of Apollo 14; but again showing surprising differences in results.

ASTRONOMY

The compiler has cited several publications of the National Aeronautics and Space Administration here rather than under Aeronautics and Space Science because they seemed to be of more special
interest to those devoted to astronomy.

Atlas and Gazetteer of the Near Side of the Moon. G. L. Gutschew-
ski and others. Natl. Aeron. and Space Admin., SP 241 (1971). 538
p. il.   033-000-00320-0
Perfectly beautiful work: the illustrations are thrilling, indexing is
perfect, and there is a short history of lunar nomenclature.

Exploration of the Solar System. A. Henderson, Jr., and J. Grey, eds.
Natl. Aeron. and Space Admin., EP-122 (1974). 67 p. il.

033-000-00581-4
This is a most remarkable document, noteworthy for the divergent
opinions of experts in the area. The compiler quotes the Foreword:
"Many shades of viewpoints exist among the contributors to this
[review], the elected officers, and the membership of the AIAA
[American Institute of Aeronautics and Astronautics]. Accordingly,
we cannot expect universal agreement with every statement and conclusion. The broad comprehensive support it has received during the
review process indicates, however, that the final product constitutes
a fair consensus from a group of informed professionals." *Conclusions* is the first part: "The purpose of this Review is to outline the
potential achievements of solar system exploration and suggest a
course of action which will maximize the rewards to mankind. A
secondary purpose is to provide . . . a sourcebook of information on
the solar system and the technology being brought to bear for its
exploration." Part III, *Our Knowledge of the Solar System,* should
be particularly interesting to the astronomer of almost any age, which
is why this is cited under Astronomy. *Technology,* and *Strategy for
Solar System Exploration* follow. There is a fine glossary.

Large Magellanic Cloud. P. W. Hodge and F. W. Wright. Smithsonian Inst. 114 p.; 168 photographic charts. Purchase from the Inst. "The first atlas and catalog developed of this important galaxy. Star clusters, emission nebulae, and variable stars are recorded [on the] charts. An accompanying booklet includes reference tables, a bibliography, and a summary of current research." Boxed.

Mariner 9 Photographs of Mars. Natl. Aeron. and Space Admin. [1972]. 16 lithographs.   033-000-00445-1
Each is 11" × 8.5"; all are framable.

Moon as Viewed by Lunar Orbiter. L. J. Kosoffsky and F. El-Baz. Natl. Aeron. and Space Admin., SP 200 (1970). 152 p. il.
         033-000-00219-0
NASA's photographs and other illustrations are superb. Here are shots of a body that has intrigued men for centuries. "The initial step in detailed knowledge . . . occurred with the invention of the telescope. A larger step came with the advent of the space age."

Our Prodigal Sun. Natl. Aeron. and Space Admin., EP 118 [1974]. 13 p.   033-000-00569-5
"Nearly all energy available to us is or was created by the sun." Another of NASA's fine booklets, especially indicated for high school students.

Quasars, Pulsars, Black Holes . . . and HEAO's. Natl. Aeron. and Space Admin., EP-120 (1974). [21] p. il.   033-000-00542-3
Another NASA beauty; fine text and superb colored plates. "Recent discoveries of startling celestial objects by high-energy astronomy have led to revolutionary new theories about energy, matter, and the origin of the universe. So fundamental are these discoveries that they may well result in major revisions to the entire structure of physics. . . . Beginning in 1977, these objects and the universe will be surveyed by a new generation of large X-rays, gamma rays, and cosmic ray instruments carried on board by high-energy astronomy observatories [HEAO's] . . ."

Strategy for the Geologic Exploration of the Planets. M. H. Carr, ed. Geol. Survey, Cir. 640 (1970). 37 p. il. Free from the Survey.

The geology of the planets bears "directly on the basic aims of lunar and planetary exploration: determination of the origin and evolution of the solar system, determination of the origin and evolution of life; and clarification of the nature of the processes shaping man's terrestrial development." The purpose of this report is to suggest guides to the orderly exploration of the planets and the assignment of priorities to specific experiments. A series of fascinating papers by experts.

AVIATION AND AERONAUTICS

Airframe and Powerplant Mechanic Airframe Handbook. Flight Standards Serv., 1972. 538 p. il.   050-007-00174-6

Prepared to "familiarize student mechanics with airframe construction, repair theory . . . from a generalized point of view." Excellent instructional illustrations.

Basic Helicopter Handbook. Flight Standards Serv., 1973. 107 p. il.   050-011-00064-0

Begins with the theory of aerodynamics, as applied particularly to helicopter operation. There follows a general introduction to the flight manual. Then come some of the hazards, etc.

Flight to Grandmother's. Fed. Aviation Admin. [1969]. [40] p. il. Free from the Admin.

One hundred and fifteen steps and activities involved in flying. Freely adapted from a color filmstrip.

Pilot's Handbook of Aeronautical Knowledge. Flight Standards Serv., 1971. 207 p. il.   050-011-00051-8

All you need to know to become a certified pilot: principles of flight, weather factors, navigation, operation, instruments, performance checking; manual operation, computer; communications, and flight planning. With sample examinations.

Plane Sense; General Aviation Information. Fed. Aviation Admin., [1970]. 27 p. il. Free from the Admin.
"To acquaint the prospective pilot and aircraft owner with some fundamental information on the regulations for owning and operating an aircraft."

BEES AND BEEKEEPING

Analysis of Beekeeping Production Costs and Returns. C. Downes and T. Cleaver. Dept. of Agr., Prod. Research Rept. 151 [1973]. 13 p.   001-000-02921-5
The number of honey bee colonies has been declining for almost twenty years. Side activities may make beekeeping profitable, however. These activities are discussed here.

Bee Flies of the World; the Genera of the Family Bombyllidae. F. M. Hull. Smithsonian Inst. 700 p. il. Purchase from the Inst.
"Since the last major study concerning the world genera in 1912, there have been many new genera created, resulting in confusion about proper names and arrangement. This study, arranged according to present concepts, includes all the genera of the family and is invaluable to specialists and entomologists in general."

Beekeeping for Beginners. Dept. of Agr., Home and Garden Bull. 158 (1974). 12 p. il.   001-000-03216-0
Strains of bees desirable; equipment necessary; hives. Needs of the bees. Making of honey. Stings. Diseases and pests.

Beekeeping in the United States. S. E. McGregor. Dept. of Agr., Agr. Handbook 335 (1971). 147 p. il.   001-000-00728-9
". . . for the established beekeeper, the extension specialist, the teacher and those who desire to know more about bees." Exhaustive work; everything from the make-up of the hive to the plants bees prefer and diseases that afflict them.

Honey Bee. T. R. Wessel. Smithsonian Inst., Smithsonian Inform. Leaflet 482 [1971]. 15 p. il. Free from the Inst.

The family—with portraits; the colony, including diagrams of the famous "dance"; the hive. There is a short section on honey, wax, and pollination.

Instrumental Insemination of Queen Bees. O. Mackensen and K. W. Tucker. Dept. of Agr., Agr. Handbook 390 (1970). 28 p. il.

001-000-01139-1

A technique for controlling mating.

Protecting Honey Bees from Pesticides. Dept. of Agr., Leaflet 544 [1972]. 6 p. il.   001-000-02467-1

Simplified Pollen Trap for Use in Colonies of Honey Bees. E. R. Harp. Dept. of Agr., ARS-33-111 (1966). 4 p. il. Purchase from the Dept.

Thermology of Wintering Honey Bee Colonies. C. D. Owens. Dept. of Agr., Tech. Bull. 1428 [1971]. 32 p. il.   001-000-01295-9

Bees do not hibernate; they cling together for warmth, and there are casualties. This booklet tells how to help the bees keep warm and reduce the number of fatalities.

Using Honey Bees to Pollinate Crops. Dept. of Agr., Leaflet 549 [1968]. 6 p. il.   001-000-00242-2

Forage, fruit, and nut and other crops. Colony strength; field distribution.

BIRDS AND WATERFOWL

Attracting and Feeding Birds. T. W. Booth, Jr., and D. W. Ffitzer. Dept. of the Interior, Conservation Bull. 1 (1973) [1972]. [11] p. il.

024-010-00330-8

How to make birds welcome; what they like to eat.

Birds of Francis Marion National Forest. E. B. Chamberlain, comp. Forest Serv. [1968]. 32 p. il. Free from the Serv.

Bird Song; Acoustics and Physiology. C. H. Greenewalt. Smithsonian Inst. 194 p. il. Purchase from the Inst.
"A study which demonstrates that the physiology and acoustics of bird vocalization are unique in the animal kingdom. Two records of bird song in back pocket."

Birds of the Northern Appalachians. E. B. Chamberlain, comp. Forest Serv. [1968]. 36 p. il. Free from the Serv.

Birds of Snake Range, Humboldt National Forest (Ogden, Utah). Forest Serv. [1970]. [12] p. il. Free from the Serv.

Birds of the Southern Appalachians. E. B. Chamberlain, comp. Forest Serv. [1968]. 36 p. il. Free from the Serv.

Checklist of Birds of the Tennessee Valley. T. C. Welborn. Tennessee Valley Authority, 1974. 26 p. Free from the Authority.

Conservation Notes. Bur. of Sport Fisheries and Wildlife.
The numbers of this group devoted to birds are particularly fine for their illustrations.

    4. America's Upland Game Birds. 1971. [6] p. il. 024-010-00241-7
    8. Migration of Birds. 1971. [8] p. il.   024-010-00242-5

Conservation Plantings for the Northeast; Invite Birds to Your Home. W. R. Hamor. Dept. of Agr., PA 940 (1969). Folder.
                                    001-000-00622-3
Lovely folder, with enchanting plans for bird houses—such pretty little houses that they seem to deserve the best of interior decoration!

Diving Ducks. J. Sien and L. DeBates. Bur. of Sport Fisheries and Wildlife [1971]. [12] p. il.   024-010-00254-9

Fine illustrations of the *second* type of duck—the *first* is the dabbler or puddle duck!

Ducks at a Distance; a Waterfowl Identification Guide. B. Hines. Bur. of Sport Fisheries and Wildlife (1963). [23] p. il. by B. Hines.
024-010-00038-4
A wonderful guide, captivatingly illustrated by a celebrated artist of wildlife.

Foreign Game Leaflets. Bur. of Sport Fisheries and Wildlife, 1970–72. A very attractive group; all of four-page size and loose-leaf format. Each title has a handsome drawing of its subject bird and includes a great deal of information about it.

    8. Eastern Gray Partridges. G. Bump. 1970. il. 024-010-00201-8
  17. Western Gray or Hungarian Partridges. G. Bump. 1970. il.
                                               024-010-00248-0
  18. Kalif Pheasants. W. H. Bohl. 1971. il. 024-010-00260-3
  19. Spotted Tinamous. G. Bump. 1971. il. 024-010-00261-1
  20. Red-winged Tinamous. G. Bump. 1971. il. 024-010-00262-0
  21. White-winged Pheasants. W. H. Bohl. 1971. il.
                                               024-010-00263-8
  22. Imperial or Black-bellied Sandgrouse. W. H. Bohl. 1971. il.
                                               024-010-00264-6
  23. Rock Partridges. W. H. Bohl. 1971. il. 024-010-00265-4
  25. Black-necked Pheasants. G. Bump. 1972. il. 024-010-00321-9
  26. Erckel's Francolins. W. H. Bohl. 1972. il. 024-010-00322-7
  27. Snow Partridges. W. H. Bohl. 1972. il. 024-010-00320-1

Nesting Helps; a Birdhouse Guide. [W. Hailcourt]. Tenn. Valley Authority, 1974. [7] p. il. Free from the Division of Forestry, Fisheries, and Wildlife Development, TVA.
Apparently reproduced from W. Hailcourt's *Field Book of Nature and Conservation* (New York: Putnam, 1961). A delightful guide, complete with plans, to making your own birdhouses. Among other things, you learn that birds like weathered wood; so don't paint your birdhouse green or red!

A Paddling of Ducks. D. Ripley. Smithsonian Inst. 256 p. il. Purchase from the Inst.
"A personal account of the author's lifelong fascination with, and observation of, waterfowl." Wonderful illustrations by F. L. Laques.

Population Ecology of Migratory Birds; Papers from the Symposium Held at the Migratory Bird Populations Station, Laurel, Maryland, Oct. 9–11, 1969. Bur. of Sport Fisheries and Wildlife, Wildlife Research Rep. 2 (1972). 273 p. il. Free from the Bur.
Sponsored by the American Institute of Biological Sciences. A group of papers of a more detailed and learned order than other titles cited in this section.

Puddle Ducks. Bur. of Sport Fisheries and Wildlife [1970]. 12 p. il.
024-010-00209-3
An undistinguished name that includes some distinguished ducks.

LIFE HISTORIES OF NORTH AMERICAN BIRDS

Life Histories of North American Birds. A. C. Bent and others. [Natl. Museum]. 18 vols. Out of print, but see below.
The compiler of this *Guide* has adopted an unusual procedure in connection with this superb series. This is: to cite the republication of an entire group by a *private* publisher: Dover Publications, Inc. The "Life Histories" were originally published as *Bulletins* of the National Museum (Smithsonian Institution), and all have long been out of print. But this is a series that should not be allowed to die. It belongs, in its entirety, in every library, and in every bird fancier's collection.

In the listing of Dover reprints that follows, the compiler has made use of that publisher's brief descriptions of the fuller coverage of each volume. For the compiler's evaluation: the group will probably never again be equaled for detailed accounts of the life habits, range, calls, nesting habits, and so on, of hundreds of American birds. Interesting anecdotal material furnished by bird watchers all over the country has enlivened the text of each of the books. Again: no library or bird lover should be without the set.

Birds of Prey. 2 vols. il.

Hawks, owls, condors, vultures, kites, eagles, falcons, etc.

Blackbirds, Orioles, Tanagers, and Allies. 549 p. il.

Includes English sparrow, bobolink, meadowlark, grackle, red-wing, cowbird, etc.

Cardinals, Grosbeaks, Buntings, Towhees, Finches, Sparrows, and Their Allies. 1889 p. il. (Originally 3 vols.)

Full information on over 110 species of sparrows and juncos; the dickcissel, crossbills, pine siskin, etc.

Cuckoos, Goatsuckers, Hummingbirds and Their Allies. 2 vols. il.

Full information on over 110 fishers, swifts, and whippoorwills, etc.

Diving Birds. 239 p. il.

Grebes, auks, loons, puffins, murres, etc.

Flycatchers, Larks, Swallows, and Their Allies. 555 p. il.

Includes peewee, martin, kingbird, phoebe, etc.

Gallinaceous Birds. 490 p. il.

Quail, grouse, partridge, ptarmigan, pheasant, pigeon, dove, turkey, bobwhite, etc.

Gulls and Terns. 337 p. il.

Skua, jaeger, kittiwake, noddy also covered.

Jays, Crows, and Titmice. 495 p. il.

Covers magpies, jays, rooks, ravens, chickadees, bush tits, nutcrackers, verdins, etc.

Marsh Birds. 392 p. il.

Coots, bitterns, rails, crakes, cranes, herons, egrets, etc.

Nuthatches, Wrens, Thrashers, and Their Allies. 475 p. il.

Creepers, wren tits, dippers, mockingbirds, etc.

Petrels and Pelicans and Their Allies. 335 p. il.

Covers albatross, fulmar, shearwater, booby, cormorant, gannet, cahow, etc.

Shore Birds. 699 p. il.

Phalaropes, snipes, woodcocks, sandpipers, plovers, curlews, etc.

Thrushes, Kinglets, and Their Allies. 452 p. il.

Robins, veeries, bluebirds, gnatcatchers (all power to these birds!), etc.

Wagtails, Shrikes, Vireos, and Their Allies. 411 p. il.
Includes pipits, waxwings, starlings, etc.
Wild Fowl. 558 p. il.
Ducks, geese, swans, mergansers, teal, widgeon, eiders, smew, etc.
Wood Warblers. 2 vols. il.
58 species.
Woodpeckers. 334 p. il.
Includes sapsucker and flicker.

BOTANY

Aquatic and Wetland Plants of the Southwestern United States. D.
S. Correll and H. B. Correll. Environ. Protect. Agency, 1972. 1777
p. il.   055-001-01770-1
A very detailed botanical guide.

**First Book of Grasses; the Structure of Grasses Explained for Be-
ginners.** A. Chase. Smithsonian Inst., 1959. 127 p. il. Purchase from
the Inst.
"Of all plants grasses are the most important to man." A richly illustrated handbook that gives those with little or no knowledge of
botany "such an understanding of the structure of grasses as will
enable them to use manuals of botany and other technical works, to
the end that our native grasses may become better known and their
worth and beauty more fully appreciated."

Grass Varieties in the United States. A. A. Hanson. Dept. of Agr.,
Agr. Handbook 170 [1972]. 124 p.   001-000-02444-2
A detailed botanical guide; in the usual sense not a "popular" book
at all.

Guide to Medicinal Plant of Appalachia. A. Krochmal and others.
Dept. of Agr., Agr. Handbook 400 (1971). 291 p. il.
                                                      001-000-01261-4
Descriptions of the plants; collecting them; processing. Includes the
mints.

Lichen Handbook; a Guide to the Lichens of Eastern North America.
M. E. Hale, Jr. Smithsonian Inst., 1961. 178 p. il. Purchase from the
Inst.

Everything the amateur or the professional will want to know about
our fascinating lichens. A very detailed chapter on the chemistry of
the subject.

Manual of the Grasses of the United States. A. S. Hitchcock; rev. by
A. Chase. Dept. of Agr., Misc. Pub. 200 (1950) [1951]. 1051 p. il.

001-000-01386-6

Definitive botanical guide, including descriptions of all grasses
known to grow in the continental United States, excluding Alaska.
Scores of genera and hundreds of species, embracing food, forage,
range, and ornamental classes.

Typical Poisonous Plants. H. W. Youngken and J. S. Karas. Public
Health Serv., 1973. 23 p. il.   017-012-00177-7
Nineteen plants, with colored portraits, from amanita to yew. Anti-
dotes and first aid are given in detail.

CARPENTRY

"Carpentry" is used here in the limited sense of small bench or
hand work.

Bleaching Wood. Forest Serv., Research Note FPL-0165 (1967). [11]
p. Free from the Serv.
Practical hints for the do-it-yourselfer.

Forest Products Laboratory Natural Finish. Forest Serv., Research
Note FPL-046 (1972). 7 p. Purchase from the Serv.

How to Make a Laminated Diving Board. Forest Serv., Forest Products Lab., Research Note FPL-088 (1964). 3 p. Free from the Forest
Serv.

Nailing Dense Hardwoods. Forest Serv., Forest Products Research Lab., Lab Note FPL-037 (1964). 3 p. Free from the Serv.

Selection and Properties of Woodworking Glues. Forest Serv., Research Note FPL-0138 [1968]. 10 p. Purchase from the Serv.

Wood Finishing; Blistering, Peeling and Cracking of House Paints from Moisture. Forest Serv., Research Note FPL SO-0125 (1970). 7 p. Free from the Serv.

Wood Finishing; Water-repellent Preservatives. Forest Serv., Research Note FPL-0124 (1968). 7 p. il. Free from the Serv.

CHILD CARE

Bibliography on Early Childhood. Project Head Start, 1970. [36] p. Free from the Project.
Several hundred citations; unannotated. Books, pamphlets, and reprints included. Very useful in spite of those missing annotations.

Boys in Fatherless Families. E. Hertzog and C. E. Smith. Children's Bur., 1971. 120 p.   017-091-00168-5
"Conceived in rather simple terms: merely to inquire whether growing up in a fatherless family is likely to affect a child adversely in ways that would interfere with achieving his full potential." A very good bibliography is included.

Child Development; Day Care. Off. of Child Develop., 1971–74. 9 parts.
A group of useful, practical handbooks; realistic, representing the consensus of over 200 individuals who are either active in the field of day care or otherwise thoroughly acquainted with it. The booklets themselves deal with various aspects of such care, from the point of view both of the social worker and of the administrator.

1. Statement of Principles. [1971]. [12] p.   017-091-00160-0

3. Serving Preschool Children. 1974. 164 p.   017-091-00196-1
4. Serving School-Age Children. D. J. Cohen and others, eds. [1972]. 71 p. il.   017-091-00165-1
5. Staff Training. R. K. Parker and L. L. Dittmann, eds. [1971]. 38 p.   017-091-00163-4
7. Administration. M. S. Host and P. B. Heller. 1971 [1972]. 167 p.   017-091-00161-8
9. Family Day Care. 1973. 118 p.   017-091-00188-0

Day Care Facts. A. L. Hart and B. Rosenberg. Women's Bur., Pamph. 16 (1973). 16 p. Free from the Bur.   029-016-00011-9
With the need for child care likely to increase, the suggestions and ideas in this booklet should be very valuable. Some existing programs—public and private—are briefly discussed.

Fun in the Making. Off. of Child Develop. [1973]. [30] p. il.
    017-090-00011-9
Absolutely charming booklet on amusements for the young child, with wonderful illustrations.

Guide for Planning Food Service in Child Care Centers. Food and Nutrition Serv., FNS-63 (1971). 22 p. il.   001-024-00175-9
Basically, sees mealtimes as part of an active and rich day. Planning the meal; suggested menus; preparing the food; purchasing hints; sanitation—among others. For preschool child care centers.

—— Supplement. 1974. [2]p. il. Free from the Serv.

Psychoanalytic Study of the Child. [Abstracts]. Natl. Inst. of Mental Health, 1972. 225 +93 p.   017-024-00275-5
National Clearinghouse for Mental Health Information Abstracts. A "comprehensive compilation of all the papers which appeared in the first 25 years of [the journal] *The Psychoanalytic Study of the Child*." One of the founders of that journal was Dr. Anna Freud. These abstracts are not only very good, they are expertly indexed (whence the extra 93 pages). Something over 1,200 abstracts.

Rights of Children; Hearing . . . [Part 1]. The Senate, 1972. 230 p. Free from the Comm.
Hearing was before the Subcommittee on Children and Youth, Committee on Labor and Public Welfare. This part deals almost entirely with the sudden infant death syndrome. There are statements of expert witnesses, and a full discussion of the possible causes of the syndrome and ways of preventing it.

School Age Child Care; a Primer for Building Comprehensive Child Care Services. G. L. Hoffman. Community Services Admin. [1972]. 22 p. il.   017-061-00031-3
Needs of the child; types of facilities and programs needed; some very practical advice. Very good general hints; not a detailed guide.

Selected References on the Abused and Battered Child. Natl. Inst. of Mental Health [1972]. 11 p.   017-024-00329-8
Coverage is 1968–72, and there are some 600 references. Unannotated and *sans* index, but invaluable for a study of an increasing problem.

Stop, Look, and Listen: Children Ahead. N. Stirling. Project Head Start and Bur. of Child Serv. Programs [1972]. 40 p. il. Free from the Bur.
A play in the "Plays for Living" group shows how stopping to listen to others helps to work out some of our conflicts.

What's So Hard about Feeding Kids? Food and Nutrition Serv., FNS-68 [1972]. [8] p. il. Free from the Serv.   001-024-00169-4

When Your Child First Goes Off to School. B. S. Brown. Natl. Inst. of Mental Health [1973]. [6] p. il.   017-024-00028-1

Who Are the Working Mothers? Women's Bur., Leaflet 37 (1972) [1973]. 9 p.   029-016-00007-1

Your Baby's First Year. Children's Bur., Pub. 400 (1963). [32] p. il.
                                                        017-091-00082-4

A durable classic dealing with the physical attention the baby needs; nutrition, sleep requirements, etc.

—— **El Primer Año de Vida de Su Bebe.** Children's Bur., Pub. 400 (Span.), 1963; reissued, 1971. 27 p. il. Free from the Bur.
Translation of the preceding title.

Your Child from 1 to 6. L. L. Dittmann. Children's Bur., Pub. 30
Repr. 1962. [98] p. il.   017-091-00069-7
First published in 1918, this guide gets better with every new edition. Your child's physical care, his activities and how to guide them, his potential.

Your Child from 3 to 4. Children's Bur., Bull. 446 (1966). [27] p. il.
                                                             017-091-00097-2
Picture story of child care. Deservedly a long-time best seller.

CIVIL DEFENSE

Civil Defense Management for Sewerage Systems; an Industrial Civil Defense Handbook. Civil Defense Off., 1970. 85 p. il. Free from the Off.
How to preserve these vital systems; or, where necessary, to make the most acceptable substitutes for them.

Disaster Operations; Handbook for Local Governments. Defense Civil Preparedness Agency, 1972. 100 p. il. Free from the Agency.

Introduction to Civil Preparedness; How Civil Preparedness Came to Be; What Civil Preparedness Is Today; Help Available and Where to Get It; and Outstanding Works. Defense Civil Preparedness Agency, 1972. 28 p. il. Free from the Agency.

Report to Congress: Disaster Preparedness, Jan. 1972. Emergency Preparedness Off., 1972. 387 p. il.   041-002-00006-9
"Comprehensive study of the types of major natural disasters ex-

perienced in the United States that offers findings and potential solutions to prevent or minimize the loss of life and damage to property."

CIVIL RIGHTS

Above Property Rights. S. F. Lawson. Civil Rights Comm., Clearinghouse Pub. 38 (1972) [1973]. 29 p. il.   005-000-00080-7
The plight of our black and other minorities as they attempt to move away from the cities' ghettoes. The federal role is discussed, its problems, and how it tries to meet them. And there are depressing statistics to show how slow that progress is.

Diminishing Barrier; a Report on School Desegregation in Nine Communities. [M. E. Sloane and others]. Civil Rights Comm., Clearinghouse Pub. 40 [1972]. 64 p.   005-000-00087-4
The communities are in Florida, Illinois, North Carolina, Ohio, and Pennsylvania. What has been done in these communities since 1954; what needs to be done. "Experience in these . . . communities strongly suggests that through patience, thoughtfulness, and a common sense of fairness, equal educational opportunities for all the Nation's children can finally be achieved." A most encouraging report of nine courageous communities.

Equal Opportunity in Employment. Civil Serv. Comm., Personnel Bibliog. Ser. 49 (1973). 170 p.   006-000-00745-7
How the Commission works toward this end.

Equal Opportunity in Housing; Manual for Corporate Employers. Housing and Urban Devel. Dept. [1973]. 53 p.   023-000-00253-1
"It would do corporations well to remember that the controversy about the nation's minorities seldom comes up in the market place. Here equality is a cost factor. What they buy greatly affects the gross yields of any corporation." The obligations and opportunities that corporations have.

Federal Civil Rights Enforcement Effort; a Reassessment: a Report
. . . Civil Rights Comm., 1973. 425 p.   005-000-00094-7
Covered here, in great detail, are efforts to enforce the law in the
areas of employment, housing, education, federally assisted programs, and the regulatory agencies involved.

**Federal Data Banks and Constitutional Rights; a Study of Data Sys-
tems on Individuals Maintained by Agencies of the United States
Government; Summary and Conclusions** . . . The Senate, 1974. 53 p.
052-070-02383-0
Prepared by the Subcommittee on Constitutional Rights of the Senate's Committee on the Judiciary.

Federal Enforcement of School Desegregation; a Report . . . Civil
Rights Comm., 1969. 123 p. Free from the Comm.
Valuable for its instances of genuine effort, on the part of the Federal Government, to fulfill obligations. For examples of the opposi-
tion the Government meets, see Appendix B.

**Federal Government's Role in the Achievement of Equal Opportu-
nity in Housing; Hearings** . . . House of Representatives, 1972. 904
p. il. Free from the House Document Room.   052-070-02400-3
Hearings before Civil Rights Oversight Subcommittee of the Committee on the Judiciary. History and documents of importance.

For All the People . . . **by All the People; a Report on Equal Opportunity in State and Local Government Employment** . . . Civil
Rights Comm., 1969. 277 p.   005-000-00007-6
Contains many valuable tables showing the occupational attainments
of minority groups, on local, state, and federal levels. Important history for all of us concerned with the advance of minority groups
among us.

**Freedom of Information Act Source Book; Legislative Materials,
Cases, Articles.** The Senate, 1974. 432 p.   052-070-02303-1

Series of articles and other material prepared by the Subcommittee on Administrative Practice and Procedure of the Committee on the Judiciary.

Government Looks at Privacy and Security in Computer Systems; Summary . . . C. R. Renninger and D. K. Branstad, eds. Natl. Bur. of Standards, Tech. Note 809 (1974). [39] p.   003-003-01239-4
Summary of a conference held at the Bureau in November, 1973. "Any confrontation between society and technology over problems of individual privacy and data confidentiality can be defused by understanding and action. The Conference . . . has contributed to both by providing an initial statement of governmental needs and problems and suggesting a broad range of activities for satisfying them." (Foreword by R. M. Davis.) The Conference discussed protection of the individual's privacy, guidelines for assessing this privacy, and the problems of managing information in automated record-keeping systems (among other things). Probably not, in its entirety, of interest to the average person, although it should be: its conclusions and suggestions are important. (In its public documents, there is evidence of praiseworthy lack of censorship on matters discussed in such conferences as this; this does not apply, of course, to any matter of the "national security." Yet even there, there is much encouraging evidence of wide freedom of thought and expression.)

Layman's Guide to Individual Rights under the United States Constitution. The Senate, 1973. 32 p.   052-070-02089-0
Prepared by the Subcommittee on Human Rights for the Senate Committee on the Judiciary.

Military Surveillance of Civilian Politics; a Report . . . The Senate, 1973. 150 p. il. Purchase from the Comm.   052-070-02387-2
Before the Subcommittee on Constitutional Rights, of the Senate's Committee on the Judiciary. Part 1 covers the nature of domestic intelligence (origins, reporting, intelligence data, storage, etc.); Part 2 deals with the legality of surveillance. "The study has been the

result of three and a half years of painstaking investigation and study. . . . Army surveillance has now been curtailed."

Military Surveillance; Hearings . . . The Senate, 1974. 397 p. Purchase from the Comm.
Before the Subcommittee on Constitutional Rights of the Senate's Committee on the Judiciary. Testimony of all types of experts and witnesses. Purpose of the investigation was to study whether the military has been used to conduct surveillance of the political activities of civilians or civilian organizations (except in those "limited situations" where the military actually has a need for such information to further a lawful objective). The expression of opinions of every shade of thought is encouraging.

Records, Computers, and the Rights of Citizens; a Report . . . Dept. of Health, Educ., and Welfare, 1973. 346 p.   017-000-00116-7
Report of the Advisory Council on Automated Personal Data Systems. Intended to "analyze the consequences of using computers to keep records about people." Points out that such computers are "destined to become the prime medium for making, storing, and using records about people." Nine chapters: origins of the systems; safeguards for privacy; uses of your Social Security number; and other aspects of the subject.

Selective Service and Amnesty; Hearings. The Senate, 1972. 671 p. Free from the Comm.   052-070-01639-6
Before the Senate Committee on the Judiciary's Subcommittee on Administrative Processes and Procedures. Purpose is twofold: ". . . first, to examine the current administration of the Selective Service Act in the light of the recommendations of this Subcommittee two years ago. . . . and second, to explore the administrative possibilities and problems in granting executive clemency to men who have chosen exile, to men who have chosen punishment, or to men who have chosen to go 'underground' rather than fulfill the obligations that the military selective service law has imposed on them." Testimony of many witnesses.

Who Will Listen? (**If You Have a Civil Rights Complaint**). Civil Rights Comm., Clearinghouse Pub. 13 (1969). 16 p.

005-000-00052-1

Directory of federal agencies to contact when you feel your rights have been violated.

Wiretapping and Electronic Surveillance; Hearings . . . House of Representatives, 1974. 275 p. Purchase from the House Document Room.

"A basic purpose of these hearings is to examine the trend toward privacy invasion, and to determine what should be done to reassert the right of the individual to be free of Government surveillance." Present protective legislation is cited; then follows a good deal of testimony by legislators, government officials, academic personnel; articles, letters, memoranda, and so on. House Judiciary Committee.

CLIMATOLOGY AND WEATHER

Climates of the United States. J. L. Baldwin. Environ. Data Serv., 1973. 113 p. il. 003-017-00211-0

Particularly valuable for its very fine maps, covering every kind of weather in every part of the United States.

Clouds. Natl. Oceanic and Atmos. Admin. [1972]. il.

003-014-00016-9

Chart.

Flash Floods. Natl. Weather Serv. [1974]. [6] p. il. 003-018-00057-1
What causes them; how to minimize their damage.

Heat Wave. Natl. Oceanic and Atmos. Admin. [1972]. [8] p. il.

003-017-00080-0

Causes; how to get more comfortable.

Homeport Story; an Imaginary City Gets Ready for a Hurricane.
Natl. Oceanic and Atmos. Admin. [1971]. 20 p. il.   003-014-00046-1
To instruct community leaders, and the communities themselves, on
what they can do to lessen the effects of a hurricane.

Hurricane, the Greatest Storm on Earth. Natl. Oceanic and Atmos. Admin. [1974]. [35] p. il.   003-018-00018-1
"No other atmospheric disturbance combines duration, size, and violence more destructively." Fascinating booklet traces the storm from
birth to death. How the Government helps predict the coming of
hurricanes, how it provides warnings. What your town and you can
do if the greatest storm on earth decides to pay a visit.

Hurricane Information and Atlantic Tracking Chart. Environ. Sci.
Serv. Admin., 1971. Folder. il.   003-018-00012-1
Safety rules, and a map of our Eastern states, so vulnerable to these
storms.

Memorable Hurricanes of the United States since 1873. A. L. Sugg
and others. Natl. Oceanic and Atmos. Admin., NWS SR-56 (1971).
52 p. il. Purchase from the Admin.
Dramatic indeed; we have had some whoppers. Their occurrence
and their toll are chronicled here.

Naming of Hurricanes. Natl. Weather Serv., 1973. [2] p. Free from
the Serv.
Tropical cyclones in the Atlantic, Caribbean, and Gulf of Mexico
have been known by girls' names since 1953. In 1960 a semi-
permanent list of four sets was established; a list enlarged in 1971
to ten sets. This will be used over and over again in the same alphabetic sequence, starting in 1981 (and presumably lasting as long as
such girls annoy our coasts). The list began in 1971 with Arlene, and
ended that year with Wallis. The year 1980 will begin with Abby
and will conclude with Willette.

National Climatic Center, Asheville, N.C. Environ. Data Serv., 1970
[1971]. [35] p. il. Free from the Serv.
Functions and activities. Includes a valuable listing of publications.

Smithsonian Meteorological Tables. R. J. List. Smithsonian Inst. 527 p. Purchase from Inst.
". . . 174 tables, index. Tables: conversion; wind and dynamical; barometric and hypsometric; geopotential and aeological; standard atmosphere and altimetry; radiation and visibility; geodetic and astronomical."

Some Devastating North Atlantic Hurricanes of the 20th Century. Natl. Oceanic and Atmos. Admin., 1973. [11] p. il.

003-017-00127-0

Eleven maps plot 61 hurricanes from August and September, 1900, to June, 1972. Areas affected, highest wind velocities recorded, deaths (for the United States only); damage done. The storm of June 14–23, 1972, was one of the costliest natural disasters in our history.

Thunderstorms. Natl. Oceanic and Atmos. Admin. [1970]. [6] p. il.

003-017-00016-8

Winter Storms. Natl. Weather Serv. [1971]. [8] p. il.

003-018-00004-1

COMMUNISM

Assault on Freedom; Compendium of Theoretical and Policy Statements by Communist Movement, Domestic and International, and by Other Organizations Committed to Violent Overthrow of Free Institutions. Part 1, 1971. Comm. on the Judiciary, The Senate, 1971. 220 p.

052-070-01279-0

Prepared for the Subcommittee to Investigate the Administration of Internal Security Act and Other Internal Security Laws of the Senate's Committee on the Judiciary.

Communist Global Subversion and American Security. Vol. 1: The Attempted Communist Subversion of Africa through Nkrumah's Ghana. The Senate, 1972. 215 p. il.

052-070-00142-9

A Report to the Subcommittee to Investigate the Administration of the Internal Security Act and Other Internal Security Laws of the Senate Committee on the Judiciary. A most valuable collection of documents and testimony by experts.

Human Cost of Communism in Vietnam; Compendium . . . The Senate, 1972. 123 p. 052-070-01400-8
Prepared for the Subcommittee to Investigate the Administration of the Internal Security Act and Other Internal Security Laws of the Senate's Committee on the Judiciary. Expert testimony includes some on the "myth of the bloodbath."

World Strength of the Communist Party Organizations; 25th Annual Report, 1973. State Dept., 1973. 158 p. il. 044-000-01488-2
Much more than a series of statistical tables. Records the legal status of the parties; gives names of leaders (where known); and also some of their activities. Does not include the United States.

CONSERVATION

Autumn Olive for Wildlife and Other Conservation Uses. P. F. Allen and W. W. Steiner. Dept. of Agr., Leaflet 458 (1972). 8 p. il.
001-000-02607-1
For attracting birds, establishing barriers; conservation; to beautify old lands; as ornamental planting. Don't eat the berries—they're for the birds! A very useful plant. The booklet covers its cultivation for the purposes noted.

Conservation Activities for Girl Scouts. Dept. of Agr., PA 1009 (1973). 31 p. il. 001-000-02593-7
A very pleasant handbook on the factors that shape—and destroy— a landscape, and how young people (of both sexes) can help preserve their wildlife heritage.

Russian Olive for Wildlife and Other Conservation Uses. A. E. Borell. Dept. of Agr., Leaflet 517 (1971). 8 p. il. 001-000-01092-1
Said to be a very valuable plant in the Western and Plains states.

Teaching Conservation through Outdoor Education Areas. Dept. of Agr., PA 837 (1970). [23] p. il.   001-000-00578-7
Development of demonstration areas where the life of the forest and the importance of conservation can be taught.

CONSTRUCTION AND CONSTRUCTION MATERIALS

Builder 1 & C. Naval Training Comm. [1974]. 353 p. il.
008-047-00165-7
Chapters on supervision, planning, estimating, scheduling; concrete construction; masonry construction; plastering, wall tile, and acoustical ceilings; heavy construction; construction inspection; maintenance inspection. As usual with so many Navy manuals, packed with practical information.

Construction Guides for Exposed Wood Decks. L. O. Anderson and others. Dept. of Agr., Agr. Handbook 432 (1972). 78 p. il.
001-000-02577-5
Choice of materials; plans; detailed drawings; many illustrations. Very fine.

Controlling Erosion on Construction Sites. Dept. of Agr., Agr. Inform. Bull. 347 [1970]. 31 p. il.   001-000-01158-8
General discussion of points to be considered. Not a detailed guide. Probably of interest to those charged with supervision and with actual planning.

Recreational Buildings and Facilities. Dept. of Agr., Agr. Handbook 438 (1972). 74 p. il.   001-000-02663-1
Cabins; barns and equipment for horses; greenhouses; recreational facilities. Reduced plans and drawings.

HOUSE

Fireplaces and Chimneys. Dept. of Agr., Farmers' Bull. 1889 (1971). 23 p. il.   001-000-01520-6

Indoor and outdoor. Reduced plans. Detailed drawings.

House Construction; How to Reduce Costs. J. O. Newman and others. Dept. of Agr., Home and Garden Bull. 168 (1970). 16 p. il.

001-000-02788-3

From planning to final stages—a manual on getting the most for your hard-earned money and then putting it to best use. Designs; interior arrangements.

Low-Cost Wood Homes for America—Construction Manual. L. O. Anderson. Dept. of Agr., Agr. Handbook 364 (1969). 112 p. il.

001-000-00747-5

Selection of materials; laying the foundations; flooring; roofing; exterior walls. Insulation; heating; interior finishing; paneling. Scores of useful reduced drawings.

Wall Siding, Installing, Finishing, Maintaining. Dept. of Agr., Home and Garden Bull. 203 (1973). 13 p. il.   001-000-02680-1
Practical working advice.

Wood-frame House Construction. L. O. Anderson. Dept. of Agr., Agr. Handbook. 73 (1970). 223 p. il.   001-000-01232-1
"Sound principles for wood-frame house construction . . . gives suggestions for selecting materials even by inexperienced builders." In addition, the book contains all sorts of construction advice, and includes many reduced construction drawings. One of the best of this type of handbook the compiler has ever seen. Covers not only construction, but painting, fire protection. (The readers in the compiler's library like this book so much that it has been necessary to purchase *eight* copies.)

MATERIALS

Building with Adobe and Stabilized-Earth Blocks. Dept of Agr., Leaflet 535 (1972). 8 p. il.   001-000-01563-0

Hardwood? Carpet? or Tile? Comparison of Flooring Costs under

Residential Conditions. D. G. Martens. Forest Serv., Research Paper NE-200 (1971). 25 p. Free from the Serv.

Maple Flooring; How Architects View It. G. R. Lindell. Forest Serv., Research Note NC-109 [1971]. 4 p. il. Purchase from the Serv.

CONSUMER GUIDES

Buying a New Sewing Machine. Dept. of Agr., PA 1044 (1973). 11 p. il.   001-000-02859-6

Consumer Bulletins. Fed. Trade Comm., 1970–74. 9 parts.
Every number in this group is based on Federal Trade Commission investigations and reports. Each tells what pitfalls to avoid in making purchases of particular commodities or services.
  1. Mail Order Insurance [1970]. [12] p. il.   018-000-00022-9
  2. Unordered Merchandise. [1970]. [6] p.   018-000-00016-4
  3. Risks in Raising Chinchillas. [1971]. 8 p. il.   018-000-00117-9
  4. Franchise Business Risks. [1972]. [11] p. il.   018-000-00140-3
  5. Freezer Meat Bargains. [1972]. [8] p.   018-000-00130-6
  6. Look for that Label. [1974]. [8] p. il.   018-000-00123-3
  7. Know Your Rights under the Fair Credit Reporting Act; a Checklist for Consumers. [1972]. [7] p.   018-000-00138-1
  8. Don't Be Gypped. [1972]. [6] p. il.   018-000-00122-5
  9. Protection for the Elderly. [1971]. [11] p.   018-000-00124-1

Consumer Guide to FDA. Food and Drug Admin., 1975. [11] p. il. Purchase from the Admin.
The Administration's authority and activities; its origin; advice on how to use its services; listing of officers and offices. Excellent guide to a most important consumer tool.

Consumer Information Series. Fed. Supply Serv., 1971–74. 18 numbers.
An extremely valuable series for the consumer. Each of the titles

tells you what to look for in a good buy, how the article should perform, and what may be right or wrong with it.

1. Automobile Batteries; Their selection and Care. 1971. 13 p. il.   022-000-00067-5
2. Paint and Painting; Selection, Preparation, Application. 1971. 24 p. il.   022-000-00066-7
3. Fire Extinguishers; ABC's and 1, 2, 3 of Selection [1971]. 10 p. il.   022-000-00068-3
4. Vacuum Cleaners. 1972. 15 p. il.   022-000-00070-5
5. Ladders; Selection, Maintenance, Proper Use. 1972. 12 p. il.   022-000-00069-1
6. Room Air Conditioners. 1972. 20 p. il.   022-000-00074-8
7. Antifreeze/Coolant. [1972]. 5 p. il.   022-000-00075-6
9. Washers and Dryers. [1972]. 22 p. il.   022-000-00079-9
10. Dishwashers. [1972]. 20 p. il.   022-000-00035-7
11. Automatic Toasters. [1972]. 10 p. il.   022-000-00078-1
12. Carpets and Rugs. [1973]. 32 p. il.   022-000-00080-2
13. Mixers and Blenders. [1973]. 8 p. il.   022-000-00077-2
14. Electric Irons. [1973]. 8 p. il.   022-000-00084-5
15. Electric Percolators. [1973]. 8 p. il.   022-003-00901-9
16. Power Hand Tools. [1973]. 24 p. il.   022-003-00902-7
17. Portable Dehumidifiers. [1974]. 6 p. il.   022-001-00055-8
18. Household Cleaners. [1974]. 11 p. il.   022-001-00059-1

Directory of State, County, and City Government Consumer Offices, July 1, 1973. Off. of Consumer Affairs, 1973. 35 p.

017-000-00140-0

Family Food Budgeting . . . for Good Meals and Good Nutrition. Dept. of Agr., Home and Garden Bull. 94 (1971). [15] p. il.

001-000-01377-7

Includes valuable tables showing nutritional requirements for the various food groups, for children and adults.

Family Food Buying; a Guide for Calculating Amounts to Buy; Comparing Costs. E. H. Dawson and others. Dept. of Agr., Home Econ. Research Rept. 37 (1969). 60 p.   001-000-02987-8

Rather novel use of mathematical tables; extremely useful in figuring household costs.

Food and Drug Administration Guides. Food and Drug Admin., 1971–74, 20 numbers, several out of print.

Aids to Compliance for Drug Industry. [1972]. 19 p. Free from the Admin.

Banned Toys. Vol. 1. Sept. 1972. [1972]. 43 p. Free from the Admin.

Listing of all banned toys and other banned articles that had been intended for use by children.

—— Suppl. Sept. 1–Nov. 30, 1972. [1973]. 10 p. Free from the Admin.

FDA Information Materials for the Food and Cosmetic Industries; Movies, Slides, Posters, Booklets, Fact Sheets. [1974]. 15 p. Free from the Admin.

FDA Introduction to Total Drug Quality. 1973. 101 p. il.
017-012-00220-0

FDA: We Want You to Know about FDA. FDA Pub. 1 1972. 24 p. il. Free from the Admin.

Federal Recordkeeping Requirements for Microwave Oven Dealers and Distributors. [1973]. [4] p. 017-015-00058-3

For Every Child Poisoned This Year, There Is an Adult Responsible. 1971. 32 p. Free from the Admin.

Milestones in U.S. Food and Drug Law History. [1972]. [2] p. Free from the Admin.

Nutrition Sense and Nonsense. [1973]. [6] p. il. 017-012-00200-5

Playing Safe in Toyland. C. Young. [1972]. [4] p. il.
017-012-00149-1

Poison Control Centers Directory. [1971]. 50 p. 017-012-00129-1

Protect Food; Stay Alert. [1972]. 8 p. il. Free from the Admin.
017-012-00151-3

Recommendations to the Commissioner for Control of Foodborne Human Salmonellosis; Report of the FDA Salmonella Task Force. [1973]. 71 p. il. Free from the Admin.

Requirements of the United States Food, Drug, and Cosmetics Act. [1972]. 55 p. 017-012-00138-6

So You Work in a Food Plant? [1972]. [12] p. il. 017-012-00146-7

Food Buying Guide for Child Care Centers. A. Cazier and O. M. Batcher. Food and Nutrition Serv., FNS 108 (1974). 43 p. il.

001-024-00190-2

Buying the right foods in quantity, and saving money as you do it.

Food Buying Guide for Type A School Lunches. Dept. of Agr., PA 270 (1972). 92 p. il. 001-000-01454-4

". . . information for planning and calculating quantities of food to be purchased and used by schools in the National School Lunch Program." Of course, applicable to schools *not* in the Program.

Food for Your Table; Let's Talk about It. Dept. of Agr. [1971]. 22 p. Free from the Dept.

Gasoline; More Miles per Gallon. Dept. of Transportation [1974]. 9 p. il. 050-000-00072-9

Very good advice on not wasting expensive gas.

Guide to Budgeting for the Family. Dept. of Agr., Home and Garden Bull. 108 (1970). 14 p. il. 001-000-01826-4

Guide to Budgeting for the Retired Couple. L. F. Mork. Dept. of Agr., Home and Garden Bull. 194 [1972]. 14 p. il.

001-000-02963-1

Helping Families Manage Their Finances. Dept. of Agr., Home Econ. Research Rept. 21 [1968]. 51 p. il. 001-000-00982-6

How to Buy Beef Roasts. Dept. of Agr., Home and Garden Bull. 146 [1974]. [16] p. 001-000-00808-1

—— **Como Comprar Bistecs.** Dept. of Agr., Home and Garden Bull. 145-S (1972). Folder. il. 001-000-02529-5

Translation of preceding title.

How to Buy Canned and Frozen Fruits. E. T. Greeley. Dept. of Agr., Home and Garden Bull. 191 (1971). [23] p. il. 001-000-01434-0

How to Buy Canned and Frozen Vegetables. E. R. Thompson. Dept. of Agr., Home and Garden Bull. 167 (1969). 23 p. il.

001-000-03377-8

Twenty-four vegetables.

How to Buy Cheese. Dept. of Agr., Home and Garden Bull. 193 (1971). [24] p. il. 001-000-01441-2

How to Buy Dairy Products. Dept. of Agr., Home and Garden Bull. 201 (1972). 15 p. il. 001-000-02595-3
Not only advice on buying; includes a detailed glossary of dairy products.

How to Buy Dry Beans, Peas, and Lentils. Dept. of Agr., Home and Garden Bull. 177 (1970). 11 p. il. 001-000-01242-8
Types of beans, peas, and lentils; purchase, storage, preparation for the table.

How to Buy Eggs. Dept. of Agr., Home and Garden Bull. 144 (1968). Folder. il. 001-000-00806-4

How to Buy Fresh Fruits. M. E. Smith. Dept. of Agr., Home and Garden Bull. 141 (1967). 23 p. il. 001-000-00803-0

How to Buy Fresh Vegetables. M. E. Smith. Dept. of Agr., Home and Garden Bull. 143 [1967]. 24 p. il. 001-000-00805-6

How to Buy Lamb. Dept. of Agr., Home and Garden Bull. 195 (1971). [16] p. il. 001-000-01457-9

How to Buy Meat for Your Freezer. Dept. of Agr., Home and Garden Bull. 166 (1969). 27 p. il. 001-000-03276-3
What to get; how much.

How to Buy Poultry. Dept. of Agr., Home and Garden Bull. 157 (1968). Folder. 001-000-00816-1

How to Use USDA Grades in Buying Food. Dept. of Agr., Home and Garden Bull. 196 [1972]. [21] p. il.   001-000-01815-9
The Government labels are there, why not use them? This booklet can be carried in a handbag.

Meat and Poultry Labeled for You. Dept. of Agr., Home and Garden Bull. 172 (1969). Folder.   001-000-00830-7

Meat and Poultry Standards for You. Dept. of Agr., Home and Garden Bull. 171 (1969). Folder. il.   001-000-02749-2

Meat and Poultry Wholesome for You. Dept. of Agr., Home and Garden Bull. 170 (1969). Folder. il.   001-000-00828-5

1975 Gas Mileage Guide for New Car Buyers; Fuel Economy Test Results for Automobiles. Fed. Energy Admin., 1974. [9] p. Purchase from the Admin.
Third year of publication. Both city-driving fuel economy and highway-driving fuel economy. Many cars cited.

Used Furniture Can Be a Good Buy. G. Pifer. Dept. of Agr., PA 1061 [1973]. 8 p. il.   001-000-02966-5

Used Sewing Machines; Good Buy. V. Ogilvy. Dept. of Agr., PA 1045 [1973]. [7] p.   001-000-02894-4

We Want You to Know What We Know about . . . Food and Drug Admin., 1972–74. 15 numbers.
This very informative group, largely in the form of handy folders, belongs not only in every library, but literally in every household—particularly one boasting smaller children. The present listing includes fifteen titles, with slight variation of title and some abbreviation; and five posters belonging to the same group, but with a slightly variant classmark. Incidentally, every drugstore in the land should have a set.

     Diagnostic X rays. [1974]. 8 p. il.   017-012-00181-5

Drugs for Food-producing Animals. [1973]. 6 p. il.
017-012-00176-9
Foodborne Illness. 1974. [9] p. il. 017-012-00189-1
Impact-resistant Eyeglass Lenses. [1974]. [6] p. il.
017-012-00164-5
Labels on Foods. [1973]. [6] p. il. 017-012-00183-1
Labels on Medicines. [1974]. [6] p. il. 017-012-00180-7
Medicines without Prescriptions. [1974]. [8] p. il.
017-012-00170-0
Microwave Oven Radiation. [1973]. [7] p. il. 017-012-00184-0
Nutrition Labels on Foods. [1973]. [6] p. il. 017-012-00190-4
Prescription Drugs. [1974]. 8 p. 017-012-00169-0
Preventing Childhood Poisonings. [1974]. [8] p. il. Purchase from Admin.
Safe Use of Eye Cosmetics. [1973]. [5] p. il. 017-012-00182-3
Salmonella and Food Poisoning [1974]. 6 p. il. 017-012-00163-7
Shocking, Isn't It? . . . Electrical Safety. 1972. Poster 26″ × 22.5″.
017-012-00155-6
Today's FDA. 1974. 6 p. il. Purchase from the Admin.

COOKING, PRESERVING, AND STORING FOOD

Although some of the titles below might seem better cited under Consumer Guides, the compiler has put them here because they contain cooking hints and recipes.

Cereals and Pasta in Family Meals; a Guide for Consumers. Dept. of Agr., Home and Garden Bull. 150 (1968). 32 p. il. 001-000-00811-1
Buying; storing; preparing; recipes.

Cooking for Two. Dept. of Agr., PA 1043 [1974]. 89 p. il.
001-000-03327-1
Recipes; helpful hints on planning and serving meals. *In large type.*

Food for the Young Couple; a Guide to Budgeting. Dept. of Agr., Home and Garden Bull. 85 (1973). 16 p. il. 001-000-02851-1
Prices are approximately up-to-date; and menus are still good.

Food Safety in the Kitchen. Dept. of Agr. [1974]. [5] p. il. Free from the Dept.

Freezing Combination Main Dishes. Dept. of Agr., Home and Garden Bull. 40 (1973). 19 p. il.   001-000-02712-3
How to freeze, and how to thaw and cook. Includes recipes.

Home Care of Purchased Frozen Foods. Dept. of Agr., Home and Garden Bull. 69 (1971). 6 p. il.   001-000-03410-3

How to Make Jellies, Jams, and Preserves at Home. Dept. of Agr., Home and Garden Bull. 56 (1971). 30 p. il.   001-000-03167-8
Essential ingredients; equipment and containers; making and storing all kinds of goodies.

Keeping Food Safe to Eat; a Guide for Homemakers. Dept. of Agr., Home and Garden Bull. 162 (1971). 12 p.   001-000-03396-4
Contains a chart of proper temperatures.

Making Pickles and Relishes at Home. Dept. of Agr., Home and Garden Bull. 92 (1970). 31 p. il.   001-000-00871-4
Many recipes, well illustrated.

Making Raisins. M. Jackson. Dept. of Agr., Science Study Aid 1 (1971). [4] p. il.   001-000-01007-7

Money-saving Main Dishes. Dept. of Agr., Home and Garden Bull. 43 (1971). 48 p. il.   001-000-01460-9
Principles of a reasonably priced cuisine, and recipes for meats, vegetables, salads, soups, sandwiches.

Nuts in Family Meals; a Guide for Consumers. Dept. of Agr., Home and Garden Bull. 176 (1971). 14 p. il.   001-000-01461-7
Kinds; storage; preparation; recipes.

Protect Food; Stay Alive. Food and Drug Admin. [1972]. [9] p. il. Free from the Admin.   017-012-00151-3
Safety, cleanliness in handling foods; making storage areas.

Quantity Recipes for Child Care Centers. Food and Nutrition Serv., FNS Ser. 86 [1973]. [92] cards, 5″ × 8″. Free from the Serv.

001-024-00170-8

Menus for large groups, of course; but there is no particular reason that they cannot be adapted to much smaller groups.

Quantity Recipes for Type A School Lunches. Dept. of Agr., PA 631 (1971). [203] cards, each 5″ × 8″. 001-000-00499-9

These are wonderful recipes, adaptable to any number and in a most handy form.

Storing Perishable Foods in the Home. Dept. of Agr., Agr. Handbook 78 (1973). 9 p. il. 001-000-02715-8

Storage needs of foods vary. This booklet describes the different types that are required.

BAKED GOODS

Breads, Cakes, and Pies in Family Meals; a Guide for Consumers. Dept. of Agr., Home and Garden Bull. 186 (1971). 30 p. il.

001-000-01380-7

Not a buying guide; this tells how and where to use pastry. Recipes included.

FISH AND SHELLFISH

Fishery Facts. Natl. Marine Fisheries Serv., FSHFA Ser., 1972–73. Interesting group. Covers the biology of the fishes; then tells how to catch and process them.

1. Redfish. G. F. Kelly and others. 1972. 18 p. il. 003-020-00056-8
2. Alaska's Fishery Resources: Pacific Herring. G. M. Reid. 1972. 20 p. il. 003-020-00057-6
3. Dungeness Crab Pots. F. W. Hipkins. 1972. 13 p. il.

003-020-00058-4

4. Inshore Lobster Fishing. J. T. Everett. 1972. 26 p. il.

003-020-00059-2

6. Alaska's Fishery Resources: Dungeness Crab. D. T. Hoopes. 1973. 14 p. il.   003-020-00079-7

FRUITS AND VEGETABLES

Apples in Appealing Ways. Dept. of Agr., Home and Garden Bull. 161 (1969). 16 p. il.   001-000-00820-0
Over 40 recipes.

Fruits in Family Meals; a Guide for Consumers. Dept. of Agr., Home and Garden Bull. 125 (1972). 30 p. il.   001-000-03265-8
Buying sensibly, and cooking interestingly.

Home Canning of Fruits and Vegetables. Dept. of Agr., Home and Garden Bull. 8 (1972). [31] p. il.   001-000-03398-9
Correct procedures to follow; directions for canning many fruits and vegetables.

Home Freezing of Fruits and Vegetables. Dept. of Agr., Home and Garden Bull. 10 (1971). 48 p. il.   001-000-02448-5
General principles and precise details on freezing many types of fruits and vegetables. How to use in family meals.

Making and Preserving Apple Cider. J. F. Robinson and others. Dept. of Agr., Farmers' Bull. 2125 (1971). 14 p. il.   001-000-02671-2

Storing Vegetables and Fruits in Basements, Cellars, Outbuildings, and Pits. Dept. of Agr., Home and Garden Bull. 119 (1973). 18 p. il.
001-000-02942-8
The method you adopt depends on your climate. If you live in Virginia, your problems will differ from those of the Minnesota housekeeper. This booklet will help you—wherever you live.

Vegetables in Family Meals; a Guide for Consumers. Dept. of Agr., Home and Garden Bull. 105 (1971). 29 p. il.   001-000-03271-2
Buying; storage; cooking—including recipes.

MEAT, POULTRY, AND EGGS

Beef and Veal in Family Meals; a Guide for Consumers. Dept. of Agr., Home and Garden Bull. 118 (1971). 30 p. il.   001-000-03363-8

Eggs in Family Meals; a Guide for Consumers. Dept. of Agr., Home and Garden Bull. 103 (1971). 29 p. il.   001-000-03269-1
How to buy, and how to cook.

Freezing Meat and Fish in the Home . . . Dept. of Agr., Home and Garden Bull. 93 (1973). 23 p. il.   001-000-02981-9
Detailed instructions.

Home Canning of Meat and Poultry. Dept. of Agr., Home and Garden Bull. 106 [1972]. 24 p. il.   001-000-02612-7

Lamb in Family Meals; a Guide for Consumers. Dept. of Agr., Home and Garden Bull. 124 [1974]. 22 p. il.   001-000-02716-6
How to choose your cut. Appetizing recipes.

Meat and Poultry Care Tips for You. Dept. of Agr., Home and Garden Bull. 174 (1970). 12 p.   001-000-01610-5

Meat and Poultry Clean for You. Dept. of Agr., Home and Garden Bull. 173 (1973). Folder. il.   001-000-02752-2

Pork in Family Meals; a Guide for Consumers. Dept. of Agr., Home and Garden Bull. 160 (1969). 28 p. il.   001-000-02707-7
Buying, storing, cooking.

Poultry in Family Meals; a Guide for Consumers. Dept. of Agr., Home and Garden Bull. 110 (1968). 30 p. il.   001-000-03338-7
Buying, storing, cooking.

Protecting Home-cured Meat from Insects. Dept. of Agr., Home and Garden Bull. 109 (1974). 6 p. il.   001-000-03212-7

MILK AND CHEESE

Cheese in Family Meals; a Guide for Consumers. Dept. of Agr., Home and Garden Bull. 112 (1972). 22 p. il.   001-000-01592-3

Cheese Varieties and Descriptions. Dept. of Agr., Agr. Handbook 54 (1969). 151 p. il.   001-000-00761-1
There are many hundreds of kinds of cheese. This book details the provenance of most of them—animal and geographic provenance.

Making Cottage Cheese at Home. Dept. of Agr., Home and Garden Bull. 129 (1967). 8 p. il.   001-000-03409-0

Milk in Family Meals; a Guide for Consumers. Dept. of Agr., Home and Garden Bull. 127 (1972). 22 p. il.   001-000-01496-0

CRIME, DELINQUENCY, AND LAW ENFORCEMENT

To Abolish the Death Penalty; Hearings . . . The Senate, 1970. 239 p. il. Free from the Comm.
Hearings held in 1968, before the Subcommittee on Criminal Laws and Procedures of the Senate's Committee on the Judiciary. Testimony, pro and con, is by experts, and makes instructive reading.

Basic Elements of Intelligence; a Manual of Theory, Structure, and Procedures for Use by Law Enforcement Agencies against Organized Crime. E. D. Godfrey and D. R. Harris. Dept. of Justice, 1972. 150 p. il.   027-000-00162-9
Bear in mind that "intelligence" here means the data collected by law enforcement agencies. Purpose of this book is to "describe the process of intelligence and to point out how law enforcement agencies may apply intelligence to control organized crime." Particularly interesting for a detailed definition of "intelligence" in this context.

Citizen Support for Law Enforcement Efforts. Bur. of Narcotics and Dangerous Drugs [1972]. 48 p. il. Free from the Bur.
What communities can do, with examples cited in helpful detail.

Correctional Treatment in Community Settings; Report on Current Research. M. Q. Warren. Natl. Inst. of Mental Health [1972]. 59 p.

017-024-00247-0

Focuses on rehabilitation during probation and parole.

Crime in the Nation's 5 Largest Cities; National Crime Panel Surveys of Chicago, Detroit, Los Angeles, New York, and Philadelphia; Advance Report. Law Enforcement Assistance Admin., 1974. 29 p. Free from the Admin.

"Information presented . . . reflects only those victimizations incurred by the residents and commercial firms of each city. . . . All data . . . are estimates. . . . A more complete report . . . will include data sampling curves and . . . technical details about the survey." There is a short glossary of terms of violence.

Criminal Justice; the Consumer's Perspective. J. D. Casper. Dept. of Justice, PR 72-9 (1972). 62 p.   027-000-00143-2

"Defendants believe that American criminal justice operates much like an assembly line . . . exemplifying characteristics similar to their own lives on the street. . . . This report attempts to explore defendants' perceptions and evaluations of American criminal justice." Seventy-one men charged with felonies in Connecticut were interviewed. Their ideas of the police, court procedures, their attorneys, the prosecutors, the judges, are examined. Conclusion: "the defendant sees himself as an object in the hands of individuals not concerned with *him*, but with production." Most remarkable study, with excellent recommendations.

Guidelines and Standards for the Use of Volunteers in Correctional Programs. I. H. Scheier and others. Dept. of Justice, 1972. 296 p. il. Free from the Dept.   027-000-00236-6

Volunteer workers probably outnumber paid workers four or five to one in these programs. A very thorough guide to efficient management of volunteers.

Improving Police/Community Relations; Prescriptive Package. R. Wasserman and others. Dept. of Justice, 1973. [116] p.

027-000-00237-4

". . . designed for the use of police administrators and their command staffs as a guide to undertaking positive steps . . . to improve police/community relations." Seven chapters.

National Strategy to Reduce Crime. Natl. Advisory Comm. on Criminal Justice Standards and Goals, 1974. 195 p. il.   027-000-00204-8
The Commission proposes as a goal for Americans a 50 percent reduction in high-fear crimes by 1983. These are: homicide, forcible rape, aggravated assault, robbery, and burglary. This report (one of five) goes into the causes of crime, examines arrest and court procedures, sentencing. An extraordinary piece of work. Many recommendations are advanced.

New Environment for the Incarcerated . . . Dept. of Justice, 1972. 32 p. il. Free from the Dept.
Three reprints from the *Prison Journal* (Vol. 51, Spring-Summer, 1971). These deal with recent correctional architecture, social psychology of the cell environment, and use of the building as a tool for therapy of the young offender. A fine piece of work.

Not the Law's Business? An Examination of Homosexuality, Abortion, Prostitution, Narcotics, and Gambling in the United States. G. Geis. Natl. Inst. of Mental Health, 1972. 262 p.   017-024-00237-2
One in the "Crime and Delinquency Issues: Monograph Series."
Summary: "Three ideas need to be reiterated: that victimless crimes often represent defined deviations singled out for reasons more subtle than those sometimes stated as justification for campaigns against them; that singling out behavioral patterns and labeling them creates designated groups and pushes such groups toward alienation if their actions are viewed as invidious; and that given such a situation there is need for tolerance and flexibility, combined with attitudes designed to encourage and reward desired behavior."

Reaching Out . . . New Breed of Worker. Human Development Off., 1974. [30] p. il.   017-066-00013-7
Describes the concept of the National Center for Youth Outreach Workers, a way of approaching youth in trouble outside established agencies; dealing directly with the adolescent.

Riots, Civil and Criminal Disorders. The Senate, 1967–70. 26 parts. The investigations reported in this massive set were under the aegis of the Committee on Government Operations (Permanent Subcommittee on Investigations). The 26 parts are without parallel in the areas they cover. Unfortunately, the general public will probably read little, if any, of them: they will appeal primarily to the student of our times (and, specifically, of the violence that characterizes it); and perhaps to the occasional college student, faced with choosing a term-paper theme. And this is a shame. These reports rank very high as oral history. Witnesses questioned in many cities all across the country testified on campus disorders, ghetto unquiet, militant organizations, and so on. The compiler of this *Guide* has not read the 5,000+ pages that constitute the full hearings, but he has read enough to learn several things—among them, great respect for the Congressional groups who conducted the investigations (both for their fairness and their knowledge of their subjects); that, whatever the cause, the situation in 1968 *was* dangerous; and that some of the rioters were sincere in their beliefs (as, in fact, they had cause to be). A detailed work, one of the longest cited in this *Guide*, to be read when one has time to absorb its social meaning; and slowly. As a firsthand account of one phase of our history, it is invaluable; it belongs in every library, especially those concentrating on modern American history. It should be borne in mind, incidentally, that the emphasis on law enforcement procedures, and the necessity for them, is the prime emphasis of the group; this was, of course, particularly true where Federal funding was involved. In the listing below, the compiler has not indicated cities where the investigations took place, or the subject or subjects taken up; a failing, but one—alas!—of space.

1. Nov. 1–3, 6, 1967. 1968. 393 p. il.   052-070-00323-5
2. Nov. 7–9, 21–22, 1967. 1968. [395-756] p. il. 052-070-00331-6
3. Nov. 29–30, Dec. 4, 1967. 1968 [757-943] p. il.

   052-070-00333-2
3A. Nov. 30, 1967. 1968. 142 p.   052-070-00332-4
5. March 19–20, 1968. 1968. [1205-1346] p. il. 052-070-00335-9
6. March 20–21, 1968. 1968. [1347-1470] p. il., 052-070-00336-7
7. May 14–16, 1968. 1968. [1471-1587] p. il. 052-070-00337-5

8. May 21–22, 27–28, 1968. 1968. [1589-1803] p. il.

052-070-00338-3

9. June 20–21, 1968. 1968. [1805-1971] p. il. 052-070-00339-1

11. June 28, July 1–2, 1968. 1968. [2217-2472] p. il.

052-070-00317-1

12. July 3, 9–10, 1968. 1968. [2473-2655] p. il. 052-070-00318-9

13. Sept. 5, Oct. 10–11, 1968. 1968. [2657-2777] p. il.

052-070-00319-7

14. Oct. 8–9, 11, 1968. 1968. [2779-2948] p. il. 052-070-00320-1

15. March 4, 1969. 1969. [2949-2975] p. 052-070-00321-9

16. May 9, 13–14, 1969. [2973-3118] p. 052-070-00322-7

17. May 27–28, 1969. 1969. [3119-3304] p. il. 052-070-00324-3

18. June 16–17, 1969. 1969. [3305-3720] p. il. 052-070-00325-1

19. June 18–25, 1969. 1969. [3721-4173] p. il. 052-070-00326-0

20. June 26, 30, 1969. 1969. [4175-4498] p. il. 052-070-00327-8

21. July 1–8, 1969. 1969. [4499-4764] p. il. 052-070-00328-6

22. July 9–16, 1969. 1969. [4765-5164] p. il. 052-070-00329-4

23. July 22–August 5, 1969. 1969. [5167-5511] p.

052-070-00330-8

24. July 15–17, 21–22, 29–30, 1970. 1970. [5313-5569] p.

052-070-00842-3

25. July 3, August 4–6, 1970. 1970. [5571-5814] p.

052-070-00843-1

Science of Fingerprints. Fed. Bur. of Investigation, 1973. 198 p. il.

027-000-00011-8

Prepared especially for law enforcement officers and agencies. Includes discussions of types of patterns and their interpretation. Classification formulas and extension of these formulas. Scarred prints. Filing, searching, and other identification work. How to take prints; the latent impression. Preparation of useful charts. Use of the camera. Many millions of prints are on file in the FBI.

DENTISTRY AND TOOTH CARE

Do You Hate to Smile [Because of the Appearance of Your Teeth]?
Medicine and Surgery Bur. [Navy]. [1973]. 23 p. il. Free from the
Bur.
Heed some of the advice, and don't be afraid to grin thereafter.

Save Your Teeth. Public Health Serv., 1973. [13] p. il.

017-041-00061-4

"Three out of four Americans who have one or more teeth suffer
from periodontal disease" and "more teeth are lost from periodontal
disease than from dental decay." The sort of valuable booklet that
should be in every home. Tells you the proper care of your teeth,
from 32 to none.

DRUGS AND DRUG ABUSE

Alternatives to Drugs; a Conference . . . May 16–18, 1972. Bur. of
Narcotics and Dangerous Drugs [1972]. 61 p. Free from the Bur.
This is the first 61 pages of the *Proceedings* cited further on. It is a
general discussion of constructive programs, on many levels—from
police to school.

Alternatives to Drugs—a New Approach to Drug Education. V. A.
Dohner. Natl. Clearinghouse for Drug Abuse Inform., 1972. 22 p.
Free from the Clearinghouse   017-024-00347-6
Reprint of an article in the *Journal of Drug Education,* 1972. ". . .
suggests the positive use of alternatives to drug abuse as a basis for
education and prevention of drug abuse. . . . The various tactics used
for drug education are discussed. They include scare tactics, scientific approach, exploration of motives . . . and providing non-chemical
alternatives for students. . . . The author describes ten 'realities' related to drug abuse which must be recognized." These "realities"
range from the pleasure induced by drugs to the observation that

"the alternatives to drug abuse are also alternatives to the distresses and discomfort which lead to any self-destructive behavior." A most stimulating paper.

Barbiturate Abuse in the United States; Report . . . B. Bayh. The Senate, 1973. 69 p.   052-070-02074-1
Report to the Subcommittee to Investigate Juvenile Delinquency. Based on hearings and investigations, 1971–72. A very thorough study of illegal sale and transfer of these drugs, followed by a state-by-state review.

Bibliography on Drug Abuse Literature, 1972. S. B. Lachter and others. Natl. Clearinghouse for Drug Abuse Inform., 1972. 39 p.
017-024-00369-7

Bibliography on Drug Dependence and Abuse, 1928–66. Public Health Serv. [1969]. [258] p. Free from the Serv.
A sort of starting point for any detailed study; more than 3,000 citations.

Current Trends in the Treatment of Drug Dependence and Drug Abuse. N. B. Eddy. Bur. of Narcotics and Dangerous Drugs [1971]. 30 p. Free from the Bur.
Valuable introductory statement, with treatments cited, and examples of treatment policies in various typical areas.

Drug Abuse and the Criminal Justice System; a Survey of New Approaches in Treatment and Rehabilitation . . . Drug Enforcement Admin. 1974. 221 p. Free from the Admin.
Prepared by the staff of ALFY (sic!) (presumably "New Life for You"). Two parts: Diversions by Criminal Justice Systems; and Drug Offenders and the Criminal Justice System: Methods and Models. For planners and administrators.

Drug Abuse; Game without Winners; a Basic Handbook for Commanders. Armed Forces Inform. Serv., DoD-GEN-33 [1972]. 72 p. il.
008-001-00091-0

Very fine and detailed and—alas!—not yet out of date. Symptoms and treatment.

Drug Abuse Prevention Material for Schools. Natl. Clearinghouse for Drug Abuse Inform. [1972]. 40 p. il.   017-024-00238-1

Drug Addiction and Abuse among Military Veterans, 1971; Hearings . . . The Senate, 1971 [1972]. 2 parts. Purchase from the Comm.
Hearings before the Subcommittee on Health and Hospitals of the Senate Committee on Veterans' Affairs. The testimony of experts is cited in full; a great deal of it is startling (and gives some idea of the horrors peculiar to the Vietnam struggle).
    Part 1. 1972. 317 p. il.
    Part 2 (1972). [319-503] p. il.

Drug Dependence and Use; a Selected Bibliography. Natl. Clearinghouse for Drug Abuse Inform., 1971; repr. 1972. 51 p.
                                        041-010-00010-0
Books and articles of 1969–70. Arranged by 18 subject categories, then alphabetically by author. Not annotated, and no index.

Drug Use in America; Problem in Perspective; Second Report of the National Commission on Marihuana and Drug Abuse. Marihuana and Drug Abuse Comm., 1973. 481 p.   052-066-00003-4
A massive study that begins by clearly defining some of the basic issues involved, personal and social. Drug-use behavior in this country is discussed: a typology of such behavior is suggested. There is a study of the social impact of drug dependence and drug-induced behavior. A most impressive bibliography (not, alas, annotated).

Drug Use and Highway Safety; a Review of the Literature. J. N. Nichols. Natl. Highway Traffic Safety Admin., 1972. 110 p.
                                        050-003-00050-7
Astonishingly detailed and fair assessment of the subject—a review

that reflects great credit on the issuing department and the compiler. Every conceivable aspect of the subject is dealt with, including effects of alcohol on the human body and how it affects very specific driving skills. The study is particularly interesting for its conclusions. There is a glossary of drug terms.

Drugs of Abuse. Bur. of Narcotics and Dangerous Drugs. [1972]. [15] p. il.   027-004-00017-2
Very fine booklet. Illustrations in color, to help with identification. Effects; fighting the habits.

Drug-taking in Youth; an Overview of the Social, Psychological, and Educational Aspects. L. G. Richards and J. H. Lander. Bur. of Narcotics and Dangerous Drugs, 1969 [1971]. 48 p.

027-004-00014-8

To give adults some understanding of the social and psychological aspects of the drug phenomenon; suggestions for further reading are included.

Efforts to Prevent Heroin from Illicitly Reaching the United States. Genl. Accounting Off., 1972. 36 p. il. Free from the Off.
Report prepared by the Bureau of Narcotics and Dangerous Drugs and the Department of State.

Fact Sheets. Drug Enforcement Admin., 1973. 67 p. Free from the Admin.   027-004-00018-1
Very fine for readers of any age. One would think they might be particularly valuable in upper high school, providing, as they certainly should, themes for many a term paper. Discussed are the trade routes of drug traffic; drug abuse; prevention of abuse; narcotic drugs; depressants; hallucinogens. Includes lists of audio-visual aids, publications. Has a vivid section on drug identification, with portraits in color of the villains. The activities of the Drug Enforcement Administration are discussed fully.

Glossary of Terms in the Drug Culture. Bur. of Narcotics and Dangerous Drugs [1971]. [15] p. Free from the Bur.
Listing of "street" terms.

Growing Up in America; a Background to Drug Abuse. A. McLeod. Natl. Inst. of Mental Health, 1973. 98 p. il.   017-024-00290-9
The tragedy of youth caught in the inner city, the suburbs—you name it. And some ways of fighting the growing evil.

Guidelines for Drug Abuse Prevention Education. Bur. of Narcotics and Dangerous Drugs [1970]. 77 p. Free from the Bur.
027-004-00016-4
Several papers by authorities. Background information; sample courses of study. An appendix in the form of a chart listing drugs, medical uses, symptoms of abuse, and a bibliography. Primarily intended to show how various schools have conducted educational programs to fight drug abuse from kindergarten through high school.

Has Anyone You Care About Changed for No Apparent Reason? Bur. of Narcotics and Dangerous Drugs [1970]. [9] p. il.
027-004-00002-4
Telltale symptoms; how to observe them; where to seek help.

Hashish Smuggling and Passport Fraud; "The Brotherhood of Eternal Love;" Hearings . . . The Senate, 1973. 118 p. il.
052-070-02147-1
Before the Subcommittee to Investigate the Administration of the Internal Security Act and Other Internal Security Laws, of the Senate's Committee on the Judiciary. Discusses the bearing of both smuggling and passport fraud on internal security. Study is focused primarily on Dr. T. Leary's "Brotherhood of Eternal Love," ("which has combined a mystical fanaticism with criminal activities," in the words of one speaker). Interesting for its reprints of advertisements, articles; and for the testimony of witnesses.

Heroin: Can the Supply Be Stopped? Report . . . W. Spong. The Senate, 1972. 28 p. Free from the Comm. on Foreign Relations.
Senator Spong's report to the Committee on Foreign Relations, made after an extensive trip in the course of which he conferred with many foreign governments on this problem.

How Was the Trip? A Play Concerned with Drug Abuse. E. Blake.
Natl. Inst. of Mental Health (1970) [1971]. 31 p.   017-024-00100-1
"Complete production guide for a 1-act play suitable for presentation by amateur drama groups, with suggestions for group discussion."

Illicit Use of Dangerous Drugs in the United States; a Compilation
of Studies, Surveys, and Polls. D. F. Berg and L. P. Broecker,
comps. Bur. of Narcotics and Dangerous Drugs, 1972. 77 p. Free
from the Bur.
A great many studies are cited, and their findings shown in tables.

Katy's Coloring Book about Drugs and Health. Bur. of Narcotics
and Dangerous Drugs, [1973]. [16 p.] il.   027-004-00011-3
Original way to teach children about drug use; for adults, as well.

Long Dark Hallway. Natl. Inst. of Mental Health [1971]. [32] p. il.
017-024-00174-1
Very touching and fine photographs tell the story of how drug
addiction is being fought by social workers in a Mexican-American
setting—and why it needs to be fought.

LSD-25; Factual Account; a Layman's Guide to the Pharmacology,
Physiology, Psychology, and Sociology of LSD. L. G. Richards and
others. Bur. of Narcotics and Dangerous Drugs, 1969 [1970]. 44 p. il.
027-004-00006-1
Superb booklet, briefly covering every important aspect of the
dangers of this drug.

Marihuana and Health; a Report to Congress . . . The Senate, 1971.
100 p.   052-070-01022-3
The report is from the Secretary of HEW to the Subcommittee on
Alcoholism and Narcotics, of the Senate Committee on Labor and
Public Works. Natural and synthetic drug; the extent and patterns
of its use; studies of its effects on animals; effects on man; social
and cultural consequences of its use. Research needs, and future
directions of research.

Marihuana and Health; 4th Annual Report to the U.S. Congress from the Secretary of Health, Education, and Welfare. Natl. Inst. of Drug Abuse [1974]. 163 p.   017-024-00416-2
A major purpose of these reports is to serve as a widely available, up-to-date compendium of scientific information bearing on the issue of marihuana and health.

Narcotics Situation in Southeast Asia; Report of a Special Study Mission. H. L. Wolff. House of Representatives, 1972. 22 p. Free from the Comm.
Prepared for the Committee on Foreign Affairs. "[Over the situation holding when a report was issued one year earlier] there is growing evidence that the situation is changing, and that the governments in the area, particularly Thailand and Burma, are making considerable progress in their fight against narcotics trade and trafficking, although much remains to be accomplished . . ." Burma, Laos, Thailand, Vietnam, Korea, Japan, Hong Kong, People's Republic of China.

National Directory, Drug Abuse Treatment Programs. Natl. Inst. of Mental Health [1972]. 54 p.   017-024-00230-5

Neonatal Narcotic Addiction. J. S. Lin-Fu. Maternal and Child Health Serv. [1969]. 11 p. Free from the Serv.

Proceedings of Alternatives to Drug Abuse Conference, Santa Barbara, Calif., May 16–18, 1972. Bur. of Narcotics and Dangerous Drugs [1972]. 2 parts. Free from the Bur.
Sixty-page summary is followed by the full transcript of the Conference, whose purpose was "to bring together people from the criminal justice system, from the education system, and from community-based drug programs, to discuss ways of more effectively preventing drug abuse by young people"; i.e., by providing acceptable alternatives to the drug habit.
    Part 1. 61 + 110 p.
    Part 2. [111-379] p.

Proper and Improper Use of Drugs by Athletes; Hearings . . . House of Representatives, 1973. 843 p. Free from the Comm.

052-070-02472-1

Before the Subcommittee to Investigate Juvenile Delinquency of the House Committee on the Judiciary.

Reference Aid; Glossary of Narcotics Terms, World Wide. Joint Publication Research Serv., 60386 (1973). 58 p. Purchase from the Serv.

Terms are in English, Arabic, French, German, Japanese, Malagasy, Polish, Portuguese, and Spanish.

Resource Book for Drug Abuse Education. M. Nellis, ed. Natl. Clearinghouse for Drug Abuse Inform. [1972]. 115 p.

017-024-00238-0

Second edition of a very fine work first issued in 1969. A selection of 24 articles from various sources on the subject. Divided into 4 parts: insights and perspectives; definitions and delineation; programs: prevention and intervention; education: principles and practices. "Intended to serve as a basis for improved understanding, trust, and communication between teacher and student about drug abuse."

Selected Bibliography on Drugs of Abuse. Natl. Inst. of Mental Health, 1970. 25 p. Free from the Inst.

Citations are not annotated.

Social Seminar Handbook: Education, Drugs, and Society. Natl. Inst. of Mental Health [1972]. 65 p. il. Free from the Inst.

017-024-00167-8

Specifics and aims of a "multi-media drug abuse educational program designed for teachers, school administrators, and other school personnel." Sees drug abuse as a community problem. It is important to remember that the suggestions and guidelines in books of this kind come from experienced, imaginative, and compassionate people who have lived and worked for years with the problem.

Special Action Office for Drug Abuse Prevention Answers the Most Frequently Asked Questions about Drug Abuse. Exec. Off. of the President, 1972. 25 p. Free from the Office.

Brief historical introduction to the problem; then general questions; sections on sedatives, hallucinogens, stimulants, narcotics, marihuana.

U.S. Heroin Problem and Southeast Asia; Report . . . John J. Brady and others. House of Representatives, 1973. 82 p. il. Free from the Comm.

Report of a staff survey team working for the Committee on Foreign Affairs. Covered here is the situation in Burma, Laos, Thailand, South Vietnam, Hong Kong, People's Republic of China, Japan, and Korea.

Wild Hemp (Marijuana); How to Control It. Dept. of Agr., PA 959 [1970]. [8] p. il. 001-000-01221-5

Grows wild in many places in this country.

World Drug Traffic and Its Impact on U.S. Security; Hearings . . . The Senate, 1972. 6 parts.

Hearings held before the Senate's Committee on the Judiciary. A detailed study of the "Drug Trail" from various parts of the world into the United States. The reports are based upon the testimony of witnesses and a mountain of documents. Separate parts are as follows:

    3. International Connection. [81-121] p. il. 052-070-01649-3

    4. Global Context; Report of General Walt. [123-197] p. il.
                              052-070-01674-4

    5. Research on Marihuana and Hashish. [199-252] p. il.
                              052-070-01672-8

    6. Machinery of Control [253-303] p. il. 052-070-01679-5

World Heroin Report; Report of Special Study Mission . . . M. P. Murphy and others, eds. House of Representatives, 1971. 46 p. il. Free from the House Document Room.

A report to the House Committee on Foreign Affairs, based on interviews by two Representatives with concerned authorities in Switzerland, France, Italy, Turkey, Iran, Thailand, South Vietnam, Hong Kong, and Japan. There is an invaluable map showing major illicit opium sources and flow throughout the world. Map contains some surprises.

World Narcotics Problem; the Latin American Perspective; Report . . . M. F. Murphy and R. H. Steele. House of Representatives, 1973. 80 p. il. Free from the Comm.
Report of a special study mission to Latin America and the Federal Republic of Germany, submitted to the House Committee on Foreign Affairs. Part 1 (Latin America) includes studies in Mexico, Colombia, Panama, Argentina, Peru, Ecuador, Bolivia, and Chile. Part 2 (Europe) covers West Germany, including use of drugs among our armed forces. The value of this kind of study cannot be sufficiently stressed.

Youthful Drug Use. R. Brotman and F. Suffet. Youth Develop. and Delinquency Prevention Admin., 1970. 39 p.   017-060-00096-1
Discussion of one of society's most puzzling problems; with many useful guidelines for turning youth's proclivities into more meaningful channels.

ECONOMIC AND POLITICAL GEOGRAPHY

The listing in this section contains titles or series published by five departments of the Government. Each of the series has a "covering" and detailed annotation. Thus the Background Notes (164 titles) and the Foreign Economic Trends (118 titles) are blanketed under one annotation each.
The Department of State generally observes the rule of updating

data, where possible, every three years. The compiler has therefore limited his citations to material no earlier than 1971–72, unless there was good reason for going further back.

The titles cited here were prepared by Government Agencies active in the field, or were compiled from data supplied by such Agencies. They may therefore be assumed to be accurate. What is, perhaps, surprising is that they make very good reading. The compiler has found them invaluable for every class of student, as well as for adult (if that is the right word!) readers. They belong not only in every kind of library, but in every literate household as well.

The Army pamphlets described as "Bibliographical Surveys" are much more than that modest designation implies. They are bibliographies: exhaustive, arranged by subject, and annotated fully and expertly. But they are also notable for very fine maps in the pocket of each title: maps that would probably be hard to match elsewhere. Each of the Surveys contains the State Department's Background Note current at the time the Survey was issued; in one or two cases a more recent edition of the Notes may be available. The entire group (or what of it remains in print) is most highly recommended for schools of any grade and for every interested reader. Bear in mind that the *latest* issue of any title you request is always sent unless you ask for a particular year.

Agriculture in the Vietnam Economy; System for Economic Survival. R. R. Daly and others. Econ. Research Serv., FDD Field Rept. 34 [1973]. 321 p. il. Free from the Serv.

Part of the tragic history of this country lies in its complete dependence on agriculture; a bad year means widespread famine and death. This is a very thorough study of the situation, meant for the serious student.

Area Handbooks. Dept. of the Army, 1969–1974.

It is somewhat ironical that this group of titles, which embraces a good many of the Government's finest publications, should be classified as pamphlets. They must be, by all odds, the most learned "pamphlets" ever published anywhere. The Handbooks are prepared by the Foreign Area Studies of the American University, in Washington, D.C. (This statement does not always apply; in certain cases the Handbooks appear to have been prepared *for* the Foreign Area Studies by an outside agency. But for ordering from the Government Printing Office, this sort of bibliographic exactitude is not necessary. The listing below is thus in certain cases simplified.) All in all, the entire group is immensely interesting, and in the experience of the compiler has not been exceeded in usefulness for students of high school and college level (as well as, of course, for the adult who has left schooling behind him). Each of the Handbooks covers the geography and economy of the area it deals with, as well as the history, ethnic composition and government of the title area.

These comments have in no way conveyed the charm with which the Area Handbooks are prepared and written: they are not simply textbooks. They go deeply into the ways, peculiarities, and customs of their subject peoples, and do much to show that these people are like ourselves.

Afghanistan. H. H. Smith and others. 1973. 453 p. il.

008-020-00461-8

Albania. E. K. Keefe and others. 1973. 223 p. il.

008-020-00362-0

Algeria. R. F. Nyrop and others. 1972. 401 p. il.

008-020-00435-9

Angola. A. B. Herrick and others. 1975. 439 p. il.

008-020-00204-6

Argentina. F. P. Munson and others. 1974. 466 p. il.

008-020-00536-3

Brazil. T. E. Weil and others. 1971. 645 p. il.   008-020-00564-9

Burma. J. W. Henderson and others. 1972. 341 p. il.

008-020-00391-3

Burundi. G. C. McDonald and others. 1973. 203 p. il.

008-020-00219-4

Ceylon. R. F. Nyrop and others. 1973. 525 p. il.

008-020-00366-2

Chad. H. D. Nelson and others. 1974. 267 p. il.   008-020-00423-5

People's Republic of China. D. P. Whitaker and others. 1973. 729 p. il. 008-020-00418-9

Republic of China. F. H. Chaffee and others. 1974. 435 p. il. 008-020-00437-5

Colombia. T. E. Weil and others. 1973. 595 p. il. 008-020-00321-2

People's Republic of Congo (Brazzaville). G. C. McDonald and others. 1973. 225 p. il 008-020-00346-8

Costa Rica. H. I. Blutstein and others. 1974. 323 p. il. 008-020-00340-9

Cuba. H. I. Blutstein and others. 1973. 505 p. il. 008-020-00375-1

Cyprus. R. F. Nyrop and others. 1973. 543 p. il. 008-020-00364-6

Czechoslovakia. E. K. Keefe and others. 1974. 321 p. il. 008-020-00408-1

Dominican Republic. 1973. p. il. 008-020-00484-7

East Germany. E. K. Keefe and others. 1972. 329 p. il. 008-020-00421-9

Ecuador. T. E. Weil and others. 1973. 403 p. il. 008-020-00449-9

El Salvador. H. I. Blutstein and others. 1972. 259 p. il. 008-020-00367-1

Ethiopia. I. Kaplan. 1974. 543 p. il. 008-020-00365-4

Germany. N. C. Walpole and others. 1974. 955 p. il. 008-020-00186-4

Ghana. I. Kaplan and others. 1975. 449 p. il. 008-020-00382-4

Greece. A. B. Herrick and others. 1970 [1974]. 357 p. il. 008-020-00443-0

Guatemala. J. Dombrowski and others. 1973. 361 p. il. 008-020-00215-1

Guyana. W. B. Mitchell and others. 1970. 378 p. il. 008-020-00218-6

Haiti. T. E. Weil and others. 1973. 189 p. il. 008-020-00486-3

Honduras. H. L. Blutstein and others 1973. 225 p. il. 008-020-00368-9

Hungary. E. K. Keefe and others. 1973. 339 p. il. 008-020-00485-5

India. Rinn-Sup Shinn and others. 1972. 791 p. il.

008-020-00185-6

Indian Ocean Territories. T. L. Stoddard and others. 1974. 160 p. il.   008-020-00393-0

Indonesia. J. W. Henderson and others. [1974]. 569 p. il.

008-020-00508-8

Iran. H. H. Smith and others. 1973. 653 p. il.   008-020-00349-2

Iraq. H. H. Smith and others. 1972. 413 p. il.   008-020-00407-3

Israel. H. H. Smith and others. 1970. 457 p. il.   008-020-00341-7

Ivory Coast. T. D. Roberts and others. 1973. 449 p. il.

008-020-00481-2

Japan. F. H. Chaffee and others. 1974. 628 p. il. 008-020-00520-7

Hashemite Kingdom of Jordan. H. C. Reese and others. 1974. 370 p. il.   008-020-00523-1

Kenya. I. Kaplan and others. 1974. 707 p. il.   008-020-00201-1

Khmer Republic (Cambodia). D. P. Whitaker. 1974. 389 p. il.

008-020-00445-6

North Korea. Rinn-Sup Shinn and others. 1974. 481 p. il.

008-020-00217-8

Republic of Korea. K. G. Clare and others. 1970. 492 p. il.

008-020-00350-6

Laos. D. P. Whitaker and others. 1974. 337 p. il.

008-020-00467-7

Lebanon. H. H. Smith and others. 1974. 352 p. il.

008-020-00320-4

Liberia. T. D. Roberts and others. 1972. 387 p. il.

008-020-00414-6

Libya. R. F. Nyrop and others. 1973. 317 p. il.   008-020-00452-9

Malagasy Republic. H. D. Nelson and others. 1973. 327 p. il.

008-020-00453-7

Malaysia. J. W. Henderson and others. 1973. 639 p. il.

008-020-00193-1

Mauritania. B. D. Curran and J. Schrock. 1972. 185 p. il.

008-020-00438-3

Mongolia. T. N. Dupuy and others. 1974. 500 p. il.

008-020-00509-6

Morocco. R. F. Nyrop and others. [1972]. 403 p. il.

008-020-00420-1

Mozambique. A. B. Herrick and others. 1974. 351 p. il.
008-020-00207-1

Nepal, with Sikkim and Bhutan. G. L. Harris and others. 1972 [1973]. 431 p. il.
008-020-00480-4

Nicaragua. J. M. Ryan and others. 1974. 393 p. il.
008-020-00327-1

Nigeria. H. D. Nelson and others. 1974. 485 p. il.
008-020-00404-9

Oceania. J. W. Henderson and others. 1973. 555 p. il.
008-020-00307-7

Pakistan. R. F. Nyrop and others. 1974. 691 p. il.
008-020-00195-3

Panama. T. E. Weil and others. 1974. 415 p. il. 008-020-00419-7

Paraguay. T. E. Weil and others. 1974. 316 p. il. 008-020-00402-2

Peripheral States of the Arabian Peninsula. 1974. 201 p. il.
008-020-00347-6

Peru. T. E. Weil and others. 1973. 429 p. il. 008-020-00436-7

Philippines. F. H. Chaffee and others. 1974. 413 p. il.
008-020-00210-1

Poland. E. K. Keefe and others. 1973. 335 p. il. 008-020-00450-2

Romania. E. K. Keefe and others. 1974. 319 p. il.
008-020-00433-2

Rwanda. R. F. Nyrop and others. 1969. 212 p. il.
008-020-00220-8

Saudi Arabia. N. C. Walpole and others. 1974. 373 p. il.
008-020-00383-2

Senegal. 1974. 489 p. il. 008-020-00521-5

Somalia. I. Kaplan and others. 1969 [1970]. 455 p. il.
008-020-00326-3

Republic of South Africa. I. Kaplan and others. 1972. 845 p. il.
008-020-00308-5

Soviet Union. E. K. Keefe and others. 1974. 827 p. il.
008-020-00335-2

Democratic Republic of Sudan. H. D. Nelson and others. 1973. 351 p. il. 008-020-00440-5

Syria. R. F. Nyrop and others. 1974. 357 p. il. 008-020-00396-4

Tanzania. A. B. Herrick and others. 1974. 522 p. il.
008-020-00206-2

Thailand. J. W. Henderson and others. 1973. 413 p. il.

008-020-00384-1

Republic of Tunisia. H. C. Reese and others. [1974]. 415 p. il.

008-020-00328-0

Republic of Turkey. T. D. Roberts and others. 1974. 438 p. il.

008-020-00496-1

Uganda. A. B. Herrick and others. 1974. 456 p. il.

008-020-00212-7

United Arab Republic (Egypt). H. H. Smith and others. 1972. 555
p. il.   008-020-00192-9

Uruguay. T. E. Weil and others. [1971]. 439 p. il.

008-020-00361-1

Venezuela. T. E. Weil and others. 1972. 525 p. il.

008-020-00381-6

North Vietnam. H. H. Smith. 1974. 494 p. il.   008-020-00202-0

South Vietnam. H. H. Smith and others. 1974. 510 p. il.

008-020-00333-6

Yugoslavia. G. C. McDonald and others. 1973. 653 p. il.

008-020-00490-1

Zaire. G. C. McDonald and others. 1971. 587 p. il.

008-020-00348-4

Zambia. I. Kaplan and others. 1974. 482 p. il.   008-020-00537-1

Background Notes. Dept. of State, 1971–75.

The Background Notes are one of the Government Printing Office's
best buys. They belong not only in every school and public library,
but even in every literate American's library. Their pagination is deceptive: a 4-page brochure is easily the equivalent of a 16-page
chapter in any book. Normally, items are updated at least every
three years, and nothing older than three years is cited below. Data
for the Background Notes are gathered by State Department personnel stationed in the many countries covered (at present the Notes
number 164). Used in conjunction with several other Government
series (see elsewhere in this section), the Notes give reliable and very
recent information on almost every aspect of any country and its
people. Fuller information (though normally not so recent) is to be
found in the very remarkable Area Handbooks; more detailed economic information, in the Foreign Economic Trends. Each of the

briefer items is most remarkable; but, on balance, the Background Notes are probably most useful for the general student and reader since they are more compact. In this listing, pagination is not cited, because it varies within narrow limits; usually it is four to eight. Latest editions are always sent.

French Territories of Afars and Issas. 1975.	044-000-99894-1
Kingdom of Afghanistan. 1972.	044-000-99891-2
People's Republic of Albania. 1973.	044-000-99823-8
Democratic and Popular Republic of Algeria. 1974.	
	044-000-99897-1
Valleys of Andorra. 1973.	044-000-99812-2
Angola. 1973.	044-000-99810-6
Republic of Argentina. 1975.	044-000-99907-2
Australia. 1973.	044-000-99784-3
Federal Republic of Austria. 1974.	044-000-99865-3
Bahamas. 1973.	044-000-99814-9
State of Bahrain. 1974.	044-000-99701-1
Bangladesh. 1973.	044-000-99765-7
Barbados. 1972.	044-000-99889-1
Kingdom of Belgium. 1973.	044-000-99806-8
Bermuda. 1972.	044-000-99870-0
Republic of Bolivia. 1972.	044-000-99873-4
Republic of Botswana. 1972 [1973].	044-000-99902-1
Federative Republic of Brazil. 1972.	044-000-99900-5
British Honduras. 1972.	044-000-99750-9
People's Republic of Bulgaria. 1973.	044-000-99819-0
Socialist Republic of the Union of Burma. 1974.	044-000-99843-2
Republic of Burundi. 1971.	044-000-99648-1
United Republic of Cameroon. 1973.	044-000-99822-0
Canada. 1975.	044-000-99903-0
Central African Republic. 1973.	044-000-99788-6
Republic of Ceylon. 1973.	044-000-99804-1
Republic of Chad. 1972.	044-000-99735-5
Republic of Chile. 1975.	044-000-91004-7
People's Republic of China. 1974.	044-000-99877-1
Republic of China. 1974.	044-000-99851-3
Republic of Colombia. 1973.	044-000-99759-2

People's Republic of the Congo (Brazzaville). 1973.

	044-000-99791-6
Republic of Costa Rica. 1975.	044-000-99912-9
Republic of Cuba. 1971.	044-000-99670-7
Cyprus. 1973.	044-000-99789-4
Czechoslovak Socialist Republic. 1974.	044-000-99856-4
Republic of Dahomey. 1975.	044-000-99905-6
Kingdom of Denmark. 1974.	044-000-99895-5
Ecuador. 1975.	044-000-99772-0
El Salvador. 1973.	044-000-99794-1
Equatorial Guinea. 1975.	044-000-99915-3
Empire of Ethiopia. 1972.	044-000-99726-6
Fiji. 1973.	044-000-91008-0
Finland. 1973.	044-000-91001-2
France. 1973.	044-000-91012-8
French Guiana. 1973.	044-000-99783-5
Gabonese Republic. 1974.	044-000-99837-8
Republic of the Gambia. 1975.	044-000-99893-9
East Germany (Soviet Zone). 1971.	044-000-99922-6
Federal Republic of Germany. 1974.	044-000-99887-4
Ghana. 1973.	044-000-99665-1
Greece. 1973 [1974].	044-000-99824-6
Guadeloupe. 1971.	044-000-99875-1
Republic of Guatemala. 1972.	044-000-91005-5
Republic of Guinea. 1974.	044-000-99669-3
Cooperative Republic of Guyana. 1974.	044-000-99852-1
Republic of Haiti. 1972.	044-000-99869-6
Republic of Honduras. 1974.	044-000-99663-4
Hong Kong. 1974.	044-000-99850-5
Hungarian People's Republic. 1972.	044-000-99693-6
Republic of Iceland. 1974.	044-000-99847-5
Republic of India. 1973 [1974].	044-000-99828-9
Republic of Indonesia. 1971 [1972].	044-000-99864-5
Iran. 1972.	044-000-99857-2
Republic of Iraq. 1974.	044-000-99861-1
Ireland. 1974.	044-000-99879-3
State of Israel. 1974.	044-000-99862-9
Italy. 1973.	044-000-99916-1

Republic of Ivory Coast. 1973.   044-000-99813-1
Jamaica. 1974.   044-000-99849-1
Japan. 1973.   044-000-99803-3
Hashemite Kingdom of Jordan. 1974.   044-000-99880-7
Republic of Kenya. 1972.   044-000-99700-2
Khmer Republic (Cambodia). 1973.   044-000-99768-1
(North) Korea. 1973.   044-000-99808-4
(South) Korea. 1974.   044-000-99831-9
State of Kuwait. 1972.   044-000-99913-7
Republic of Lebanon. 1975.   044-000-99898-0
Kingdom of Lesotho. 1975.   044-000-99896-3
Liberia. 1973.   044-000-91003-9
Libyan Arab Republic. 1972.   044-000-99868-8
Principality of Liechtenstein. 1974.   044-000-99859-9
Luxembourg. 1973.   044-000-99802-5
Macao. 1972.   044-000-99844-1
Malagasy Republic. 1973.   044-000-99792-4
Republic of Malawi. 1974.   044-000-99829-7
Malaysia. 1973.   044-000-99815-7
Republic of Maldives. 1974.   044-000-99883-1
Republic of Mali. 1971 [1972].   044-000-99855-6
Malta. 1972.   044-000-99878-5
Martinique. 1974.   044-000-99845-9
Islamic Republic of Mauritania. 1974.   044-000-99853-0
Mauritius. 1974.   044-000-99867-0
Mexico. 1973.   044-000-91002-1
Monaco. 1972.   044-000-91013-6
Mongolian People's Republic. 1972.   044-000-99749-5
Morocco. 1973.   044-000-99678-2
Mozambique. 1973.   044-000-99798-3
Republic of Nauru. 1973.   044-000-99644-8
Kingdom of Nepal. 1973.   044-000-99635-9
Netherlands. 1973.   044-000-99832-1
Netherlands Antilles. 1974.   044-000-99625-1
New Zealand. 1973.   044-000-99775-4
Republic of Nicaragua. 1975.   044-000-99901-3
Republic of Niger. 1973 [1974].   044-000-99827-1
Nigeria. 1975.   044-000-99911-1

Kingdom of Norway. 1974.	044-000-99858-1
Oman. 1975.	044-000-99917-0
Pakistan. 1975.	044-000-99886-6
Panama. 1974.	044-000-99888-2
Republic of Paraguay. 1974.	044-000-99863-7
Republic of Peru. 1972.	044-000-99742-8
Republic of the Philippines. 1974.	044-000-99871-8
Polish People's Republic. 1974.	044-000-99838-6
Qatar. 1972.	044-000-99872-6
Socialist Republic of Romania. 1975.	044-000-99914-5
Republic of Rwanda. 1973.	044-000-99767-3
Republic of San Marino. 1973.	044-000-99825-4
Saudi Arabia. 1973.	044-000-99769-0
Republic of Senegal. 1974.	044-000-99882-3
Seychelles. 1973.	044-000-99786-0
Republic of Sierra Leone. 1972.	044-000-99854-8
Singapore. 1973.	044-000-99800-9
Somali Democratic Republic. 1974.	044-000-99841-6
South Africa. 1973.	044-000-99799-1
Southern Rhodesia. 1972.	044-000-99743-6
Spain. 1973.	044-000-99774-6
Spanish Sahara. 1974.	044-000-99846-7
Sri Lanka (Ceylon). 1973.	044-000-99804-1
Sudan. 1973.	044-000-99919-6
Surinam. 1971.	044-000-91007-1
Swaziland. 1973.	044-000-99909-9
Kingdom of Sweden. 1975.	044-000-99906-4
Switzerland. 1973.	044-000-99826-2
Syrian Arab Republic. 1974.	044-000-99840-8
United Republic of Tanzania. 1974.	044-000-99890-4
Kingdom of Thailand. 1973.	044-000-99764-9
Republic of Togo. 1974.	044-000-99821-1
Tonga. 1975.	044-000-91006-3
Trinidad and Tobago. 1973.	044-000-99781-9
Tunisia. 1973.	044-000-99801-7
Turkey. 1971.	044-000-99683-9
Republic of Uganda. 1974.	044-000-99839-4
Union of Soviet Socialist Republics. 1973.	044-000-99770-3

United Arab Emirates. 1975.	044-000-91009-8
United Kingdom. 1973.	044-000-99920-0
Upper Volta. 1973.	044-000-99771-1
Oriental Republic of Uruguay. 1972.	044-000-99720-7
Vatican City. 1973.	044-000-99918-8
Venezuela. 1974.	044-000-99830-1
(North) Viet-Nam. 1974.	044-000-99836-0
Republic of Viet-Nam. 1974.	044-000-99874-2
Independent State of Western Samoa. 1974.	044-000-99860-2
People's Democratic Republic of Yemen. 1974.	044-000-99881-5
Yemen Arab Republic. 1975.	044-000-99906-4
Socialist Federal Republic of Yugoslavia. 1974.	044-000-99835-1
Republic of Zaire. 1975.	044-000-99921-8
Republic of Zambia. 1974.	044-000-99834-3

Communist China; a Bibliographical Survey. Dept. of the Army, Pamph. 550-9 (1971). 253 p.   008-020-00351-4

Communist Eastern Europe; an Analytical Survey of the Literature. Dept. of the Army, Pamph. 550-8 (1971). 367 p. il.

008-020-00352-2

Communist North Korea; a Bibliographic Survey. Dept. of the Army, Pamph. 550-11 (1971). 130 p.   008-020-00376-0

Country Demographic Profiles, ISP-30 Series. Bur. of the Census, 1973–74.
The ethnic make-up and percentages are discussed in the titles that follow. There are demographic maps, probably hard to locate elsewhere.

1. Costa Rica. W. G. Duncan and D. L. Wolf. 1973. 10 p.
003-024-00124-1
—— Spanish ed. 1974. 17 p. Free from the Bur.
2. Ghana. W. G. Duncan. 1973. 10 p.   003-024-00232-9
3. Republic of China, Taiwan. W. G. Duncan. 1974. 10 p.
003-024-00255-8

Estimates and Projections of the Population of the U.S.S.R., by Age and Sex: 1950 to 2000. G. Baldwin. Dept. of Commerce, 1973. 29 p.

003-024-00112-8

International Population Report P-91/23, prepared by the Economic Analysis Bureau. Included here not only for its general interest, but as an excellent example of the profound statistical analyses made by so many Federal agencies.

Insular Southeast Asia; Australia, Indonesia, Malaysia, New Zealand, Philippines, Singapore; a Bibliographic Survey. Dept. of the Army, Pamph. 550-12 (1971). 419 p. il.   008-020-00394-8

Introduction to Antarctica. Dept. of the Navy, 1969. 54 p. il.

008-040-00046-0

Very fine; there is a brief, annotated bibliography.

Latin America and the Caribbean; Analytical Survey of the Literature. Dept. of the Army, Pamph. 550-7 (1969). 319 p. il.

008-020-00533-9

Magnificent overview of this large area. The pamphlet consists of a detailed bibliography, *plus* the State Department's Background Notes for the South American countries included, *plus* over 35 wonderful maps prepared for the U.S. Army Topographic Command. Some of the Background Notes have been updated. This extraordinary pamphlet is one of several available on global areas—all very fine.

Peninsular Southeast Asia; a Bibliographic Survey of the Literature ... Dept. of the Army, Pamph. 550-14 (1972). 424 p. il.

008-020-00428-6

Included are Burma, Cambodia, Laos, and Thailand.

Potential and Promise of the Arctic. Dept. of the Interior, 1970. 24 p. il.   024-000-00477-1

A "special report to the people." Largely an album of splendid color photographs, with explanatory text.

Ryukyu Islands; a Bibliography. N. D. King. Dept. of the Army, Pamph. 550-4 (1967). 105 p.   008-020-00191-1

Selected Annotated Bibliography of Environmental Studies of Iraq, Jordan, Lebanon, and Syria. V. J. Creasi and others, comps. Dept. of the Air Force, Environ. Tech. Applications Center, Tech. Note 70-5 (1970). 26 p. Purchase from the Center.

Selected Annotated Bibliography of Environmental Studies of Poland. A. L. Smith, Jr., comp. Dept. of the Air Force, Environ. Tech. Applications Center, Tech. Note 70-6 (1970). 52 p. Purchase from the Center.

Selected USSR and Eastern European Economic Data. Dept. of Commerce, 1974. 66 p. Free from the Dept.　　　003-025-00021-7
An overview of developing trade relations with these areas. Market data; commodity composition and trade; their trade with us; population and rates of growth; agricultural and industrial growth. Drawn from very reliable sources, and again invaluable for the student. (Prepared by the East-West Trade Bureau.)

Soviet Economic Prospects for the Seventies; a Compendium . . . Joint Econ. Comm., 1973. 776 p.　　　052-070-01853-4
Compiled for the Joint Economic Committee by the Congressional Research Service. J. P. Hardt, chief planner, "invited papers designed to meet the interests of the Committee and the Congress in an up-to-date body of data and interpretative comment on the domestic economy of the Soviet Union, including the record of recent economic development, and its relations with the outside world." Forty-two experts have contributed 30 papers divided into: plan and policy; resource claims of Soviet military establishment; industry; agriculture; consumption; human resources and education; foreign economy. There are papers on pollution, the Soviet petroleum industry, consumer welfare, housing, demographic trends, labor, education, U.S.S.R.–Western industrial cooperation, Soviet foreign aid. There is an extensive study of economic developments in the period 1959–66, with detailed statistical tables in an end pocket. It is impossible in a brief annotation to do justice to the scope and quality of this work, which the compiler considers one of the finest Congressional studies of recent years. The study deserves the widest possible circulation among scholars, libraries, and the general inter-

ested public. A very valuable additional feature is a chart of the committee apparatus of the Communist Party of the Soviet Union as of April 1, 1973—complete with names.

ECONOMICS

Anatomy of Inflation. Bur. of Labor Statistics, Rept. 373 (1970). 24 p. Free from the Bur.

"The term inflation really describes the state of the Nation's whole price and cost structure. The anatomy of inflation should be viewed in terms of a complicated network of commodity and service prices, wages and other costs of production, and asset values." To explain further the quality of this fine booklet, the compiler is in serious danger of quoting the whole Introduction to it. Most highly recommended.

Foreign Economic Trends and Their Implications for the United States. Bur. of International Commerce, 1973–75. Purchase from the Dept. of Commerce.

This immensely valuable group may be ordered, in single numbers or in its entirety, from the National Technical Information Service, Springfield, Va. 22161. The "FET's" are, generally, of specific interest only to a segment of the international business community, rather than to the individual "uninitiated" reader. (But see below!) The compiler has, therefore, cited only those titles of interest to the former. Titles are normally issued every six months; their information is thus very much up to date. Number of pages and the stock number for each title differ with each issuance of that title; for this reason the compiler has not cited pages or dates. (However, when the reader orders any of the group, he will receive the *latest* edition.) The Bureau of International Commerce provided most of the listing that follows. The brief description of the group furnished by the Bureau of International Commerce runs: "This series of commercial reports from the U.S. Foreign Service posts, U.S. Department of State, present current business and economic developments, with latest economic indicators, in over 100 countries [129 are listed below] which offer a present or potential market for U.S. goods and services . . ." The Bureau's remarks are intended for a commercial and trade audience; it should be emphasized, however, that the titles are of value even to students and readers of general backgrounds, their interest is by no means confined to commerce. They contain information on population, ethnic groups, history, and so on. The compiler has found them of inestimable value in working with all grades of students. The listing below was carried through April, 1975. In the citations, the number to the left refers to the date of the latest revision available.

75-018. Afghanistan.
73-074. Algeria.
73-069. Angola.
75-005. Argentina.
74-113. Australia.
74-139. Austria.
74-128. Bahamas.
75-009. Bahrain.
74-040. Bangladesh.
74-101. Barbados.
74-136. Belgium.
75-038. Belize.
74-109. Bermuda.
74-107. Bolivia.
73-039. Botswana.
74-126. Brazil.
75-035. Bulgaria.
75-016. Burma.
74-091. Burundi.
75-027. Cameroon.
74-117. Canada.
74-071. Central African Republic.
74-132. Chad.
75-002. Chile.
75-034. Republic of China.
74-100. China (Taiwan).
75-014. Colombia.

75-019. Costa Rica.
73-071. Cyprus.
74-029. Czechoslovakia.
74-010. Dahomey.
75-021. Denmark.
74-115. Dominican Republic.
74-016. Ecuador.
74-141. El Salvador.
74-013. Ethiopia.
75-030. Fiji.
73-142. Finland.
74-137. France.
74-060. French West Indies.
74-118. Gabon.
74-043. Germany, Democratic Republic.
74-131. Germany, Federal Republic.
74-087. Ghana.
74-116. Greece.
75-033. Grenada.
74-121. Guatemala.
75-032. Guinea.
74-102. Guyana.
74-104. Haiti.
75-023. Honduras.
74-135. Hong Kong.
74-072. Hungary.

74-124. Iceland.
74-125. India.
74-106. Indonesia.
74-123. Iran.
74-133. Ireland.
75-039. Israel.
74-120. Italy.
74-034. Ivory Coast.
74-127. Jamaica.
75-015. Japan.
74-079. Jordan.
74-080. Kenya.
74-129. Korea.
75-004. Kuala Lumpur.
75-037. Kuwait.
74-047. Laos.
75-012. Lebanon.
74-024. Liberia.
73-028. Libya.
74-074. Luxembourg.
74-075. Malagasy Republic.
74-084. Malawi.
75-004. Malaysia.
74-060. Martinique,
    Guadaloupe,
    French Guinea.
74-119. Mexico.
75-031. Morocco.
74-089. Mozambique.
74-105. Nepal.
74-112. Netherlands.
74-138. Netherlands Antilles.
75-029. New Zealand.
75-013. Nicaragua.
74-032. Niger.
74-134. Nigeria.
75-024. Norway.
75-008. Sultanate of Oman.

74-114. Pakistan.
74-142. Panama.
74-067. Paraguay.
75-022. Peru.
74-140. Philippines.
74-017. Poland.
73-063. Metropolitan Portugal.
74-093. Romania.
74-103. Rwanda.
74-141. San Salvador.
75-007. Saudi Arabia.
74-099. Senegal.
74-095. Sierra Leone.
75-003. Singapore.
75-020. Somali.
75-011. South Africa.
74-098. Spain.
74-021. Sri Lanka.
74-004. Sudan.
74-097. Surinam.
74-130. Sweden.
74-122. Switzerland.
74-094. Tanzania.
74-070. Thailand.
74-082. Togo.
74-050. Trinidad and Tobago.
75-010. Tunisia.
74-143. Turkey.
73-098. Turks/Caicos Islands.
73-129. Uganda.
75-017. United Kingdom.
75-025. Upper Volta.
74-030. Uruguay.
75-026. U.S.S.R.
75-028. Venezuela.
75-028. Yugoslavia.
74-068. Zaire.
74-065. Zambia.

Improving Marketing Systems in Developing Countries; an Approach to Identifying Problems and Strengthening Technical Assistance. M. Kriesberg and H. Steele. Econ. Research Serv., For. Agricultural Econ. Rev. 93 (1972). 85 p. Free from the Serv.

"A systematic approach to the analysis of marketing in developing countries . . . points out where research and technical assistance would be useful. It focuses particularly on means of measuring marketing efficiency and on identifying problems that need to be dealt with in improving efficiency."

Inflation; on Prices and Wages Running Amok: Readings. Cost of Living Council [1973]. 24 p. il.   041-014-00022-9

Very fine, especially as an introduction for the noneconomist. What inflation is; who gets hurt by it; what causes it; what the Government can do—and "what would *you* do?"

Material Needs and the Environment, Today and Tomorrow; Final Report. Natl. Comm. on Materials Policy [1973]. [312] p. il.

052-003-00005-9

Study undertaken for the purpose of "developing a national materials policy of broad dimensions . . . a policy, as we see it now, that must of necessity embrace the entire national resources scene—materials, energy, and the natural environment." The Commission makes five important recommendations, based on a profound study of many aspects of the economy.

Productivity and the Economy. Bur. of Labor Statistics, Bull. 1779 (1973). 65 p. il.   029-001-01070-2

A chartbook, divided into 3 parts: how productivity has developed over time; changes in factors that are influenced by productivitity; trends in factors that influence productivity.

Resource Scarcity, Economic Growth, and Environment; Hearings . . . Joint Econ. Comm., 1974. 192 p. il.   052-070-02367-8

Before the Subcommittee on Priorities and Economy in Government. Very fine; testimony of witnesses, and reprints of many pertinent articles.

EDUCATION

Bilingual Education Act; Hearings . . . House of Representatives, 1974. 484 p. Free from the Comm.
Hearings before the General Subcommittee on Education of the House Committee on Education and Labor. Detailed testimony from educators and others who have worked in this area.

Career Education; Implications for Minorities; Proceedings . . . Off. of Educ., 1973. [104] p. Free from the Off.
A national conference held in Washington, D.C., February 1–3, 1973.

Education Directory, 1973–74: Higher Education. H. E. Poole. Off. of Educ. [1974–75]. 570 p.   017-080-01392-4
The citation of the *Education Directory* is complicated by the fact that different parts (or volumes) are not always published together. This 1974 publication lists institutions in the United States and its outlying areas that offer at least a two-year program of college-level studies in research. Requirements and criteria for listing in the directory are stated in detail in the Introduction. Curricula are not given in detail. There is a full citation of officers of each school, including deans.

Education of the Culturally Different; a Multicultural Approach . . . a Handbook for Educators. J. D. Forbes. Off. of Educ., 1969. 64 p.
017-080-00705-3
Like many of the more recent titles of the Office of Education, based on a very wide and practical experience and intended to lend you a hand. Remember, this is for a teacher facing a particular problem and challenge.

Educational Research in Europe; Report . . . House of Representatives, 1971. 574 p. il. Free from the Subcomm. on Education.
Covered here are France, Norway, Great Britain, and Poland.

EDUCATION 113

Educational Revolution in China. R. D. Berendsen. Off. of Educ. [1973]. 52 p.   017-080-01228-6
"Summarizes the course of the 'education revolution' which was initiated in the Spring of 1960, and provides a compact analysis of the impact of this wide-ranging upheaval on the organization and condition of the educational enterprise of that country [China]. . . . There can be little doubt that the period covered by this study encompasses one of the most extraordinary sets of events in educational change in contemporary times . . . the report traces [in brief outline] the repudiation of the former school system, the virtual suspension of regular school activities for persons up to 4 years, and the gradual piecing together of a new kind of educational establishment more nearly in line with the view of Chairman Mao Tse-tung."

Educational Technology; Hearings . . . House of Representatives, 1972. 368 p. Free from the Comm.
Hearings before the Labor and Education Committee. Partly a reprint of a most remarkable work (*The Fourth Revolution,* published by McGraw-Hill, New York, 1973). The book was a report (and recommendations) of the Carnegie Commission on Higher Education. Following this partial reprint, the hearings include testimony and discussion by highly qualified educators.

Educational Technology and the Teaching-learning Process; a Selected Bibliography. J. S. Berthold and others, comps. Health Professions Educ. and Manpower Training Bur., 1969. 56 p. Free from the Bur.
". . . an introduction to the literature on the teaching-language process and on the new approaches in the field of teaching technology . . ."; i.e., the applications of technology in teaching, *not* the teaching of technological subjects. About 1,000 references, largely annotated.

Five Communities; Their Search for Equal Education. Civil Rights Comm., Clearinghouse Pub. 37 [1973]. 55 p.   005-000-00078-5
How communities in Michigan, California, North Carolina, and Florida are tackling the problem. The disappointments—and the glimmer of hope.

High School Volunteers. Natl. Student Volunteer Program, AC-TION. [1972]. 60 p. il.   056-000-00005-4
A manual written for school officials who want to learn more about the recent emergence of high school volunteer programs in the community.

How Teachers Make a Difference. Off. of Educ. [1971]. 166 p. il.
017-080-00813-1
Teachers may inspire—or fail to inspire—certain pupils. This book may help many a teacher join the inspiring group.

Institutional Viability: the Final Report and Recommendations of the Administration and Supervision National Field Task Force on the Improvement and Reform of American Education. Off. of Educ., 1974. 112 p.   017-080-01330-4
J. R. Tanner was chairman of the Task Force. The Task Force investigated several problems of education. It was one of six task forces established by the Department of Education "to contribute directly to the Office of Education's intensified efforts to help improve the nation's school systems and the preparation of the people who staff them." Other such task forces dealt with administration and supervision; basic studies; community relations; the Council of Chief State School Officials; teachers. "Windows to the bureaucracy," they assess recruiting techniques and abilities; and they make suggestions. For educators and administrators; and vital to them.

New Technology and Education; Selected References . . . L. M. Pearce and H. A. Miller, comps. House of Representatives, 1971. 140 p. Free from the Comm.
Prepared for the Subcommittee on Science, Research and Development of the Committee on Science and Astronautics. Probably 2,000 references, unannotated, are arranged in three parts: (1) relating to issues, problems, and future uses of education in general; (2) various uses of a variety of specific media; and (3) alternative methods of organization of instruction.

PREP Reports. [Off. of Educ. and] Natl. Inst. of Education, 1971–72
This very stimulating group originated in the Office of Education

and has been completed (so far) by the National Institute of Education. The objective of all the titles has remained the reporting of educational programs and innovative ideas—in which both Government agencies have succeeded admirably. Through the courtesy of the National Institute of Education the compiler is able to provide a perfect annotation of the whole group: "PREP (Putting Research into Educational Practice) is a series of reports that synthesize and interpret the significant findings of educational research and development and current practice for the practitioner. Written in non-research language, the reports are targeted to specific educational audiences—school administrators, teachers, school board members, teacher educators, and curriculum specialists—for use in modifying existing educational programs or developing new ones." The compiler earnestly hopes this wonderful series is not yet over. One of the most praiseworthy efforts of our Government is in the field of education.

1. Instructional Television Facilities; a Guide for School Administrators and Board Members. K. E. Oberholtzer. [1972]. 19 p.
017-080-00975-7

2. Reading and the Home Environment; the Principal's Responsibility. C. B. Smith and others. [1972]. 23 p. 017-080-00978-1

3. Establishing Central Reading Clinics; the Administrator's Role. C. B. Smith and others. [1972]. 77 p. 017-080-00982-0

6. Bilingual Education. J. G. Cooper and others. [1972]. 51 p.
017-080-01013-5

7. School-Community Relations; Research for School Board Members. J. D. Wilson and others. [1972]. 44 p. 017-080-01056-9

8. Teacher Militancy, Negotiations, and Strikes; Research for School Board Members. S. B. Sentelle. 1972. 20 p.
017-080-01057-7

9. Job-oriented Programs for the Disadvantaged. T. W. Banta and others. [1972]. 63 p. 017-080-01021-6

10. Seminar on Preparing the Disadvantaged for Jobs; a Planning Handbook. T. W. Banta. [1972]. 42 p. il. 017-080-00987-1

11. Research on Elementary Mathematics. M. Suydam and C. A. Riedesel. [1972]. 45 p. 017-080-00996-0

12. Paraprofessional Aides in Education. C. H. Rittenhouse. [1972].

38 p. 017-080-01014-3

13. Sharing Educational Services. R. Jongeward and F. Heesacker. [1972]. 77 p. 017-080-01039-9

14. Social Studies and the Disadvantaged. J. C. McLendon and others. [1972]. 46 p. 017-080-01006-2

15. Student Participation in Academic Governance. L. H. Robinson and J. D. Shoenfeld. [1971]. 47 p. 017-080-01018-6

16. Individualized Instruction. J. V. Edling. [1972]. 71 p.
017-080-00979-0

17. Microteaching. D. W. Allen and others. [1972]. 31 p.
017-080-00994-3

18. Reinforcing Productive Classroom Behavior; a Teacher's Guide to Behavior Modification. E. M. Glaser and I. G. Sarason. [1972]. 24 p. il. 017-080-01060-7

19. Migrant Education. J. G. Schnur. 1972. 33 p. il.
017-080-01002-0

20. Teacher Recruitment and Selection. D. L. Bolton. [1972]. 35 p. il. 017-080-01017-8

21. Teacher Evaluation. D. L. Bolton. [1972]. 40 p. il.
017-080-01037-2

22. Readiness Test for Disadvantaged Preschool Children. W. Walker. [1972]. 35 p. il. 017-080-01012-7

23. Educational Cooperatives. L. W. Hughes and others. [1972]. 65 p. il. 017-080-01030-5

24. School-Community Relations and Educational Change. [D. Weiler and J. Guertin]. [1971]. 52 p. 017-080-00983-8

26. Black Studies in Community Colleges. J. Lombardi and E. A. Quimby [1971]. 31 p. 017-080-01088-7

27. Year-round Schools; 45-15 Plan. [1971]. 24 p. il.
017-080-00995-1

29. New Products in Education. [1971]. 31 p. il.
017-080-01089-5

32. Job Placement and Followup of Secondary School Vocational Education Students. M. D. Miller and W. E. Budke. [1972]. [64] p. 017-080-01092-5

34. Evaluating College Classroom Teaching Effectiveness. W. W. Ronan. [1972]. 32 p. 017-080-01024-1

38. Developing Specifications for a Low-Cost Computer System for Secondary Schools. G. Kleiner. [1972]. 65 p. il.

017-080-01102-6

Recurrent Education. S. J. Mushkin, ed. Natl. Inst. of Health, 1974. [346] p.   017-080-01277-4
Papers from a Georgetown University conference, 1973. "Recurrent education is one of the most important alternative educational approaches to have emerged in recent times. . . . it makes it possible to alternate between leisure, work, and education in a way that avoids the rigid sequence that characterizes the structure of educational systems in most cities." (Foreword.)

Research and Training Opportunities Abroad and Foreign Curriculum Consultants in the United States, 1975–76; Programs to Help Strengthen American Education in Foreign Languages, Area Studies, and World Affairs. Off. of Educ., 1974. 34 p.   017-080-01309-6
The funding of such educational projects; applications and requirements.

Role of Campus Security in College Setting. S. Gelber. Dept. of Justice, 1972 [1973]. 209 p.   027-000-00172-6
Probably not for the general reader; for personnel charged with keeping peace on our campuses. The history of campus security bodies is briefly touched on (Yale had the first, in 1894). The book discusses the "role of the campus security officer in terms of historical origins, legal structures, and operational functions. It provides an appraisal of the security officer by four components of the educational system. Recommendations include a model which has three primary elements: patrol, investigation, and student services."

Teachers Talk about Their Feelings. E. M. Bowen. Natl. Inst. of Mental Health, 1973. 35 p.   017-024-00291-7
"An unusual and frank account from some young teachers concerning their feelings during their early days of teaching." The hope is to extrapolate from *their* feelings enough to be of service to the feelings and attitudes of others.

Toward Equal Educational Opportunity; Report . . . The Senate, 1972. 440 p. 052-070-01686-8
The report was prepared for the Select Committee on Equal Educational Opportunity.

EDUCATION ABROAD

Education in Thailand; Some Thai Perspectives. A. Tapingkae and L. J. Setti. Off. of Educ. [1972]. 118 p. il. 017-080-00960-9

Educational Reform and Renewal in Contemporary Spain. W. W. Brickman. Off. of Educ., 1972. 80 p. 017-080-01052-6

Educational System of Israel. A. Apanasewicz and S. M. Rosen. Off. of Educ., 1971. 9 p. il. 017-080-00806-8

ELECTRONICS

Basic Electronics. Naval Personnel Bur. [1971]. 2 vols.
008-047-00134-7

1. 1971. 566 p. il.
   It has 29 chapters, dealing with fundamental devices such as transistors, electron tubes; and communications theory.
2. 1971. 323 p. il.
   This is more advanced; it deals with oscillators, pulse forming, cavity resonators, transmitting devices, receivers.

Communications—Electronics Terminology. Air Force, Air Force Manual 11-1 (1970). 320 p. 008-070-00005-9
Advanced text.

ENERGY AND POWER RESOURCES

Clean Energy from Coal Technology. Office of Coal Research [1974]. 43 p. il. 024-014-00068-1

Six percent of the world's population, we consume about one third of its commercial energy supply—about 10 to 1 on a global per capita basis. But coal is only 17 percent, oil and gas 78 percent, of our energy source. By 2000, demand for fossil fuels will double. How we produce, and misuse, and what the Office of Coal Research is trying to do to correct our costly, damaging ways.

Conservation and Efficient Use of Energy; Joint Hearings . . . House of Representatives, 1973. 4 parts.   052-070-02086-5
Before "Certain Subcommittees" of the Committee on Government Operations and the Committee on Science and Astronautics. Very detailed study of how we lay waste our powers; what our resources are (or may be); how industry and science spend these resources, and what they do to help maintain and renew them. A study for the serious student.

1. 463 p. il.
2. [465-809] p. il. Free from the Comm.
3. [811-1504] p. il. Free from the Comm.
4. [1505-1952] p. il. Free from the Comm.

Conservation and Efficient Use of Energy; 26th Report of the Committee on Governmental Operations. House of Representatives, 1974. 133 p.   052-071-00428-9
Study made by the Subcommittee on Conservation and Natural Resources. A thorough discussion of what we must do after wasting so much of our natural energy heritage. Recommendations.

Energy Crisis and Small Business. House of Representatives, 1973: 61 p. il. Free from the Comm.
Prepared for the Permanent Select Committee on Small Business. In six parts: Current Petroleum Investigation; Industry Structure; Barriers to Entry; a Summary; . . . Cooperation Rather than Competition; Industry Performance; Causes of the Petroleum Shortage.

Energy and Environment; Electric Power. Council on Environ. Quality, 1973. 58 p. il.   041-011-00019-0

". . . the use of energy damages the environment . . . the production and use of energy pollute our air, befoul our streams, and damage our land. . . . This report considers the elements underlying our growing demand for energy and the environmental implications of the complex energy systems for meeting this demand." Four chapters: trends in our demand for energy; electric power and the environmental impacts of the fossil-fueled and nuclear systems in use today; improved efficiency systems and energy conservation will reduce environmental damages and slow our use of energy resources; and how electric energy demand forecasts can be combined with data on the environmental impacts of energy systems to yield an estimate of projected environmental consequences. Many detailed figures and statistics.

——— 4th Annual Report . . . Council on Environ. Quality, 1973. 499 p. il.   041-011-00020-3
"Land use control is perhaps the most pressing environmental issue before the nation . . ." This report sets forth in great detail the more recent work of the Council. Very fine.

Energy Facts. W. Griffin, comp. House of Representatives, 1973. 539 p. il.   052-070-02160-8
Prepared for the Subcommittee on Energy of the Committee on Science and Astronautics; compiled by the Congressional Research Service of the Library of Congress.

Energy from Oil Shale; Technical, Environmental, Economic, Legislative, and Policy Aspects of an Undeveloped Energy Source; Report. House of Representatives, 1973. 66 p. Free from the Comm.
Prepared for the Subcommittee on Energy of the Science and Astronautics Committee by the Congressional Research Service, Library of Congress. The "purpose is to summarize information on oil shale which has a bearing on legislation [pending] . . . discusses some of the policy issues involved." There is an immense amount of valuable statistical and informational data on uses of shale oil, economics of the industry, etc., and there is a detailed discussion of legislative issues involved.

Energy-related Research and Development. The Senate, 1975. 131 p.   052-070-02849-1
Prepared for the Aeronautical and Space Sciences Committee. Demonstrates dramatically the major role that the various technologies developed for aeronautical and space purposes can play in solving critical national problems like the energy crisis. A most thorough discussion.

Energy Resource Program of the United States Department of the Interior. Dept. of the Interior, 1974. 274 p. il.   024-000-00794-4
Prepared by the Office of Research and Development. Section A deals with strategies; Section B, with tactics. Together, these "provide a comprehensive review of why certain technologies will be employed and how the results will be applied." An "overview of the nation's energy system . . . proposed research . . . and budget requirements."

Fuel and Energy Resources, 1972; Hearings. House of Representatives, 1972. 2 parts.
Before the Committee on Interior and Insular Affairs. A detailed study of our reserves and expenditures of coal, natural gas, oil, and nuclear energy. ". . . bringing together material of many existing studies, and applying it to the problem we face today." Testimony of a great many qualified experts: government administrators (Federal to local), industry and labor leaders, scientists, conservationists. In short, a study of Americans as "energy gluttons." Part 2 contains biographical material on many of the witnesses.

Part 1. 448 p.   052-070-01548-9
Part 2. [449-944] p.   052-070-01593-4

Gasoline and Fuel Oil Shortage; Hearings . . . The Congress, 1973. 290 p. il.   052-070-01999-9
Before the Subcommittee on Consumer Economy of the Joint Economic Committee. A discussion of the problem from an unusual point of view: that of the small operator, such as a gas station operator, who is being faced with forced closing because the major oil

companies do not supply his needs. (This is only one aspect of a complex problem studied in detail in this publication.)

Geothermal Energy Research, Development, and Commercial Demonstration Act of 1973; Geothermal Energy Research, Development and Demonstration Act of 1974; Hearings . . . House of Representatives, 1974. 544 p. Free from the Comm.   022-003-90697-5

Before the Subcommittee on Energy of the House Science and Astronautics Committee. A discussion of both "the great potential of hot dry rock formations and geopressured fields and the need for an accelerated technical effort to realize this potential . . ." The pertinent pending legislation is cited in full (pp. 2-10 and 476-98). Most of the hearings, however, are taken up with the testimony of experts, and reprints of articles and other data. Includes very fine maps.

Geothermal Resources [the Potential for the Production of Power from Geothermal Resources]; Hearings . . . The Senate, 1973–74. 2 parts. Free from the Comm.

A superb study by the Subcommittee on Water and Power Resources of the Committee on Interior and Insular Affairs (if "study" is the proper word for hearings): testimony of experts; reprints of pertinent and important literature; detailed statistical tables. The Hearings are not only on potential, but on Government policies (including taxation) involved in research into this energy potential.

    Part 1. 1973. 290 p. il.
    Part 2. 1974. [291-771] p. il.

Home Energy Saving Tips. Natl. Bur. of Standards [1974]. [4] p. Free from the Bur.

How to Start an Energy Management Program. Dept. of Commerce [1973]. [8] p. il.   003-000-00414-7

Major Natural Pipelines . . . Fed. Power Comm., 1974.
    015-000-00309-0

A colored map, 13″ × 19″, updated at frequent intervals. There is one later than the date shown above, in all probability. This will be sent on your order.

NASA and Energy. Natl. Aeron. and Space Admin., EP-121 (1974). 15 p. il.   033-000-00567-9
NASA is working on (among infinite other possibilities) direct solar heating and cooling; wind generation of electricity; electric power from solar thermal energy; solar cells; clean and renewable fuels; locating additional fuel deposits; more efficient use of fuel; use of ocean temperature differentials. How soon will results show? ". . . sooner than we think if we mount the right kind of effort." (Perhaps five to ten years.)

Natural Steam for Power. Geol. Survey, 1974. [11] p. il.
024-001-00244-2
Sources; sites; why they occur; geothermal energy may prove "the most important [source of energy] in many areas." Types; properties.

Nuclear Energy Resources; a Geologic Perspective. J. C. Olson and others. Geol. Survey [1974]. 15 p. il. Free from the Survey.
024-001-02497-7
Importance of our energy-producing resources, and the story of how they are created and exploited. ". . . technology has developed a nuclear power-producing capability that provides less than one percent of the nation's electric energy today . . ." But this figure will rise to 21 percent in 1980, and to 38 percent by 1990.

Oil Shale; a Potential Source of Energy. [D. C. Duncan]. Geol. Survey, 1975. 16 p. il.   024-001-02204-4
An oil "locked in rock." In the United States, such locked reserves probably exceed 2,000 billion barrels of petroleum.

Potential for Energy Conservation; Substitutes for Scarce Fuels; Staff Study. Emergency Preparedness Off. [Exec. Off. of the President]. 1973. [114] p. il.   041-002-00010-7

Potential for Energy Production from Geothermal Resources; Report . . . The Senate, 1973. 40 p. 052-070-02114-4
Report of the Subcommittee on Water and Power Resources, Senate Committee on Interior and Insular Affairs. ". . . greater attention must be given to unconventional energy sources which have been largely ignored in the past. Geothermal energy, the energy of the earth's natural heat, is among the most promising. . . . It has been estimated that as much as 400,000 megawatts of electric generating capacity based upon geothermal energy could be installed in the United States by the year 2000 . . ." Expert testimony.

Questions and Answers about Nuclear Power Plants. Environ. Protection Agency, 1973. [25] p. il. 055-000-00106-5
From "What kind of power plants are there?" to "Hasn't there been a controversy over the capability of emergency . . . cooling systems in reactors to prevent an accident?" Includes a list, by states, of nuclear power plants operating in 1973.

Residential Energy Conservation; a Summary Report. Dept. of Housing and Urban Develop., 1974. 28 p. il. Free from the Dept.
"The energy which we use in our homes accounts for approximately one-fifth of our total national energy consumption." The Baltimore-Washington areas were used as the "geographic and climatic" areas to be studied in depth. The booklet shows plans for apartments in low- and high-rise buildings; how they can be oriented, and designed, to consume less fuel. Charts show the effects of design on energy consumption in residences modified to meet more scientific findings.

Water Demands for Expanding Energy Development. G. H. Davis and L. A. Wood. Geol. Survey, Cir. 703 (1974). 14 p. Free from the Survey.
"Water is used in providing energy for mining and reclamation of mined land, insite processing, transportation, refining, and conversion of fuels to other forms of energy." This circular tells how much of our water goes into these various industrial applications.

Winter U.S.A.: **Staying Warm and Saving Money.** S. R. Aucain. Off. of Econ. Opportunity, OEO Pamph. 6143-1 [1974]. [14] p. il. Free from the Off.
Winterproofing from attic down: doors, windows, fireplaces, etc.

ENERGY RESEARCH AND DEVELOPMENT ADMINISTRATION

The one-time Atomic Energy Commission became the Energy Research and Development Administration as of January 19, 1975. First title below, in addition to listing the Information Booklets, briefly describes the functions and activities of ERDA. The newest title for the listing below is *Order Form for Information Booklets* from ERDA. Since they are still called Information Booklets, the compiler has not altered the title below.

Information Booklets. n.d. Order from the Admin.
This group, certainly one of the two or three most remarkable issued by the United States Government, now numbers (still in print) 37. The ERDA divides these into several areas of interest and emphasis. The title "Information Booklet" is essentially a new one; the group has appeared as "Understanding the Atom Series" and as "World of the Atom Series." The preferred form is now definitely IB (Information Booklets). The entire set of titles is of immense value to anyone interested in what is going on in atomic research and in its applications, and this in spite of the fact that most of the titles are several years old. They are all written by experts in the field; readers will recognize many of the authors' names, if they have even a slight acquaintance with the history of science.

It must be acknowledged that the compiler has leaned somewhat more than heavily upon the annotations supplied by the AEC in its older descriptive brochure *(Order Form for AEC Information Booklets)*. His excuse is that *those* annotations were done by experts.

For an up-to-date index to the Information Booklets, write to the Energy Research and Development Administration.

IB-002. A Bibliography of Basic Books on Atomic Energy. 1971. 58 p. il.
A reading list of 172 commercially available books.

IB-004. Computers. W. R. Corliss. 1973. 93 p. il.
How electronic brains work.

IB-006. Nuclear Terms; a Glossary. 80 p.
Definitions of 400 terms.

IB-008. Electricity and Man. I. Asimov. 1972. 46 p. il.
Brief history of energy production, and a discussion that puts electricity production and our society in perspective.

IB-009. Atomic Energy and Your World. S. Glasstone and S. J. Thomas. 1970. 57 p.
How atomic energy is produced and how its peaceful uses are helping to build a better world.

IB-010. Atomic Pioneers. Book 1: From Ancient Greece to the 19th Century. R. Hiebert and R. Hiebert. 1970. 66 p. il.
The contributions of 25 scientists (or at least those interested in science) from Pythagoras to Berzelius. This group, incidentally, now has three volumes; a fourth is contemplated. The entire set of volumes belongs in every library, private and public. Invaluable to students of almost every age and grade.

IB-011. Atomic Pioneers. Book 2: From the Mid-19th to the Early 20th Century. R. Hiebert and R. Hiebert. 1971. 94 p. il.
From Prout to Hahn; 26 scientists.

IB-012. Atomic Pioneers. Book 3: From the Late 19th to the Mid-20th Century. R. Hiebert and R. Hiebert. 1973. 99 p. il.
Twenty-three men and one woman are discussed.

Worlds within Worlds. I. Asimov. 1972.
This set of three volumes by a justly celebrated writer includes a total of 172 pages covering the history of nuclear energy from the ancient Greeks to modern times. It is, incidentally, a most valuable commentary on Greek "science" and what we mean by the term today. Titles of the three volumes are:

IB-014. Atomic Weights; Energy; Electricity. 63 p. il.

IB-015. Mass and Energy; the Neutron and the Structure of the Nucleus. [65-115] p. il.

IB-016. Nuclear Fission; Nuclear Fusion; Beyond Fusion. [116-172] p. il.

IB-017. Teleoperators; Man's Machine Partners. W. R. Corliss. 1972. 47 p. il.

Describes machines that add to man's strength, his reach, and his ability to work in hostile environments.

IB-018. First Book of Information Science. J. Becker. 1974. 91 p. il.

Information science is the study of how man communicates with man. It is concerned with discovering better ways to get the right information quickly to the person who needs it, and with retrieving information, once it is stored in libraries and other depositories. This booklet is a primer on information science.

IB-102. Atoms in Agriculture. T. S. Osborne. 1963. 24 p. il.

Developing new plants, growing in better ways, controlling pests.

IB-106. Genetic Effects of Radiation. I. Asimov and T. Dobzhansky. 1966. 49 p. il.

How radiation affects reproductive cells and succeeding generations. By a formidable pair of scientists.

IB-110. Preserving Food with Atomic Energy. V. Pizer. 1970. 43 p. il.

How atomic radiation preserves food for long periods of time.

IB-116. Radioisotopes and Life Processes. W. E. Kisieleski and R. Baserga. 1967. 50 p. il.

How radioisotopes are used in biological research.

IB-309. The Mysterious Box: Nuclear Science and Art. B. Keisch. [1970]. 39 p. il.

A fictional mystery story involving lost treasure is used to explain the nuclear techniques and instruments that can

determine the age of oil paintings. Incredibly interesting.
IB-310. Lost Worlds: Nuclear Science and Archeology. B. Keisch. 1973. 54 p. il.
A fictional mystery is used to explain nuclear techniques and instruments that can determine the age of archeological artifacts. The book is a sequel to the preceding title.

BIOLOGY

IB-101. Animals in Atomic Research. E. R. Ricciuti. 1969. 54 p. il.
Use of laboratory animals for medical research. Includes rules for humane use of animals by secondary students and scientists.
IB-109. Your Body and Radiation. N. A. Frigerio. 1967. 78 p. il.
Ionizing radiation effects on living tissues.

CHEMISTRY

IB-301. Chemistry of the Noble Gases. C. L. Chernick. 1967. 48 p. il.
Research that led to the startling ability of these six gases to form compounds.
IB-302. Cryogenics, the Uncommon Cold. H. L. Laquer. [1967]. 59 p. il.
Low-temperature research and its applications.
IB-303. Atomic Fingerprint; Neutron Activation Analysis. B. Keisch. 1972. 56 p. il.
Identifying traces of elements by their "atomic fingerprints."
IB-308. Synthetic Transuranium Elements. E. K. Hyde. 1964. 44 p. il.
How eleven new elements were created by man, and how they are used.

THE ENVIRONMENT

IB-201. Atom and the Ocean. E. W. Seabrook Hull. 1968. 61 p. il.
How atomic energy is used in oceanographic research.

IB-202. Atoms, Nature, and Man. N. O. Hines. 1966. 57 p. il.
How man-made radiation affects the environment.

IB-304. Nuclear Clocks. H. Faul. 1968. 61 p. il.
How nuclear energy is used to measure the age of early man and his artifacts and to date ancient geological formations.

IB-306. Radioisotopes in Industry. P. S. Baker and others. 1965. 49 p. il.
A survey of numerous applications.

IB-307. Rare Earths; the Fraternal Fifteen. K. A. Gschneider, Jr. 1964. 46 p. il.
Their history, structure, properties, and uses.

IB-414. Nature's Invisible Rays. J. Kastner. 1973. 44 p.
Current research involving the radiation that has existed on earth since the beginning of time.

NUCLEAR REACTORS

IB-501. Atomic Fuel. J. F. Hogerton. 1964. 40 p. il.
Its fabrication and uses.

IB-502. Atomic Power Safety. J. F. Hogerton. 1964. 38 p. il.
Devices and designs for safe operation of nuclear power plants.

IB-503. First Reactor. C. Allerdice and others [1967]. 44 p. il.
Dramatic story of the first controlled nuclear chain reaction.

IB-505. Nuclear Power Plants. R. L. Lyerly and W. Mitchell III. 1973. 55 p. il.
How and where they are used today to generate electricity; their operation, economics, and their future.

IB-507. Nuclear Reactors. J. F. Hogerton. [1970]. 54 p. il.
Broad survey of types and uses.

IB-508. Radioactive Wastes. C. H. Fox. [1969]. 46 p. il.
Disposal of wastes generated in the nuclear industry.

IB-510. Nuclear Reactors for Space Power. W. R. Corliss. 1971.
47 p.
How small reactors are employed to power equipment in
space vehicles.

IB-511. Sources of Nuclear Fuel. A. L. Singleton, Jr. [1968]. 67 p.
il.
Mining, milling, and refining of the nuclear industry's raw
materials.

IB-512. Thorium and the Third Fuel. J. M. Dukert. 1970. 46 p. il.
Research involving this important nuclear fuel.

IB-513. Breeder Reactors. W. Mitchell III and S. E. Turner. 1971.
47 p. il.
Research involving reactors that produce more fuel than
they consume.

PHYSICS

IB-401. Accelerators. W. J. Kernan. [1969]. 57 p. il.
Machines for exploring the structure of the atom.

IB-402. Atomic Particle Detection. H. Hellman. 1970. 54 p. il.
Methods and machines used to observe elementary
particles.

IB-403. Controlled Nuclear Fusion. S. Glasstone. [1974]. 88 p. il.
Research on a vast source of power for the future.

IB-404. Direct Conversion of Energy. W. R. Corliss. 1964. 34 p. il.
Producing electricity without generators.

IB-405. Elusive Neutrino. J. Bernstein. [1969]. 79 p. il.
Discovery of, and research involving, this important elementary particle of nature.

IB-406. Lasers. H. Hellman. [1969]. 57 p. il.
Atomic light phenomena in research and industry.

IB-407. Microstructure of Matter. C. E. Swartz. 1967. 60 p. il.
Story of the fundamental particles.

IB-410. Electron. G. Thomson. 1972. 90 p.
Explains what is known about this building block of nature.

IB-411. Power from Radioisotopes. W. R. Corliss and R. L. Mead. 1971. 55 p. il.
Long-lived compact generators of electric power for remote, unattended locations.

IB-412. Space Radiation. W. R. Corliss. [1967]. 58 p. il.
Radiation from beyond our atmosphere.

IB-413. Spectroscopy. H. Hellman. [1968]. 60 p. il.
Element analysis, using the optical spectrum.

IB-415. Mystery of Matter. W. G. Pollard. [1970]. 58 p. il.
Fascinating search for the key to the structure of matter.

IB-416. Inner Space; the Structure of the Atom. S. Glasstone. 1972. 99 p.
History and present-day knowledge of the principles and concepts of atomic structure.

Nuclear Engineering in Your Future. 20 p. il. Free from the Comm. Prepared for the American Society for Engineering Education under the sponsorship of the AEC. So wonderfully illustrated you forget you are learning a great deal about energy, space exploration, water supply, health, transportation.

ENVIRONMENT AND ECOLOGY

All Around You; an Environmental Study Guide. Land Management Bur. [1973]. 177 p.   024-011-00043-7
Largely in question-and-answer form. "Activities . . . begin in the classroom and move outside to the schoolyard, the town, and natural or rural areas. All of these places afford good opportunities for environmental study."

America the Beautiful; a Collection of America's Trashiest Humor. A. Hamilton, comp. Public Health Serv., 1970. [62] p. il.
017-000-00009-8
From B.C. right up to the present; accompanied by very amusing

and admonitory remarks. What your favorite cartoonists think of you, environmentally speaking.

American Environment; a Home Study Course. Soil Conservation Serv., 1973. 153 p. il. Free from the Serv.
In loose-leaf form, for insertion in a three-ring binder. An immensely absorbing way of studying the subject by yourself (although it is supposedly for "technical" people). Suggested readings, and directions how to proceed. A mistake to think it is limited in use.

Children's Edition of Selected Publications on Environment. Environ. Protection Agency [1973]. [10] p. Free from the Agency.

Common Environmental Terms; Glossary. G. J. Stoddard. Environ. Protect. Agency, 1973. 22 p. Free from the Agency.
055-001-00456-7

Congress and the Nation's Environment; Environmental and Natural Resources of the 93rd Congress. W. D. Bowman, comp. The Senate, 1975. 950 p.   052-070-01716-3
There have been two previous such reports, compiled by the Environmental Policy Division, Congressional Research Service, Library of Congress for the Committee on Interior and Insular Affairs. A detailed study for the student. Twelve chapters—from energy and fuels to natural hazards; what the 93d Congress did relating to the Natural Environmental Policy Act of 1969.

Conservation Yearbooks. Dept. of the Interior, 1966–73.
The Conservation Yearbooks are very different from the Yearbooks of the Department of Agriculture. For one thing, they are much shorter; for another, their coverage is always of a particular aspect of the Department of Interior's work (conservation, water, soil, and so on). Within these limits, the Yearbooks are fine indeed. They are particularly notable for wonderful photographs of our national wildlife heritage. The compiler has noted them together here because their one main theme *is* conservation.
    2. The Population Challenge . . . What It Means to America. 1970.
       80 p. il.   024-000-00444-9

3. Third Wave . . . America's New Conservation. 1966. 128 p. il.
024-000-00445-7

4. Man . . . an Endangered Species? 1968. 100 p. il.
024-000-00446-5

5. Its *Your* World . . . the Grassroots Conservation Story. 1969. [96] p. il.   024-000-00447-3

7. Our Living Land; U.S. Department of the Interior Environmental Report. 1971. 96 p. il.   024-000-00613-1

8. Indivisibly One; Our Environment and Our Natural Resources. [1972]. 96 p. il.   024-000-00751-1

9. In Touch with People. 1973. 128 p. il.   024-000-00792-8

Don't Leave It All to Experts; the Citizen's Role in Environmental Decision Making. Environ. Protection Agency [1972]. 20 p. il.
055-003-00048-3
"Designed to stimulate environmental action by citizen groups." What such groups can do; what they should know. Includes relations with the press.

Environment and Community; an Annotated Bibliography. Dept. of Housing and Urban Develop., 1971. 66 p.   023-000-00176-4
Arrangement is by 16 subjects. Relevant films, periodicals, and organizations are included as supplements. Books, reports, articles, and bibliographies are included. "Emphasis is on the environment of American cities and settled communities."

Environmental Bibliography. R. A. Hussey, ed. Environ. Protection Agency, 1974. 29 p.   055-000-00141-3
Selected and annotated. Entries are almost entirely of 1971–73. Forty-six books are expertly reviewed. The 1971 edition, with much shorter annotations, is included here, (pp. 25-29). Fine for a library that wants a basic purchase list.

Environmental Planning and Geology. D. R. Nichols and C. C. Campbell, eds. Dept. of Housing and Urban Develop. [1971]. 204 p. il.   023-000-01195-6
In three parts: problems to be faced (such as seismic hazards, mineral resources, waste disposal); distribution of responsibility for solving

these problems (Federal, state, local levels); and engineering geology in urban planning.

Environmental Quality; the First Annual Report of the Council on Environmental Quality, Together with the President's Message to Congress. Council on Environ. Quality, 1970. 326 p. il.

041-011-00001-7

The President's message occupies 11 pages; the report, 326 pages. This is one of these reports in which a very great deal of information can be found (some possibly difficult to find elsewhere and some of it not too palatable).

Environmental Quality; the Second Annual Report of the Council on Environmental Quality, August 1971. Council on Environ. Quality [1971]. 360 p. il.   041-011-00005-0

Legislation proposed and passed—but much more, including a discussion of status and trends. For anyone who wants to know the situation and what our Government is trying to do about it.

Fairest One of All. Forest Serv. [1973]. 32 p. il.   001-001-00311-5

Lovely color shows endangered, unique, species; and presents proposals for their preservation. A booklet for young and old.

Fitness of Man's Environment. R. C. McAdams. Smithsonian Inst. 250 p. Purchase from the Inst.

"A study of man's relationship to his environment based on papers delivered at the Smithsonian's 1967 annual symposium. Contributors include René Dubos, Paul Goodman, Philip Johnson, Ian L. McHarg, and others in discussions of what has gone wrong with our environment and suggestions for improvements in the future."

Fun with the Environment. Fun As You Learn Book for Kids Who Care About the Environment. Environ. Protect. Agency [1973]. [16] p. il.   055-000-00100-6

The heck with the kids! Learn yourself, via a most engagingly written and illustrated book.

Hand of Man on America. D. Plowden. Smithsonian Inst. 136 p. il. Purchase from the Inst.
"The changing image of America as seen by a photographer-writer who is deeply concerned about the esthetic and environmental damage resulting from modernization . . ."

Glossary of Aquatic Ecological Terms. J. E. Matthews, comp. Water Program Operations Off., 1972. [72] p. Free from the Off.

Human Habitat and Health; Proceedings of the Congress on Environmental Health, American Medical Association . . . Bur. of Community Management, 1973. 211 p. Free from the Bur.
Papers that "indicate the variety of influences that are present in our physical and social environments and their consequences in terms of human health."

Impact of Growth on Environment; Hearings . . . House of Representatives, 1973. 158 p. Free from the Comm.
Before the Subcommittee on Air and Water Pollution, Committee on Public Works. ". . . securing the benefits of growth without also becoming its victims." Effects of population growth on every aspect of our lives: the economy, health, pollution. Testimony of experts in many areas.

Improving Our Environment. Natl. Aeron. and Space Admin. [1973]. [7] p. il. Free from the Admin.
How NASA's work contributes in almost every area of environmental improvement. See other NASA folders and publications for a more detailed discussion.

Man and Animal; Changing Concepts. J. W. Carroll. Bur. of Sport Fisheries and Wildlife, 1970. 13 p. il. Free from the Bur.
A most interesting paper on what man has thought in the past and thinks *now* about his relation to the animal kingdom.

Managing Our Environment; a Report on the Ways Agricultural Research Fights Pollution. Dept. of Agr., Agr. Inform. Bull. 351

[1972]. 48 p. il. 001-000-01587-7
Deals with water and soil pollution primarily; we do not ordinarily associate much noise with farms. Incidentally, there is a great deal about how *food* pollution can be reduced.

Miniature Environments; Environmental Education Guidebook. Bur. of Outdoor Recreation [1971]. 20 p. il. 024-016-00069-2
How to build a terrarium, a small plant and wildlife sanctuary; and how to use them educationally. Charming and practical.

National Environmental Study Area; Guide. Natl. Park Serv. [1972]. 57 p. il. 024-005-00484-0
Definition of, and suggested uses for, areas that lend themselves "to the study of the processes and dynamics of man's whole environment."

National Range Resources; a Forest-Range Environmental Study. Forest Serv., Forest Resource Rept. 19 (1972) [1973]. 147 p. il.
001-001-00237-2
"Systems study designed to explore the current [1970] and prospective production of resources and the role of grazing forest and range ecosystems—the forest-range of the 48 coterminous United States. . . . concepts and procedures developed, information assembled, and policy attitudes evaluated." One and two tenths billion acres constitute 34 major ecosystems. Contains an immense amount of valuable information.

Once There Lived a Wicked Dragon; an Environmental Coloring Book . . . for Children and Adults. F. Finan. Environ. Protection Agency, 1974. 30 p. il. 055-002-00106-8
Charming for children and instructive for all of us.

Patterns and Perspectives in Environmental Science. Natl. Science Foundation, NSF Ser. 73-2 (1973). 426 p. 038-000-00147-7
Prepared as a companion volume, a supplement, to the 3d Annual Report of the National Science Foundation's *Environmental Science —Challenge for the Seventies* (1971). "[The purpose is] to assemble,

in one place, enough material to permit the identification of fundamental patterns that might help us in appraising the status of environmental science today." In no less than 11 parts: from the solar-terrestrial system; dynamics of the solid state; climatic changes; dynamics of the Atlantic Ocean system; severe storms; precipitation and regional weather phenomena; natural resources, forestry and agriculture; aquatic ecosystems; terrestrial ecosystems; environmental contaminants; human adaptation to environmental stress. A superb work.

Plants, People, and Environmental Quality; a Study of Plants and Their Environmental Functions. G. O. Robinette. Natl. Park Serv., 1972. 136 p. il. 024-005-00479-3
Captivating and extremely informative: plants and their functions in our environment—architectural uses, engineering uses, climatological uses—to name a few.

Population Resources and the Environment. R. G. Ridker, ed. Comm. on Population Growth and the American Future, Research Rept. 3 [1972]. 377 p. il. 052-058-00003-1
In two parts: Part I: Resources and the Environmental Consequences of Population Growth, includes effect of population growth on the economy, waste water and recovery, adequacy of nonfuel minerals and forest resources, energy, agriculture, water needs, urban scale and environmental quality, ecological perspectives. Part II: Two Other Views: Environmental Cost of Economic Growth; Impact of Population Growth, presents divergent views.

Promoting Environmental Quality through Urban Planning and Controls. E. J. Kaiser and others. Environ. Protect. Agency, EPA-600/5-73-015 (1974). 475 p. il. 055-001-00761-2
In four sections: Introduction; Changing Awareness and Practices; Promising Approaches; Conclusions. ". . . focuses on the changing awareness and current practices in promoting environmental quality through urban planning and controls in local and metropolitan planning agencies . . ." A very complete treatise on practical application of ideas.

Teaching Materials for Environmental Education; Investigating Your Environment. Forest Serv., 1973. 69 p. il.   001-001-00234-8
A series of lessons plans; the ecosystem as a whole, and some of its component parts. Another of the Government's teachers' guides of great value, not only in planning courses, but in seeing them through meaningfully.

Toward a New Environmental Ethic. Environ. Protect. Agency [1971]. 24 p. il.   055-000-00031-0
Problem of air pollution control, cleaning up the water supply, solid waste management, radiation, pesticide damage, noise abatement. The role of the Agency in all of these. Excellent colored photographs emphasize every point.

Tropical Forest Ecosystems in Africa and South America; a Comparative Review. B. J. Meggers and others, eds. Smithsonian Inst. 328 p. il. Purchase from the Inst.
". . . the first systematic comparison of the major lowland tropical forest areas of Amazonia and Africa that remain, to a large extent, unaltered by modern intrusions. By contrasting these two tropical ecosystems, this volume aims to enlighten administrators and developers, as well as the layman, to the interrelationships of the natural environment that are critical to the development of the areas."

Working Toward a Better Environment; Career Choice. Environ. Protection Agency, 1974. 15 p. il. Purchase from the Agency.
Careers in the environment protection area—equipment operation; use of environmental technology; environmental technology and education; environmental science and research. Brief description of each category in these fields. Planning your career. Appendixes list colleges and universities offering courses; governmental agencies active in environmental management; sources of career information.

Your World, My World; a Book for Young Environmentalists. Environ. Protect. Agency, 1973. 48 p. il.   055-000-00079-4
Captivatingly illustrated in color, this booklet explains all kinds of

pollution to youngsters. Youngsters? Most of us can learn from this booklet.

ETHNIC GROUPS IN THE UNITED STATES

Bibliography on Ethnicity and Ethnic Groups. R. Kolm, ed. Natl. Inst. of Mental Health, 1973. 250 p.   017-024-00287-9
Four hundred and fifty-one annotated references; over 1,100 not annotated. Very thoroughly indexed.

Directory for Reaching Minority Groups. Apprenticeship and Training Bur., 1973. 214 p.   029-006-00005-9
Alphabetic, by city and state. Names, addresses, and telephone numbers of organizations and individuals who are "able to reach minority groups and tell them about job training and job opportunities."

To Know or Not to Know; Collection and Use of Racial and Ethnic Data in Federal Assistance Programs; Report. Civil Rights Comm., 1973. 90 p.   005-000-00084-0
Blunt statement by the Commission precedes this detailed program on collecting and using pertinent data: "It is apparent to the Commission that denial of equal opportunity in Federal assistance programs will continue as long as Agencies persist in basing their confidence in the nondiscriminatory character of their programs on *ad hoc* and even haphazard observations." The present work details fairer criteria for collecting data.

National Roster of Minority Consulting Professional Firms, Feb., 1973. Minority Business Enterprise Off., 1973. 121 p. Free from the Off.
A consulting service is defined here as one "operated for profit, which aims to perform professional, analytic, scientific, or technical work," and which delivers as end product a "plan, study, or other document rather than tangible goods or property." Further, such a firm is one owned at least 50 percent by minority group members (or the equivalent). Minority groups are: blacks, Spanish-speaking

surnamed Americans, Orientals, American Indians, Eskimos, Aleuts, or other socially or economically disadvantaged persons. The work is an impressive alphabetic listing followed by very useful indices by state, subject.

Racism in America and How to Combat It. A. Downs. Civil Rights Comm., Clearinghouse Pub., Urban Ser. 1 (1970). 43 p. il.

005-000-00033-5

"Nature of racism." Strategy for overcoming prejudices is outlined.

AMERICAN INDIANS AND ESKIMOS

American Indian Calendar. Bur. of Indian Affairs [1974]. 47 p. il.

024-002-00044-6

Listing of events among the various tribes and on reservations; of great interest to the traveler who wants to see what has survived among our oldest inhabitants. By the time this *Guide* appears, a later edition of the *Calendar* will probably be available. This later edition will be supplied when you order the *Calendar*.

American Indian Civil Rights Handbook. Civil Rights Comm., Clearinghouse Pub. 33 (1972). 96 p. il. Free from the Comm.

005-000-00077-7

Answers to Your Questions about American Indians. Bur. of Indian Affairs, 1974. 42 p. il.   024-002-00040-3

Their numbers, religious practices, languages, legal status.

Bark Canoes and Skin Boats of North America. E. T. Adney and H. I. Chappelle. Smithsonian Inst., 1964. 242 p. il. Purchase from the Inst.

Adney died in 1950, leaving very extensive notes, photographs, and sketches to the Mariners' Museum, in Newport News, Va. Howard Chappelle organized the "massive literary heritage" into this captivating book.

Civil Rights of the American Indians. Civil Rights Comm., Clearinghouse Pub. 35 (1972). [11] p.   005-000-00075-1
Based upon the much more detailed book *American Indian Civil Rights Handbook*, which see above.

Folklore of the North American Indians; an Annotated Bibliography.
J. C. Ullom, comp. Library of Cong., 1969. 126 p. il.

030-001-00005-2

One hundred and fifty-two items. Annotations are descriptive and critical, averaging close to 200 words each. General background and eleven specific Indian culture areas.

Indian and Mexican Americans; a Selective Annotated Bibliography.
Naval Personnel Bur., 1972. 42 p. il. Free from the Bur.
Beautifully designed and annotated work. Covers Indians (past and present): their mythology, religion, arts and crafts; their history, including Pre-Columbian). Thirty volumes are cited for the United States and Alaska. In a second section the Mexican-American is discussed (the second largest of our minority groups). A prefatory note says that "books by and about Mexican-Americans are scarce, although their supply is expanding fairly rapidly."

Indians of . . . Bur. of Indian Affairs [1968–72].
A group that covers the history of the tribes living in seven areas. Notable for their excellent make-up and illustrations. Recommended for students of any age. The economic status, history, and reservations of each Indian group in the states or areas cited are covered thoroughly.

Arizona [1968]. 24 p. il.	024-002-00010-1
Central Plains. [1968]. 20 p. il.	024-002-00012-8
Dakotas. [1968]. 20 p. il.	024-002-00013-6
Lower Plateau. [1968]. 24 p. il.	024-002-00017-9
New Mexico. [1968]. 20 p. il.	024-002-00019-5
North Carolina. [1972?]. 12 p. il.	024-004-00028-4
Oklahoma. 1968. 16 p. il.	024-002-00021-7

Indians of Texas in 1830. J. L. Berlandier; J. C. Ewers, ed.; P. R. Leclercq, tr. Smithsonian Inst. 209 p. il. Purchase from the Inst.

"An account of the Indian tribes of Texas by a French scientist who traveled through the area as a member of a Mexican boundary expedition. Done under Berlandier's direction and based on his sketches, were marvelous watercolors showing the people of sixteen tribes. They are reproduced with this first appearance in English of a long-forgotten historically valuable manuscript."

Navajo Political Process. A. W. Williams, Jr. Smithsonian Inst., 1970. 75 p. il. Purchase from the Inst.   047-001-00103-6

"Based on historical and contemporary documents maintained by the Navajo Tribe and the Bureau of Indian Affairs, this is a study of Navajo political structures and their incorporation into the Navajo way of life."

Number of American Indians by Counties of the United States, 1970. Bur. of the Census, United States Maps GE-50-49 (1973).

003-024-00101-2

Map, 30" × 42".

Socio-economic Profile of American Indians in Arizona and New Mexico; Staff Report, 1: Albuquerque/Phoenix Hearings. Civil Rights Comm., 1972. [110] p. il. Free from the Comm.

Not for casual reading. A detailed, statistical investigation of the position this group occupies—and of the groove in which it is expected to operate.

Source Directories. Dept. of the Interior. Free from Indian Arts and Crafts Board, Department of the Interior.

The two pamphlets cited below tell you what groups, and what individuals, can supply native American arts and crafts.

1. Indian Eskimo Organizations Marketing Native American Arts and Crafts. [1973]. 5 p. il.
2. Indian and Eskimo Individuals Marketing Native American Arts and Crafts. [1973]. 5 p. il.

States and Their Indian Citizens. T. W. Taylor. Bur. of Indian Affairs [1972]. 307 p. il. 024-002-00024-1
Covers development, present status, and possible future of relations between Indians and Federal and state governments. Included is a large colored map of Indian lands. There is much supplemental material; and a selected bibliography.

You Asked about . . . Bur. of Indian Affairs [1971]–1973. Free from the Bur.
A group of informational leaflets, from one to four leaves in length, intended to cite facts briefly, or to give information about where further work may be done.

  Helping Indians. [1973].
  Indian Museums. [1971].
  Pictures of Indians. 1973.
  Tribal Claims against the United States. [1973].

BLACK AMERICANS

Afro-Americans in the Far West; a Handbook for Educators. J. D. Forbes. Off. of Educ. [1970]. 106 p. 017-080-00702-9
Emphasizes that, in the largest sense, "we are all Afro-Americans." Important material on the impact of our whites on blacks, and the contributions the blacks have made to white culture.

Black Americans; a Decade of Occupational Change. S. S. Small and others. Bur. of Labor Statistics, Bull. 1760 [1972]. 26 p. il.
029-001-00967-4

Brief review of the position of the black American in the decade 1960–70. Excellent charts and statistical tables from many agencies.

Black Heritage: the American Experience; a Selected Annotated Bibliography. Naval Personnel Bur., 1972. 57 p. il. Purchase from the Bur.
Very fine piece of work. The general background is a moving state-

ment of the Navy's allegiance to the idea that black Americans form a vital part of our past and our future.

Black Panther Party; Its Origin and Development as Reflected in Its Official Weekly Newspaper "The Black Panther Black Community News Service"; Staff Study . . . House of Representatives, 1970. 142 p. il.   052-070-00987-0
Study undertaken by the Committee on Internal Security. And a most valuable source it is, since it contains many specific quotations as well as a number of cartoons (these last chiefly political in nature).

Booker T. Washington; Appreciation of the Man and His Times. B. Mackintosh. Natl. Park Serv., 1972. 78 p. il.   024-005-00282-1
One of the Service's "Historical Series." An excellent biography for adult and younger readers. Cites the many places with which Washington's name is associated.

Families for Black Children; Search for Adoptive Parents; an Experience Survey. E. Herzog and others. Children's Bur., 1972. 79 p.
017-091-00157-0
The fate of minority children is a particularly hard one. Here the rewards of kindness, as well as some of the difficulties of exercising it, are pointed out.

—— 2. **Programs and Projects.** A. L. Sandusky and others. [1972]. 67 p. il.   017-091-00166-1
"Collection of abstracts describing salient features of some twenty programs and projects already in progress throughout the country, together with a general statement of some of the recurrent themes."

"Glimmer of Their Own Beauty"; Black Sounds of the Twenties. Natl. Portrait Gallery, 1971. [30] p. il. Free from the Gallery.
047-006-00004-0
Harlem in the jazz age, told largely through the lives and activities of Louis Armstrong and others. Fine photographs.

List of Free Black Heads of Families in the 1st Census of the United

States, 1790. D. L. Newman, comp. Natl. Archives and Records Serv., Spec. List. 34 (1973). 44 p. Free from the Serv.

A listing of free blacks (called "other persons" than whites or Indians who were taxed). Included are figures for all the then Atlantic seaboard states, as well as Kentucky and Tennessee. (Note that census figures for Delaware, Georgia, Kentucky, Tennessee, and Virginia were probably destroyed in the War of 1812.) For various reasons, no accurate count of free blacks in 1790 can be made; but some of the figures cited in this booklet may surprise Northerners. (It is interesting that slaves are enumerated only; i.e., no family information is cited.)

Me; (from the Children of the Deep South Comes a Cry for Help that Cannot be Ignored). H(attie) M(ay) and L. Heine. Off. of Econ. Opportunity, Pamph. 4100-7 (1969). 40 p. il. Free from the Off.

Hattie May is thirteen years old. Her touching drawings are made the basis for a picture lesson in sociology and plain human compassion.

Negro Population as Percent of Total Population by Counties of the United States, 1970. Bur. of the Census, United States Map GE-50-48 (1973). 003-024-00103-9

Colored map, 30" × 42".

Negro in the United States; Selected Bibliography. D. B. Porter, comp. Library of Congress, 1970. 313 p. 030-000-00044-7

Symbionese Liberation Party; Study. House of Representatives, 1974. 13 p. Free from the Comm.

Study by the Internal Security Committee.

MEXICAN AMERICANS

Mexican-American Education; a Selected Bibliography . . . Supplement 2. A. D. Link. Off. of Educ., 1972. [350] p. 017-080-01063-1

Mexican American Education Study. Civil Rights Comm., 1971–74. 6 parts.

An extraordinarily honest and detailed study of the price paid by this minority group for *being* a minority group. Each of the six reports covers five Southwestern states, and each is separately annotated below.

1. Ethnic Isolation of Mexican Americans in the Public Schools of the Southwest. 1971. 102 p. il.   005-000-00059-9
   Based on a 1968 survey made by the Department of Health, Education, and Welfare.
2. The Unfinished Education; Outcome for Minorities in Five Southwestern States. Mexican American Ser., 1971. 101 p. il.
                                                    005-000-00068-8
   ". . . attention is focused on the performance of the schools in Arizona, California, Colorado, New Mexico, and Texas as reflected in the achievements of their pupils."
3. The Excluded Student; Educational Practices Affecting Mexican Americans in the Southwest. 1972. 86 p. il.
                                                    005-000-00074-2
   "The dominance of Anglo values is apparent in the curricula on all education levels."
4. Mexican Education in Texas; a Function of Wealth. 1972. 53 p. il.   005-000-00079-3
   A catalog of deficiencies in the schools of this state, where this minority is concerned.
5. Teachers and Students; Differences in Teacher Interaction with Mexican American and Anglo Students. 1972. 68 p. il.
                                                    005-000-00093-9
   ". . . focuses on the denial of . . . opportunities. . . . The picture of verbal interaction that emerges . . . is one in which Mexican American students are neglected in comparison to Anglo students."
6. Toward Quality Education for MAs. C. P. de Buriraza and others. 1974. 98 p. Purchase from the Civil Rights Commission.

Stranger in One's Land. Civil Rights Comm., Clearinghouse Publ. 19 (1970). 49 p. il.   005-000-00029-7
Plight of the Mexican American, who faces language barriers, job shortages, minimal educational opportunities.

We the Mexican Americans; Nosotros Los Mexico Americanos. Bur. of the Census [1970]. [17] p. il.   003-024-00197-7
In English and Spanish. The minority groups; their growth; some of their history; their living conditions, jobs, education. How *you* can help them.

FARM BUILDINGS AND EQUIPMENT

Feedlot and Ranch Equipment for Beef Cattle. R. L. Davis and W. F. Edgerly. Dept. of Agr., Farmers' Bull. 1584 (1963). 19 p. il.   001-000-02764-6
Plans for many types of equipment for feeding, watering; silos, etc.

Fences for the Farm and Rural Home. M. S. Timmins, Jr. Dept. of Agr., Farmers' Bull. 2247 (1971). 26 p. il.   001-000-01236-3
Selection of materials; types of fences; gateways; maintenance. Construction details.

Foundations for Farm Buildings. N. C. Teter. Dept. of Agr., Farmers' Bull. 1869 (1967). 32 p. il.   001-000-00016-1
Recommendations for the design and laying down of good foundations. How to choose the right site for them. Construction; cost estimating. Maintenance, repair, remodeling.

Home Treatment of Fence Posts. Tennessee Valley Authority, 1973. 12 p. il. Free from the Div. of Forestry, Fisheries and Wildlife Dept., TVA.

Lightning Protection for the Farm. M. S. Timmins, Jr. Dept. of Agr., Farmers' Bull. 2136 (1967). 18 p. il.   001-000-00037-3

Roofing Farm Buildings. Dept. of Agr., Farmers' Bull. 2170 (1969). 28 p. il.   001-000-02830-8
Types of roofing; installation; repair.

Standby Electric Power for the Farm. L. E. Campbell. Dept. of Agr., Leaflet 480 (1965). 8 p. il.   001-000-00210-4
How to use auxiliary equipment if the necessity arises.

Use of Concrete on the Farm. Dept. of Agr., Farmers' Bull 2203. (1970). 30 p. il.   001-000-03373-5
Ready and job-mixed. Concrete structures, pavements, bridges, walls. Repair.

FARMING

Here are included only the most general titles dealing with farming on the broadest scale. For specific problems and aspects, of farming, the reader is referred to the Index.

Facts for Prospective Farmers. K. H. Myers. Dept. of Agr., Farmers' Bull. 2221 (1971). 22 p. il.   001-000-01535-4
"Primarily for the person with little or no farming knowledge or experience who expects farming to provide the major part of his, and his family's income." Types of farms; financing; getting started; sources of information.

Family-Farm Records. J. Vermeer and I. R. Starbird. Dept. of Agr., Farmers' Bull. 2167 (1968). 22 p. il.   001-000-03196-1
Five different types of records are described.

Father-Son Agreements for Operating Farms. Dept. of Agr., Farmers' Bull. 2179 (1970). 18 p. il.   001-000-03187-2
Terms used in such agreements; hints on avoiding family friction.

Know Your Soil. Dept. of Agr., Agr. Inform. Bull. 267 (1970). 16 p. il.   001-000-01212-6
How a soil survey is made; and why it is vital to a farmer to have such a survey made.

Mulch Tillage in Modern Farming. W. A. Hayes. Dept. of Agr., Leaflet 554 (1971). Folder. il.   001-000-01231-2

Part-Time Farming. O. J. Scoville. Dept. of Agr., Farmers' Bull. 2178 (1971). 14 p. il.   001-000-03336-1

The advantages and some of the possible problems; choice of land and equipment; profitable farm activities.

What Are Cooperatives? Dept. of Agr., FCS-67 (1970). [12] p. il. Free from the Farmer Cooperative Service, Dept. of Agriculture

What Is Farm Conservation Plan? Dept. of Agr., PA 629 [1973]. 8 p. il. Free from the Dept.
How to develop your own written conservation plan for your farm in the event the Government will not.

What Young Farm Families Should Know about Credit. L. A. Jones. Dept. of Agr., Farmers' Bull. 2135 (1971). 20 p. il.

001-000-02614-3

Credit; types of loans; where to borrow; costs.

FIRST AID AND SAFETY

Case for Seat Belts; Experimental and Statistical Evidence. Natl. Highway Traffic Safety Admin., 1973. 13 p.   050-003-00102-3

Employee Accident Prevention Handbook. Bur. of Mines, 1972. 223 p. il. Free from the Bur.
A very fine handbook for anyone. Includes helpful illustrations.

First Aid for Flooded Homes and Farms. Dept. of Agr., Agr. Handbook 38 (1974). 31 p. il.   001-000-03186-4
Immediate first aid for the home, for clothing, for furnishings; avoidance of trouble with rodents and other pests. Rehabilitation and other services.

First Aid for Mineral and Allied Industries. J. S. Kelly. Bur. of Mines, 1971. 191 p. il.   024-004-00883-1
Practical guide for care of injured workers, with far wider application than accidents in mines. Helpfully illustrated.

Handle Yourself with Care; Accident Prevention for Older Amercans. [D. J. Lewis.] Admin. on Aging [1969]. [20] p. il.

017-062-00011-5

——**Instructor's Guide.** D. J. Lewis and R. J. Winsor. Admin. on Aging [1969]. 46 p.

With reasonable precaution, older people can be active and lively. These booklets tell them (and their teacher) how to liven things up safely.

Horse Safety Guidelines. Dept. of Agr., PA 1033 (1973). 16 p. il.

001-000-02812-0

If you really want a horse, learn how to handle one safely.

Horse Sense on Backcountry Trips. D. Miller and F. Talbott. Forest Serv., 1970. [16] p. il. Free from the Serv.

Kitchen Ranges in Fabric Fires. A. K. Vickers. Natl. Standards Bur., Tech Note 817 (1974). 17 p. Free from the Bur.

003-003-01265-3

One of those useful publications where an abstract of the monograph is included. Danger of lack of caution around kitchen ranges: female victims of fires outnumbered male by three to one. And reaching over and leaning against the stove caused the majority of fabric fires.

Natural Radiation Exposure in the United States. D. T. Oakley. Off. of Radiation Programs, ORP/SD 72-1 (1972). 68 p. Free from the Off.

"Natural background constitutes the greatest source of radiation in the world's population. This exposure is by no means uniform for all individuals, but varies because of a number of influencing factors." Probably not for the average reader; informational, but technical and statistical. Should, however, be in all libraries.

Outdoor Safety Tips. Dept of Agr., PA 887 (1971). [13] p. il.

010-000-03427-8

Food and water requirements; minimizing fire hazards; first aid.

Overboard with Chest Waders, Hip Boots, or Rain Gear. R. O.
Parker, Jr. Natl. Marine Fisheries Serv., Fishery Leaflet 635 (1971).
[6] p. il.   003-020-00005-3
None of these will cause you to drown if you don't panic. This
booklet tells you how to preserve your presence of mind.

Pool Drownings and Their Prevention. D. P. Webster. Health Serv.
and Mental Health Admin. [1972]. 14 p. il. Free from the Admin.
017-018-00014-1

**Radiation Safety and Protection in Industrial Applications; Pro-
ceedings of Symposium, Aug. 16–18, 1972.** H. F. Klein, ed. Bur.
of Radiological Health, 1972. 307 p. il.   017-015-00042-7
General and specific problems of radiation safety; recommends
solutions and standards.

Rescue Skills and Techniques. Defense Civil Preparedness Agency,
Student Manual SM 14.2 (1972). 81 p. il. Free from the Agency.

Safety Belt Instructional Booklet. B. E. Haughey and others. Natl.
Highway Traffic Safety Admin. [1972]. 25 p. il.   050-003-00077-9

Safety Handbook. Soil Conservation Serv. [1969]. 147 p. il. Free
from the Serv.
Intended for Department of Agriculture employees, but an immensely valuable first aid guide for anyone.

Safety and Survival in an Earthquake. Geol. Survey, 1969. [12] p. il.
024-001-00001-6
What you can do before, during, and after such an event: as a
citizen, a householder, a father. Graphically illustrated to prove its
points.

Snow Survey; Safety Guide. Dept. of Agr., Agr. Handbook 137
(1974). 60 p. il.   001-000-03182-1
First aid (of all kinds) for the lost or injured snow traveler. Detailed,
invaluable advice.

Space Benefits: Safety. Natl. Aeron. and Space Admin., 1972. Folder. Free from the Admin.
We are today "leading safer lives thanks to space technology." Another of NASA's proofs of the practical applications of space research.

Teach Children Fire Will Burn. Children's Bur., Pub. 471 (1969) [1971]. 24 p. il.   017-091-00152-9
The annual total of child injury and death is appalling. Follow the simple directions here, and show your children (not by direct example) that fire is dangerous.

Teaching Children about Safety Belts; Grades K-3. J. A. Klingensmith and others. Natl. Highway Traffic Safety Admin., 1973. 32 p. il.   050-003-00100-7

In Time of Emergency; a Citizen's Handbook on [Peacetime] Disasters. Defense Civil Preparedness Agency, Handbook H-14-B [1973]. 41 p. il. Free from the Agency.
Peacetime disasters: fires, floods, earthquakes, etc. Care of the sick and the wounded.

Tornado Preparedness Planning. Natl. Weather Serv., 1973. 26 p. il.   003-017-00215-2
Hints on building; on safety features in the house.

Tornado Safety Rules. Natl. Weather Serv., 1971. 1 p. il.
003-018-00023-7

Volatile Substances; Some Questions and Answers. Natl. Inst. of Mental Health [1972]. 6 p.   017-024-00123-0

What to Buy in Child Restraint Systems. Natl. Highway Traffic Safety Admin. [1971]. [16] p. il.   050-003-00052-3

Working with Ammonia. Natl. Inst. for Occupational Safety and Health [1973]. Folder. il. Free from the Inst.

Working with Chlorine. Natl. Inst. of Occupational Safety and Health, 1973. [6] p. il. Free from the Inst.

Young Children and Accidents in the Home. Children's Bur., 1974. 28 p. il.   017-091-00191-0

FISH, SHELLFISH, AND FISHING

Angler's Guide to Sharks of the Northeastern United States, Maine to Chesapeake Bay. J. G. Casey. Fish and Wildlife Serv., Cir. 179 (1964). 32 p. il.   024-010-00017-1

Catfish Farming; a New Farm Crop. R. A. Grizzell, Jr., and others. Dept. of Agr., Farmers' Bull. 2244 (1969). 22 p. il.
        001-000-01294-1
Channel, blue, and white catfish.

Commercial Clams of the North American Pacific Coast. M. H. Amos. Fish and Wildlife Serv., Cir. 237 (1966). 18 p. il. Free from the Serv.

Earthworms for Bait. U.S. Fish and Wildlife Serv., Leaflet FL-23 (1970). 5 p. Free from the Serv.
Collecting, raising, storing, harvesting. Control of pests.

Edible Land Snails in the United States. L. T. Dees. Bur. of Sport Fisheries and Wildlife, Resources Pub. 91 (1970). 8 p. il.
        024-010-00220-4
These snails are not an unmixed blessing; they can cause damage to plants before gourmets get them.

Map, Line, and Sinker. [E. C. Palfery]. Geol. Survey [1973]. [7] p. il.   024-001-02394-6
How the Survey helps the interested angler in determining bottom conditions of man-made water bodies.

Marine Fishes of the North Atlantic. W. Watanabe and others. Natl. Marine Fisheries Serv., 1971.   032-000-00027-4 Poster, 48″ × 30″.

Our Changing Fisheries. S. Shapiro, ed. Natl. Marine Fisheries Serv. [1971]. 534 p. il.   032-000-00046-1

Sport Fishing U.S.A. D. Saults and others, eds. Bur. of Sport Fisheries and Wildlife, 1971. 464 p. il.   024-010-00235-2 Forty or so essays on the joys—and the techniques—of fishing, by an impressive roster of experts. One could wish the color were better. The book is enchanting and deserves the best.

Trout Farming; Could Trout Farming Be Profitable for You? P. M. Scheffer and L. D. Marriage. Dept. of Agr., Leaflet 552 (1969). 8 p. il.   010-000-00244-9

True Pikes. E. G. Karvelis. U.S. Fish and Wildlife Serv., Fishery Leaflet 569 (1965). 11 p. il. Free from the Serv.

Turtle Trapping. U.S. Fish and Wildlife Serv., Fishery Leaflet 190 (1964). 6 p. il. Free from the Serv.

FORAGE CROPS, GRASSES, AND RANGELANDS

Culture and Use of Grain Sorghum. W. H. Ross and O. J. Webster. Dept. of Agr., Agr. Handbook 385 (1970). 30 p. il.
010-000-01089-1
A member of the grass family. Planting, control, harvest, and—of course—diseases and pests.

Grass; the Rancher's Crop. J. S. McCorkle. Dept. of Agr., Leaflet 346 (1967). 8 p. il.   010-000-00174-4 How to start it, and see it through its growing pains.

Nation's Range Resources; a Forest-Range Environmental Study. Forest Serv., Res. Rept. 19 (1972) [1973]. 147 p. il.

001-001-00237-2

"Purpose was to assemble information about all of the nation's range and to develop a technology for its evaluation that would serve the planning needs of the Forest Service." Some 1.2 billion acres in 48 coterminous states are categorized in 34 major ecosystems.

One Hundred Native Forage Grasses in 11 Southern States. H. L. Leithead and others. Dept. of Agr., Agr. Handbook 389 (1971). 216 p. il.   010-000-01138-3
Distribution; applications; care and management.

Seeds of Native and Naturalized Vetches of North America. C. R. Gunn. Dept. of Agr., Agr. Handbook 392 (1971). 42 p. il.

010-000-01141-3

A detailed botanical guide.

Sericea Lespideza; Its Use and Management. W. J. Guernsey. Dept. of Agr., Farmers' Bull. 2245 (1970). 29 p. il.   010-000-01035-2
Has a special place in Southern states, where it is useful in soil and water conservation, among other things.

FOREST FIRES AND FIREFIGHTING

Fire Extinguishing Equipment. U.S. Postal Serv., Facilities Handbook S-10 (1970). 26 p.   039-000-00142-0
Learn to use this equipment; you can't always find an easy way out.

Fireline Handbook. Forest Serv., 1971. [161] p. il.

001-001-00076-1

Preventing and controlling forest fires.

Fire Weather . . . a Guide for the Application of Meteorological Information to Forest Fire Control Operations. M. J. Schroeder

and C. C. Buck. Dept. of Agr., Agr. Handbook 360 (1970). 229 p. il.   001-000-01093-0
Exhaustive study of atmospheric conditions that breed and feed fire.

Forest Fire Detection. E. W. Zimmerman. Forest Serv., 1969. 25 p. il.   001-001-00006-0
How the Forest Service locates a fire—not always an easy job.

Protecting the Forests from Fire. Dept. of Agr., Agr. Inform. Bull. 130 (1969). 32 p. il.   001-000-00624-0
Our forests suffer over 300 fires a day.

Wildfire; a Story of Modern Fire-fighting. Dept. of Agr., PA 993 [1972]. [28] p. il.   001-000-02598-8
How forest fires are fought, told with dramatic color photographs.

You and Forest Fires. Dept. of Agr., PA 64 (1972). [16] p. il. Free from the Dept.
Some frightful statistics. In 1969 over 10,000 square miles of forest burned—an area equal to New Jersey and Delaware combined! Causes of such fires; prevention and control.

FORESTRY

American Woods. Forest Serv., 1970–74.
A group of titles that, like the earlier Useful Woods group (see below) comes in looseleaf form for easy inclusion in a notebook: a fact that leads one to hope the American Woods group will go on approximately forever. They are of handsome format; each carries a full-length portrait of the subject tree, and a careful drawing of its leaf. In addition to the pictorial charm, each book is filled with botanical data: the types of soil the tree grows in, where it grows, what age it attains; and (not exactly botanical data) how it can be used. The entire set is indicated for every student and every tree lover.

American Beech (*Fagus grandifolia*). 1974. 8 p. il.

001-001-00379-4

American Chestnut (*Castanea dentata*). J. R. Saucier. 1973. 6 p. il.

001-001-00305-1

American Holly (*Ilex opaca*). R. M. Krinard. 1973. 5 p. il.

001-001-00336-1

American Sycamore (*Platanus occidentalis*). R. G. McAlpine and M. Applefield. 1973. 7 p. il.

001-001-00326-3

Ash (*Fraxinus* spp.). H. A. Stewart and J. E. Krajicek. 1973. 7 p. il.

001-001-00321-2

Aspen (*Populus tremuloides* and *P. grandidentata*). J. R. Jones and D. C. Markstrom. 1973. 8 p. il.

001-001-00308-5

Baldycypress (*Taxodium distichium*). H. E. Kennedy, Jr. 1972. 5 p. il.

001-001-00348-4

Birch (*Betula* spp.). R. L. Brisbin and D. L. Sonderman. 1973. 11 p. il.

001-001-00332-8

Black Locust (*Robinia pseudoacacia*). R. H. McAlister. 1971. 6 p. il.

001-001-00068-0

Black Walnut (*Juglans nigra*). E. F. Landt and R. E. Phares. 1973. 7 p. il.

001-001-00314-0

Black Willow (*Salix nigra*). W. K. Randall. 1973. 6 p. il.

001-001-00344-1

Buckeye (*Aesculus octandra; A. glabra*). J. E. Duff. 1973. 8 p. il.

001-001-00307-7

Butternut (*Juglans cinerea*). J. G. Schroeder. 1972. 6 p. il.

001-001-00222-1

Eastern Hemlock (*Tsuga canadensis*). R. L. Brisbin. 1970. 8 p. il.

001-001-00062-1

Eastern Redcedar (*Juniperus virginiana*). E. R. Ferguson and E. R. Lawson. 1974. 6 p. il.

001-001-00376-0

Eastern Spruce (*Picea* spp.). M. D. Ostrander. 1974. 10 p. il.

001-001-00374-3

Eastern White Pine (*Pinus strobus*). M. D. Ostrander. 1971. 4 p. il.

001-001-00067-1

Elm (*Ulmus* spp.). P. Y. S. Chen and R. C. Schlesinger. 1973. 7 p. il.

001-001-00325-5

Flowering Dogwood (*Cornus florida*) A. L. Mignery. 1973. 5 p. il. 001-001-00335-2

Hackberry (*Celtis* spp.). G. W. Smalley. 1973. 7 p. il. 001-001-00322-1

Hickory (*Carya* spp.). D. R. Phillips. 1973. 7 p. il. 001-001-00333-6

Incense-Cedar (*Libocedrus decurrens*). P. M. McDonald. 1973. 7 p. il. 001-001-00337-9

Jack Pine (*Pinus banksiana*). E. M. Carpenter and D. A. Perala. 1973. 6 p. il. 001-001-00334-4

Oak (*Quercus* spp.). G. A. Cooper and R. F. Watt. 1974. 9 p. il. 001-001-00320-4

Osage Orange (*Maclura pomifera*). J. D. Burton. 1973. 7 p. il. 001-001-00315-8

Pecan (*Carya* spp.). A. Clark III. 1973. 8 p. il. 001-001-00324-7

Ponderosa Pine (*Pinus ponderosa*). E. S. Kotok. 1973. 6 p. il. 001-001-00341-7

Port-Orford-Cedar (*Chamaecyparis lawsoniana*). J. W. Henley. 1973. 6 p. il. 001-001-00320-4

Redwood (*Sequoia sempervirens*). 1974. 8 p. il. 001-001-00373-5

Sitka Spruce (*Picea sitchensis*). R. O. Woodfin, Jr. 1973. 7 p. il. 001-001-00319-1

Sweetgum (*Liquidamber styraciflua*). C. B. Briscoe. 1973. 6 p. il. 001-001-00339-5

Tupelo (*Nyssa* spp.). W. N. Darwin, Jr. 1972. [8] p. il. 001-001-00079-5

Western Redcedar (*Thuja plicata*). E. S. Kotok. 1973. 8 p. il. 001-001-00342-5

Western White Pine (*Pinus monticola*). E. S. Kotok. 1973. 6 p. il. 001-001-00343-3

Yellow Poplar (*Liriodendron tulipifera*). C. B. Vick. 1973. 7 p. il. 001-001-00304-2

Arkansas Forest Resource Patterns. C. C. Van Sickle. Forest Serv., Research Bull. SO-24 (1970). 34 p. il. Free from the Serv.

Artificial Reforestation Practices for the Southwest. G. H. Schubert and others. Dept. of Agr., Agr. Handbook 370 (1970). 25 p. il.
010-000-00754-8
Seed requirements; site preparation; planting; care.

Atlas of United States Trees. Vol. 1: Conifers and Important Hardwoods. E. L. Little, Jr. Dept. of Agr., Misc. Pub. 1146 (1971). [310] p. il.
010-000-01026-3
From *Abies amabilis* to yew (*Taxus brevifolia*). Maps show the occurrence of the trees throughout our country. Wonderful work. Limited, perhaps, in interest to enthusiastic botanists and libraries —which is a shame. More of us should buy and study works of this nature.

Bristlecone Pine; Its Phenology, Cone Maturity, and Seed Production. G. H. Schubert and W. J. Rietveid. Forest Serv., Research Note RM-180 [1971]. 7 p. il. Free from the Serv.
The oldest living thing on earth. This contains detailed botanical information. For a more popular title, see the following entry.

Bristlecone Pine, Nature's Oldest Living Thing. Forest Serv. [1970]. [4] p. il. Free from the Serv.
Interestingly enough, the tree *looks* its age: gnarled, bent, etc.

Chemical Control of Plant Growth. Dept. of Agr., Sci. Study Aid 7 [1972]. 23 p. il.
010-000-02708-5
A "science kit" that teaches a great deal in a few interesting, well-illustrated "lessons."

Decorative Plants of Appalachia; Source of Income. T. C. Nelson and M. J. Williamson. Dept. of. Agr., Agr. Inform. Bull. 342 (1970). 31 p. il.
010-000-01094-8
Not a raiser's handbook; a botanical guide.

Direct-seeding Pines in the South. H. J. Derr and W. F. Mann, Jr. Dept. of Agr., Agr. Handbook 391 (1971). 68 p. il.
010-000-01140-5
The exact details of what is described as a "versatile" technique.

Forest Atlas of the Northeast. H. W. Lull. Forest Serv., 1968. 46 p. il. Free from the Serv.   001-001-00306-9

Forest Atlas of the Northwest. H. W. Lull. Forest Serv., 1968. 46 p. il. Free from the Serv.

Forest Atlas of the South. Forest Serv., 1969. 27 p. il. Free from the Serv.

Forest Resources of Mississippi. C. C. Van Sickle and D. D. Van Hooser. Forest Serv., Research Bull. SO-17 (1969). 34 p. il. Purchase from the Serv.

Forest Resources of Tennessee. P. A. Murphy. Forest Serv., Research Bull. SO-35 (1972). 33 p. il. Free from the Serv.

Forest Service Health and Safety Code; Your Guide to Safe Practices. Forest Serv., 1970. 420 p. il.   001-001-00042-6
Meant for foresters, with their particular interests and problems; but actually a great deal of it is applicable to a variety of dangerous situations.

Forestry Comes to America. Forest Serv. [1971]. [16] p. il. Free from the Serv.

Forestry Schools in the United States. Forest Serv. [1974]. 32 p. il.   001-001-00351-4

Forests Forever. Forest Serv. [1973]. 6 p. il.   001-001-00007-8

Forests in South Dakota. G. A. Choate and J. S. Spencer, Jr. Forest Serv., Research Bull. INT-8 (1968). 40 p. il. Free from the Serv.

Genetic Variation; Key to Superior Trees. G. K. Stephenson and E. B Snyder. Forest Serv., 1969. 12 p. il. Free from the Serv.

Genetics Are Sex. Forest Serv. [1971]. [20] p. il. Free from the Serv.

Guidelines for Establishing Forestry Cooperatives. G. P. Dempsey and C. B. Markeson. Forest Serv., Research Paper NE-133 (1969). 38 p. il. Purchase from the Serv.

How to Grow Christmas Trees in the South. P. Touliatos and others. Forest Serv. [1971]. 16 p. il. Free from the Serv.

How a Tree Grows. Forest Serv., 1970. 8 p. il.   001-001-00057-4
Tree grows from leaves, crown, trunk, roots. Very clear and instructive drawings.

Human Behavior Aspects of Forest and Wildlife Conservation; an Annotated Bibliography. D. R. Potter and others, eds. Forest Serv., Genl. Tech. Rept. PNW 4 (1973). 288 p. Free from the Pacific Northwest Forest and Range Experiment Sta., Portland, Oreg.
"Covers non-biological or human aspects of forest and wildlife conservation, including sportsman characteristics, safety, law enforcement, professional and sportsman education . . ." There are 995 references, from a tremendous variety of sources. An attempt to tie together a widely diversified literature in its human aspects. Because of its very breadth, a book difficult to annotate adequately.

Indiana's Timber. J. S. Spencer, Jr. Forest Serv., Research Bull. NC-7 (1969). 61 p. il. Free from the Serv.

In Your Service; the Work of Uncle Sam's Forest Rangers. Dept. of Agr., Agr. Inform. Bull. 136 (1971). [23] p. il.   010-000-01369-6
One sixth of our forests can grow useful trees. The work of the Rangers in caring for such lands is described here.

Kansas Woodlands. C. D. Chase and J. K. Strickler. Forest Serv., Research Bull. NC-4 (1968). 50 p. il. Free from the Serv.

"Let It Grow" Treatment for Timber; Is It Economically Worth While? D. P. Worley. Forest Serv., Research Paper NE-157 (1970). 37 p. il. Purchase from the Serv.

Managing the Family Forest. G. G. Mark and R. S. Dimmick. Dept. of Agr., Farmers' Bull. 2187 (1971). 61 p. il.

010-000-01366-1

One out of every ten Americans owns a bit of family forest. This booklet tells how to increase the value of these holdings.

Maple Sirup Production from Bigleaf Maple. R. H. Ruth and others. Forest Serv., Research Note PNW-181 (1972). 12 p. Free from the Station (see below).

A fine publication very difficult to cite: its full producer is the Forest Products Laboratory, Madison, Wis.; its full citation is Research Note FPL–Pacific North West Forest and Range Experiment Station, Portland Oreg., Research Note PNW-181.

Materials to Help Teach Forest Conservation. Forest Serv. [1973]. 8 p. il. Free from the Serv.

Men Who Matched Mountains; the Forest Service in the Southwest. E. A. Tucker and G. Fitzpatrick. Forest Serv., 1972. 293 p. il.   001-001-00249-6

A "chronology of and by a few of the men who quite literally blazed the trail, and of the fulfillment, frustration, and fun they found along the way." Spans almost seventy-five years, and is good.

National Forest Landscape Management; Vol. 1. Dept of Agr., Agr. Handbook 434 (1973). [77] p. il.   001-000-02583-0

Publication of the Forest Service. Superb photographs illustrate several salient points in landscape preservation, design, and development. Excellent.

National Forest System Areas as of June 30, 1972. Forest Serv. [1972]. 20 p. il. Free from the Serv.

Detailed listings, including acreage. Does not describe facilities of campsites.

National Forest Wildernesses and Primitive Areas; National Forests. Forest Serv. [1973]. 12 p. il. Free from the Serv.

001-001-00245-3

Oklahoma Forest Industries. D. F. Bertelson. Forest Serv., Res. Bull. SO-45 [1973]. 16 p. il. Purchase from the Serv.

Planting Black Walnut for Timber. F. B. Clark. Dept. of Agr., Leaflet 487 (1971). 10 p. il.   010-000-02670-4
Requires care; but can profitably be grown in ten or twelve states.

Proceedings, Research on Coniferous Forest Ecosystems; First Year Progress in the Coniferous Forest Biome. J. F. Franklin and others, eds. Forest Serv., 1972. 322 p. Order from the Serv.
Proceedings of a symposium held in March, 1972. Discusses "probably the largest and most complete single effort at ecosystem analysis being carried out in the Western United States." Exhaustive study in five parts; work that shows the relationship between this class of tree and the soil and water conditions prevailing. Also shows what proper planting and care can do.

Public Land Statistics, 1974. Bur. of Land Management 1974. 191 p. il.   024-011-00053-4
Statistics on area, land disposition and use, food management, outdoor recreation and wildlife, range management, minerals, protection, surveys, adjudication, administration, and finance.

Ranger 'Rithmetic for First and Second Grade Teachers. Forest Serv., 1966; repr. 1971. 12 p. il. Free from the Serv.
This, and the following titles in the group, contain problems meant to show young people about forest conservation; but it is a mistake to think they are so limited. Any young person would like them and would learn something about our forests at the same time. Usually, the titles contain something like 24 problems; their

page limits are 11-12 pages, and all are illustrated. (This title is for third grade.)
——Fourth Grade.
——Fifth Grade.
——Sixth Grade. 1972.
——Seventh Grade. 1966 [1971.] 12 p. il.

Silvicultural Systems for the Major Forest Types of the United States. Dept. of Agr., Agr. Handbook 445 (1973). 114 p.

010-000-02816-2

Pacific Northwest, Pacific Southwest, and Northern Rocky Mountain trees, Central and Southern Rocky Mountain trees; North Central, Northeastern, Southeastern, and Southern trees—all are briefly described for their use and their beauty.

Silviculture Guide for Northern Hardwoods in the Northeast. W. B. Leak and others. Forest Serv., Research Paper NE-143 (1969). 34 p. il. Free from the Serv.

Silviculture of Oaks and Associated Species; Summary of Current Information . . . Forest Serv., Research Paper NE-144 (1970). 66 p. il. Purchase from the Serv.
The large-scale growth and care of oak forests.

Site Preparation and Reforestation of Droughty Acid Sands. R. M. Burns and E. A. Hobb. Dept. of Agr., Agr. Handbook 426 (1972). 60 p. il. 010-000-02470-1
How to convert land from scrub oak and wiregrass to the production of marketable pine.

Timber Resources of Kentucky. D. A. Gansner. Forest Serv., 1968. 97 p. il. Free from the Serv.

Timber Resources of Maine. R. H. Ferguson and N. H. Kingsley. Forest Serv., Research Bull. NE-20 (1970). 193 p. il. Free from the Serv.

Timber Resources of New York. R. H. Ferguson and C. E. Mayer. Forest Serv., Research Bull. NE-20 (1970). 193 p. il. Purchase from the Serv.

Timber Resources of Ohio. N. P. Kingsley and C. E. Mayer. Forest Serv., Research Bull. NE-19 (1970). 137 p. il. Free from the Serv.

Timber Resources of Pennsylvania. R. H. Ferguson. Forest Serv., Research Bull. NE-8 (1968). 147 p. il. Free from the Serv.

Timber Resources of Vermont. N. P. Kingsley and J. E. Barnard. Forest Serv., Research Bull. NE-12 (1968). 117 p. il. Free from the Serv.

A Tree Hurts, Too. Forest Serv. [1973]. 28 p. il.   001-001-00338-7
Lovely booklet, with striking colored drawings, showing how a tree "hurts" as it is cut, neglected, "wanes," dies. For children, a real find; for adults, a sharp reminder. The tree, incidentally, dies not only externally, but internally. Many cross sections of wood in various diseased conditions are shown in color. Most highly recommended.

Trees of the Forest; Their Beauty and Use. Dept. of Agr., PA 613 [1971]. [24] p. il.   001-000-03451-1
How the forest grows; some of its mighty denizens: the great firs, the huge pines. Enchanting illustrations.

Trees of Puerto Rico and the Virgin Islands; Second Volume. E. L. Little, Jr., and others. Dept. of Agr., Agr. Handbook 499 (1974). 1024 p. il.   010-000-02884-7
Staggering botanical work.

Useful Trees of the United States. Forest Serv., 1971–74.
A beautiful and immensely useful collection; in loose-leaf form for convenience. Each title covers every aspect of its subject tree: where it grows, how it looks, what its uses are. The entire group

is recommended unreservedly, for students of every age and grade; and not only for schools, but for every library. Almost all titles are four pages.

American Beech (*Fagus grandifolia*). 1974. il.	001-601-00379-4
American Elm (*Ulmus americana*). 1973. il.	001-001-00325-5
Baldycypress (*Taxodium distichium*). 1972. il.	001-001-00348-4
Black Locust (*Robinia pseudoacacia*). 1971. il.	001-001-00068-0
Black Walnut (*Juglans nigra*). 1973. il.	001-001-00314-0
Eastern Hemlock (*Tsuga canadensis*). 1971. il.	001-001-00062-1
Eastern White Pine (*Pinus strobus*). 1971. il.	001-001-00067-1
Ponderosa Pine (*Pinus ponderosa*). 1973. il.	001-001-00341-7
Redwood (*Sequoia sempervirens*). 1974. il.	001-001-00373-5
Sitka Spruce (*Picea sitchensis*). 1973. il.	001-001-00319-1
Sweetgum (*Liquidamber styraciflua*). 1973. il.	001-001-00339-5
Western Red Cedar (*Thuja plicata*). 1973. il.	001-001-00342-5
Western White Pine (*Pinus monticola*). 1973. il.	
	001-001-00343-3
Yellow Poplar (*Liriodendron tulipifera*). 1973. il.	
	001-001-00304-2

Uses for Sawdust, Shavings, and Waste Chips. J. M. Harkin. Forest Serv., Research Note FPL-0208 (1969). 37 p. il. Purchase from the Serv.

Veneer Species That Grow in the United States. J. F. Lutz. Forest Serv. Research Rept. FPL-167 (1972). 127 p.   001-001-00330-1 Describes properties of 156 tree species that affect their manufacture and use as veneer or products made from veneer. Each species is rated for use in general categories of construction plywood, decorative or face veneer, inner poles of decorative panels, or container veneer and plywood. Very thorough.

What the Forest Service Does. Forest Serv. [1970]. 4 p. Free from the Serv.

FUR ANIMALS

Risks in Raising Chinchillas. Federal Trade Comm., Consumers Bull. 3 [1971]. 8 p.   018-000-00117-9
Don't be fooled by ads that pretend raising chinchillas is easy. Read in this booklet of the pitfalls (and the *real* profits) before you decide to branch out into this difficult business.

Northern Fur Seal. R. C. Baker and others. Bur. of Commercial Fisheries, Cir. 336 (1970). 19 p. il. Free from the Bur.
Distribution; movements; some account of processing and selling.

GEMS

Gems in the Smithsonian. P. E. Desautels. Smithsonian Inst., 1965. 74 p. il. Purchase from the Inst.
"The Smithsonian's dazzling gem collection displays more than 1000 items, including the Hope diamond and the Star of Asia. This beautifully illustrated book describes gem cutting techniques, gem lore, and other aspects of gemology."

Man-made Crystals. J. E. Arem. Smithsonian Inst. 112 p. il. Purchase from the Inst.
"A companion to *Gems in the Smithsonian,* this handsomely illustrated book explores the fantastic and colorful world of crystals and crystal growth, from the glitter of synthetic gems to the awesome capabilities of lasers and microcircuitry. Including a How-to-Grow-Crystals-at-Home section, it explains growing techniques, uses, and the technology's history and significance for the future."

GEOLOGY

Absorption of Gold by Plants. H. T. Shacklette and others. Geol. Survey, Bull. 1314-B (1970). 23 p. il.   024-001-00220-5
The next time you make vegetable soup, watch for the gold flakes!

Active Faults of California. Geol. Survey, 1972. [15] p. il. Free from the Survey. 024-001-02496-9
An impressive listing of the surface faulting, 1836–1968. Map of the fault lines.

Ancient Lavas in Shenandoah National Park Near Luray, Virginia. J. C. Reed, Jr. Geol. Survey, Bull. 1265 (1969). 43 p. il.

024-001-00150-1
Excellent popular explanation of a difficult subject.

Antarctic and Its Geology. Geol. Survey, 1970. [15] p. il. Free from the Survey. 024-001-00233-7
Particularly interesting for its discussion of the great ice cap.

Atlantic Continental Shelf and Slope of the United States. Geol. Surv., Prof. Paper 529. 13 parts, 1966–1974.
The publications of the Geological Survey, like those of so many of the Governmental agencies, range in appeal from simplified versions of difficult subjects—which are aimed at students in almost every grade of school, as well as the less-informed, but interested, amateur—to profound and lengthy studies, the quality of which is unsurpassed. The Shelf is the home of a good proportion of our population, stretching, as it does, from Canada to Florida; secondly, it possesses a dramatic interest in that it ends abruptly in a 20,000-foot drop into the "Atlantic Abyss." (One has to sail across this "Abyss" to appreciate the difference between a few hundred feet in depth and 20,000 feet!) Unfortunately, only three parts of the "Atlantic Continental Shelf" group remain in print.

J. Petrology of the Sand Fraction of Sediments, Northern New Jersey to Southern Florida. J. D. Milliman. 1972. 40 p. il.

024-001-02066-1
K. Sand-Size Fraction of Bottom Sediments, New Jersey to Nova Scotia. J. V. A. Trumbull. 1972. 45 p. il. 024-001-02185-4
M. Texture of Surface Sediments from New Jersey to Southern Florida. C. D. Hollister. 1973. 23 p. il. 024-001-02432-2

Atlas of Volcanic Phenomena. Geol. Survey, 1971.

024-001-01202-2

Twenty colored posters, each 21.4" × 15.8".

Bedrock Geology of Rhode Island. A. W. Quinn. Geol. Survey, Bull. 1295 (1971). 68 p. il. 024-001-01077-1

Changes in Stratographic Nomenclature by the Geological Survey, 1972. G. V. Cohee and W. B. Wright. Geol. Survey, Bull. 1394-A, (1974). 93 p. il. 024-001-02450-1

Continental Drift; the Evolution of a Concept. U. B. Marvin. Smithsonian Inst. 256 p. il. Purchase from the Inst.
". . . reviews the early scientific and polemical debates on continental drift. Today, although most scientists and laymen appear persuaded of the truth of the new global tectonics, none of the later pieces of evidence or interpretations has gone unchallenged."

Colorado River Region and John Wesley Powell. Geol. Survey, Prof. Paper 669 (1969). 145 p. il. 024-001-00844-1
In four parts: A: John Wesley Powell, Pioneer Statesman of Federal Science, by M. C. Rabbitt; B: Stratified Rocks of the Grand Canyon, by E. D. McKee; C: Geologic History of the Colorado River, by C. B. Hunt; D: The Rapids and the Pools—Grand Canyon, by L. B. Leopold. Part A is a brief survey of Powell's work in its historical, mid-nineteenth century setting; parts B, C, and D are very recent evaluations of the geology of the Canyon, with comments on Powell's early work. Actually, these latter parts amount to a discussion of recent geological findings and theories; Powell is almost casually mentioned. Very fine photographs, geological cross sections, tables of geological names, etc. For the most part, even part A is not primarily a biography. A very fine work, but not for the amateur.

Contribution of Ranger Photographs to Understanding the Geology of the Moon. N. J. Trask. Geol. Survey, Prof. Paper 599-J (1972). 16 p. il. 024-001-02111-1

Earthquake History of the United States. J. L. Coffman and C. A. von Hake, eds. Environ. Data Serv., 1973. 208 p. il.

003-019-00019-5

North Dakota seems to have been exempt, and a few other states have gotten off comparatively easily. But beginning in the 1600s, we have had a hard time of it. Appalling photographs (starting on the cover with poor Charleston on August 31, 1886), a number of sober listings of dates for each of the major geographical areas, and a fine text make this a fascinating book.

Earthquakes. L. C. Pariser. Geol. Survey, 1974. 19 p. il. Purchase from the Survey.

Colorfully illustrated booklet; what earthquakes are; what they have done to us through the ages; likely areas; measuring; predicting. Excellent geological cross sections.

Elevations and Distances in the United States. Geol. Survey [1973]. 23 p. il. 024-001-00349-0

Ferdinand Vandiveer Hayden and the Founding of the Yellowstone National Park. Geol. Survey [1973]. 45 p. il.

024-001-02396-2

One of our earliest Western explorers and scientists.

Geologic Setting of the John Day Country, Grant County, Ore. T. F. Thayer. Geol. Survey, 1974. 23 p. il. Purchase from the Survey.

Beautifully illustrated history of northeast Oregon, including fine geologic maps and cross sections.

Geologic Time; the Age of the Earth. W. L. Newman. Geol. Survey, 1975. 20 p. il. 024-001-00260-4

Fine illustrations and colored geological cross sections show the major divisions of our planet's time from Cenozoic to Precambrian. Atomic time scale, with some fascinating examples of its applications, from a cloth wrapping of a mummified man (over 2,000 years old) to Morton gneiss (3,600,000,000 years old). Age of the earth is estimated as at least 4,500,000,000 years.

Geological Framework and Petroleum Potential of the Atlantic Coastal Plain and the Continental Shelf. J. C. Maher and E. P. Applin. Geol. Survey, Prof. Paper 659 (1971). 98 p. il.

024-001-01083-6

"A summary of the regional structure and stratigraphy of the Mezozoic rocks with special reference to petroleum exploration." Includes 17 large folded maps in pocket.

Geology of Great Smoky Mountains National Park, Tennessee and North Carolina. P. J. King and others. Geol. Survey, Prof. Paper 587 (1968). 23 p. il. 024-001-00732-1

Geysers. Geol. Survey, 1971. 23 p. il. 024-001-02029-7
The geological origin of geysers, with facts on some famous ones and where they occur.

Gold Content of Water, Plants, and Animals. R. S. Jones. Geol. Survey, Cir. 625 (1970). 15 p. Free from the Survey.

Gold in Igneous, Sedimentary, and Metamorphic Rocks. R. S. Jones. Geol. Survey, Cir. 610 (1969). 28 p. Free from the Survey.

Gold in Meteorites and the Earth's Crust. R. S. Jones. Geol. Survey, Cir. 603 (1968). 4 p. Free from the Survey.

Great Ice Age. Geol. Survey, 1972. 15 p. il. 024-001-02039-4
The dimensions of the Ice Age; how it can be traced. (And get ready, another may be on the way!)

Interior of the Earth. Geol. Survey, 1975. [7] p. il. 024-001-02607-4
Excellent drawing of our earth from crust to core. And the usual fine explanation.

John Wesley Powell; Soldier, Explorer, Scientist. Geol. Survey, 1969. 24 p. il. Free from the Survey.   024-001-02395-4
Contemporary photographs of a great frontiersman and scientist, along with fascinating text.

Landforms of the United States. [J. T. Hack]. Geol. Survey, 1975. [15] p. il.   024-001-02192-7
Geological maps show the physiographic regions and provinces of the coterminous 48 states. Plus a fine text.

Large Rivers of the United States. K. T. Iseri and W. B. Langbien. Geol. Survey, Cir. 686 (1974) [1975]. 10 p. Free from the Survey.
Our 28 largest rivers; their drainage areas; stream length; sources and mouths.

Mountains and Plains; Denver's Geological Setting. [D. E. Trimble and others.] Geol. Survey, 1975. 23 p. il.   024-001-00224-8
Text and good drawings (including cross sections of rocks). Lovely booklet.

Our Changing Continent. Geol. Survey, 1968. 15 p. il. Free from the Survey.   024-001-02033-5
Wonderful folder illustrates the gigantic geologic changes that have shaped the continent.

Peat Deposits of Southeastern New York. C. C. Cameron. Geol. Survey, Bull. 1317-B (1971). 32 p. il.   024-001-00982-0

Principal Rivers & Lakes of the World. Natl. Ocean Survey, 1973. 25 p. il. Free from the Survey.
". . . to provide nontechnical information. . . . The contents are a compilation of data from many sources developed primarily to answer inquiries by the National Ocean Survey for general information . . ." For any interested reader, of almost any age or background. Excellent photographs; material on the origin, formation, geologic features, and so on; and a valuable listing of the planet's

leading rivers with their length, drainage areas, flow. Similar listing
for lakes shows their areas, depth, and length.

Recent Activity of the Glaciers of Mount Rainer, Washington. R. S.
Sigafoos and E. L. Hendricks. Geol. Survey, Prof. Paper 387-B
(1972). 24 p. il.   024-001-02179-0
Investigation of the chronology of terminal and lateral moraines
of eight glaciers; botanical evidence of glacier activity. Seven
plates of exemplary quality accompany the text.

**River and Rocks; the Geologic Story of Great Falls and the Po-
tomac River Gorge.** Geol. Survey, 1970. 46 p. il.   024-001-00002-4
How this spectacular natural feature—close to the Capital—was
formed, with a good deal of geology (made easy) of the Eastern
mountain systems thrown in.

San Andreas Fault. Geol. Survey, 1973. 10 p. il.   024-001-02032-7
The shift along this fault caused the great earthquake and fire of
San Francisco on April 18, 1906.

Seismic Hazards and Land-Use Planning. D. R. Nichols and J. M.
Buchanan-Banks. Geol. Survey, Cir. 690 (1974). 38 p. il. Free from
the Survey.
"Outlines those earthquake-induced geologic conditions that could
be hazardous, the type of problems they pose, how information
can be obtained to assess the degree of hazard, and some possible
implications to land use."

Studying the Earth from Space. Geol. Survey [1971]. 18 p. il.
024-001-02060-2

Tree Rings; Timekeepers of the Past. Geol. Survey [1973]. 15 p.
il. Free from the Survey.   024-001-02449-7
Geologists, of course, are particularly interested in the evidence
these rings afford. That statement should be corrected, perhaps:
archeologists would probably beat the geologist to the evidence. At
any rate, *you* would do well to buy the booklet.

United States Geological Survey. Geol. Survey [1974]. 27 p. il. Free from the Survey.
Its organization; what it does. A new national center for the Geological Survey has been built in Reston, Virginia.

Volcanoes. [C. Anderson]. Geol. Survey, 1974. [9] p. il.

024-001-00261-2

Wonderful, colorful, introductory brochure. Fine for all of us.

Volcanoes of the United States. Geol. Survey, 1969. 19 p. il.

024-001-00262-1

Maps; cross sections. Activity confined to Hawaiian Islands, Aleutian Islands, Alaskan Peninsula, and Cascade Mountains. Colored drawings show the interior of the earth's crust that is so troublesome.

THE HANDICAPPED

American Profile; What States Are Doing (and Can Do) to Hire the Handicapped. President's Comm. on Employment of the Handicapped [1971]. 74 p. Free from the Comm.
A state-by-state listing of hiring practices; what facilities each state has and does not have. Valuable appendices show sample state legislation, as guides to those seeking similar laws in have-not states. Primarily of interest to administrators and workers with the handicapped.

A Bright Future; Your Guide to Work. R. W. Flanagan. President's Comm. on Employment of the Handicapped, 1970. [33] p. il. Purchase from the Comm.
In cooperation with the National Association for Mental Health. A very fine little introduction, especially valuable for a directory of state contacts.

Careers for the Homebound. President's Comm. on Employment of the Handicapped [1974]. 16 p. Free from the Comm.

Developing Programs for the Rural Handicapped. E. J. Nieder-frank. Dept. of Agr., PA 961 (1970). [16] p. Free from the Dept.
". . . some suggestions to help members of state and local organizations in developing programs for aiding the handicapped." By a rural sociologist with the Extension Service.

Feeding the Child with a Handicap. Childrens Bur., 1973. 19 p. il.   017-029-00025-8

Group Treatment for Parents of Handicapped Children. H. L. Beck. Maternal and Child Health Serv., 1973. 24 p.   017-121-00008-7
"Group treatment is particularly well suited to the task of aiding the parents of the handicapped children." How such groups operate, and some of their activities.

Handicapped Child in Your Home. Children's Bur. [1973]. [16] p. il.   017-091-00189-8
Wonderful little booklet on care of your handicapped child—done with the sympathy one has come to expect of so many Government health agencies.

Hearing Aids. E. L. R. Corliss. Natl. Standards Bur., Mono. 117 (1970). 24 p. il.   003-003-00751-0
Includes a list of aid centers, by state.

How Federal Agencies Have Served the Handicapped, 1973. President's Comm. on Employment of the Handicapped, 1974. 43 p. Free from the Comm.
How a Presidential committee works—in this instance, through HEW, the Department of Labor, Veterans Administration, Department of Agriculture, Department of Transportation, Department of Housing and Urban Development, Department of Commerce, and the Civil Service Commission. What cooperation with all of these agencies has done for the handicapped.

How to Get a Job. W. A. Fraenkel and others. President's Comm. on Employment of the Handicapped [1972]. 29 p. il. Free from the Comm. 052-003-00087-3

Choosing the right kind of work if you are handicapped or are working with the handicapped; looking for the job; going on an interview; starting work; 100 job possibilities for you. A remarkably helpful booklet, not alone to the handicapped.

Opening Doors for the Handicapped; Publicity Guide and Activities Calendar for State and Local Committees on Employment of the Handicapped. President's Comm. on Employment of the Handicapped, 1973. [36] p. il. Free from the Comm.

". . . to help statewide and local communities participate in a coordinated publicity campaign to gain as much visibility as possible for their handicapped neighbors . . ." How to prepare releases. Includes a listing of publicity materials, publications, films, exhibits. Very fine.

Productive Employment of the Disadvantaged; Guidelines for Action. E. M. Glaser and H. L. Ross. Manpower Admin., Research and Develop. Findings 15 (1973). [191] p. Free from the Admin.

Primarily for the employer who wishes to give work to the disadvantaged. Involvement in programs; recruiting, screening, hiring; orienting supervisors; conducting upgrading programs; etc.

Rehabilitating the Person with Spinal Cord Injury; a Source Book. Veterans Admin., Inform. Bull. IB-11-31 [1972]. 58 p. il.

051-000-00063-3

"Spinal cord injury is a catastrophic disability." This very practical and detailed program guide shows you how to help the injured person meet his problems—problems of "overwhelming magnitude." The physical and sexual needs of the patient, his sociopsychological attitudes (and those of the persons around him); helping him to find and perform work. Very fine.

Talking Book Machines. Library of Cong., 1970. 16 p. il. Free from the Libr.

Edison predicted, in 1878, that his phonograph might be used to read books to the blind. This booklet is a discussion of how his prediction has become a reality, and how the Library of Congress helps the unseeing.

Talking Books and Cerebral Palsy. Library of Cong., 1973. Folder. Purchase from the Library.

Volunteers Who Produce Books: Braille, Large Type, Tape. Library of Cong., 1970 [1971]. 69 p. il. Free from the Libr.
Directory by states.

Volunteers with Vision. Library of Cong., Div. of Blind and Handicapped, 1972. Folder. Purchase from the Library.
The Library makes available many services that can extend the horizons of the handicapped.

Work and How to Get It. President's Comm. on Employment of the Handicapped. [9] p. il. Purchase from the Comm.
The choices; rehabilitation; how to look for work; how to act on the job; where to start—the proper places to visit (those cited here are in or near Washington, D.C.); what the cited agencies do (a great deal, indeed, and *for nothing!*).

HANDICRAFTS AND HOBBIES

COINS, MEDALS, AND PAPER CURRENCY

Counterfeiting and Forgery. Secret Serv. [1970]. Folder. il. Free from the Serv.

Domestic and Foreign Coins Manufactured by Mints of the United States, 1793–1973. Bur. of the Mint. [1973]. 138 p.

                                        048-005-00017-9
Hobbyist's guide to the issues; no prices cited.

Facts about United States Money. T. A. Dubinsky, ed. Treasury Dept., [1973]. 28 p. il.   048-000-00231-5
History of the various denominations; specific paper and other content; coining; seals; portraits and buildings described. Particularly recommended for schools.

Medals of the United States Mint Issued for Public Sale. K. M. Fallor and E. Hayden. Bur. of the Mint, [1972]. 312 p. il.
048-004-00497-6
Over 300 historic medals from 1776 to the present.

CRAFTS

American Crafts; a Rich Heritage and Rich Future. [W. R. Seymour.] Dept of Agr., PA 1026 [1972]. 16 p. il. Free from the Dept.
Practical advice on how to organize your community to exploit our crafts heritage.

Beautiful Junk. D. Warner and J. Quill. Project Head Start, 1967. 12 p.il.   017-092-00004-9
"Use necessity as your guide . . ." How to combine and convert all sorts of odds and ends to serve constructive purposes. Illustrated with inventive wit.

Crafts, Techniques in Occupational Therapy. Dept. of the Army, Tech. Manual 8-290 (1971). [525] p. il.   008-020-00397-2
Ceramics; mosaics; plastics; weaving; rug making; leatherwork; printing; woodworking. Wonderful practical guide.

How PEG Helps the Hobbyist Who Works with Wood. H. L. Mitchell. Forest Serv., 1972. 20 p. il. Free from the Serv.
001-001-00303-4

Natural Dyes in the United States. R. J. Adrosko. 158 p. il. Smithsonian Inst. Purchase from the Inst.

"Beginning with a discussion of dyes used in America during the 18th and 19th centuries, this book combines historical background with a manual of dye recipes designed to draw students and craftsmen into further exploration . . ."

POSTAGE STAMPS

History of United States Postage Stamps, Postal Cards, and Stamped Envelopes. U.S. Postal Serv., Public Inform. Ser. 3 [1970]. 14 p. il. Free from the Serv.

Postage Stamps of the United States; an Illustrated Description of All United States Postage and Special Service Stamps [Issued by the Post Office from July 1, 1947–June 30, 1970]. U.S. Postal Serv., 1970. 241 p. il.   039-000-00224-8
A must for every collector. Please note the new name of the Post Office Department.

Stamp Collecting: How and Why. U.S. Postal Serv., 1972. [11] p. Purchase from the Serv.
Beautiful folder, with illustrations in color. Tells you what appears on what denominations. Eugene O'Neill, for example, is on a 1973 dollar stamp.

United States Postage Stamps; an Illustrated Description of All United States Postage and Special Services Stamps. U.S. Postal Serv., 1972. 52 p. il.   039-000-00243-4

United States Postage Stamps. Trans. 3. U.S. Postal Serv., 1974. 64 p.   039-000-00251-5
Includes information about new stamps issued from February, 1972, to December, 1973.

United States Postage Stamps & Postal Stationery. U.S. Postal Serv., 1972. 20 p. il. Purchase from the Serv.
Another beautiful brochure. Tells how stamps and other postal commodities are designed and produced (and reproduced). No stamp buff should be without this booklet.

HEALTH

Army Medical Specialist Corps. R. S. Anderson, ed. Army Med. Serv., 1968. 648 p. il.   008-023-00006-9
A detailed guide: every kind of first aid, hospital procedures and activities. The sort of medical guide every individual, and certainly every library, should have. Diseases are described; treatment is outlined. Not intended to take the place of the doctor, of course.

Arteriosclerosis; Report by the National Heart and Lung Task Force . . . Natl. Heart and Lung Inst., 1971 [1972]. 2 vols.
                                                                017-043-00005-6
An excellent statement of the problems of this very prevalent disability, and how medicine is working to fight them.
  1. 47 p.
  2. 365 p. il.

Bacteria; the Littlest Cells. Natl. Inst. of Allergy and Infectious Diseases [1970]. [20] p. il.   017-044-00001-0
Instructive. Amusingly illustrated.

Cerebral Vascular Disease and Strokes. Public Health Serv. [1969]. 19 p. il.   017-002-00011-2

Epidemiology of Epilepsy; a Workshop. M. Alter and W. A. Hauser. Natl. Insts. of Health, NINDS Mono. 14 (1973). 167 p. il.
                                                                017-049-00041-1
Nine main topics in 28 chapters: selected studies, untapped sources of data; host characteristics and risk; genetics; selected types of seizures; efficiency of diagnostic procedures; treatment facilities; definitions.

Epilepsia; Esperanza en la Investigacion. Natl. Insts. of Health, 1972. 27 p. il.   017-049-00046-1

Epilepsy; Hope through Research. Natl. Inst. of Neurological Diseases and Stroke [1972]. 26 p.il.   017-049-00035-6

Eye, Ear, Nose and Throat Specialist. Dept. of the Army, Tech. Manual 8-234 (1970). [184] p. il. Purchase from the Dept.
General anatomy and physiology; diseases and trauma; clinical procedures. Hearing aids; there is a chapter on the nature of sound.

Facts about Trichinosis. Dept. of Agr., ARS-91-72 (1969). 16 p. il. Free from the Dept.

Feet First; Booklet about Foot Care for Older Persons and People Who Have Diabetes. Health Professions Education and Manpower Training Bur. [1970]. 45 p. il.   017-041-00011-8

Flu. Natl. Inst. of Allergy and Infectious Diseases [1974]. [12] p. il.   017-044-00015-0

Food Allergy. Natl. Insts. of Health [1973]. [11] p. Free from the Inst.   017-044-00012-5

Hearing Loss; Hope through Research. Natl. Inst. of Neurological Diseases and Stroke [1973]. 35 p. il.   017-049-00042-9

Hepatitis. Natl. Inst. of Allergy and Infectious Diseases [1973]. [14] p. il.   017-024-00352-2

How You Can Handle Pressure. Natl. Inst. of Mental Health [1973]. [6] p.   017-024-00355-1

Introduction to Physical Fitness; Includes Self-testing Activities, Graded Exercises, and a Jogging Program. [President of the United States]. [1973]. [26] p. il. Free from the President's

Council on Physical Fitness and Sports.   017-000-00122-1
Forty-five percent of all adult Americans do not get enough exercise. For those who feel they need it, this booklet is most highly recommended; its illustrations are helpful.

Muscular Dystrophy; Hope through Research. (In Spanish.) Pub. Health Serv., 1971. 22 p. il.   017-049-00016-0

National Institute of Neurological Diseases and Stroke; Mission & Publications for the Public. Natl. Inst. of Neurological Diseases and Stroke, 1973. Folder. Free from the Inst.
Part of the gigantic health complex that runs through several towns in Maryland and Virginia. Serious visitors are welcome; and one wishes every American could see what the Department of Health, Education, and Welfare is doing to advance his health!

Occupational Health Manual [Improvement, Treatment, Prevention]. Med. and Surgery Bur., the Navy, 1972. 192 p.il.   008-045-00014-3
"While aimed primarily at the Naval Medical Officer, the information contained in the Manual could be of valuable assistance to anyone responsible for the administration of an Occupational Hospital." Not a first aid handbook; a very thorough administrative guide.

Preventing Lead Poisoning in Children. J. S. Lin-Fu. Off. of Child Develop. [1973]. [7] p. il. Free from the Off.

———**Cuidado! La Pintura de Plomo Envenena.** Maternal and Child Health Serv. [1971]. [4] p. il.
Spanish translation of preceding title.

Proceedings; NIH Acupuncture Research Conference. H. P. Janerick, ed. Natl. Inst. of General Medical Sciences, 1973 [1974]. 145 p. Free from the Inst.   017-043-00030-7
Proceedings of a 1973 conference. Over 40 papers cover use of acupuncture in treatment of chronic pain, experimental pain, as

surgical anesthesia, other clinical applications. Physiological responses are studied. Acupuncture *loci* are explained.

Que Es Diabetes? A. P. Covarrubias. Social Security Admin., 1974. [36] p. il. Free from the Admin.
Marvelously illustrated booklet. The causes, manifestations, and means of control are discussed and illustrated.

Research Explores Nutrition and Dental Health. Natl. Inst. of Dental Research, 1970. [19] p. il.   017-047-00002-7

Ringworm, Including Athlete's Foot. Center for Disease Control [1973]. [4] p. Free from the Center.

Rubella. Public Health Serv., 1970. 8 p.   017-029-00011-8
German measles to you.

Selected Bibliography on Death and Dying. J. J. Vernick. Natl. Inst. of Health and Human Devel. [1970]. 59 p.   017-045-00051-2
Contains 1,494 references, well-indexed. Not annotated.

Sickle Cell Anemia; a Medical Review. J. S. Lin-Fu. Maternal and Child Health Serv., 1972. 26 p. Free from the Serv.
Genetics; pathophysiology; pathological findings; clinical manifestations; laboratory manifestations; screening; diagnosis; prognosis; management. Sickle cell trait. Very fine bibliography.

Sickle Cell Anemia and Sickle Cell Trait. Dept. of Labor, 1973 [1972]. [6] p. il. Free from the Dept.

Sudden Infant Death Syndrome; Selected Annotated Bibliography, 1960–71. Natl. Inst. of Child Health and Human Develop. [1972]. 58 p.   017-046-00016-1

Syncrisis; Dynamics of Health; an Analytic Series on Interactions of Health and Socioeconomic Development. Dept. of Health, Educ., and Welfare, 1972–74.

Not for the average reader, probably; but, used with data furnished by many other Departments and agencies (dealing with housing, education, law, trade) of very great interest to the serious student of foreign areas.

1. Panama. P. O. Woolley, Jr., and others. [1972]. 205 p.
017-000-00098-5
2. Honduras. P. O. Woolley, Jr., and others. 1972 [1973]. 73 p. il.
017-000-00099-3
3. Perspectives and Methodology. P. O. Woolley, Jr., and others. 1972. 62 p. il.
017-000-00107-8
An explanation of the theory and practices employed in preparing these booklets.
4. Philippines. P. O. Woolley, Jr., and others. 1972. 134 p.
017-000-00108-6
5. El Salvador. P. O. Woolley, Jr., and others. 1972. 53 p.
017-000-00111-6
6. Haiti. L. G. Beamer and others. 1972. 42 p.   017-000-00155-8
8. Ethiopia. R. A. Britanak and others. [1974]. 189 p.
017-000-00130-2

Tracking Diseases from Nature to Man. Public Health Serv., 1968. 54 p. il.   017-023-00031-4
Winged carriers, four-footed foes, fish: a depressing array of nature is against us. This booklet tells new ways of tracing the damage our many friends do us.

Watch Your Blood Pressure. Natl. Insts. of Health, 1972. 28 p. il. Purchase from the Institutes.
Publication of the High Blood Pressure Information Center, part of the National Institutes of Health.

What Are the Facts about Genetic Disease? Natl. Inst. of General Medical Sciences, 1974. [33] p. il. Free from the Inst.
The most ubiquitous of all human maladies. This is an unusually fine, and very reassuring, booklet, filled with good advice.

X-ray Examinations . . . a Guide to Good Practice. Public Health Serv. [1971]. 28 p. il.   055-005-00003-6

Primarily for physicians and trained personnel—but should interest a great many others.

Your Medicare Handbook. Social Security Admin., 1974. 31 p.
017-070-00247-1
Everything you need to know.

ARTIFICIAL ORGANS AND TRANSPLANTS

Cardiac Replacement: Medical, Ethical, Psychological and Economic Implications; a Report by Ad Hoc Task Force on Cardiac Replacement. Public Health Serv., 1969. 93 p. il.
017-043-00002-1
Extraordinary discussion of a moot question.

Totally Implantable Artificial Heart: Legal, Social, Ethical, Medical, Economic, Psychological Implications; a Report . . . Natl. Heart and Lung Inst., 1973. 250 p. il. Free from the Inst.
017-043-00029-3
A fine coverage of every aspect of the problems of implanting a heart, by the Artificial Heart Assessment Panel of the National Heart and Lung Institute.

CANCER

Breast Self-Examination. Natl. Cancer Inst., 1974. [12] p. il.
017-042-00080-7
Monthly self-examination is detailed.

Cancer of the Colon and Rectum. Natl. Cancer Inst. [1973]. Folder.   017-042-00052-1
Four-page introduction to symptoms, diagnosis, treatment, and research now under way.

Cancer of the Larynx. Natl. Cancer Inst., 1973. [4] p.
017-042-00053-0

Cancer of the Mouth. Natl. Cancer Inst. [1973]. 6 p.

017-042-00054-8

Cancer of the Skin. Natl. Cancer Inst., 1972 [1973]. 7 p.

017-042-00047-5

Cancer Story; a Brief Look at Science and Cancer. Natl. Cancer Inst., 1970 [1973]. 52 p.   017-042-00078-5
Short account of some of the research being done.

Childhood Leukemia; a Pamphlet for Parents. Pub. Health Serv., 1972. 26 p.   017-042-00041-6

Make Breast Examination a Health Habit. Natl. Cancer Inst., 1974. [9] p. il. Purchase from the Inst.

Science and Cancer. M. B. Shimkin. Natl. Insts. of Health [1973]. 159 p. il.   017-042-00071-8
"A medical scientist explains the nature of neoplastic disease, and the efforts of science and medicine to control it."

Special Viral Cancer Program. J. B. Moloney. Natl. Cancer Inst., 1972. 425 p. il. Free from the Inst.

SMOKING

Cigarette Smoking; Some Questions and Answers. Natl. Inst. of Mental Health [1971]. Folder. il.   017-024-00154-6

Health Consequences of Smoking. Health Services and Mental Health Admin., 1973. 249 p.   017-023-00064-1
Seventh of the famous series. Cites continuing evidence of the hazards of smoking cigarettes; and, for the first time, contains some evidence that pipe and cigar smoking may also be hazardous.

Health Consequences of Smoking; Report of the Surgeon General, 1972. Health Services and Mental Health Admin., 1972. 158 p. il.

017-023-00051-9

Six times since 1964 there have been reports of this type. The 1972 edition contains information on diseases and disorders diagnosed as resulting from too much smoking; their treatment, etc. And this edition confirms the original 1964 conclusion that "cigarettes are a major cause of death and disease."

1970 Bibliography on Smoking and Health. Pub. Health Serv. [1973]. 351 p.   017-023-00085-3
Some 1,500 annotated references drawn from 1970 literature in many languages.

Physician Talks about Smoking. Natl. Clearinghouse for Smoking and Health, 1971. 24 p. il. Free from the Clearinghouse.
What a doctor tells you *free* is worth listening to. Somehow, for one thing, the advice seems nearer to home.

Smoker's Aid to Non-Smoking; a Scorecard. Natl. Clearinghouse for Smoking and Health, 1971. [5] p. il.   017-022-00187-0
A sort of sporting introduction supposed to be good for 58 days—during which you keep tabs on your weaning away from the "filthy habit."

Tar and Nicotine Content of Cigarettes. Federal Trade Comm. [1973]. 2 p.   017-023-00090-0
A card, 4″ × 9″, measures and ranks the tar and nicotine content of cigarettes by brand.

Unless You Decide to Quit, Your Problem Isn't Going to Be Smoking; Your Problem Is Going to Be Staying Alive. Center for Drug Control, 1972. Free from the Center.   017-023-00069-1

VENEREAL DISEASES

Syphilis; a Synopsis. Public Health Serv., 1967 [1968]. 133 p. il. Purchase from the Serv.
"The purpose of this book is to bring to its readers a concise presentation of current knowledge and recent developments in the diagnosis and treatment of syphilis." Supplemented by visual aids.

VD and You. Public Health Serv. [1973]. [6] p. il.

017-023-00068-3

Avoid it, if possible; if you can't, do the right thing. This booklet tells you how to do both.

What You and Your Community Can Do about VD. Center for Disease Control. [1974]. [6] p. il. Free from the Center.

017-023-00075-9

VISION DISORDERS

Cataract. Natl. Eye Inst. [1973]. Folder.   017-050-00009-5

Corneal Disease. Natl. Eye Inst. [1973]. [3] p.   017-050-00007-9

Refractive Errors. Natl. Eye Inst. [1973]. [3] p.   017-050-00008-7

Retinitis Pigmentosa. Natl. Eye Inst. [1973]. [3] p.   017-050-00005-2

HISTORIC DOCUMENTS AND FACSIMILES

Bill of Rights. Genl. Services Admin. [1958].   022-002-00022-8
Poster, 38″ × 31″.

Constitution of the United States. Natl. Archives and Records Serv. [1958]. 38″ x 31″.   022-002-00023-6
Facsimile suitable for framing.

Documents from America's Past; Reproductions of Historical Documents in the National Archives. Natl. Archives Serv. [1972]. 21 p. Free from the Serv.
A catalog of the Service's reproductions, with prices. The sort of catalog that should be mandatory in every school.

Great Seal of the United States. Dept. of State, 1964. 2 p.

044-000-00022-9

The design of the seal, and what each part means.

HOME MAINTENANCE AND REPAIR

Condensation Problems in Your House; Prevention and Solution.
Agr. Dept., Agr. Inform. Bull. 373 (1974). 39 p. il. 001-000-03318-2
Factors in the problem, from concealed sources of condensation
to faulty insulation. How to meet existing problems. A good working bibliography and a glossary of terms.

Equipment for Cooling Your Home. Agr. Dept., Home and Garden
Bull. 100 [1970]. 7 p. il. 001-000-00772-6
Fans; water systems; air conditioning; heat pumps. Brief intro-
duction to all.

Exterior Painting. Dept. of Agr., Home and Garden Bull. 155 (1968).
12 p. il. 001-000-00815-3
Selecting the proper paint for the proper location; then applying it.

Finding and Keeping a Healthy House. R. C. Biesterfeldt and
others. Forest Serv., Genl. Tech. Rept. SO-1 (1973). 20 p. il.
Free from the Serv. 001-000-03263-1

First Aid for Flooded Homes and Farms. Dept. of Agr., Agr.
Handbook 38 [1973]. 28 p. il. 001-000-03186-4
Problems that may develop in the heating, electrical, and mechanical
equipment. Salvaging woodwork; salvaging books, furniture, clothing. Maintaining the food supply. Controlling insects and rodents.

Focus on Furniture; an Important Element in Housing. Housing
and Urban Develop. Dept., 1971. 41 p. il. Free from the Dept.
"Innovative approaches" to the question of furnishing on a low
or moderate budget. Many illustrations.

Handbook for the Home; Yearbook of Agriculture, 1973. J. Hayes,
ed. Dept. of Agr., 1973. 388 p. il. 001-000-02960-6
". . . a guide to helping families use their incomes to best ad-

vantage." Divided into: "Families," "Dwellings," "Furnishings," "Communities." Like all yearbooks of this Department, unmatchable and invaluable. One is especially impressed by the coverage of the Yearbooks of Agriculture.

How to Paint a Room, Step by Step. Public Housing Admin., 1964. [4] p. il.   023-002-00001-9
How not to paint yourself into a corner.

Interior Painting in Homes and around the Farm. Dept. of Agr., Home and Garden Bull. 184 (1971). 12 p. il.   001-000-01171-5

Plumbing for the Home and Farmstead. H. L. Garver and J. W. Rockey. Dept. of Agr., Farmers' Bull. 2213 (1971). 20 p. il.
                                                    001-000-03334-4
Water-supply piping; drainage piping; pipe fitting; service building piping. Practical illustrations.

Selecting and Financing a Home. Dept. of Agr., Home and Garden Bull. 182 (1972). 24 p. il.   001-000-02475-2
How to estimate costs and avail yourself of loan services.

Simple Plumbing Repairs for Home and Farmstead. Dept. of Agr., Farmers' Bull. 2202 (1972). 14 p. il.   001-000-02684-4
Repairs of water faucets; frozen water pipes; clogged drains; and other common emergencies.

Use of Hardwood Flooring in Mobile Homes. D. G. Martens and L. J. Koenick. Forest Serv., Research Paper NE-172 (1970). 10 p. Free from the Serv. Agr. Dept.

When You Return to a Storm-damaged Home. Fed. Disaster Assistance Admin. [1973]. [9] p. il. Free from the Admin.
                                                    023-000-00161-6
Important hints: drying; restoring electrical supplies; heating problems; water supply and plumbing; salvage and repair.

Wood Decay in Houses; How to Prevent and Control it. Dept. of Agr., Home and Garden Bull. 73 (1969). 17 p. il.

001-000-00856-1

Detailed practical advice.

Wood Finishing; Painting Outside Wood Surfaces. Forest Serv., Research Note FPL-0123 [1972]. 4 p. Free from the Serv.

Your 4-H Home Furnishings Program; Make It Meaningful, Appealing, Forward-looking. G. Hoffman. Dept. of Agr., PA 606 (1970). [15] p. il. Free from the Dept.
Charming guide that first outlines some principles of good taste, and then engages the help of the whole family in carrying them out to improve the looks and life of your home.

HORTICULTURE

Bottle Garden. Agr. Research Serv., 1972. [4] p. il. Free from the Serv.
Lots of fun growing things in a very restricted space.

Green Scene; a Program of the National Park Service; Care and Maintenance of Common Household and Office Plants; a Home Gardener's Handbook. F. Hecht and M. L. Anderson. Natl. Park Serv., 1973. 61 p. il.   024-005-00536-6
Very fine indeed. First come a good many pages of general advice on raising such plants; then individual instructions on 17 particular plants (ending with the Zebra plant).

Growing Plants without Soil for Experimental Use. M. Blankendaal and others. Dept. of Agr., Misc. Pub. 125 (1972). 17 p. il.

001-000-02657-7

This means their growth in many environments that lack soil—cracked rock, vermiculite, and coarse sand.

Mulches for Your Garden. Dept. of Agr., Home and Garden Bull. 185 (1971). Folder. il.   001-000-01172-3

FLOWERS AND FLOWERING TREES

Each of the booklets cited below tells you where, when, and how to start your flowers or trees, and how to maintain them during favorable months, as well as how to nurse them through unfavorable ones.

Growing Azaleas and Rhododendrons. Dept. of Agr., Home and Garden Bull. 71 (1970). 8 p. il.   001-000-03405-7

Growing Dahlias. Dept. of Agr., Home and Garden Bull. 131 (1970). 8 p. il.   001-000-02490-6

Growing Flowering Annuals. H. M. Cathey. Dept. of Agr., Home and Garden Bull. 91 (1970). [16] p. il.   001-000-03411-1

Growing the Flowering Dogwood. Dept. of Agr., Home and Garden Bull. 88 (1970). [8] p. il.   001-000-01901-5

Growing Flowering Perennials. H. M. Cathey. Dept. of Agr., Home and Garden Bull. 114 (1970). 32 p. il.   001-000-00783-1
Planning your perennial garden; planting; starting perennials indoors.

Growing Gardenias. Dept. of Agr., Home and Garden Bull. 152 (1971). 8 p. il.   001-000-03469-3
An evergreen that grows as far north as the Coastal Plains of Virginia.

Growing Hollies. Dept. of Agr., Home and Garden Bull. 130 (1967). 8 p. il.   001-000-00793-9

Growing Iris in the Home Garden. Dept. of Agr., Home and Garden Bull. 66 (1971). 8 p. il.   001-000-03192-9

Growing Magnolias. Dept. of Agr., Home and Garden Bull. 132 [1973]. 8 p. il.   001-000-02738-7

Growing Pansies. Dept. of Agr., Home and Garden Bull. 149 (1970). [8] p. il.   001-000-02574-1

Growing Peonies. H. M. Cathey. Dept. of Agr., Home and Garden Bull. 126 (1971). [12] p. il.   001-000-01283-5

Roses for the Home. Dept. of Agr., Home and Garden Bull. 25 (1970). 24 p. il.   001-000-01511-7
Types of roses; purchasing; planting; care. Winter protection. And the inevitable insects and diseases.

Spring Flowering Bulbs. H. M. Cathey. Dept. of Agr., Home and Garden Bull. 136 (1971). 14 p. il.   001-000-00798-0
Amaryllis to tulip.

Summer Flowering Bulbs. H. M. Cathey. Dept. of Agr., Home and Garden Bull. 151 (1971). 16 p. il.   001-000-00812-9
These do well in almost all parts of our country. Discussed here are achimenes, allium, amaryllis, begonia, caladium, calla, canna, dahlia, day lily, gladiolus, gloxinia, iris, ismene, lilium hybrid, lycoris, montbretia, peony, tigridia, tuberose, etc. (That long listing of flower types is meant to illustrate, for readers of this *Guide,* the Government's thorough coverage of any subject it tackles.)

FRUIT GROWING

A berry is "any small, succulent fruit," and the compiler wants no complaints from professional botanists. (However, he is aware that in classing tomatoes as "vegetable," he is probably wrong; but see his remarks under "Vegetable Gardening.") There are few annotations in the listings below; it may be assumed that all the titles follow a similar pattern: they tell you where, when, and how to plant your crop; how to nurse it through bad times; and how to reap its riches.

Commercial Strawberry Growing in the Pacific Coast States. G. F. Waldo and others. Dept. of Agr., Farmers Bull. 2236 (1971). 22 p. il.   001-000-00089-6
In California, Oregon, and Washington.

Dwarf Fruit Trees; Selection and Care. Dept. of Agr., Leaflet 407 (1971). 8 p. il.   001-000-03226-7

Growing American Bunch Grapes. Dept. of Agr., Farmers' Bull. 2123 [1973]. 22 p. il.   001-000-03266-6

Growing Blackberries. J. W. Hull and F. J. Lawrence. Dept. of Agr., Farmers' Bull. 2160 [1972]. 18 p. il.   001-000-03472-3

Growing Cherries East of the Rocky Mountains. Dept. of Agr., Farmers' Bull. 2185 (1967). 30 p. il.   001-000-03279-8

Growing Raspberries. Dept. of Agr., Farmers' Bull. 2165 (1971). 14 p. il.   001-000-01486-2

Muscadine Grapes; Fruit for the South. Dept. of Agr., Farmers' Bull. 2157 (1973). 14 p. il.   001-000-03166-0

Muskmelons for the Garden. Dept. of Agr., Leaflet 509 (1968). Folder. il.   001-000-00223-6

Strawberry Culture, Eastern United States. Dept. of Agr., Farmers' Bull. 1028 [1972]. 20 p. il.   001-000-03162-7

Strawberry Varieties in the United States. G. M. Darrow and D. H. Scott. Dept. of Agr., Farmers' Bull. 1043 (1967). 16 p. il.
                                                                                                001-000-01501-0
Twenty-seven main varieties make up 97 percent of the strawberries we eat.

Why Fruit Trees Fail to Bear. Dept. of Agr., Leaflet 172 (1971).
Folder.   001-000-01590-7

LANDSCAPING AND LAWN CARE

Better Lawns: Establishment, Maintenance, Renovation, Lawn
Problems, Grasses. Dept. of Agr., Home and Garden Bull. 51
(1971). [30] p. il.   001-000-03476-6
Putting the lawn down; keeping it looking good. Weeds, insects,
diseases—all those things that undo your good work. Soil composition in relation to choice of grass type.

Color It Green with Trees; a Calendar of Activities for Home
Arborists. Dept. of Agr., PA 791 (1972). [16] p. il.
                                                       001-000-01557-5
Pains of the winter months are lightened by preparations for the
coming growing season.

Growing Boxwoods. Dept. of Agr., Home and Garden Bull. 120
(1971). 15 p. il.   001-000-01163-4

Growing Ground Covers. Dept. of Agr., Home and Garden Bull.
175 (1970). 16 p. il.   001-000-00833-1

Growing Ornamentals in Urban Gardens. H. M. Cathey. Dept. of
Agr., Home and Garden Bull. 188 (1971). 22 p. il.
                                                       001-000-01329-7
Plotting the garden; choosing the right plants; cultivation and
care.

How to Buy Lawn Seed. Dept. of Agr., Home and Garden Bull.
169 (1969). Folder.   001-000-01286-0
What kinds are available; which is best suited for your land; how
to nurse the growing grass.

Landscape for Living; the Yearbook of Agriculture, 1972. J.
Hayes, ed. Dept. of Agr., 1972. [376] p. il.   001-000-02441-8

Tells the novice and the skilled home landscaper how to improve the environment with plants. Includes chapters on the ecology of plant life, matching plants with their surroundings, the selection and protection of new plants; new ways to utilize plants, as well as where to go for further information. As is usual with this series, the text is preceded by most attractive sets of color plates.

Lawn Diseases; How to Control Them. K. W. Kreitlow and F. V. Juska. Dept. of Agr., Home and Garden Bull. 61 (1971). 14 p. il.
001-000-02786-7
Leaf spot, foot spot, rust, falling out, fairy rings, slime, molds—lawns have a hard time of it. Dogs and other pets don't help much. This Bulletin tells how to cheer up your grass.

Lawn Insects; How to Control Them. A. M. Vance and B. A. App. Dept. of Agr., Home and Garden Bull. 53 (1971). 23 p. il.
001-000-01264-9
The excellent advice given here is not, of course, limited to home lawns; it applies to any expanse of grass that requires grooming.

Lawn Weed Control with Herbicides. Dept. of Agr., Home and Garden Bull. 123 (1971). 24 p. il.   001-000-01165-1

Protecting Shade Trees During Home Construction. Dept. of Agr., Home and Garden Bull. 104 (1971). [8] p. il.   001-000-01309-2

Pruning Ornamental Shrubs and Vines. Dept. of Agr., Home and Garden Bull. 165 (1969). 16 p. il.   001-000-00823-4
Prune to improve the health of your plants, control their size, and increase flower display.

Selecting Fertilizers for Lawns and Gardens. Dept. of Agr., Home and Garden Bull. 89 (1973). Folder. il   001-000-02739-5

Selecting Shrubs for Shady Areas. Dept. of Agr., Home and Garden Bull. 142 (1970). 16 p. il.   001-000-03272-1
Thirty-two kinds; their cultivation and care.

Shade Trees for the Home. Dept. of Agr., Agr. Handbook 425 (1972). 48 p. il.   001-000-02496-5
Characteristics, selection, planting and care; lists of trees by region; descriptions of these. Full and careful indexes.

Trees for Shade and Beauty; Their Selection and Care. Dept. of Agr., Home and Garden Bull. 117 (1970). 8 p. il.

001-000-01606-7

PLANT AND TREE DISEASES

Controlling Diseases of Raspberries and Blackberries. Dept. of Agr., Farmers' Bull. 2208 (1971). 13 p. il.   001-000-03366-2

Controlling Dodder in Fodder. J. H. Dawson and others. Dept. of Agr., Farmers' Bull. 2211 (1971). 16 p. il.   001-000-01443-9

Diseases of Forest and Shade Trees of the United States. G. H. Hepting. Dept. of Agr., Agr. Handbook 386 (1971). 658 p. il.

001-000-01135-9

Everything from *Abies amabilis* to *Umbellaria californica*. Seed; foliage, root; trunk diseases. Very fine handbook.

Dutch Elm Disease and Its Control. R. R. Whitten and R. N. Swingle. Dept. of Agr., Agr. Inform. Bull. 193 (1964). 12 p. il.

001-000-03442-1

This disease was unknown in America prior to the 1930s; no known cure has yet been found. The only method is to prevent spread of the beetle that causes it. Some authorities think all our elms are doomed; what a dismal prospect to those of us old enough to remember the tree in its unrivaled beauty!

Fungal Control of Smut Diseases of Cereals. J. G. Maseman. Agr. Research Serv., CR 41-68 (1968). 36 p. Free from the Serv.

Maple Diseases and Their Control; a Guide for Homeowners. Dept. of Agr., Home and Garden Bull. 81 (1970). 8 p. il.   001-000-03490-1

Rice Diseases. J. G. Atkins. Dept. of Agr., Farmers' Bull. 2120
[1972]. 14 p. il.   001-000-02483-3

Tomato Diseases and Their Control. T. H. Barksdale and others.
Dept. of Agr., Agr. Handbook 203 [1972]. 109 p. il.

001-000-02466-3

VEGETABLE GARDENING

Strictly speaking, asparagus is a member of the *lily* family; mint,
beets, parsley (among others below) are *herbs;* sweet potatoes are
roots; potatoes are *tubers,* and so on. But they are all members of
the vegetable kingdom. Which is why the compiler has not included the *herbs* under a separate heading "Herb Gardening," the
asparagus under the heading "Flower Gardening."

Growing Vegetables in the Home Garden. R. E. Wester. Dept. of
Agr., Home and Garden Bull. 202 [1972]. 49 p. il.

001-000-02604-6

Minigardens for Vegetables. Dept. of Agr., Home and Garden Bull.
163 (1970). 12 p. il.   001-000-03219-4
A windowsill, a balcony, a doorstep—all can afford enough space
for the little gardens described here.

Teacher's Guide to Minigardens. C. Jackson. Dept. of Agr., Sci.
Study Aid 2 (1971). 3 p.   001-000-02906-1
Ways to use the preceding title as a "basis for learning activities."

SPECIFIC CROPS

Barley; Origin, Botany, Culture, Winter Hardiness, Genetics, Uti-
lization, Pests. Dept. of Agr., Agr. Handbook 338 (1968). 127 p. il.
Free from the Dept.
Very detailed: history, culture; weeds, insect pests; diseases. Botany.

Commercial Greenhouse Production of Greenhouse Tomatoes. A. K.
Stoner. Dept. of Agr., Agr. Handbook 382 (1971). 32 p. il.

001-000-00382-8

Commercial Growing of Asparagus. Dept. of Agr., Farmers Bull. 2232 (1971). 22 p. il. 001-000-03443-0
Climate for growth; varieties; cultivation; harvesting. Insects and diseases.

Growing Cauliflower and Broccoli. Dept. of Agr., Farmers' Bull. 2239 (1971). [12] p. il. 001-000-03408-1

Growing Ginseng. L. Williams. Dept. of Agr., Farmers' Bull. 2201 (1968). 8 p. il. 001-000-02779-4

Growing Table Beets. Dept. of Agr., Leaflet 360 (1971). Folder. il. 001-000-03170-8

Growing Tomatoes in the Home Garden. A. K. Stoner. Dept. of Agr., Home and Garden Bull. 180 (1971). 12 p. il.

001-000-02463-9

Rhubarb Production. Dept. of Agr., Leaflet 555 (1972). 8 p. il.

001-000-03342-5

Rice in the United States; Varieties and Production. Dept. of Agr., Agr. Handbook 289 (1973). 154 p. il. 001-000-02717-4
Everything about the types: their breeding, cultivation; seeding; irrigation, harvesting. Weeds; diseases.

Sweetpotato Culture and Diseases. C. E. Steinbauer and L. J. Kushman. Dept. of Agr., Agr. Handbook 388 (1971). 74 p. il.

001-000-01136-7

HOUSEKEEPING

Clean Beds for a Clean House. Dept. of Agr., PA 830 [1967]. [4] p. il. 001-000-00569-3

Clean Electric Ranges for a Clean House. Dept. of Agr., PA 829 [1972]. [8] p. il. 001-000-00568-5

Clean Gas Ranges for a Clean House. Dept. of Agr., PA 828 [1967]. [8] p.   001-000-01123-5

Clean Refrigerator for a Clean House. Dept. of Agr., PA 733 [1972]. [8] p. il. Free from the Dept.   001-000-00529-4

Clean Upholstered Furniture for a Clean Home. Dept. of Agr., PA 827 [1967]. [4] p. il.   001-000-00567-7

Cleaning Kitchen Ranges. Adapted by G. Pifer. Dept. of Agr., PA 1072 [1973]. [2] p. il.   001-000-03065-5

Cleaning Metal Furniture. Adapted by G. Pifer. Dept. of Agr., PA 1070 [1973]. [2] p. il.   001-000-03068-0

Cleaning Windows, Mirrors, Other Glass. Adapted by G. Pifer. Dept. of Agr., PA 1065 [1973]. [2] p. il.   001-000-03061-2

Cleaning Wood Furniture. Adapted by G. Pifer. Dept. of Agr., PA 1066 (1973).   001-000-03059-1

11 Ways to Reduce Energy Consumption and Increase Comfort in Household Cooling. Natl. Stand. Bur. [1971]. [20] p. il.
      003-000-00876-1

Floors; Care and Maintenance. Post Off. Dept., Facilities Handbook, Ser. S-3 (1969). 35 p.   039-000-00144-6
Properly, of course, for postal employees, but full of useful information about general cleaning (including a stain-removal chart).

Get Rid of Garbage and Trash . . . for a Clean House. Dept. of Agr., PA 826 (1967). [4] p. il.   001-000-01122-7
Every little thing helps.

Have a Sparkling Clean Kitchen Sink. Adapted by G. Pifer. Dept. of Agr., PA 1071 [1973]. [2] p. il.   001-000-03066-3

Home Energy Saving Tips from NBS. Natl. Stand. Bur. [1974]. [4] p. Free from the Bur.

How to Clean the Bathroom. Adapted by G. Pifer. Dept. of Agr., PA 1063 [1973]. [2] p. il.   001-000-03062-1

How to Clean Floors. Adapted by G. Pifer. Dept. of Agr., PA 1068 [1973]. 4 p. il.   001-000-03058-2

How to Clean Rugs and Carpets. Adapted by G. Pifer. Dept. of Agr., PA 1069 [1973]. [2] p. il.   001-000-03067-1

How to Clean Walls, Ceilings, Woodwork. Adapted by G. Pifer. Dept. of Agr., PA 1064 [1973]. [2] p. il.   001-000-03063-9

How to Prevent and Remove Mildew; Home Methods. Dept. of Agr., Home and Garden Bull. 68 (1971). 12 p. il.   001-000-01548-6

Make Dishwashing Easy. Adapted by G. Pifer. Dept. of Agr., PA 1067 [1973]. [2] p. il.   001-000-03060-4

Products and Tools for Cleaning. Adapted by G. Pifer. Dept. of Agr., PA 1073 (1973) [2] p. il.   001-000-03064-7

Removing Stains from Fabrics; Home Methods. Dept. of Agr., Home and Garden Bull. 62 (1968). 32 p. il.   001-000-00850-1

Sanitation in Home Laundering. Dept. of Agr., Home and Garden Bull. 97 (1971). 8 p. il.   001-000-01488-9

7 Ways to Reduce Fuel Consumption in Household Heating through Energy Conservation. Natl. Stand. Bur. [1971]. 9 p. il.
003-003-01086-3

Soaps and Detergents for Home Laundering. Dept. of Agr., Home and Garden Bull. 139 (1971). 8 p. il.   001-000-01318-1

Staying Warm and Saving Money. S. B. Aucoin. Off. of Econ. Opportunity, OEO Pamph. 6143-1 (1974). [16] p. Free from the Off.

When to Do House Cleaning Jobs. Dept. of Agr., PA 724 [1972]. Folder. il. Free from the Dept.   001-000-00530-8

HOUSE PLANNING AND DESIGN

Architectural Design for Crime Prevention. O. Newman. Justice Dept., 1973. 214 p. il.   027-000-00161-1
"Residential complexes can be designed to deter robbery, vandalism, and other crime." (Foreword.)

Design Guide for Home Safety [Guideline 1]. Teledyne Brown Engineering, Huntsville, Ala. Dept. of Housing and Urban Develop., 1972. [177] p. il.   023-000-00201-9
"Clear, concise, and readily usable guide to the design of safer homes." Helpful illustrations.

Designs for Low-Cost Homes; House Plan FS-FPL [Ser.]. Forest Serv., [1970].
   1. Dec. 1969 [1970]. 9 sheets, each 18″ × 24″. Plan for rambler, 3 bedrooms. Designed by L. O. Anderson.   001-001-00009-4
   2. Dec. 1969 [1970]. 9 sheets, each 18″ × 24″. Plan for one-and-a-half-story home, 3 large bedrooms. Designed by L. O. Anderson.   001-001-00010-8
   3. Dec. 1969 [1970]. 8 sheets, each 18″ × 24″. Plan for rambler, one bedroom and spare room. Designed by L. O. Anderson.

                    001-001-00011-6
   4. Dec. 1969 [1970]. 9 sheets, each 18″ × 24″. Plan for two-story home, 4 large bedrooms. Designed by L. O. Anderson.

                    001-001-00012-4
   5. Dec. 1969 [1970]. 10 sheets, each 18″ × 24″. Plans for 2-bedroom rambler or expandable two-story home. Designed by L. O. Anderson.   001-001-00008-6

Designs for Low-Cost Wood Homes. L. O. Anderson and H. F. Zornig. Dept. of Agr., Agr. Handbook 364 (1969) [1970]. 28 p. il.

001-000-00747-5

Interior layout; plans are obtainable from the Superintendent of Documents.

Designs for Low-Cost Wood Homes; House Plan FS-SE [Ser.]. Forest Serv. 1969 [1970].

One annotation will serve for the entire group of house plans cited here and following. The publications themselves contain reduced plans for full-scale plans which are obtainable from the Forest Service. All are adapted to their sites in a striking way, all appear roomy, and all are reasonable in price. The six plans cited immediately below are by L. O. Anderson and H. F. Zornig.

1. Dec. 1969 [1970]. 5 sheets, each 18" × 24". Plan for rural home; 3 bedrooms. Designed by H. F. Zornig. 001-001-00013-2

2. Dec. 1969 [1970]. 4 sheets, each 18" × 24". Plan for rural home; 2 bedrooms and bunk room. Designed by H. F. Zornig.

001-001-00014-1

3. Dec. 1969 [1970]. 5 sheets, each 18" × 24". Plan for 3-bedroom pole-supported house, plus carport and storage room if constructed on steep enough slope. Designed by H. F. Zornig.

001-001-00015-9

4. Dec. 1969 [1970]. 7 sheets, each 18" × 24". Plan for tubular home; 3 bedrooms. Designed by H. F. Zornig.

001-001-00016-7

5. Dec. 1969 [1970]. 6 sheets, each 18" × 24". Plan for round house; 3 bedrooms. Designed by H. F. Zornig.

001-001-00017-5

6. Dec. 1969 [1970]. 6 sheets, each 18" × 24". Plan for hillside duplex; Gothic type arches; 2-story; 2-bedroom houses. Designed by H. F. Zornig. 001-001-00018-3

FPL Designs Meet Family Housing Needs. G. E. Sherwood. Forest Serv., Res. Paper FPL-173 (1972). [28] p. il. Purchase from the Serv.

Kitchen Planning. Dept. of Housing and Urban Develop., Training Handbook 4075.3 (1973). 22 p. il. Free from the Dept.
Planning to save space and your legs. Reduced plans are included.

Kitchen Planning Guide. D. L. Moore. Fed. Housing Admin., Tech. Standards Training Guide 2 (1969). 24 p. il. Free from the Admin.
Basic principles of design; use of planning concepts in evaluating existing kitchens and in designing the well-planned kitchen. Very good illustrative drawings.

Know the Soil You Build On . . . Dream House or Nightmare? A. A. Klingebiel. Dept. of Agr., Agr. Inform. Bull. 320 (1967). 13 p. il.
001-000-00655-0
Things can happen to your structures if you don't make sure your soil can sustain their weight and maintain their proper position.

Low-Cost Wood Homes For Rural America . . . Construction Manual. L. O. Anderson. Dept. of Agr., Agr. Handbook 364 (1969). 112 p. il. 001-000-00747-5
This covers in detail every aspect of construction; many reduced drawings.

Planning Your Home Lighting. Dept. of Agr., Home and Garden Bull. 138 (1968). 22 p. il. 001-000-00800-5
Right fixtures, right positions.

Three-Bedroom Framehouse. Dept. of Agr., Misc. Pub. 1279 (1974). [2] p. il. 001-000-03206-2

HOUSING AND URBAN PLANNING

Citizen and Business Participation in Urban Affairs; A Bibliography. Dept. of Housing and Urban Develop., 1970. 84 p.
023-000-00089-0

Condominiums; Their Development and Management. A. D. Grezzo. Dept. of Housing and Urban Develop., 1972. 71 p.
023-000-00202-7

A suddenly popular way of buying your home. This booklet tells how they must be capably managed to work right. Practical hints to the sometimes perplexed buyer.

How to Improve Your Community by Attracting New Industry. Econ. Develop. Admin., 1972. 44 p. il.   003-011-00052-6
"This publication shows how a community can effectively wage a campaign to attract industrial prospects."

HUD International Briefs . . . Dept. of Housing and Urban Develop., 1970–73.
"Brief is designed for the exchange of housing and urban development information from both foreign and domestic sources. Its contents, as the name implies, touches only on highlights and pertinent information. Where information is digested from a larger paper, availability of the complete work is indicated on the last page of the issue." Like so many self-analyses by Government departments, this one is much too modest. The Briefs afford a look into a phase of foreign (and domestic) life probably difficult to trace easily elsewhere. Several numbers in the group are annotated briefly; others speak pretty plainly for themselves. Please note that there are slight variants in title; and the compiler has shortened some.

1. Program Report. 1. Housing and Urban Development—U.S.A.: a Look at Major Domestic Problems and Methods of Solution . . . 1971. 16 p. il.   023-000-00173-0
   Such factors as population trends and patterns; their effects on housing; the role of the Federal Government; research and development; "Operation Breakthrough"—a brief guide to these and many other aspects of the subject.
2. Program Report: Urban Transportation in the Renewal of American Cities; an Information Paper . . . [1971]. [12] p. il.   023-000-00174-8
   How transportation hurts cities; planning for coordinated improvement.
4. Research and Technology: Operation Breakthrough: its

Origin, Objectives, and Implementation. 1971. 11 p.

023-000-00181-1

". . . outlines the housing situation in the U.S.A. . . . Broad objectives of the Program aimed at improving the process of housing . . ." A report of a meeting of building contractors.

6. Housing and Urban Development in Japan; an In-Depth Report on Japan made By a Team of Housing Experts from HUD as Part of the Japanese-American Bilateral Agreement for the Exchange of Information on Housing and Urban Development. 1971. [48] p. il.   023-000-00185-3
Conventional Japanese housing; how the Japanese are adapting to change. A most remarkable and interesting study.

7. Design for Livability; Livability Problems Arising from the Proper Orientation to Sunlight. 1971. 7 p. il.

023-000-00186-1

Making the maximum use of position and plot.

8. Urban Development in Iran [R. Warburton]. 1971. [24] p. il.   023-000-01190-5
Historical highlights; something of the land and the people; the incubus of tradition; planning for the future.

9. Seasonal Unemployment in the Construction Industry: How Subsidies and Scheduling of Works Projects by [European] Governments Cut Individual Unemployment and Allow Building Contractors to Operate During the Winter Months. [1970]. 16 p. il.   023-000-00187-0

10. Homeownership in the United States; a Short History of Private Homeownership . . . and the Eventual Role of the Federal Government. 1971. 11 p. il.   023-000-00182-9

11. Tenant Involvement in Public Housing; Reshaping the Social and Physical Environment of Housing for Low-Income Families in the United States; and a Report of the Philadelphia Experience. 1971. 11 p.   023-000-00183-7

12. Housing and Urbanism in Marxist China; a Portent and Prognosis. W. Mannis. 1972. 11 p. il.   023-000-00193-4
In view of the apparent uncertainty of recent events, the progress is remarkable.

13. Cooperative Housing in the U.S.A. 1972. 11 p. il.

> 023-000-00195-1

Historical study; valuable for its listing of cooperative housing organizations.

15. Housing and Urban Development in Sweden; a Report of the First U.S. Mission to Sweden under a Bilateral Agreement between the U.S. Department of Housing and Urban Development and the Swedish Building Commission. 1972. 34 p. il.   023-000-00197-7

17. New Communities in the United States; the American Approach to New Towns. 1973. 32 p. il.   023-000-00252-3
Begins with America's "unloved" cities; traces our changing attitudes; and ends on a hopeful note. Very fine photographs.

18. Housing and Urban Development in the United Kingdom; with a Bibliography by A. Wells. 1972. 20 p. il.

> 023-000-00198-5

It is interesting to compare American and English attitudes.

19. Transportation Innovations in New Communities Abroad; Some Foreign Approaches to Public Transportation. 1973. 15 p. il.   023-000-00225-6

Operation Breakthrough; Mass Produced and Industrialized Houses; a Bibliography. Dept. of Housing and Urban Develop. [1970]. 72 p.   023-000-00088-1
Selective, annotated bibliography exploring the "application of modern technology" to building.

Revitalizing Older Houses in Charlestown [Mass.]. G. Stephen and R. Rettig. Dept. of Housing and Urban Develop. [1973]. 28 p. il.

> 023-000-00222-1

"Right to a Decent Home . . .": Housing Improvement Initiatives for Public Welfare Agencies. Social and Rehab. Serv., 1970. 40 p. il.

> 017-065-00001-7

Millions of Americans depend on public assistance for housing. This "guide"—with telling illustrations—shows how many of these Americans live now, and how they might live if better care were provided. **Role of Water in Urban Planning and Management.** W. J. Schneider, Jr. and others. Geol. Survey, Cir. 601-H (1973). 10 p. il. Free from the Survey.

HUNTING

Atlas of Southern Forest Game. L. K. Halls and J. J. Stransky. Forest Serv., 1971. 24 p. il. Free from the Serv.

Conservation Practices—Signs of Good Hunting and Fishing. Dept. of Agr., PA 1012 [1972]. 31 p. il.   001-000-02573-9
The good huntsman and the good fisherman do not waste game—or their own time and equipment. This booklet is chockful of practical advice—obviously by experts who love their pastimes.

Handling Your Big-Game Kill. Forest Serv., 1967. [9] p. il. Free from the Serv.
How to cut up the kill, skin it, bone it, and prepare the edible parts.

INTERNATIONAL AFFAIRS

Arms Control and Disarmament Agreements, 1959–1972. Arms Control and Disarmament Agency, 1972. 119 p. Free from the Agency.   002-000-00041-5
Text of the agreements only.

Ataturk and Turkey; a Bibliography, 1919–1938. A. Bodurgil. Library of Congress, 1974. 74 p.   030-020-00011-1

Greece, Spain, and the Southern NATO Strategy; Hearings . . . House of Representatives, 1971. 582 p.   052-070-01303-6
Hearings before a Subcommittee of the Committee on Europe. Very valuable study, with reprints of many articles that have appeared on this subject.

Homemaking Handbook for Village Workers in Many Countries.
Dept. of Agr., PA 953 (1971). 237 p. il.   044-001-00030-6
Aimed at a special group—workers among the deprived abroad—
which nevertheless has a compelling place in such a "guide"
as the present one, since it tells what the United States is doing, in a
very practical way, to help our world neighbors. A very moving
book.

International Terrorism; Hearings . . . House of Representatives,
1974. 219 p. Purchase from the Comm.
Hearings before the Subcommittee on the Near East and South
Asia, of the House Committee on Foreign Affairs. Expert testimony
and reproductions of articles and other data.

**New China Policy; Its Impact on the United States and Asia; Hear-
ings . . .** House of Representatives, 1972. 310 p.
                                             052-070-01640-0
Before the Subcommittee on Asian and Pacific Affairs of the
House's Committee on Foreign Affairs. Detailed study of every aspect of the recent Chinese détente and its effects on many nations,
including our own. In five chapters, covering strategic and general considerations of the new China policy; its impact on the
Republic of China, on Korea and Thailand, and on Japan; an exile's
view of the People's Republic.

Perspectives on Ocean Policy; Conference . . . Natl. Sci. Found.,
1974 [1975]. 436 p. il.   038-000-00211-2
"One objective has been to achieve a synthesis, as well as an analysis, of all the related aspects of what one might call the new era of
ocean politics—all of those aspects revolving around the uses of
ocean space and its resources, including the legal, military, scientific, technological, ecological, and economic aspects, as they affect
the patterns of interest, conflict, and alignment and the patterns of
accommodation. . . . The second objective has been to relate this
synthesis and analysis to the components of a new . . . regime for
the use of the oceans, and to relate all these aspects of the new era
of ocean politics to U.S. ocean policy options." A superb study.

Policy Aspects of Foreign Investment by U.S. Multinational Corporations. Internatl. Comm. Bur., 1972. 86 p. Free from the Bur.
Six chapters: overview; impact on employment; transfer of technology; response of U.S. foreign direct-investment countries; impact on balance of payments; political implications. The multinational corporation is described as "a bold and imaginative and necessary response of United States business to the inexorable pressures of international commerce."

Questions and Answers about UNESCO. Dept. of State [1970]. 20 p. Free from the Dept.
Answers your questions about the United Nations Scientific, Educational, and Cultural Organization: its organization, what it does and has done, and our relations with it.

Select Chronology and Background Documents Relating to the Middle East. The Senate, 1969. 287 p.   052-070-00292-1
Hearings before the Foreign Relations Committee. Contains both American statements and agreements and reports and speeches dealing with the situation. Good basic *primary* material.

U.S. Participation in the U.N.; Report by the President to the Congress for the Year 1971. Dept. of State, Intern. Org. and Conf. Ser. 104 [1972]. 238 p.   044-000-01437-8
One of a long series, this one is divided into five main parts: maintenance of peace and security; economic, social, and humanitarian developments; trusteeship and dependent areas; legal developments; and budget and administration. Valuable appendices cover the UN's internal system. For a library that wants a file on foreign developments, this entire group (i.e., predecessors and followers) is recommended.

KOREAN WAR

Combat Actions in Korea. R. A. Gugeler. Dept. of the Army [1970]. 252 p. il.   008-029-00003-2
Firsthand accounts by men who saw action.

United States Army in the Korean War. Dept. of the Army, 1961–72. 3 vols.

Here the compiler of this *Guide* has fallen back upon the latest most excellent "Publications of the U.S. Army Center of Military History." As in the magnificent group dealing with the United States Army in World War II, this set contains works both on logistics and supply and on the fighting front. The latter, as is perhaps to be expected, are the more "exciting" chronicles. And finally, the compiler has once again availed himself of the masterly annotations furnished in the "Publications."

1. South to the Naktong, North to the Yalu. R. E. Appleman. 1961. 813 p. il. 008-029-00079-2
   Detailed account of the first five months of the Korean War; vividly describes the disheartening days of setback and withdrawal in the Pusan perimeter, MacArthur's landing and drive northward that crushed the Koreans, and the stiffening of enemy resistance as the UN forces neared the Yalu and the Manchurian border.

2. Truce Tent and Fighting Front. W. G. Hermes. 1966. 571 p. il. 008-029-00001-6
   Covers the intricate and frustrating truce negotiations at Kaesong and Panmunjom from July, 1951, to July, 1953, between the UN forces and the Chinese Communist forces, and affords an insight into Communist tactics and strategy at the bargaining table. Describes some of the bitter hill fighting that continued to claim lives in spite of the truce; and includes a detailed account of the large scale prisoner riots at Koje-do.

3. Policy and Direction: the First Year. J. F. Schnabel. 1972. 443 p. il. 008-029-00083-1
   Developments in Korea from August, 1945, to the outbreak of war in June, 1950, this volume examines definitely the major policy decisions and planning actions in Washington and Tokyo through June, 1951. A broad outline of combat operations is included.

U.S. Marine Operations in West Korea, 1950–53. Marine Corps, 1972.

5. Operations in Korea. R. Meid and J. M. Yingling. 1972. 643 p. il. 008-055-00059-9

LABOR

Brief History of the American Labor Movement. Bur. of Labor
Statistics, Bull. 1000 (1970). 143 p. il.   029-001-00388-9
An excellent account (certainly not too "brief"), and a valuable
table of events, 1778–1969.

Handbook of Labor Statistics, 1974. Bur. of Labor Statistics, Bull.
1735 (1972). 400 p.   029-001-01314-1
Entirely statistical; but indispensable for libraries.

Important Events in American Labor History, 1778–1971. Dept. of
Labor [1971]. 35 p. il.   029-000-00132-4
From something resembling a strike of angry New York journeyman
printers in 1778 to February, 1971. Reprint from Bureau of Labor
Statistics *Bulletin* 1000.

Labor Day; How It Came About; What It Means. Dept. of Labor
[1969]. [5] p. Free from the Dept.
Brief account of events that led up to its original proclamation,
September 29, 1912, and of those responsible for it.

Labor Law and Practice in . . . Bur. of Labor Statistics, 1968–72.
Of this group (all BLS reports), at least 65 have been issued
since 1961. Some 15 remain in print, but since a number of these
are over a decade old, and others reflect statistics and information
gathered when different governments were in power, a word of
explanation is due as to why the compiler has included these older
titles. The fact is, that, as a whole, the group constitute a sort of
truncated "Area Handbooks" (of the Defense Department), and
they are not adequately or fairly labeled simply "Labor Law and
Practice." All of them have much valuable information on the
geography, ethnic groups, and natural resources of the subject
countries; this information is probably still valid and valuable, and
certainly much of it is not easily come by. They all include, also,

information on social factors, manpower, and relations between labor and government that will now, of course, be true only for the more recent titles. Listing is by country. There are very slight variants in title.

Argentina. R. C. Hayes and N. A. Halvonik. [1969]. 65 p. il.
029-001-00368-4
Belgium. C. Reynolds and C. S. McEwen. 1970. 85 p. il.
029-001-00381-1
Republic of China (Taiwan). T. Bleecker. 1972. 72 p. il.
029-001-00955-1
Colombia. G. A. Sallas. 1972. 89 p. il. 029-001-01007-9
Dominican Republic. G. A. Sallas. 1968. 39 p. il.
029-001-00367-6
Great Britain, H. M. Douty. 1972. 89 p. il. 029-001-00960-7
Kingdom of Greece. J. Clarke. 1968. 139 p. il.
029-001-00361-7
Iceland. F. A. Groemping. 1970. 38 p. il. 029-001-00501-6
Japan. K. Braun. 1970. 64 p. il. 029-001-00493-1
Republic of Korea. T. Bleecker. [1969]. 45 p. il.
029-001-00372-2
Laos. T. Bleecker and D. Bell. [1970]. 52 p. il.
029-001-00371-5
Uruguay. R. C. Hayes. 1971. 88 p. il. 029-001-00711-6
Venezuela. G. A. Sallas. [1972]. 71 p. il. 029-001-00694-2
Republic of Viet-Nam (South Viet-Nam). M. B. Zuzik. 1968. 85 p. il. 029-001-00362-5
Zaire. C. A. Reynolds. 1972. 85 p. il. 029-001-00900-3

Labor-Management Relations in Europe; Results . . . House of Representatives, 1972. 506 p. il. Free from the House Document Room.
A field investigation by the Special Subcommittee on Labor of the House's Committee on Education and Labor. Conditions in Italy, France, and the United Kingdom are reported. There are many pertinent reprints from original sources, and much material of a firsthand kind probably difficult to find elsewhere.

Labor Offices in the United States and Canada. Employment Standards Admin., Bull. 177 (1972). 84 p. Free from the Admin.
"Labor office" is used very broadly, and usefully; included are labor boards, separate commissions, and so on, with functional responsibility for such programs as workmen's compensation, employment manpower, industrial relations. By state and province, with personnel cited.

Labor in the U.S.S.R. E. Nash. Bur. of Labor Statistics, Rept. 414 (1972). 50 p. il. Purchase from the Bur.

Suggestions for Control of Turnover and Absenteeism. Dept. of Labor, 1972. 55 p. il. 029-000-00161-8
Aims to make management aware of conditions that cause employees to be dissatisfied, and makes suggestions for correcting poor working conditions. Appendix includes a number of useful sample forms.

LANGUAGES

The listing below contains 42 titles, representing grammars or guides to 39 languages. With one exception the titles were issued by either the Department of State or the Department of the Army. The Department of State covers 32 languages; the Army Department covers 3. These latter are of a popular phrase-book type, very useful to anyone thinking of traveling in the countries covered. One Spanish grammar has been published by the Immigration and Naturalization Service. It will be noted that many of the titles are older than the limits set for this edition of this *Guide*—but languages do not change all that rapidly. All of these titles are heartily recommended: they represent quite an unorthodox way of learning a language.

Adapting and Writing Language Lessons. E. W. Stevick. Dept. of State, 1971. 450 p. il. 044-000-01365-1
Prepared with the cooperation of the Office of Education. How to

go about preparing a useful and sensible grammar in almost any foreign tongue.

Foreign Versions, Variations, and Diminutives of English Names; Foreign Equivalents of United States Military and Civilian Titles. Immig. and Natur. Serv. [1973]. 54 p.   027-002-00130-3
In: Bulgarian, Croatian, Czechoslovak, Estonian, Finnish, French, German, Greek, Hungarian, Italian, Latvian and Lithuanian, Norwegian, Polish, Portuguese, Rumanian, Russian (this in English script), Serbian, Slovenian, Spanish, Swedish, Ukrainian, Yiddish.

AMHARIC

Basic Course. 2 vols. Dept. of State, 1964–65.   044-000-00251-5
   1 (units 1-50). 1964. 500 p.
   2 (units 51-60). 1965. 502 p.

CANTONESE

Cantonese; Basic Course. 2 vols. E. L. Boyle and others. Dept. of State, 1970.
   1 (lessons 1-15). 392 p.   044-000-01268-5
   2 (lessons 16-30). 410 p.   044-000-01269-3

FINNISH

Finnish Graded Reader. A. R. Bell and A. A. Koski. Dept. of State, 1968. [752] p. il.   044-000-00294-9

FRENCH

French; Basic Course (Units 1-15). D. Desberg and others. Dept. of State, 1960. 315 p.   044-000-00257-4

French; Supplementary Exercises for Basic Course (Units 1–15). R. J. Salazar and associates. Dept. of State, 1967. 712 p.

044-000-00256-8

FULA

Basic Course. Dept. of State, 1965. 489 p.   044-000-00259-1

GERMAN

German; Basic Course (Units 13–24). S. A. Brown and others. Dept. of State, 1965 [1966]. [335-710] p. il.   044-000-00260-4

German; Programmed Introduction. W. R. Van Buskirk and associates. Dept. of State, 1971. 647 p.   044-000-01353-3

GREEK

Greek; Basic Course. 3 vols. S. Obolensky and others. Dept. of State, 1967–69.
   1. 1967. 327 p.   044-000-00262-1
   2. 1968. [329-528] p.
   3. 1969. [529-736] p.   044-000-00263-9

HEBREW

Hebrew; Basic Course. J. A. Reif and H. Levinson. Dept. of State, 1965 [1966]. 552 p. il.   044-000-00265-5

HINDI

Hindi; Active Introduction. D. N. Sharma and J. W. Stone. Dept. of State, 1970. 131 p. il.   044-000-01271-5

HUNGARIAN

Hungarian; Basic Course. 2 vols. Dept. of State, 1962–64.
   1 (units 1-12). 1962. 266 p.   044-000-00266-3
   2 (units 13-24). 1964. 340 p.   044-000-01272-3

Hungarian Graded Reader. I. Mihalyfy and A. A. Koski. Dept. of
State, 1968. 592 p. il.   044-000-00295-7
Some knowledge of the language is assumed.

INDONESIAN

Indonesian; Newspaper Reader. J. M. Harter and others. Dept. of
State, 1968. 271 p.   044-000-00293-1
Interesting piece of work. News item is given in Indonesian, with an
Indonesian glossary. There is also a glossary at the end of the book.
This does not assume previous knowledge.

ITALIAN

Italian; Guide to the Spoken Language. Dept. of the Army, Tech.
Manual 30-303, 1963. 62 p.   008-020-00464-2

JAPANESE

Japanese; Guide to the Spoken Language. Dept. of the Army, Tech.
Manual 30-341, 1964. 60 p.   008-020-00374-3

KIRUNDI

Kirundi; Basic Course. Dept. of State, 1965. 526 p.
                           044-000-00267-1

KITUBA

Kituba; Basic Course. Dept. of State, 1963. 470 p.

044-000-00268-0

KOREAN

Korean; Basic Course. 2 vols. B. N. Park and C. T. Kay. Dept. of State, 1968–69.
  1. 1968. 500 p.   044-000-00269-8
  2. 1969. 560 p.   044-000-00270-1

LAO

Lao; Basic Course. W. G. Yates and others. 2 vols. Dept. of State, 1970–71.
  1. 1970. 423 p.   044-000-01273-1
  2. 1971. 366 p.   044-000-01369-0

LINGALA

Lingala; Basic Course. Dept. of State, 1963. 295 p.

044-000-00271-0

LUGANDA

Luganda; Basic Course. F. K. Kamoga and E. W. Stevick. Dept. of State, 1968. 345 p.   044-000-00272-8
"A collection of materials which can be useful in the interaction between teachers and students."

Luganda; Pretraining Program. E. W. Stevick and F. K. Kamoga.
Dept. of State, 1970. 246 p. il.   044-000-01274-0
To be used in conjunction with the first 20 lessons in the preceding
title.

MORÉ

Moré; Basic Course. M. Lehr and others. Dept. of State, 1966. 340 p.
044-000-00273-6

PORTUGUESE

From Spanish to Portuguese. J. L. Ursch. Dept. of State, 1971.
91 p.   044-000-01363-1
The transition from a knowledge of Spanish to a knowledge of
Portuguese is very easy. Pronunciation, however, is vastly different.

RUSSIAN

Russian; Active Introduction. N. de la Cruz and R. A. C. Goodison.
Dept. of State, 1973. 138 p. il.   044-000-01487-4

SERBO-CROATIAN

Serbo-Croatian; Basic Course. 2 vols. C. T. Hodge and others.
Dept. of State, 1965–68.
  1 (units 1-25). 1965. 633 p.   044-000-00274-4
  2 (units 26-50). 1968. [635-1304] p.   044-000-00275-2

SHONA

Shona; Basic Course. Dept. of State, 1965. 519 p.
044-000-00276-1

SPANISH

Practical Spanish Grammar for Border Patrol Officers. J. G. Friar and G. W. Kelly. Immigration and Naturalization Serv., 1968. 225 p.   027-002-00114-1
One of the finest grammars this compiler has seen.

Spanish; Basic Course. 3 vols. Dept. of State, 1959–69.
   1 (units 1-15). 1959. 699 p.   044-000-00278-7
   2 (units 16-30). 1959. 716 p.   044-000-00279-5
   3 (units 31-55). 1969. 465 p.   044-000-00277-9

Spanish; Programmed Course; Vol. 2. V. Arbelaez G. and others. Dept. of State, 1970. 614 p.   044-000-00281-7

——**Instructor's Manual; Vol. 2.** V. Arbelaez G. and others. Dept. of State, 1970. [145-223] p.   044-000-01275-8

SWAHILI

Swahili; Active Introduction; General Conversation. E. W. Stevick and others. Dept. of State, 1966. 150 p. il.   044-000-00283-3

Swahili; Basic Course. Dept. of State, 1963. 560 p. 044-000-00285-0

Swahili; Geography and Land. E. W. Stevick and others. Dept. of State, 1966. 130 p. il.   044-000-00284-1

TAGALOG

Tagalog; Guide to the Spoken Language. Dept. of the Army, Tech. Manual 30-340. 86 p.   008-020-00535-5

THAI

Thai; Basic Course. 2 vols. W. G. Yates and A. Tryon. Dept. of State, 1970.
    1. 326 p. il.   044-000-01277-4
    2. [327-738] p. il.   044-000-01278-2

TURKISH

Turkish; Basic Course. 2 vols. Dept. of State, 1966–68.
    1 (units 1-30). 1966. 385 p.   044-000-00287-6
    2 (units 31-50). 1968. [387-745] p.   044-000-00286-8

TWI

Twi; Basic Course. Dept. of State, 1963. 224 p.   044-000-00288-4
The language of Ghana.

VIETNAMESE

Basic Course. E. H. Jordan and others. 2 vols. Dept. of State, 1967.
    1 (guide to pronunciation and lessons 1-10). 328 p.
                                  044-000-00289-2
    2 (lessons 11-15). 321 p.   044-000-00290-6

Vietnamese Familiarization Course. N. Hy-Quang and others. Dept. of State, 1969. 232 p.   044-000-00291-4

YORUBA

Yoruba; Basic Course. Dept. of State, 1963. 343 p.
                                  044-000-00292-2

LITERATURE

Carl Sandburg. M. Van Doren. Library of Cong., 1969. 83 p.

030-016-00013-1

One of the Gertrude Clark Whittal Lectures. An appreciation of Sandburg the man and poet by an eminent literary figure.

Children and Poetry; Selective, Annotated Bibliography. V. Haviland and W. J. Smith, comps. Library of Cong., 1969. 67 p. il. Free from the Library. 030-000-00018-8

Children's Books . . . List of Books for Preschool through Junior High School Age. V. Haviland and L. B. Watts, comps. Library of Cong., 1969–75.

A carefully chosen and annotated listing of about 200 books per year, for various levels. Nominations and acceptance are by *ad hoc* committees who go through hundreds of books: picture books, picture story books, books for the middle group (those of seventh grade or so), poetry, arts and hobbies, history, biography, science and nature, and so on. The titles finally picked are arranged by subject (approximately as just cited); and any children's library that doesn't have at least the last two or three issues may go stand in the corner.

1968. [1969]. 16 p.	030-001-00034-6
1969. [1970]. 16 p.	030-000-00035-4
1970. [1971]. 16 p.	030-001-00039-7
1971. [1972]. 16 p.	030-001-00045-1
1972. [1973]. 16 p.	030-001-00054-1
1973. [1974]. 16 p.	030-001-00058-3
1974. [1975]. 16 p.	030-001-00062-1

Cultural Drama: Modern Identities and Social Ferment. W. S. Dillon, ed. Smithsonian Inst., 1974. 330 p. Purchase from the Inst. "The essays in this book, based upon material delivered at the Fourth International Symposium sponsored by the Institution, revolve around the interdependent themes of diversity, identity, protest, and change. Leading educators, cultural observers, sociologists, and historians are represented."

Louisa May Alcott; a Centennial for Little Women; an Annotated, Selected Bibliography. J. C. Ullom. Library of Cong., 1969. 91 p. il.
030-001-00003-6
Books (and editions) about Miss Alcott, carefully annotated; 171 items. Many illustrations taken from her published works.

Louise Bogan: a Woman's Words. W. J. Smith. Library of Cong., 1972. 81 p. 030-016-00017-3
A very fine bibliography of her works.

LIVESTOCK

Raising Livestock on Small Farms. Dept. of Agr., Farmers' Bull. 2224 (1972) [1973]. 22 p. il. 001-000-01617-2
Chickens and turkeys, ducks and geese; squabs. Dairy cows, goats, sheep, rabbits, hogs—on a small scale.

DISEASES

Anthrax in Livestock; How to Fight It. Dept. of Agr., PA 431 (1968). 8 p. il. Free from the Dept.

Cattle Scabies. Dept. of Agr., Picture Story 261 (1972). 4 p. il. Free from the Dept.

Common Liver Fluke in Sheep. Dept. of Agr., Leaflet 492 (1969). 8 p. il. 001-000-03475-8
Parasite of goats, cattle, wild rabbits, and other vermin-loaded animals, as well as sheep.

Fescue Foot in Cattle; What to Do About it. R. C. Buckner and D. E. LaBore. Dept. of Agr., Leaflet 546 (1971). Folder. il.
001-000-01453-6
Disease develops in cattle that feed on fescue.

Foot Rot of Sheep. Dept. of Agr., Farmers' Bull. 2206 (1972). 16 p. il.   001-000-02404-3

Is Brucellosis Vaccination Necessary? Dept. of Agr., PA 1007 [1972]. [6] p. il.   001-000-02480-9
Very honest appraisal of disadvantages and advantages; brucellosis vaccination will help about 65 percent of your livestock; but it has side effects.

Marek's Vaccine on Target. Dept. of Agr., Picture Story 273 (1973). 6 p. il. Free from the Dept.

Protect against Tuberculosis; Do's and Don'ts for Swine, for Cattle, for Poultry. Dept. of Agr., PA 1025 [1973]. Folder. Free from the Dept.

Questions and Answers on Equine Infectious Anemia (Swamp Fever). Dept. of Agr., PA 805 [1974]. 6 p. il. Free from the Dept.

Rinderpest . . . Highly Contagious Virus Disease of Cattle. Dept. of Agr., PA 944 (1970). Folder. il. Free from the Dept.

Sick Pigs? Suspect Cholera First. Agr. Research Serv. [1971]. 16 p. il. Free from the Serv.

Swine Brucellosis; How to Eradicate It; How to Validate Your Herd and Area. Dept. of Agr., PA 964 [1972]. Folder. Free from the Dept.

Swine Identification for Disease Eradication. Dept. of Agr., Picture Story 260 (1972). 4 p. il. Free from the Dept.

VEE of Horses . . . Disease on the Move. Dept. of Agr., PA 1004 (1973). Folder. il. Free from the Dept.
Venezuelan equine encephalomyelitis; apparently a 1971 import, and a very serious threat to horses.

What You Can Do about Bovine Mastitis. Dept. of Agr., Farmers' Bull. 2253 (1973). 14 p. il.   001-000-02964-9

Most costly beef disease for dairymen. How to recognize the symptoms; examining the animal. Looking for causes of spread of the disease.

Wiping Out Exotic Newcastle Disease. Dept. of Agr., Picture Story 270 (1973). 6 p. il. Free from the Dept.

SPECIFIC ANIMALS

CATTLE

Beef Cattle Breeding. K. E. Gregory Dept. of Agr., Agr. Inform. Bull. 286 (1969). 55 p. il.   001-000-02962-2
Genetic considerations; selection; housing; keeping records, etc.

Beef Cattle Breeds. Dept. of Agr., Farmers' Bull. 2228 (1968). 28 p. il.   001-000-03395-6
Descriptions and full-length portraits of various types.

Beef Cattle; Dehorning, Castrating, Branding, and Marking. R. T. Clark and others. Dept. of Agr., Farmers' Bull. 2121 (1971). [16] p. il.   001-000-01340-8

Farm Beef Herd. E. J. Warwick and P. A. Putnam. Dept. of Agr., Farmers' Bull. 2126 (1969). 16 p. il.   001-000-03341-7
Selecting the stock; feeding and care; breeding.

Raising a Few Cattle for Beef. Dept. of Agr., Leaflet 542 (1966). 8 p. il. Purchase from the Dept.

GOATS

Dairy Goat for Home Milk Production. Dept. of Agr., Leaflet 588 (1968). 8 p. il. Free from the Dept.
How to develop a very small flock; i.e., one or two.

HORSES

Breeding and Raising Horses. M. E. Ensminger, Jr. Dept. of Agr., Agr. Handbook 394 (1972). 81 p. il.   001-000-01347-5

Horsemanship and Horse Care. M. E. Ensminger. Dept. of Agr., Agr. Inform. Bull. 353 (1972). 50 p. il.   001-000-01475-7
Breeds; selecting a breed; riding equipment; showing the horse; feeding; grooming. Care of the foal. Diseases and parasites.

RABBITS

Commercial Rabbit Raising. R. B. Casady and others. Dept. of Agr., Agr. Handbook 309 (1971). 69 p. il.   001-000-01376-9
Choosing the breed; the rabbitry and its equipment; reproduction (always such a problem with rabbits); marketing; preparation of the skins.

SHEEP

Docking, Castrating, and Ear Tagging Lambs. Dept. of Agr., Leaflet 551 [1974]. 8 p. il.   001-000-03183-0

Earning a Living with Sheep. J. T. Hall. Dept. of Agr., Extension Serv. ESC-576 (1973). 33 p. il. Free from the Serv.

SWINE

Breeds of Swine. Dept. of Agr., Farmers' Bull. 1263 (1968). 10 p. il.
001-000-01027-1
Sort of porcine portrait gallery: new and old faces; or rather, views from various angles. Not a raiser's or breeder's manual.

Hog Castration. Dept. of Agr., Leaflet 473 (1965). 6 p. il.
001-000-00208-2

Meat-Type Hog. Dept. of Agr., Leaflet 429 (1971) [1972]. 8 p. il.
001-000-01902-3
"Thickly muscled, long, and lean." Raising him, feeding, marketing him.

Slaughtering, Cutting, and Processing Pork on the Farm. Dept. of Agr., Farmers' Bull. 2138 (1973). 48 p. il.   001-000-02952-5
Detailed, grisly photographs of the entire processes; but if we are to have pork chops in the city, *somebody* has to do this.

MAPS AND MAPMAKING

The United States Government publishes a great many maps indeed. Since many of these are very specific, either in area or intent, the compiler has listed only those that should have wide appeal and should be in every public library. For a guide to the types of maps published by the Government, the reader is referred to:

Types of Maps Published by Government Agencies. Geol. Survey [1972]. [2] p.
The reader's particular attention is called to the maps issued by the Central Intelligence Agency, over 45 of which are now in print. The Agency hopes, ultimately, to have maps of every important world area. Some of the Agency's maps have gone out of print; the compiler hopes these will reappear.

American Revolution, 1775–83; an Atlas of 18th Century Maps and Charts; Theaters of Operation. W. B. Greenwood, comp. Naval Operations Off. [1972]. 85 p. 20 maps and charts.   008-046-00043-3
This booklet reviews the history of cartography, and includes a selected bibliography of the subject. The maps (18" × 23") are historically incomparable. Although not in color, they can be beautifully framed. Incidentally, the state of the art of cartography two centuries ago may surprise you.

Atlas of Physical, Economic, and Social Resources of the Lower Mekong Basin. Internatl. Develop. Agency, 1968. 257 leaves. il.
                                                          044-001-00006-3
A "very model" of an atlas. Contains not only superb maps, but all sorts of economic, ethnic, and social information. Must be updated in some respects; but by all means buy it.

Descriptive List of Treasure Maps and Charts in the Library of Congress. D. A. Wise, comp. Library of Cong. [1974]. 30 p. il.
                                                          030-004-00012-4

Geologic Maps, Portraits of the Earth. Geol. Survey, 1972. 19 p.
il.   024-001-02191-9
How these are prepared, what they show, and how they can instruct almost anyone who can read. Very fine.

**Guide to the History of Cartography; Annotated Listing of Refer-
ences on the History of Maps and Mapmaking.** W. W. Ristow,
comp. Library of Cong., 1973. 96 p.   030-001-00055-9

How Topographic Maps Are Made. Tennessee Valley Authority,
1972. 28 p. il. Free from the Authority.
From the manuscript—made from aerial surveys—through the complicated printing process. The emergence of one such map is
illustrated.

Issues in the Middle East; Atlas. Central Intelligence Agency, 1973.
40 p. il.   041-015-00046-2
In the best tradition of the CIA maps cited below. Every aspect
of recent activities and production.

Maps. Central Intelligence Agency, 1971–74.
These maps, which cover single countries in every sector of the
globe, are perhaps the finest the compiler has ever seen. To begin
with, they show topographic features, land features, main rivers,
and so on. In addition, they show, in smaller detail, such features
of the areas as natural vegetation (tropical forest, for example, in
Brazil), land use (grazing, and so on), population, administrative
divisions, and economic regions, temperature range, and precipitation, and in very helpful detail, economic activity. In other words,
they combine in a single format the factors of several kinds of
map. Their value to students cannot be overrated. According to the
Central Intelligence Agency, in Washington, 54 had been issued
through December, 1974. Only those still in print are listed. The
entire set belongs not only in every library, but in every literate
household.

Afghanistan. [1971]. 18″ x 30″.   041-015-00017-9
Brazil. [1973]. 23″ x 26″.   041-015-00052-7

Bulgaria. 1972. 23" x 30".   041-015-00006-3
Cambodia. [1972]. 24" x 18".   041-015-00004-7
Cyprus. 1972. 17" x 25".   041-015-00025-0
Ecuador. [1973]. 14" x 23".   041-015-00045-4
Egypt. [1971]. 16" x 36".   041-015-00024-1
Ethiopia. [1972]. 18" x 25".   041-015-00022-5
East Germany. 1973. 17" x 23".   041-015-00050-1
Guinea. [1973]. 21" x 26".   041-015-00042-0
Guyana. [1973]. 16" x 22".   041-015-00044-6
Honduras. [1973]. 19"x 22".   041-015-00048-9
Hungary. [1973]. 19" x 18".   041-015-00031-4
Iceland. 1973. 17" x 18".   041-015-00040-3
India with Sikkim and Bhutan. 1973. 23" x 29".
                                              041-015-00051-8
Indonesia. [1972.] 22" x 30".   041-015-00027-6
Iran. [1973.] 17" x 29".   041-015-00039-0
Italy. [1973.] 20" x 26".   041-015-00056-0
Ivory Coast. [1972]. 18" x 28".   041-015-00011-0
Liberia. 1973. 16.5" x 23".   041-015-00057-8
Malta. [1973]. 11" x 17".   041-015-00041-1
Martinique and French Guiana. 1972. 23" x 15".
                                              041-015-00014-4
Mauritius. [1972]. 11" x 15".   041-015-00005-5
Mexico. [1972]. 22" x 31".   041-015-00019-5
Morocco. [1973]. 18" x 29".   041-015-00036-5
Nigeria. [1972]. 26" x 23".   041-015-00034-9
North Korea. [1972]. 27" x 23".   041-015-00030-6
Pakistan. [1973]. 17" x 28".   041-015-00054-3
Philippines. [1973]. 21" x 25".   041-015-00060-8
Poland. 1973. 16.5" x 25.5".   041-015-00058-6
Portugal. [1972]. 22" x 24".   041-015-00018-7
Russia. 1972. Set of two maps.   041-015-00012-8
Map 1 (19" x 30") is U.S.S.R. proper. Map 2 (23" x 30") shows
population, ethnic groups, etc.
Senegal and Gambia. [1972]. 20" x 23".   041-015-00023-3
Seychelles. [1971]. 11" x 9".   041-015-00008-0
Singapore. [1973]. 8" x 16".   041-015-00038-1
South Korea. 1973. 19" x 25".   041-015-00053-5

South Vietnam. 1972. 24" x 28".   041-015-00021-7
Sweden. [1973]. 20" x 18".   041-015-00037-3
Tunisia [1972]. 22" x 21".   041-015-00015-2
Uruguay. [1974]. 18" x 23".   041-015-00059-4
Yemen (Aden). [1973]. 19" x 27".   041-015-00043-7
Yemen (San'a'). 1973. 21" x 20".   041-015-00033-1
Yugoslavia. [1973]. 17" x 27".   041-015-00035-7

Maps; Their Care, Repair, and Preservation in Libraries. C. E. LeGear. Library of Cong., 1956. 75 p. il. Purchase from the Library.

People's Republic of China: Atlas. Central Intelligence Agency, 1971. 82 p. il.   041-015-00010-1
Perhaps only the CIA could prepare an atlas of this quality. It divides China into six areas, and gives you every conceivable kind of information about each: geography, population, industry, agriculture, administrative divisions—even the correct Chinese pronunciations! Also highways, waterways; climate; mines and minerals. Superb.

Three Maps of Indian Country: 1, Probable Location of Indian Tribes North of Mexico about A.D. 1500; 2, Culture Areas and Approximate Location of American Tribes Today; 3, Indian Reservations under Federal Jurisdiction. Bur. of Indian Affairs [1971]. [2] p. Free from the Bur.

Tools for Planning Topographic Maps. Geol. Survey [1971]. 15 p. il.   024-001-02047-5

Topographic Maps. Geol. Survey, 1969. 20 p. il. Free from the Survey.
Such maps "record in conventional, readable form the physical characteristics of the terrain as determined by precise engineering surveys and measurements." The well-illustrated story of how such maps are made.

MEDICINE

For a thorough coverage of current works on this subject, the reader is referred to *Index Medicus*, a monthly index of something like 2,000 medical journals. (The *Index* is published by the National Library of Medicine.) However: bear in mind, that much of the material indexed in *Index Medicus* may be available only in large libraries. It is published in a tremendous variety of languages.

Anticancer Agents Recently Developed in the People's Republic of China. C. P. Li. John E. Fogarty Internatl. Center for Advanced Study in the Health Sciences [1973]. 255 p. il.   017-053-00017-5
One of an excellent group on developments in China in the field of medicine.

Army Medical Department Handbook of Basic Nursing. Army Dept., Tech. Manual 8-230 (1970) [1971]. [632] p. il.

008-020-00336-1
Basics of physiology and anatomy; of drug administration; fundamental nursing; outpatient care.

Bibliography of the History of Medicine; No. 7, 1971. Natl. Library of Med. [1973]. 263 p.   017-052-00147-7

Chinese Herbal Medicine. C. P. Li. John E. Fogarty Internatl. Center for Advanced Study in the Health Sciences, 1974. 120 p.
017-053-00032-9

Evolution of Preventive Medicine in the United States Army, 1607–1939. S. Bayne-Jones. Dept. of the Army, 1968. 255 p. il.
008-023-00005-1
Army medicine goes away back (in this case to Jamestown, Va.). Much of the material in this book might be difficult to trace elsewhere.

Information Sources for the Neurosciences. Natl. Inst. of Neurological Diseases and Stroke [1973]. [114] p.   017-049-00049-6
Audio-visual aids; bibliographies; abstracts; journals; informational centers.

Medicine and Public Health in the People's Republic of China. J. R. Quinn, ed. John E. Fogarty Internatl. Center for Advanced Study in the Health Sciences, 1973. 333 p. il. Free from the Center.
017-053-00011-6
One chapter deals with the history of Chinese medicine; others with health care organization and administration, problems of health, nutrition, infectious and parasitic diseases, cancer research, mental illness. And, of course, a full chapter on acupuncture.

Social and Psychological Aspects of Applied Human Genetics; a Bibliography. J. R. Sorenson, comp. John E. Fogarty Internatl. Center for Advanced Study in the Health Sciences [1973]. 98 p.
017-053-00012-4
"A selective compilation of books and articles [which emphasize how] within the past few decades, discoveries in basic science and developments in medical technology have significantly increased the role of human genetics in medical practice and daily life." About 1,000 unannotated references, in five sections. Very fine.

Soviet Medicine; Bibliography of Bibliographies. John E. Fogarty Internatl. Center for Advanced Study in the Health Sciences, 1973. 46 p.   017-053-00015-9
Bear in mind this is a bibliography of bibliographies; done, of course, with the usual excellence of the International Center.

Witchcraft and Medicine (1484–1793). J. Nemec. Natl. Inst. of Mental Health [1974]. 10 p. il. Free from the Inst.
Fascinating text and fine reproductions from old woodcuts: some show the harsh treatment accorded those suspected of witchcraft prior to the French Revolution.

MENTAL HEALTH AND ILLNESS

Art Therapy; a Bibliography. L. Gantt and M. S. Schmal [and others]. Natl. Inst. of Mental Health, 1974. 148 p.

017-024-00383-2

Almost 125 citations, many abstracted briefly, deal with the use of art therapy as a means of self-expression and communication.

Autism: 4th Annual Meeting of the National Society for Autistic Children . . . Proceedings. Natl. Inst. of Mental Health, 1973. 161 p. il.

017-024-00345-0

Held in Flint, Mich. Series of fine papers dealing with problems of language and communication, community planning, education, handicrafts for the autistic.

Behavior Modification in Child and School Mental Health; Annotated Bibliography on Applications with Parents and Teachers. D. G. Brown. Natl. Inst. of Mental Health [1971] (repr. 1972). 41 p.

017-024-00159-7

Behavioral Sciences and Mental Health; an Anthology of Program Reports. E. A. Rubinstein and G. V. Coelho, eds. Natl. Inst. of Mental Health [1970]. 419 p. il.

017-024-00095-7

Collection of twenty-five reports, arranged in five sections: development of behavior; brain function; learning process; influence of biology on behavior; and effect of personal and cultural factors on behavior. Up to the usual unmatchable standard of NIMH.

Bibliography on Suicide and Suicide Prevention, 1897–1957, 1958–1970. N. L. Farberow, comp. Natl. Inst. of Mental Health [1972]. [285] p.

017-040-00342-1

Bibliography of 4,722 items compiled to meet the need for scientific investigation of the subject. Author and subject indexes.

Current Ethical Issues in Mental Health. M. F. Shore and S. E. Golans, eds. Natl. Inst. of Mental Health, 1973. 55 p.

017-024-00293-3

An astonishing work, in which contributors do not hesitate to come to grips with thorny issues. Based on a Workshop at the 47th Annual Meeting of the American Orthopsychiatric Association in San Francisco, March, 1970.

Directory of Halfway Houses for the Mentally Ill and Alcoholics. Natl. Inst. of Mental Health, 1973. 133 p.   017-024-00283-6
A directory by states.

Directory of Institutions for Mentally Disordered Offenders. W. C. Eckerman. Natl. Inst. of Mental Health [1972]. 24 p.

017-024-00236-4

"A listing of mental and correctional institutions providing psychiatric care for adult mentally disturbed offenders." A work of marginal popular interest, probably; but useful in certain libraries.

Early Childhood Psychosis: Infantile Autism; Childhood Schizophrenia and Related Disorders; an Annotated Bibliography, 1964–1969. C. Q. Bryson and J. M. Hingtgen. Natl. Inst. of Mental Health, 1971. 127 p.   017-024-00264-0
"Current and comprehensive compilation of the relevant literature pertaining to theory, research, and treatment, without emphasis on any specific school of thought. It should be a useful tool for those who work to alleviate suffering caused by childhood psychosis."

Facts about Autism. Natl. Inst. of Mental Health [1973]. [8] p. il.

017-024-00259-3

Facts about College Mental Health. Natl. Inst. of Mental Health [1972]. 13 p.   017-024-00257-7
Discusses some of the problems of students; and supplies some possible answers.

It's Good to Know about Mental Health. Natl. Inst. of Mental Health [1973.] 11 p.   017-024-00337-9

Indubitably; this booklet tells you what to look for and what may be done about it.

Latino Mental Health; Bibliography and Abstracts. A. M. Padilla and P. Aranda, comps. Natl. Inst. of Mental Health [1974]. 288 p.
017-024-00316-6
"Latino" means here all those groups usually identified as Spanish-speaking, Spanish-surnamed, or of Spanish origin. Particularly interesting because it deals exclusively with the mental health of the Latino minority.

Lithium in the Treatment of Mood Disorders. A. A. Gattozzi. Natl. Inst. of Mental Health, 1970. 99 p.   017-024-00367-1
Lithium as a psychoactive drug, particularly useful in the manic phase of manic-depressive illnesses.

Mental and Emotional Illnesses in the Young Child. B. S. Brown. Natl. Inst. of Mental Health [1971]. 12 p. il. Purchase from the Inst. Intended primarily as a sympathetic guide for those who deal with children with such illnesses. Not in depth; a practical guide to how to act in most situations.

Mental Health Consultation to Programs for Children; a Review of Data Collected from Selected U.S. Sites. F. B. McClung and A. A. Stunden. Natl. Inst. of Mental Health [1972]. 60 p.
017-024-00192-9
Period of coverage is 1968–69. Purpose is "to review and analyze community programs, practices, and procedures of the mental health consultants in order to generate an in-depth, empirically devised, conceptual formula which will assist in the development of new programs of training research . . ." Data from ten states were used. The report reviews pertinent literature; describes procedures and the conceptual model used in the study; evaluates moral and philosophic aspects of consultations as now practiced.

National Institute of Mental Health. Natl. Inst. of Mental Health, 1970. [21] p. il. Free from the Inst.   017-024-00023-0

The work accomplished by the Institute and its various affiliated Institutes. The Institute "administers the Federal Government's major program of support for the nation's work in mental health . . . in research, in training, in services." The magnitude of the various institutes' work can only be grasped by a visit to the widespread installations . . .

Nationwide Survey of Mental Health and Correctional Institutions for Adult Mentally Disordered Offenders. W. C. Eckerman. Natl. Inst. of Mental Health [1972]. 93 p.   017-024-00263-1

Analyzes data collected on the mental health problems of criminals, including the characteristics of the institution, system, and treatment programs involved. Makes suggestions for improvement, where these may be indicated.

Promoting Mental Health in the Classroom; a Handbook for Teachers. K. R. P. Todd. Natl. Inst. of Mental Health, 1973. 87 p.

017-024-00286-1

Intended to help teachers at all grade levels "learn to appreciate, implement, and teach to their pupils the causal or understanding approach to human behavior." A detailed "seminar" guide; not a series of essays. Recommended for the teacher.

Recreation for Autistic and Emotionally Disturbed Children. M. A. Dewey. Natl. Inst. of Mental Health [1973]. 18 p. il.

017-024-00308-5

How to start the children in programs; toys for their use; arts and crafts; dramatics; sports—these among others.

Schizophrenia: Is There an Answer? Natl. Inst. of Mental Health, 1972. 16 p. Free from the Inst.

More than 3,000,000 Americans, at one time or another, have suffered the symptoms: and one half of our hospital beds are occupied by schizophrenic patients. This is a general discussion of the nature of the disease, how it is treated, what prospects for a cure really are.

Social Change and Human Behavior; Mental Health Challenges of the Seventies. C. V. Coelho and E. A. Rubinstein, eds. Natl. Inst. of Mental Health [1972]. 237 p. il.   017-024-00248-8
Multidisciplinary approach to social change and "future shock." Ten articles by leading biologists, psychologists, and social scientists.

Special Report: Schizophrenia. L. R. Mosher and D. Feinsilver. Natl. Inst. of Mental Health. 1971. 40 p.   017-024-00140-6
Citations of general sources dealing with the present state of study of schizophrenia, in an effort to discover causes and determine treatment.

Suicide among Youth; Review of Literature, 1900–1967. R. H. Seiden. Natl. Inst. of Mental Health [1969]. 62 p. il.
017-024-00038-8
A valuable bibliographic essay.

Suicide Prevention in the '70's. H. L. P. Resnik and B. C. Hathorne. Natl. Inst. of Mental Health, 1973. 109 p. 017-024-00226-7
"Reports the results of a Conference of some 50 leaders and students in the field." Contains, among other things, several very detailed bibliographies.

Voluntary Agency & Community Mental Health Services. Natl. Inst. of Mental Health, 1973. 33 p. il.   017-024-00328-0
". . . primarily for the citizen concerned with the organization and delivery of community health services." It includes not only a listing of such agencies already in existence (from whose experience you may learn), but a valuable cross section of community services: alcoholism, child and youth care, rehabilitation, home care, referral, education and counseling—and so on. A most impressive work.

Women and Mental Health; Selected Annotated References, 1970–73. P. E. Cromwell, ed. Natl. Inst. of Mental Health [1974]. 247 p.   017-024-00405-7

"Designed to provide information on the social, economic, and psychological pressures on women and to show the diversity, or lack, of expert opinion on female psychological and sociocultural processes. The material was selected from the behavioral science literature and audiovisual resources. It is intended to serve as a background and reference source for mental health professional and paraprofessionals, behavioral scientists, and community action groups." (From the Preface.) The bibliography is divided into 21 subject groups, from Abortion to Widowhood, and includes 810 expertly annotated citations. The work has already proved of great value to the compiler in his work with students.

MENTAL RETARDATION

About Jobs and Mentally Retarded People. President's Comm. on Employment of the Handicapped (and Natl. Assn. for Retarded Children). [1972]. 38 p. Free from the Comm.
For parents and friends: "to give them some notion of the world of work and the world of preparation for work." For rehabilitation counselors, employment placement specialists and psychologists and social workers. For employers who hire or plan to hire the handicapped. And, it is hoped, for the retarded themselves. Very valuable. Includes a "Directory of State Contacts."

Adoption of Mentally Retarded Children. U. M. Gallagher. Children's Bur. [1968]. [6] p. Free from the Bur.
A wonderfully charitable thing to do; but be aware of what you may face in doing it.

Bibliography on Speech, Hearing, and Language in Relation to Mental Retardation, 1900–1968. M. Peins. Maternal and Child Health Serv. [1970]. 156 p. Free from the Serv.

017-029-00004-5

Comprehensive bibliography for those concerned with the communication process of the mentally retarded.

Central Processing Dysfunctions in Children: a Review of Research.
J. C. Chalfant and M. A. Scheffelin. Natl. Inst. of Neurological
Diseases and Stroke, NINDS Mono. 9 (1969). 148 p.

017-049-00002-0

"Phase three of a three-phase project." Phase one is "minimal
brain dysfunction" (see title further along on this subject). This
third phase, of which the report is here printed, deals with learning disabilities of children whose dysfunctions are all too often
unrecognized. Dysfunctions in the analysis of sensory information;
in its synthesis; dysfunctions in symbolic operations. These are
discussed in detail.

Guide to Job Placement and Mental Retardation. W. A. Fraenkel.
Off. of the President. [1974]. 16 p. il. Free from the President's
Comm. on Employment of the Handicapped.

**Learning Disabilities Due to Minimal Brain Dysfunction; Hope
through Research.** Public Health Serv. [1971] 21 p. il.

017-002-00126-7

Causes of such defects and what parents can do to minimize the
effects of the damage.

Malnutrition, Learning, and Intelligence. H. G. Birch. President's
Comm. on Mental Retardation, 1973 [1974]. [26] p. Free from
the Comm.
Paper presented at a Leadership Institute held in Charleston,
S.C., in 1973. A brief introduction to a tragic subject.

Mental Retardation Source Book . . . 1972. Dept. of Health,
Educ., and Welfare, 1972. 127 p. Free from the Dept.
Not for the average reader; crammed with important statistics
covering every state, every kind of mental disorder (i.e., the number of people who have such disorders).

**MR 72; Islands of Excellence; Report of the President's Com-
mittee on Mental Retardation.** President's Comm. on Mental Retardation [1973]. [55] p. il. Free from the Comm.

The sixth annual report. How the family is trained to accept tragedy; what the community can do; help from the Committee.

Selected Reading Suggestions for Parents of Mentally Retarded Children. K. A. Gorham and others, comps. Children's Bur., 1970. 58 p.   017-091-00149-9
About 150 citations, annotated.

Transportation and the Mentally Retarded. President's Comm. on Mental Retardation, 1972. 58 p. il. Free from the Comm.

040-000-00285-5
How the problem can be met, with illustrations from areas that have successfully coped with it.

Very Special Child; Conference on Placement of Children in Special Education Programs for the Mentally Retarded. President's Comm. on Mental Retardation [1971]. 32 p. il. Free from the Comm.   040-000-00283-9
A number of brief commentaries by those active in the field. A very touching book that points up the need for the care of the "special child." Illustrations are by retarded youngsters.

What Is Mongolism? Natl. Inst. of Child Health and Human Develop. [1973]. [7] p.   017-046-00018-7

METRIC SYSTEM

Brief History and Use of the English and Metric Systems of Measurement, with a Chart of the Modernized Metric System. Natl. Bur. of Standards, Pub. 304A (1970). [4] p. il.   003-001-01073-1
Excellent brief account and explanation. For a much more detailed story see "A Metric America" below.

A Metric America; a Decision Whose Time Has Come: a Report to Congress. Natl. Bur. of Standards, Spec. Pub. 345 (1971). 170 p. il.   003-003-00884-2

An exhaustive study of the increasingly isolated position we occupy in a world where few nations now employ the "customary" system of measurements. There is a detailed discussion of the difficulties of converting to the metric system, and of the very great advantages of doing so—and some practical advice as to how that step can be accomplished.

Metric Conversion Card. Natl. Bur. of Standards, Spec. Pub. 365 [1972.] Card. 003-003-01068-5

Some References on Metric Information, with Charts on All You Need to Know about Metric; Metric Conversion Factors. Natl. Bur. of Standards, Spec. Pub. 389 (1973). 11 p. il. Free from the Bur. 003-003-01219-0
Bibliography and list of organizations marketing metric materials for educators. Tables of conversion from our present system of measurements. Comes with a small plastic conversion card, a six-inch comparison scale, and six pertinent pamphlets. A bargain.

MILITARY SCIENCE

Command and Commanders in Modern Military History; Proceedings of the Second Military History Symposium, U.S. Air Force Academy, March 2–3, 1968. W. Geffen, ed. Air Force, 1971 [1972]. 340 p. 008-074-00003-8
The second edition, enlarged. Series of papers on the growth of modern military thought and some of the men behind that growth.

Soldiers and Statesmen; Proceedings of the Fourth Military History Symposium, USAF Academy, Oct. 22–23, 1970. M. D. Wright and L. J. Paszek, eds. Air Force, 1973. 211 p. il.
008-070-00335-0
"Statecraft through the ages has called upon the soldiers and statesmen to play vital roles in attaining the preeminent goal of national security." The history of military thought from the Congress of Vienna to the post-World War II world.

Soviet Military Thought. Air Force, 1973–74.

So far, the Air Force has commissioned the translation of five treatises by Soviet writers on strategy and modern war. They afford quite an insight into the Lenin-Marx way of interpreting world events (past and future).

1. The Offensive (Soviet View). A. A. Siderenko. [1973]. 228 p.
   008-070-00329-5
   Originally published in Moscow, 1970.
2. Marxism-Leninism on War and the Army (Soviet View). B. Byely and others. [1974]. 335 p.   008-070-00338-4
   Originally published in Moscow, 1972.
4. Basic Principles of Operational Art and Tactics (Soviet View). V. Ye. Savkin. [1974]. 284 p. il.   008-070-00342-2
   Originally published in Moscow, 1972.
5. Philosophical Heritage of V. I. Lenin and Problems of Contemporary Warfare (Soviet View). A. S. Milovidov and V. G. Kozlov, eds. [1974]. 229 p.   008-070-00343-1
   Originally published in Moscow, 1972.

MINING AND METALLURGY

Analysis of Strip Mining Methods and Equipment Selection. Off. of Coal Research, Research and Devel. Report 61, Interim Rept. 7 [1973]. 134 p. il.   024-014-00063-1

Particularly interesting because it examines the problem of the rapid depletion of "easily minable" coal reserves and what this problem will mean economically and ecologically when we have to dig deeper into the ground to reach the lower reserves.

How to Mine and Prospect for Placer Gold. J. M. West. Bur. of Mines, Inform. Cir. 8517 [1971]. 42 p. il.   024-004-00964-1

Sage advice: if you must try for gold, go West!

Mineral Facts and Problems. Bur. of Mines, Bull. 650 (1970). 1291 p. il.   024-004-00665-0

Fourth edition of a "standard reference work with respect to mineral commodities" contains signed articles on over 90 energy sources, ferrous and nonferrous minerals, and nonminerals—from gold and lead to molybdenum and yttrium.

Minerals Yearbook, 1972. Bur. of Mines, 1972–76. 3 vols.
Despite the gap of three years since the publication of Vol. 1 of this excellent group, the entire set is known as the 1972 Minerals Yearbook. The separate volumes are cited below, with annotations taken from the forewords to each volume.

1. Metals, Minerals, and Fuels. 1976. 1392 p.   024-004-01779-1
   "Contains chapters on virtually all metallic, nonmetallic, and mineral fuel commodities important to the domestic economy. In addition, it contains a general review chapter on the mineral industries, a statistical summary, and a chapter on technological trends."
2. Minerals Yearbook, 1972. 1972 Area Reports, Domestic. 1972. 816 p.   024-004-01745-7
   ". . . contains chapters on the mineral industry of each of the 50 states, the U.S. island possessions in the Pacific Ocean and the Caribbean Sea, the Commonwealth of Puerto Rico, and the Canal Zone. The volume also has a statistical summary, identical to that in Volume I."
3. Minerals Yearbook, 1972. 1975. Area Reports, International. 1103 p.   024-004-01755-4
   "Contains the latest available mineral data on more than 100 foreign countries, and discusses the importance of minerals to the economies of the nations. A separate chapter reviews minerals in general and relationships to the world economy."

Mining and Mining Claims in National Forest Wildernesses. Bur. of Mines, 1971. 19 p. il. Free from the Bur.
Some questions and answers; a map shows likely sites.

Patenting a Mining Claim on Federal Lands; Basic Procedures. Bur of Land Management, 1970. [12] p. Free from the Bur.

Principal Gold-producing Districts of the United States. A. H. Koschmann and M. H. Bergendahl. Geol. Survey, Prof. Paper 610 (1968). 283 p. il.   024-001-00780-1

Arranged by state. A "description of the geology, mining history, and production of the major gold-mining districts in 21 states." Great deal of interesting historical material.

Prospecting for Gold in the United States. Geol. Survey [1973]. [15] p. il. 024-001-02036-0
If you feel you must prospect, learn something of the hows and wheres.

MUSIC

Eric Dolphy; a Musical Biography and Discography. V. Simosko and B. Tepperman. Smithsonian Inst. 164 p. il. Purchase from the Inst.
". . . a musical biography of black jazz musician and composer, Eric Dolphy, whose career was still on the ascent when he died in 1964. It includes a discography of Dolphy's complete recordings . . ."

Harpsichords and Clavichords. C. A. Hoover. Smithsonian Inst., 1969. 42 p. il. Purchase from the Inst.
This charming booklet illustrates and describes some of the fine instruments in the Institution's collection; virginals, clavichords, and harpsichords are included. Many of them are objects not only of great ingenuity but of great beauty.

Music Machines, American Style; Catalog of Exhibition. C. A. Hoover and others. Natl. Museum, 1971. 140 p. il.
047-000-00182-0
"Drawing from the Smithsonian's collection of more than 4000 music and music reproducing instruments . . . [this is] a multifaceted chronology, interrelating each textual part to numerous illustrations. . . . [and] given in a perspective designed to show their development as it corresponded to the overwhelming social and technological events that have occurred since the mid-nineteenth century."

NATIONAL PARKS, MONUMENTS, AND HISTORIC SITES

Many titles in this section antedate the ostensible dates of this edition, but they are still valid and good reading.

Areas Administered by the National Park Service and Related Properties as of January 1, 1974. Natl. Park Serv. [1974].

024-005-00287-1

Alphabetic listing of hundreds of public areas: acreage (federal and nonfederal), outstanding characteristics, postal addresses. Breakdown is by natural area, historical area, recreational area, cultural area, and national capital parks. In Part 2, sites declared eligible for inclusion are cited by state.

Back-Country Travel in the National Park System. Natl. Park Serv. [1971]. 40 p. il.   024-005-00267-7

A book about areas "unreachable by auto." Planning your outing; listing of the parks with their rules and regulations, as well as their attractions.

Camping in the National Park System. Natl. Park Serv., 1975. [28] p. il.   024-005-000573-1

An alphabetic listing of sites showing their seasons, facilities, fees, and so on. Valuable for anyone.

Discovering Prince William Forest. B. Perry. Natl. Park Serv. [1973]. 24 p. il.   024-005-00502-1

Ferdinand Vandiveer Hayden and the Founding of Yellowstone National Park. Geol. Survey [1973]. 45 p. il.   024-001-02396-2

Historical Handbook Series. Natl. Park Serv., 1957–69.

Only one title has been added to this exceptional series since the third edition of this *Guide*. Of the older titles, No. 1 has appeared under 1969 imprint, enlarged. The remaining titles remain what they have always been: among the most informative and engaging titles published by the National Park Service. The Handbooks are uniformly well-written. They deal with historic sites, areas, and events from many stages of our national history (and prior to that). Illustrations are generally good and numerous; those reproduced from old drawings and photographs are especially interesting. The booklets will fascinate everyone—from elementary grades up.

1. Custer Battlefield National Monument, Montana. R. M. Utley. 1969. 94 p. il.   024-005-00160-3
   The new issue of this title has been greatly enlarged over the first. There is a full account of the battle of the Little Bighorn River, a description of the whole monument area, and considerable biographical material.

2. Jamestown, Virginia: the Townsite and Its Story. C. E. Hatch, Jr. 1957. 54 p. il.   024-005-00170-1
   The site of the first permanent English settlement in the United States, with an account of archeological work done there for many years.

3. Ford's Theatre and the House Where Lincoln Died. S. W. McClure. 1969. 40 p. il.   024-005-00226-0
   The Civil War President was shot in the theater and died very shortly afterward in the house described here. Included in this booklet is a contemporary account of Lincoln's last hours.

4. Saratoga National Historical Park, New York. C. W. Snell and F. F. Wilshin. 1961. 36 p. il.   024-005-00189-1
   Detailed account of the battle, and description of remaining and restored sites and structures.

5. Fort McHenry National Monument and Historic Shrine, Maryland. H. I. Lessem and G. C. Mackenzie. 1961. 38 p. il.
                                                          024-055-00191-3
   Much historical, biographical, and musical information; story of a battle, a patriot, and a national anthem.

6. Custis Lee Mansion, the Robert E. Lee Memorial, Virginia.

M. H. Nelligan. 1962. 48 p. il. 024-005-00192-1
Double biography: Arlington and its owners.

7. Morristown National Historical Park; a Military Capital of the American Revolution. M. J. Weig and V. B. Craig. 1961. 44 p. il. 024-005-00194-8
Morristown was the site of an Army encampment during two critical winters of the Revolution.

9. Gettysburg National Military Park, Pennsylvania. F. Tilberg. 1962. 64 p. il. 024-005-00196-4
The battle in considerable detail, and a guided tour of structures and sites associated with it.

10. Shiloh National Military Park, Tennessee. A. Dillahunty. 1961. 47 p. il. 024-005-00161-1
Spirited account of the battle, and an illustrated tour of the area.

12. Fort Sumter National Monument, South Carolina. F. Barnes. 1962. 47 p. il. 024-005-00163-8
Interesting for its accounts of the bombardments and for contemporary photographs.

14. Yorktown and the Siege of 1781. C. E. Hatch, Jr. 1957. 59 p. il. 024-005-00165-4
Scene of the surrender of Lord Cornwallis, after a prolonged siege.

15. Manassas (Bull Run) National Battlefield Park, Virginia. F. F. Wilshin. 1961. 48 p. il. 024-005-00227-8
Site of two famous battles of the Civil War. "The first shall be ever memorable as the opening engagement of that great conflict, while the second, fought approximately a year later, paved the way for Lee's first invasion of the North."

17. Independence National Historical Park, Philadelphia, Pa. E. M. Riley. 1956. 68 p. il. 024-005-00167-1
Particularly interesting for its fine series of portraits.

18. Fort Pulaski National Monument, Georgia. R. B. Lattimore. 1961. 56 p. il. 024-005-00168-9
This gigantic pile is associated with some of the most interesting skirmishes of the Civil War.

19. Fort Necessity National Battlefield Site, Pennsylvania. F.

Tilberg. 1961. 44 p.   024-005-00169-7
Story of the fort associated with the early career of George
Washington and with the defeat of General Braddock.

20. Fort Laramie National Monument, Wyoming. D. L. Hieb.
1961. 48 p. il.   024-005-00171-9
At first a fort for fur trappers, then a stopping post for those
traveling the Oregon Trail. "Perhaps no other single site is
so intimately connected with the history of the Old West
in all its phases."

21. Vicksburg National Military Park, Mississippi. W. C. Ever-
hart. 1961. 60 p. il.   024-005-00228-6
Grant's campaign against the city, with a sharp account of
the siege and fall.

23. Bandelier National Monument, New Mexico. K. A. Wing.
1961. 44 p. il.   024-005-00173-5
An extensive prehistoric Indian site.

24. Ocmulgee National Monument, Georgia. G. D. Pope, Jr.
1961. 58 p. il.   024-005-00174-3
Story of the excavation of Indian mounds near Macon, and
of the varied and important finds made there.

25. Chickamauga and Chattanooga Battlefields, Chickamauga
and Chattanooga National Military Park, Georgia-Tennessee.
J. R. Sullivan. 1961. 60 p. il.   024-005-00229-4
"In and around strategically important Chattanooga, Ten-
nessee, in the autumn of 1863, there occurred some of the
most complex maneuvers and hard fighting of the Civil War."

26. George Washington Birthplace National Monument, Virginia.
J. P. Hudson. 1961. 44 p. il.   024-005-00175-1
The story of the Washington family plantation in Westmore-
land County.

28. Scotts Bluff National Monument, Nebraska. M. J. Mattes.
1961. 64 p. il.   024-005-00177-8
Celebrated landmark on the Great North Platte Valley trunk-
line of the Oregon Trail.

30. Guilford Courthouse National Military Park, North Carolina.
C. T. Reid. 1961. 40 p. il.   024-005-00179-4

Site of an important battle of the American Revolution, one
that marked the turn of the tide for the patriots' fortunes.

31. Antietam National Battlefield Site, Maryland. F. Tilberg.
1961. 60 p. il.   024-005-00180-8
Describes the scene and the events of the battle that ended
Gen. R. E. Lee's first invasion of the North, September,
1862.

32. Vanderbilt Mansion National Historic Site, New York. C. W.
Snell. 1961. 52 p. il.   024-005-00228-6
History of this mansion on the Hudson River, with a de-
tailed, illustrated description of the mansion and its grounds.

33. Richmond National Battlefield Park, Virginia. J. P. Cullen.
1961. 46 p. il.   024-005-00182-4
Sites of some of the greatest battles of the Civil War.

34. Wright Brothers National Memorial. O. G. East. 1961. 64 p.
il.   024-005-00183-2
This booklet is much more than a simple description of this
site; it is actually a detailed story of one of the earliest and
greatest chapters in aeronautical history.

35. Fort Union National Monument, New Mexico. R. M. Utley.
1962. 68 p. il.   024-005-00184-1
Located on the Santa Fe Trail, this fort played a very important role in military and civilian ventures between 1851
and 1891. A fascinating chapter in the history of the Old
West.

36. Aztec Ruins National Monument, New Mexico. J. M. Corbett.
1963. 66 p. il.   024-005-00185-9
An archeological study of the Four Countries area, where
New Mexico, Colorado, Utah, and Arizona meet in a common boundary at right angles.

37. Whitman Mission National Historic Site, Washington. E. N.
Thompson. 1964. 92 p. il.   024-005-00183-2
Site of a mission founded among the Indians in 1836 by
Marcus and Narcissa Whitman; after about a decade their
mission was destroyed, and they were murdered, by the
Indians.

38. Fort Davis National Historic Site, Texas. R. Utley. 1965.
    62 p. il.   024-005-00187-5
    This fort guarded the Trans-Pecos segment of the southern
    route to California from 1854 to 1891. As in so many of the
    Historical Handbook Series, contemporary drawings and pho-
    tographs are specially interesting.

39. Fredericksburg, Chancellorsville, Wilderness, and Spotsyl-
    vania Court House, Where One Hundred Thousand Fell.
    J. P. Cullen. 1966. 56 p. il.   024-005-00188-3
    These areas in Virginia witnessed some of the bloodiest
    fighting of the Civil War.

40. Golden Spike. R. M. Utley and F. A. Ketterson, Jr. 1969.
    58 p. il.   024-005-00190-5
    The spike was driven at 12:47 P.M., May 10, 1869, to join
    the railroads that came from the East and the West. "The
    Pacific Railroad had become a reality."

Independence National Historic Park, Philadelphia, Pa. Natl. Park
Serv., 1956. 68 p. il.   024-005-00167-4

National Forest Wildernesses and Primitive Areas, National Forests.
Forest Serv., 1973. [24] p. il.   001-001-00245-3
Generally descriptive, with relevant statistics. Fine map shows the
forest wildernesses and primitive areas in the Western states.

National Park Guide for the Handicapped. Natl. Park Serv.
[1971]. 79 p. il.   024-005-00286-3
For those in any way incapacitated, an invaluable guide to parks
and areas that offer special treatment and facilities.

National Park System. Natl. Park Serv., 1972. 2 vols. [Vol. 2
out of print]. Vol. 1. 164 p. il.   024-005-00538-2
The objective of the study was the definition of a national park system, and identification of gaps in our present system.

National Parks and the American Landscape. W. H. Truettner
[and R. Bolton-Smith]. Natl. Coll. of Fine Arts, 1972. 141 p. il.
                                                047-003-00015-6

Published to accompany an exhibit of the National Collection of Fine Arts; but this "catalog" stands amply on its own. There is a very fine introduction, and then profuse and wonderful illustrations. Some of the illustrations are in color.

National Register of Historic Places, 1969. Natl. Park Serv., 1972. 352 p. il.   024-005-00294-4
Lovely work, prepared by a Department part of whose duties is to guard our heritage. The *National Register* includes more than 110 sites. In this edition there are the customary fine photographs.

Place Where Hell Bubbled Up; the History of the First National Park. D. A. Clary. Natl. Park Serv., 1972. 68 p. il.
    024-001-00486-1
Lovely photographs and fine essay on Yellowstone National Park.

Recording Historic Buildings. H. J. McKee, comp. Natl. Park Serv., 1970. 165 p. il.   024-005-00235-9
Principles for reporting and recording historic structures. Many illustrations.

Saguaro National Monument, Ariz. N. Shelton. Natl. Park Serv., [1972]. il.   024-005-00292-8
Simple account of the national beauty of this area, with many fine illustrations.

Signers of the Declaration; Historic Places Commemorating the Signing of the Declaration of Independence. C. W. Snell, J. O. Littleton, and others, eds. Natl. Park Serv., 1973. 310 p. il.
    024-005-00496-3
Superb book, filled with portraits, biographies, drawings, maps. Should be in every school, in fact in *every*, library—private and public.

Soldier and Brave; Historic Places Associated with Indian Affairs and the Indian Wars in Trans-Mississippi West. R. G. Ferris, ed. Dept. of the Interior, Natl. Survey of Historic Sites and Buildings, vol. 12 (1971). 453 p. il.   024-005-00236-7

The usual well-told history and the usual very fine reproductions of contemporary illustrations and maps. Highly recommended.

Yellowstone Wildlife. Natl. Park Serv. [1972]. [32] p. il.

024-005-00474-2

NAVIGATION

Coast Guard Aids to Navigation. U.S. Coast Guard, 1972. 27 p. il. Free from the Coast Guard.

Emergency Repairs Afloat; Boatman's Pocket Guide to: Trouble Shooting; Emergency Repairs; How to Stay Afloat; Recommended Basic Hand Tools and Spare Parts. U.S. Coast Guard, 1973. Folder. Free from the Coast Guard.
This folder manages to cram an unbelievable amount of good advice into its few pages.

Great Lakes Pilot, 1974. Natl. Ocean Survey [1974]. 629 p. il. Purchase from Lake Survey Center.

Historically Famous Lighthouses. U.S. Coast Guard, 1972. 88 p. il. Free from the Coast Guard.
Fifty-six lighthouses from 22 states, including Alaska and Hawaii. A surprising number of these are quite old. This booklet sometimes cites original costs for these structures: an economic comparison depressing indeed. The salary of one keeper appointed by President John Quincy Adams was fixed at $450 per annum in 1828.

Light Lists. U.S. Coast Guard, 1975.
These titles cover marine lights and other aids to navigation maintained by, or under the authority of, the Coast Guard. They are intended to furnish information on aids that can conveniently be shown on charts. They are *not* intended to be used in the place of charts and coast pilot guides, and they should not so be used. They list buoys, fog signals, lights, day beacons, light ships, radio beacons, and loran stations.

1. Atlantic Coast from St. Croix River, Maine, to Little River, S.C. 1975. 551 p. il.   050-012-00087-5
2. Atlantic and Gulf Coast, Little River, S.C., to Rio Grande, Tex., and the Antilles. 1975. 511 p. il.   050-012-00088-3
3. Pacific Coast and Pacific Islands. 1975. 315 p. il.
   050-012-00089-1
4. Great Lakes, United States and Canada. 1975. 191 p. il.
   050-012-00090-5
5. Mississippi River System of the United States. 1975. 340 p. il.
   050-012-00091-3

Marine Aids to Navigation. U.S. Coast Guard, 1971. 27 p. il. Purchase from the Coast Guard.
Basic principles "underlying the marking of coasts and waterways of the United States, with lights, day beacons, fog signals, radio bearing, loran, and buoys."

Radar Navigation Manual. E. B. Brown. Naval Oceanographic Off., H. O. Pub. 1310 (1971) [1972]. [172] p. il. Purchase from Defense Mapping Agency.
Basic radar system; characteristics of radar equipment. Not a book for a beginner!

Rules of the Road: Great Lakes. U.S. Coast Guard, 1972. 79 p. il. Free from the Coast Guard.

Rules of the Road: International and Inland. U.S. Coast Guard, 1972. 114 p. il. Free from the Coast Guard.

Tidal Currents. Coast and Geodetic Survey [1969]. 21 p. il. Free from the Survey.
What these currents are: types, rhythms, duration, velocity.

United States of America Nautical Chart Symbols and Abbreviations. Coast and Geodetic Survey, Chart 1. [1968]. il. Purchase from the Survey.

NOISE AND NOISE CONTROL

Harmful Intruder; Noise in the Home. Environ. Protect. Agency
[1972]. Folder. 055-000-00074-3
Sources of home noises and some hints on reducing them.

**Public Hearings on Noise Abatement and Control, Conducted by
the Office of Noise Abatement and Control.** Environ. Protection
Agency, 1971–72. 8 vols. Free from the Agency.
A massive study; an example of Government research and investigation at their very best. The hearings cited below were conducted
in a number of cities throughout the country over a period of
months, in 1971. Several hundred witnesses were heard: experts
from industry, from universities, and from many professional and
nonprofessional fields. Their testimony constitutes a staggering compilation of facts and data on every aspect of the noise problem—
from its effect on animals and humans, building structures, and
wildlife to planning for its control.

    1. Construction Noise, Atlanta, Ga. [1972]. 187 p. il.

	055-000-00037-9
2.	055-000-00085-9
4.	055-000-00036-1
6.	055-000-00038-7
8.	055-000-00039-5

**Report on Aircraft-Airport Noise; Report of the Administrator of
the Environmental Protection Agency.** The Senate, 1973. 116 p.
052-070-01936-1
A report to the Public Welfare Committee, the Senate.

Transportation Noise and Its Control. Dept. of Transportation,
1972. 27 p. 050-000-00057-5

NUTRITION AND NUTRITIONAL DISORDERS

Annotated Bibliography on Maternal Nutrition. Maternal and Child Health Serv., 1970. 199 p.   017-029-00007-0
About 1,000 annotated citations directed to physicians, nutritionists, and "other persons concerned with applying the research findings reported in the literature . . ." Listing was prepared from a careful scanning of *Index Medicus* for the years 1958–68; but only articles in English are included. Another example of the very fine bibliographies now so widely available from, and expanding the work of, many of our official agencies.

Conserving the Nutritive Values in Foods. Dept. of Agr., Home and Garden Bull. 90 (1971). 16 p. il.   001-000-00869-2
These vary greatly in stability. Learn how to keep them as long as possible in vegetables, fruits, canned foods, meats, etc.

Eat a Good Breakfast to Start a Good Day. Dept. of Agr., Leaflet 268 (1972). Folder. il.   001-000-01583-4

Energy Value of Foods . . . A. L. Merrill and B. K. Watt. Dept. of Agr., Agr. Handbook 74 (1955) [Slightly rev. 1973.] 105 p.
                001-000-02770-1
The 1973 revision consists of an insert of four pages; otherwise, the exhaustive tables of hundreds of foods are intact. There is an introductory essay devoted to the nutritional value of foods.

Family Fare; a Guide to Good Nutrition. Dept. of Agr., Home and Garden Bull. 1 (1973). 91 p. il.   001-000-03280-1
Recipes from apples to waffles. But much more: how to balance necessary nutrients in appetizing ways.

Fats in Food and Diet. R. M. Leverton. Dept. of Agr., Agr. Inform. Bull. 361 [1974]. 10 p.
                001-000-03358-1

Food for the Family with Young Children. Dept. of Agr., Home and Garden Bull. 5 (1973). 16 p. il.   001-000-02944-4
The food plan; proper nutrition; menus.

Food for Fitness; Daily Food Guide. Dept. of Agr., Leaflet 424 (1973). 8 p. il.   001-000-02882-1

Food for Us All; Yearbook of Agriculture, 1969. J. Hayes, comp. Dept. of Agr., 360 p. il.   001-000-00116-7
Food from the farm to you. Forty-seven essays by experts. Instructive reading and wonderful illustrations. "In a nation with the greatest food capacity ever achieved—and ability in fact to produce considerably more than domestic and foreign markets can absorb—one might assume that food for us all would have long ago been achieved; yet it has not." (Foreword by C. M. Hardin, Secretary of Agriculture.)

Food for Your Table; Let's Talk About It. Dept. of Agr., 1971. 22 p. il.   001-024-00157-1
That is, what you should eat, and how much.

Food Guide for Older Folks. Dept. of Agr., Home and Garden Bull. 17 (1974). 19 p. il.   001-000-03321-2
Discusses categories of food and gives sample recipes and menus.

Food Is More than Just Something to Eat. Dept. of Agr. [1973]. 20 p. il. Free from the Dept.

Food Selection for Good Nutrition in Group Feeding. B. B. Peterkin. Dept. of Agr., Home Econ. Res. Rept. 35 (1972). 32 p.
001-000-02633-0

Food and Your Weight; Let's Talk about It. L. Page and L. J. Fincher. Dept. of Agr., Home and Garden Bull. 74 (1973). 37 p. il.
001-000-02603-8
Let's talk about how much food you need, and what.

Good Foods Coloring Book. Dept. of Agr., PA 912 (1973). [31] p. il.   001-000-02940-1
For kids, of course—but what adult can resist it?

Guide to Nutrition and Food Service for Nursing Homes and Homes for the Aged. M. C. Coble [and E. T. Aitken]. Community Health Serv. [1971]. 111 p. il.   017-001-00392-1
Not only complete nutrition tables, both for the well and the ill, but many tempting recipes to excite the tired appetite of the elderly.

How Food Affects You. Fed. Extension Serv. [1970]. 31 p. il.
001-005-00002-2
Lessons in nutrition taught via cartoons and explanatory text.

Nutrition and Aging; a Selected, Annotated Bibliography, 1964–72. M. D. Simko and K. Colitz. Admin. on Aging [1973]. 42 p.
017-062-00080-8

Nutrition and Disease—1973; Hearings . . . The Senate, 1973. 4 parts.
Concerned with various types of diet (notably Dr. Atkins's and the Zen macrobiotic) and their use. Expert testimony. Select Comm. on Nutrition and Human Needs.
    1. Obesity and Fad Diets. 148 p. il.   052-070-01835-6
    2. Sugar in Diet, Diabetes, and Heart Disease. [145-278] p.
052-070-01875-5
    3. Appendix to Hearings . . . [279-403] p. il.   052-070-01876-3
    4. Diabetes and the Daily Diet. 1974. [405-478] p.
052-070-02298-1
A notable feature of the hearings (Part 1) is the reproduction of many advertisements promising spectacular loss of weight, with fetching pictures to "prove" the claims.

Nutrition, Development, and Social Behavior. D. J. Kallen, ed. Public Health Serv., 1972. 386 p.   017-046-00014-4
Proceedings of a 1972 conference. "It has been estimated that three

hundred million children [in the world] suffer from malnutrition."
(Various types of malnutrition exist in the United States.) This is a
series of papers on the effects of such malnutrition on physical
growth and maturation. Over 20 papers.

Nutrition Education; Hearings . . . The Senate, 1972–73. 8 parts.
Before the Select Comm. on Nutrition and Human Needs. "We
take better care of our automobiles than we do of our bodies. . . .
The hearings that begin today will focus on one of the underlying
problems causing widespread nutritional ignorance—inadequacy
of nutritional education. Are we a nation of nutritional illiterates?"
The Hearings are as follows.

    1. Overview; Consultants' Recommendations. 1972 [1973]. 60 p.

        052-070-01736-8

    1A. Appendix. 1972. [61-138] p. il.   052-070-01737-6

    2. Overview; Federal Program. 1973. [139-191] p.

        052-070-01740-6

    2A. Appendix. 1972 [1973]. [199-253] p. il.   052-070-01741-4

    3. TV Advertising of Food to Children. 1973. [255-368] p.

        052-070-01748-1

    4. TV Advertising of Food to Children. 1973. [369-447] p.

        052-070-01809-7

    5. TV Advertising of Food to Children. 1973. [449-546] p.

        052-070-01818-6

    6. Phosphate Research and Dental Decay. 1973. [547-596] p.

        052-070-01877-1

    7. School Nutrition Education Progress. 1973. [597-662] p.

        052-070-02037-7

    8. Broadcast Industry's Responsibility to TV Advertising. 1973.
    [663-712] p.   052-070-02046-6

Nutrition Research in the USSR, 1961–1970. W. H. Fitzpatrick.
Public Health Serv., 1972. 143 p.   017-053-00005-1
Based on original Soviet research published within the last decade.
Physiological processes; nutrition; enzymes; diet therapy; food sci-
ence. Each section has a detailed bibliography. (A publication of the

John E. Fogarty International Center for Advanced Study in the Health Sciences.)

Nutrition Sense and Nonsense. Food and Drug Admin. [1973]. 6 p. il.   017-012-00200-5
Exposes some of the myths of what you should and should not eat, both for health and a healthy figure.

Nutritive Value of Foods. Dept. of Agr., Home and Garden Bull. 72 (1974). 41 p.   001-000-01528-1
Tables of values of scores of foods, with revealing caloric information.

Studies of Human Need; Prepared by the Select Committee on Nutrition and Human Needs. The Senate, 1972. 229 p.

052-070-0512-2
Seattle was chosen as the area for an intense study of hunger, housing, and human requirements.

Toward the New; a Report on Better Foods and Nutrition from Agricultural Research. E. M. Adams and others. Dept. of Agr., Agr. Inform. Bull. 341 (1972). 60 p. il.   001-000-01565-6
Quite a marvelous introduction to what agriculture contributes to our well-being: better food and nutrition for all the world.

OCCUPATIONS AND CAREERS

Apprentice Training; Sure Way to a Skilled Craft. Manpower Admin. [1974]. 8 p. il.   029-006-00007-5
What such training is; how it helps you in getting (and holding) a good job.

Career Profiles of Forestry, Conservation, Ecology, Environmental Management. Forest Serv. [1973]. [16] p. il.   001-001-00356-5
A fine little guide for those contemplating any forestry career; charmingly illustrated.

Career in Veterinary Medicine. Bur. of Health Manpower Educ. [1974]. 10 p. il. Free from the Bur. 017-040-00352-8

Directory of Federal Job Information Centers, Sept. 1973. Civil Serv. Comm., Pamph. BRE-9 (1973). Folder. Free from the Comm. Listing, by state, of these information centers.

Directory of Local Employment Security Offices. . . . Manpower Admin., 1973. 102 p. Free from the Admin.
Strictly a directory: by state, then alphabetically by town, with addresses. Functions of agencies briefly described, as well as the occupational groups they serve. For use by those who know the meaning of the codes employed.

Employment Testing; Guide Signs, Not Stop Signs. M. Kandel. Civil Rights Comm., Clearinghouse Pub. 10 (1968). 30 p.
005-000-00021-1
A study, based on real cases, intended to show that tests valid for one ethnic group trained for a particular job do not necessarily hold for other groups; and that a positive attitude must be taken toward results of any such tests, especially where the disadvantaged are involved.

FDA Chemist. Food and Drug Admin. [1974]. 8 p. il. Free from the Admin.

FDA Microbiologist. Food and Drug Admin. [1974]. 8 p. il. Free from the Admin.

Forest Service Career Guide; Professional Opportunities in Natural Resource Management, Planning, and Research. Dept. of Agr., Misc. Pub. 1282 (1974). [16] p. il. 001-000-03258-5

Guide to Local Occupational Information, 1973. Dept. of Labor, 1973. 176 p. Purchase from the Dept.
". . . a directory of selected State employment services, brochures,

bulletins, and other releases intended to provide current local occupational information for use in designing programs . . ."

Health Careers Guidebook; 3rd Edition. Dept. of Labor, 1972. 166 p. il. 029-000-00158-8
Current occupational information; an overview. Career planning; financial aid; descriptions of health occupations (opportunities, training, prospects). Salary charts and referral lists. And—thank God!—an index.

How to Pay for Your Health Career Education; Guide for Minority Students. Health Resources Admin. [1974]. [12] p. Free from the Admin. 017-041-00064-9

Improving Employee Performance. Civil Serv. Comm., Personnel Bibliog. 45 [1974]. 95 p. 006-000-00662-1

Job with the Forest Service: a Guide to Nonprofessional Employment. Dept. of Agr., Misc. Pub. 843 (1972). [20] p. il.
001-000-03429-4
It is interesting to note how many of our young people want to get back "to the soil and trees."

Jobs for Which a High-School Education Is Usually Required. Bur. of Labor Statistics, 1973. [16] p. Free from the Bur.
Many of the occupations cited are from the 1972–73 *Occupational Outlook Handbook.* Seventeen fields and their possibilities are briefly explained and explored: qualifications and training; employment opportunities and trends.

Jobs for Which Junior College, Technical, Institute, or Other Specialized Training Is Usually Required. Bur. of Labor Statistics, 1973. [9] p. il. Free from the Bur.

Journalist 1 & C. Naval Personnel Bur., 1970. 399 p. il.
008-047-00076-6

Primarily for naval personnel, of course. Begins with a study of establishing community relations; then on to scientific—and other—writing, news photography, TV program production. Obviously has wide application among us civilians.

Mathematics and Your Career. Bur. of Labor Statistics, 1972. Folder. il. Free from the Bur.

Merchandising Your Job Talents. Dept. of Labor, 1974. 26 p. il.

029-000-00220-7

How to appraise yourself; prepare a résumé; the letter of application. Sources of job information. The interview.

1973 Examinations for Foreign Service Officer Careers. Dept. of State, 1973. [37] p. il. Purchase from the Dept.

Applying; qualifying; career types. The examination: written; sample questions.

Occupational Outlook Handbook, 1972–73 Edition. Bur. of Labor Statistics, Bull. 1700 (1973). 879 p. il. 029-001-01083-4

Job description and employment outlook of over 800 occupations, to enable people to plan careers intelligently. "Discusses the nature of work in different occupations, as well as earnings, job prospects . . . education and training requirements." Basic reference source for vocational counselors and manpower planners, as well as the individual job seeker. A handy "Sources of Additional Information" follows each occupation. New edition now available.

Science and Your Career. Bur. of Labor Statistics [1970]. [8] p. il. Free from the Bur.

So You Want to Be a Forester? C. E. Randall. Forest Serv. [1972]. 24 p. Free from the Serv.

Who can blame you? But this at least tells you how, your duties, your pleasures, your *hard work*.

Summer Jobs in Federal Agencies. Civil Serv. Comm., Oct. 1972. [49] p. il. Free from the Comm.
Departments and Agencies interested; job types; salaries and allowances. Where to write. Does not include specific job descriptions.

Working for the USA; How to Apply for a Civil Service Job; What the Government Can Offer You as a Federal Worker. Civil Serv. Comm., Pamph. BRE-37 (1974). 35 p.   006-000-00891-7
Introductory: job opportunities, qualifications, salaries.

OCEANOGRAPHY

Glossary of Oceanographic Terms. B. B. Baker and others, comps. U.S. Naval Oceanographic Off., SP-35 (1966). 204 p. il. Purchase from the Defense Mapping Agency.
Definitions of technical terms used in oceanography and allied marine sciences taken from the fields of physics, chemistry, biology, geology, geophysics, geography, mathematics, and meteorology.

Marine Geology; Research beneath the Sea. Geol. Survey [1969]. 14 p. il. Free from the Survey.
Another of the Survey's excellent pamphlets; an invaluable introduction.

Marine Mammals; Hearings . . . House of Representatives, 1971. 584 p. Free from the House Document Room.   052-070-01423-7
Hearings before the Merchant Marine and Fisheries Committee. The book includes many statements by experts in the field of conservation of endangered sea mammals. These statements include statistics. (One could wish Congressional hearings were printed in larger type; filled with interesting material, they are often physically tiring to read.)

Marine Resources Development . . . a National Opportunity. Dept. of the Interior [1969]. [60] p. il. Free from the Dept.

How we remove and utilize materials (and various animals) from our waters at a rate of over $2,000,000,000 annually. Fine photographs, drawings.

Our Living Oceans; Secrets of the Sea. Natl. Marine Fisheries Serv., 1973. [7] p. il. Free from the Serv.
Too bad it's so short. Even so, it manages to show how the sea has reluctantly yielded up its wealth, its secrets, and the some of its potential. Charming pamphlet. Let's hope for a much longer version!

Our Nation and the Sea; a Plan for National Action. Off. of the President, 1969. 305 p. il. 040-000-00111-5
Certainly one of the most fascinating books cited in this *Guide*. Not a running account, containing, as it does, scores of recommendations made by a commission authorized by Congress in 1966 to undertake an exhaustive investigation of our nation in relation to the seas around us. The Commission's recommendations are, of course, firstrate; but they do not constitute the real interest of this book. *That* lies in the wonderful essays and the data cited to support the recommendations; every conceivable aspect of marine ecology is discussed, and enchantingly. The reader may well conclude that if he is not an oceanographer, he is wasting his time.

Windows in the Sea. M. C. Link. Smithsonian Inst. 198 p. il. Purchase from the Inst.
"The step-by-step evolution of an underwater research vessel, the *Johnson Sea-Link*, is told in a readable, knowledgeable way by an eye-witness . . ."

PATENTS, COPYRIGHT, AND TRADEMARKS

General Information about Patents. Patent Off., 1975. 41 p.
003-004-00522-0

General Information Concerning Trademarks. Patent Off., 1975. 28 p. il.   003-004-00009-1
How the law operates to protect your ideas.

General Information on Copyright. Copyright Off., Cir. 1 (1973). 11 p. Free from the Off.
The law in very general terms.

Guide for Patent Draftsmen. Patent Off., 1975. 19 p. il.

003-004-00521-1

Problems particular to this particular work.

PESTS

Aquatic Pests on Irrigation Systems; Identification Guide. W. E. Otto and T. R. Bartley. Bur. of Reclamation, 1965 [repr. 1972]. 72 p. il.   024-003-00069-8
Plants and other pests in lovely color. Fine guide.

Be Safe from Insects in Recreational Areas. J. A. Fluno and D. E. Weidhaas. Dept. of Agr., Home and Garden Bull. 200 [1972]. 6 p. il.   001-000-02511-2

Control of Starfish; Hearing before the Subcommittee on Territories and Insular Affairs of the Committee on Interior and Insular Affairs, United States Senate, 91st Congress, 2nd Sess. The Senate. [1970]. 58 p. Free from the Comm.
The Crown of Thorns starfish is causing widespread damage among the Pacific Islands by eating up live coral.

Controlling the Brown Recluse Spider. W. J. Gladney. Dept. of Agr., Leaflet 556 (1973). [8] p. il.   003-000-02950-9

Controlling Chiggers. Dept. of Agr., Home and Garden Bull. 137 [1973]. 12 p. il.   001-000-02949-5

Controlling the Eastern Tent Caterpillar. Dept. of Agr., Home and Garden Bull. 178 (1973). [6] p. il.   001-000-02778-6

Controlling Fleas. Dept. of Agr., House and Garden Bull. 121 (1971). 6 p. il.   001-000-01164-2

Controlling Wasps. Dept. of Agr., Home and Garden Bull. 122 (1972). 8 p. il.   001-000-02440-0
Hornets; yellow jackets; *Polistes,* mud daubers, and the cicada group—all are wasps. Beneficial, they destroy harmful insects; but they must be watched. Learn how.

Device and Technique for Handling Red Squirrels. C. H. Halvorson. Bur. of Sport Fisheries and Wildlife, Spec. Sci. Rept., Wildlife Ser. 159 (1972). 10 p. il. Free from the Fish and Wildlife Serv.

Grasshopper Control. Dept. of Agr., Farmers' Bull. 2193 (1973). 11 p. il.   001-000-02822-7
Heaviest infestation is in the Western two thirds of the country—which must make us Easterners wonder.

Hormigas Blancas, Plaga y Moho; Inspectione Su Casa Contra los Insectos y la Podredumbre. Dept. of Housing and Urban Devel. 1973. [6] p. Free from the Dept.

Lead, Pesticides, Man and Environment. Pesticides Programs Off. [1973]. 67 p. il. Free from the Off.

Suppression of Pest Population with Sterile Male Insects. W. Klassen and J. F. Creech. Dept. of Agr., Misc. Pub. 1182 [1971]. [8] p.   001-000-01146-4

FOREST

Eastern Forest Insects W. L. Baker. Dept. of Agr., Misc. Pub. 1175 (1972). 642 p. il.   001-000-01145-6

A gigantic, frightening compendium, with alluring pictures, and the proper names of so many of your friends!

Finding and Using Natural Enemies of the Gypsy Moth. Dept. of Agr., Picture Story 272 [1973]. [6] p. il. Free from the Dept.

Gypsy Moth; a Major Pest of Trees. Dept. of Agr., PA 1006 [1973]. [12] p. il.   001-000-02844-8
A deadly moth indeed. Its offspring cost us 400,000 acres of timber annually.

Gypsy Moth, Threat to Southern Forests. Forest Serv. [1971]. 12 p. il. Free from the Serv.

Help Destroy Gypsy Moths. Dept. of Agr., PA 974 [1973]. Folder. Free from the Dept.

Six-spined Engraver Beetle. W. M. Ciesla. Forest Serv., Forest Pest Leaflet 141 (1973). 6 p. il.   001-001-00353-1
Favors almost a half of our Eastern and Central states forests with its careful chiseling.

GARDEN AND FIELD

Alfalfa Weevil; How to Control It. Dept. of Agr., Leaflet 368 (1971). 8 p. il.   001-000-00180-9
The nation's most valuable hay crop, and one of its enduring enemies.

Aphids on Leafy Vegetables; How to Control Them. W. J. Reid, Jr., and F. P. Cuthbert, Jr. Dept of Agr., Farmers' Bull. 2148 (1972). 16 p. il.   001-000-00044-6
This garden pest, of which most specimens are about 1/16" long, lives about one month—but what a month! Your peaches, cabbages, etc., feel the full impact of that month. Methods of control are described.

Biology of the Japanese Beetle. W. E. Fleming. Dept. of Agr., Tech. Bull. 1449 (1972). 129 p. il.   001-000-01524-9
A very detailed work; intended for those who don't mind close acquaintance with this pest, and who hope their studies will help get him out of our lives.

Control of Caterpillars on Commercial Cabbage and Other Cole Crops in the South: Cabbage, Broccoli, Cauliflower, Collards, Kale. W. J. Reid, Jr., and F. P. Cuthbert, Jr. Dept. of Agr., Farmers' Bull. 2099 [1971]. 24 p. il.   001-000-01439-1
Natural control, and some of the newer insecticides.

Controlling Insects in Farm-stored Grain. Dept. of Agr., Leaflet 553 (1971). 8 p. il.   001-000-01312-2

Controlling the Japanese Beetle. Dept. of Agr., Home and Garden Bull. 159 (1973). 16 p. il.   001-000-02794-8
Has been with us since about 1910. Close-up, handsome photographs.

Controlling the Mexican Bean Beetle. Dept. of Agr., Leaflet 548 [1968]. 8 p. il.   001-000-03252-6

Controlling Mole Damage. Bur. of Sport Fisheries and Wildlife, Leaflet 325 (1970). 4 p. il. Free from the Fish and Wildlife Serv.

Cotton Insect Scout; How He Can Help You. Dept of Agr., Extension Serv. ESC 571 [1972]. [4] p. il. Free from the Dept.

Golden Nematode of Potatoes and Tomatoes. Dept of Agr., PA 816 (1970). Folder. il.   001-000-03247-0

Insects on Deciduous Fruits and Tree Nuts in Home Orchard. P. H. Schwartz, Jr. Dept. of Agr., Home and Garden Bull. 190 [1972]. 30 p. il.   001-000-01387-4

Khapra Beetle; Pest of Stored Grains and Cereal Products. Dept. of Agr., PA 436 [1972]. 6 p. il. Free from the Dept.

Periodical Cicada: "17-Year Locusts." Dept. of Agr., Leaflet 540
(1971). 8 p. il. Free from the Dept.
Arrives at thirteen- or seventeen-year intervals.

Protecting Corn from Blackbirds. R. T. Mitchell and J. J. Linehan.
U.S. Fish and Wildlife Serv., Wildlife Leaflet 476 (1967). [8] p.
Free from the Serv.
Red-winged blackbirds and grackles are chief offenders. Handsome
drawings of culprits and advice on minimizing their damage.

Soybean Cyst Nematode. Dept. of Agr., PA 333 [1968]. [4] p. il.
Free from the Dept.

Stored Tobacco Insects; Biology and Control. Dept. of Agr., Agr.
Handbook 233 [1971]. 43 p. il.   001-000-01384-0

Strawberry Insects . . . How to Control Them. Dept. of Agr.,
Farmers' Bull. 2184 (1973). 17 p. il.   001-000-03402-2

Tomato Fruitworm; How to Control It. Dept. of Agr., Leaflet
367 (1973). Folder. il.   001-000-02761-1

HOME

Ants in the Home and Garden; How to Control Them. Dept. of
Agr., Home and Garden Bull. 28 [1973]. 8 p. il.   001-000-03168-6

Biological Factors in Domestic Rodent Control. R. Z. Brown. Public
Health Serv., 1969. 32 p. il. Free from the Serv.
A training guide in the Rodent Control Series.

Cockroaches; How to Control Them. Dept. of Agr., Leaflet 430
(1971). 8 p. il.   001-000-01470-6
There are 55 varieties.

Control of Domestic Mice & Rats. B. F. Bjornson and others. Public
Health Serv., 1969. 41 p. il. Free from the Serv.

We may have 100,000,000 rats in this country—almost one for every two of us!

Controlling Household Pests. Dept. of Agr., Home and Garden Bull. 96 (1971). 32 p. il.   001-000-01273-8
"Some household pests have an incredible ability to escape extermination." Learn how to thwart their ability.

Controlling Mosquitoes in Your Home and on Your Premises. J. A. Fluno. Dept. of Agr., Home and Garden Bull. 84 (1972). 8 p. il.
001-000-02429-9
Habits; control, including sprays and repellents.

Controlling Wood-destroying Beetles in Buildings and Furniture. L. H. Williams and H. R. Johnston. Dept. of Agr., Leaflet 558 (1973). 8 p. il.   001-000-02895-2

Finding and Keeping a Healthy House. [R. C. Biesterfeldt and others.] Dept. of Agr., PA-1284. 1974. [22] p. il. Purchase from the Dept.
How to buy—then how to preserve against the multitudinous insects that try to make you regret your purchase. Describes these pests and their work—not their elimination. Most amusingly illustrated. A good buy.

House Fly; How to Control It. Dept. of Agr., Leaflet 390 [1972]. 8 p. il.   001-000-03467-7

Imported Fire Ant; Rural and Residential Pest. Dept. of Agr., PA 592 [1973]. [7] p. il. Free from the Dept.

Insects and Related Pests of House Plants; How to Control Them. G. V. Johnson and F. F. Smith. Dept. of Agr., Home and Garden Bull. 67 [1972]. 16 p. il.   001-000-01577-0

Kill Those Flies for a Clean House. Dept. of Agr., PA 832 [1972]. Folder.   001-000-02701-8

Kill Those Roaches for a Clean House. Dept. of Agr., PA 833
(1972). Folder.   001-000-02667-4

**Protecting Log Cabins, Rustic Work, and Unseasoned Wood from
Injurious Insects in the Eastern United States.** R. A. St. George.
Dept. of Agr., Farmers' Bull. 2104 (1973). 18 p. il.

001-000-02736-1

Beetles; wood borers.

Protecting Woolens against Clothes Moths and Carpet Beetles.
Dept. of Agr., Home and Garden Bull. 113 [1971]. 8 p. il.

001-000-01472-2

Safe Use of Pesticides in Home and Garden. Dept. of Agr., PA-589
(1972). Folder. il.   001-000-02584-8

Silverfish and Firebrats; How to Control Them. Dept. of Agr.,
Leaflet 412 [1973]. [6] p. il.   001-000-03188-1
Insects with a high protein, sugar, and starch diet, in other words,
disturbingly like many of us. These insects require very special in-
hospitality, detailed here.

USDA Fights the Fire Ant. Dept. of Agr., Picture Story Ser. 265
[1973]. [4] p. il. Free from the Dept.

LIVESTOCK, POULTRY, AND BEES

Chicken Lice; How to Control Them. Dept. of Agr., Leaflet 474
(1972). 8 p. il.   001-000-01514-1
Spraying; dusting; dipping. Treatment of chicken houses.

Controlling the Great Wax Moth, Pest of Honeycombs. Dept. of
Agr., Farmers' Bull 2217 [1972]. 10 p. il.   001-000-02465-5

Fight against Cattle Fever Ticks. Dept. of Agr., PA 475 [1973].
10 p. il.   001-000-02777-8

Fowl Tick; How to Control It. Dept. of Agr., Leaflet 382 (1972).
[6] p. il.   001-000-03163-5

Horse Bots; How to Control Them. Dept. of Agr., Leaflet 450
[1973]. 8 p. il.   001-000-02787-5
Common bot fly, throat bot fly, and nose bot fly. Damage and
control.

Screwworm. Dept. of Agr., Picture Story Ser. 259 (1972). [6] p. il.
Free from the Dept.

Toxicity of 45 Organic Herbicides to Cattle, Sheep, and Chickens.
J. S. Palmer. Dept. of Agr., Prod. Research Rept. 137 [1972].
41 p. il.   010-000-01502-8
Discussion of several broad types and their effects.

PHOTOGRAPHY

Method for Filing Black and White Photographs. R. E. Griffiths,
Jr. Bur. of Sport Fisheries and Wildlife, Wildlife Leaflet 490
(1969). 3 p. il. Free from the Bur.

Photographer's Mate 3 & 2. Bur. of Naval Personnel, 1971. 679 p.
il.   008-047-00146-1
A technical manual for Naval photographers that covers optics,
filters, exposure, processing and printing of black and white, color,
and motion picture photography.

POLLUTION

Air pollution is only one of several types of pollution. This *Guide*
carries material on food pollution, land pollution (often known, in
the literature, as soil pollution), noise, and water pollution, in
addition to the citations of material on air pollution. The chief
Government agency dealing with the pollutions covered in this
Guide is the Environmental Protection Agency. This Agency

issues several broad classes of material: the popular titles meant for a comparatively uninformed public; the very good, detailed bibliographies dealing with every aspect of every type of pollution; and the technical titles of interest, probably, only to professional environmentalists. As regards the popular material, the listing below is probably complete for recent material. For the technical publications of the EPA, the listing is only intended to serve as a guide to both the breadth and the number of such publications. For a complete listing of the Agency's publications, the reader will do well to write to the Agency for its free "List of Publications."

Action for Environmental Quality; Standards and Enforcement for Air and Water Pollution Control. Environ. Protect. Agency, 1973. [21] p. il.   055-000-00087-5
A booklet all of us should read. It deals with the need for laws on pollution; tells how such laws are enforced. The points made in the booklet are emphasized and illustrated by excellent colored photographs that show how much beauty we still possess, to save if we will.

AIR

Air Pollution Advice for the Elderly. Environ. Protect. Agency [1972]. 8 p. il. Free from the Agency.

Air Pollution Damages Trees. D. D. Davis [and others]. Forest Serv., 1973. 32 p. il.   001-001-00349-6
Very valuable work that shows the damage caused by a variety of chemicals.

Aircraft Emissions; Impact on Air Quality and Feasibility of Control. Environ. Protect. Agency [1973]. 99 p. il. Free from the Agency.
For the informed reader only; a detailed report of how a study was organized, carried through, and its results interpreted.

Air Quality and Automobile Emission Control . . . The Senate, 1974. Three parts.

The three parts were prepared by a coordinating committee on air quality studies of the National Academy of Sciences:

1. 130 p.   052-070-02498-4
2. 511 p. il.   052-070-02515-8
3. 137 p. il.   052-070-02516-6

Asbestos and Air Pollution; an Annotated Bibliography. Environ. Pollution Control Off., AP-82 (1971). 101 p.   055-000-00011-5
One hundred and sixty abstracts, expertly annotated.

Automobile Fuels and Air Pollution; Report of the Panel on Automobile Fuel and Air Pollution. Dept. of Commerce, 1971. 32 p. il.

003-000-00307-8

Covers pollutants from additives, fuels. Briefly discusses suggested methods of control; the implications of lead removal from gas, and other fuel modifications. Fine; but for the expert.

Chlorine and Air Pollution; an Annotated Bibliography. D. H. Farr and others. Environ. Protect. Agency, AP-99 (1971). 113 p.

055-003-00018-1

Cleaner Engines for Cleaner Air; Progress and Problems in Reducing Air Pollution from Automobiles. Genl. Accounting Off. (report to Congress by the Comptroller General of the United States), 1972. 65 p. il. Purchase from the Off.

Compilation of Air Pollutant Emission Factors. Air and Water Programs Off., AP-42 (1973). [302] p. il.   055-003-00060-2
". . . reports data available on those atmospheric emissions for which sufficient information exists to establish realistic emission factors." External combustion sources, solid waste disposal, internal combustion engine sources, evaporation loss sources, chemical process industry pollutants, metallurgical products, mineral products, the petroleum industry, and wood processing are all discussed. There is a great deal of technical data; but don't let that scare you—this is a superb work.

———Supplement 1. 1973. [28] p. il. 005-003-00066-1
———Supplement 2. 1973. [20] p. il. Free from the Off.
005-003-00068-8

Cost of Air Pollution Damage; a Status Report. L. B. Barrett and T. E. Waddell. Environ. Protect. Agency. AP-85 (1973). 73 p. il.
055-003-00055-8
Analysis of cost studies made in the past, used to develop an estimate of the national cost for pollution damage. Required a very considerable survey of the literature, both published and unpublished.

Cost of Clean Air; Annual Report of the Administrator of the Environmental Protection Agency to the Congress of the United States. The Senate, 1974. [303] p. Purchase from the Senate Document Off. Senate Document 93-122.
This is the fourth such report to the Congress, and it presents in great detail the costs, actual and projected, of protecting our environment from various pollutions. ". . . the Environmental Protection Agency estimates that the total national investment cost for the period 1971–1979 due to the Clean Air Act will be $47 billion. Of this $23 billion will be attributable to mobile sources, $13 billion to fossil fuel burning sources, and $11 billion to industrial sources." This very detailed breakdown of costs is probably only for the expert; and, incidentally, for those with good eyes. Part III is "Mobile Source Emission Control"; IV is "Industrial Source Control Costs," including among others the chemical and metal industries; Part V is "Fossil Fuel Burning Sources"; and Part VI is "Benefits of Air Pollution Control."

Environmental Lead and Public Health. R. E. Engel and others. Environ. Protect. Agency, AP-90 (1971). 34 p. 055-003-00002-5
A health study in some detail.

The Flake and His Secret Plan. Community Environ. Management Bur. [1973]. [16] p. il. 017-032-00018-6
Kids will love this and learn from it. Flake is a monstrous paint chip which, loose, can cause poisoning.

Indoor-Outdoor Air Pollution Relationships: a Literature Review.
F. B. Benson and others. Environ. Protect. Agency, AP-112 (1972).
73 p.   055-003-00043-2
". . . very few data have been gathered on indoor pollution, especially in view of the importance of the problem. The data that are
available are compiled and analyzed in this report. Based on a review of the literature, it was possible to infer relationships between
indoor and outdoor pollution and to identify factors that affect
these relationships . . ." This is not a bibliography, but an evalua-
tive review of literature—and all the more valuable for that. There
is, of course, a full citation of the sources from which the review
was drawn.

Lead and Air Pollution; a Bibliography with Abstracts. Environ.
Protect. Agency, EPA-450/1-74-001 (1974). 431 p.

055-001-00724-8

Mercury and Air Pollution; a Bibliography with Abstracts. Air
Programs Off., AP-114 (1972). 59 p.   055-003-00045-9
About 150 citations, obviously abstracted by experts. Thoroughly indexed. Sources of mercury pollution; measurements of effects on all
kinds of life; standards and criteria for judgment and improvement
of the air.

Mercury in the Environment. Geol. Survey, Prof. Paper 713 (1970).
67 p. il.   024-001-00944-7
Amounts of this deadly element in particular areas and districts.
(Derives particular interest from the stir about the lowering
"ozone" belt.)

Nationwide Air Pollutant Emission Trends, 1940–70. J. H. Caven-
der and others. Environ. Protect. Agency, AP-115 (1973). 52 p.

055-003-00058-1
". . . to provide current estimates of nationwide emissions for the
five major pollutants; sulfur oxide, particulates, carbon monoxide,
hydrogens, and nitrous oxides.

Pollution; Its Impact on Mental Health; a Literature Survey and Review of Research. Natl. Inst. of Mental Heath, 1972. 81 p.

017-024-00243-7

A survey of research trends and needs, with comments by a task force of the American Psychiatric Association. Then follow over 100 abstracts, dealing with four broad subjects. Excellent.

Proceedings of Southern Conference on Environmental Radiation Protection from Nuclear Power Plants. Environ. Protect. Agency, 1972. 236 p. il. Free from the Agency.

The Conference was held April 21, 22, 1971. "Specifically . . . techniques used to identify and monitor radionuclides contained in liquid and gas effluents produced. . . . and to specify pathways through which radioactive materials released . . . may reach the population. Such information assists in determining the dose that may be contributed . . . by the nuclear power industry." Eleven papers and a panel discussion. Of very wide interest, and certainly for all libraries.

Slash Fire Air Pollution. L. Fritschen and others. Forest Serv., PNW-97 (1970). 42 p. il. Free from the Serv.

Some Aspects of Air Pollution: Odors, Visibility, and Art. B. W. Peckham. Public Health Serv. [1969]. 13 p. Free from the Serv.

Modest booklet that deals with many aspects of pollution, some of which might not occur to most of us.

Steel Industry and Environmental Quality; Sub-Council Report. Natl. Industrial Pollution Control Council. [1972]. 26 p. il.

052-054-00040-1

Trees for Polluted Air. Dept. of Agr., Misc. Pub. 1230 [1973]. 12 p. il.

001-000-02959-2

WATER

Hydrologic Implications of Waste Disposal. W. J. Schneider. Geol. Survey, Cir. 601-F (1970). 10 p. il. Free from the Survey.
One part of a series "intended to show relevance of water facts to water problems of urban areas, and to examine the adequacy and the existing base of water information."

International Conference on Ocean Pollution; Hearings. The Senate, 1972. 126 p. Free from the Comm.
Before the Subcommittee on Oceans and Atmosphere, of the Commerce Committee. Among the witnesses were Scott Carpenter, Jacques Cousteau, Hugh Downs, and Thor Heyerdahl. Their testimony is quoted in full. Dr. B. Commoner makes a point worth remembering: "that which goes away from our immediate environment ends up in the ocean, and . . . the death of the ocean will be the death of us all."

Oil Spill, Long Island Sound, March 21, 1972; Environmental Effects. Water Program Operations Off., Oil and Hazardous Materials Program Ser. OHM 73-06-001 (1973). 136 p. il.   055-001-00645-4
For reasons as yet unknown, this area is now clearing—at least in the deeper waters. There is, in fact, no proven connection between the disappearance of certain types of life at those depths and this particular spill.

Pollution of Lake Erie, Lake Ontario, and the International Section of the St. Lawrence River. Internatl. Joint Comm., Canada and the United States (1970). 174 p. il.   044-000-01335-5

Water, Man, and Nature. Bur. of Reclamation, 1972. 27 p. il.
                                                                024-003-00077-9
A symposium sponsored by the Bureau of Reclamation and the American Institute of Biological Sciences. Deals with the ecological impact of water resource development.

PONDS

How to Build a Farm Pond for Fish Production. Soil Conservation Serv. [1969]. [4] p. il. Free from the Serv.

Make Your Farm Pond Safe; Prevent Drownings. Dept. of Agr., PA-396 [1970.] [4] p. il. Free from the Dept.

Ponds and Marshes for Wild Ducks on Farms and Ranches in the Northern Plains. W. H. Hamer and others. Dept. of Agr., Farmers' Bull. 2234 (1968). 16 p. il.   001-000-00087-0
Making—or improving—a farm pond to attract wildfowl.

Ponds for Water Supply and Recreation. Dept. of Agr., Agr. Handbook 387 (1971). 55 p. il.   001-000-01137-5
Invaluable. Purpose of ponds: water, fishing, recreation. How to make one.

Trout Ponds for Recreation. L. D. Marriage and others. Dept. of Agr., Farmers' Bull. 2249 (1971). 13 p. il.   001-000-01533-8
Amazing amount of information: types of trout; stocking; feeding. Selecting the site; planning the size; maintaining water quality.

Warm-Water Fishponds. O. W. Dillon, Jr., and others. Dept. of Agr., Farmers' Bull. 2250 (1971). 14 p. il.   001-000-01455-2
Choice of site; construction; maintenance, stocking; weed control.

POULTRY AND POULTRY FARMING

Home Grown Honkers. H. H. Dill and F. B. Lee, eds. Bur. of Sport Fisheries and Wildlife [1970]. 154 p. il. Free from the Bur.
These are Canada geese.

Raising Ducks. W. J. Ash. Dept. of Agr., Farmers' Bull. 2215 (1969). 14 p. il.   001-000-00070-5
Breeds; incubation; brooding; nutrition; diseases; marketing.

Raising Geese. Dept. of Agr., Farmers' Bull. 2251 [1972]. 14 p. il.

001-000-01584-2

Raising Guinea Fowl. Dept. of Agr., Leaflet 519 (1970). [8] p. il.

001-000-02984-3

In Texas, Oklahoma, Missouri, North Carolina, Florida, Mississippi, Alabama, Kentucky, Tennessee, Georgia.

Wild Ducks on Farmland in the South. W. W. Neely and V. E. Davison. Dept. of Agr., Farmers' Bull. 2218 (1971). 14 p. il.

001-000-00073-0

Ducks in fresh water ponds, brackish water areas, marshland. The foods they like are discussed.

POVERTY

Green Power: Consumer Action for the Poor. Off. of Econ. Opportunity, 1969. [66] p. il Purchase from the Off.

How communities can help themselves. It is hard to describe the great value—and charm—of this sort of get-together advice now so common a feature of many Government agencies.

Ladders of Opportunity; the Way Out of Poverty through Community Action. Off. of Econ. Opportunity, 1968. [24] p. il. Free from the Off.

Told through 32 cases.

Studies of Human Need . . . The Senate, 1972. 229 p.

052-070-00512-2

Prepared by the Select Committee on Nutrition and Human Needs. A thorough examination of problems posed by the present economic crisis. Deals with economic needs—unemployment insurance, public assistance, food stamps and banks; hunger; school lunch programs; reform of public welfare; rural housing needs, and so on. Summary points out "the extent of housing and [other] need in the United States is substantially greater than is recognized . . ." The specific study area here is Seattle, Wash.; but, actually, only in a rather minor sense, since figures for the entire country are discussed.

PREGNANCY, INFANT CARE, AND FAMILY PLANNING

Eat Well for Your Baby Who Is on the Way. Children's Bur. [1969]. [4] p. il.   017-091-00061-1
Nutritional hints to keep the upcomer healthy (as well as yourself).

If You're Not Ready for Another Baby. Off. of Econ. Opportunity, Pamphlet 6130-4 (1969). [16] p. il. Purchase from the Off.

Infant Care. [A. F. North]. Children's Bur., Pub. 8 (1973) [1972]. 72 p. il.   017-091-00179-1
The sixth edition of a classic. First appeared in 1914, and has sold some 60,000,000 copies. Care of the young child under every kind of condition.

Planning Your Pregnancy. Off. of Econ. Opportunity, Pamphlet 6130-5 [1969]. [15] p. il. Free from the Off.
Hints on spacing your offspring to arrive at propitious times.

Prenatal Care. M. W. Brown. Children's Bur., Pub. 4 (1962; reissued, 1972). 92 p. il.   017-091-00187-1
A very fine work: everything the mother should know to insure the birth of a healthy child.

Social Worker and Family Planning. J. F. Gorman, ed. Maternal and Child Health Serv. [1971]. 127 p.   017-030-00007-8
The social worker's activities "in the context of maternal and child health services." A series of papers read at a 1969 Conference.

So You're Going to Be a New Father? Children's Bur., 1973. [31] p. il.   017-091-00190-1
"There has always been a great deal of literature on how to cope

with the advent of a new baby in the family, but most of it was addressed to the mother. . . . The father traditionally seemed to get left out or forgotten, not only at the dramatic moment of birth itself, but all along the line during the pregnancy." Some corrective ideas.

Sudden Infant Death Syndrome; Hearings . . . House of Representatives, 1974. 154 p. Free from the Comm.
Before the Subcommittee on Public Health and Environment, House Committee on Interstate and Foreign Commerce.

Women and Their Pregnancies; the Collaborative Prenatal Study of the National Institute of Neurological Diseases and Stroke. Natl. Insts. of Health, 1972. 540 p. il.   017-049-00038-1
A comprehensive, specialized analysis whose "primary focus has remained the establishment of association between prenatal events and organic neurological defects of the offspring." Ostensibly for medical libraries, but this compiler has found that the public wants access to the type of information in this book.

PRINTING

Guide for Typing ARS Manuscripts to Be Printed in the Department Series. Agr. Research Serv., 1974. 32 p. il. Free from the Dept. of Agr.
Very complete guide to preparing, say, a term paper or a longer thesis. The advice on spacing, heads, and so on has much wider application than to the Agricultural Research Service.

Pioneer Imprints from Fifty States. R. J. Trienens. Library of Cong., 1973. 87 p. il.   030-000-00059-1
"Takes for its subject the Library's earliest examples of printing from within present-day boundaries of each state of the Union, providing for each in turn (1) a brief statement about the origin of printing; (2) identification of the Library's earliest examples; and (3) in-

formation, if available, about the provenance of these rarities." From Massachusetts (1640) to Alaska (1868). Beautiful reduced illustrations of each early imprint. Lovely and informative book.

United States Government Printing Office Style Manual. Govt. Printing Off., 1973. 548 p. il.   021-000-00068-0

PSYCHOLOGY AND PSYCHIATRY

Included here are *curative* studies of mental illness, and general works on psychology.

Acquisition and Development of Values; Perspectives on Research; Report of Conference . . . Natl. Insts. of Health, 1969. 65 p. Free from the Insts.
Thirteen excellent papers—"overall objectives . . . improvement of the quality of human life through greater scientific understanding of developmental processes and the [effect] of research on these complex problems." A series of "summaries" that compare various cultures and classes, deal with the measurement of cultural and moral values, etc. Very interesting.

Bibliography on Human Intelligence . . . an Extensive Bibliography. L. Wright. Natl. Inst. of Mental Health [1969]. 222 p.
                017-024-00046-9
Six major and nineteen minor categories. Extraordinary listing, unfortunately not annotated.

Biological Rhythms in Psychiatry and Medicine. G. G. Luce. Natl. Inst. of Mental Health, 1970. 183 p. il.   017-024-00052-3
Examines the subtle fluctuations in "energy, mood, well-being, and performance" to which we are all subject, and assesses their medical significance. There are sections on sleep and dreaming. The scope, influence, and development of rhythms, as well as the possible physical and psychological manifestations, are discussed.

Brain Death; a Bibliography with Key-Word and Author Indexes.
A. J. Smith and others, eds. Natl. Inst. of Neurological Diseases and Stroke, NINDS Bibliog. Ser. 1 (1972). 30 p. Free from the Inst.

017-049-00034-8

A result of the "urgent need to redefine the death of an individual in terms of brain death . . ." Sixteen topical divisions—from general aspects through diagnostic aids, to moral, ethical, and religious aspects. Valuable indeed—but, remember, not annotated.

Chairside Psychology in Patient Education; a Self-Instruction Course. R. L. Weiss and R. V. Swearingen. Bur. of Health Professions Educ. and Manpower Training, 1969. 200 p. il.

017-041-00006-1

The potential uses of this book are much greater than the authors modestly suppose; it is meant for a wider audience than dental students and aides. Among other things, it employs a new technique of explication that makes for most interesting reading and development of thought.

Cognitive and Mental Development in the First Five Years of Life; a Review of Recent Research. P. Lichtenberg and D. G. Norton. Natl. Inst. of Mental Health, 1970. 111 p.   017-024-00092-2
The important work described here was done under grants from the National Institute of Mental Health.

Computer Applications in Psychotherapy; Bibliography and Abstracts. K. Taylor, comp. Natl. Inst. of Mental Health, 1970. 92 p.

017-024-00045-1

Summaries of 176 articles and papers on the application of computer technology to work in psychology and psychiatry. Author and subject indexes.

Cooperative Studies in Psychiatry; an Annotated Bibliography Summarizing Fifteen Years of Cooperative Research in Psychiatry, 1956–1970. Veterans Admin., IB 11-3 (1970). 64 p. Purchase from the Admin.

One hundred and fifty cooperative projects are discussed, with citations of journals where the full material appeared. The citations are often in great detail.

Facts about Group Therapy. Natl. Inst. of Mental Health [1972]. 9 p. il.   017-024-00256-9

International Directory of Investigators in Psychopharmacology. Natl. Inst. of Mental Health [1972]. 439 p. Free from the Inst.
"To facilitate communication among researchers in the scientific community." Biographic section; geographic index; index of research activities; index of major fields covered. Highly technical, and will appeal only to those actively engaged in such research.

Report on the XYZ Chromosomal Abnormality. Natl. Inst. of Mental Health, 1970. 55 p.   017-024-00091-4
The relation of the extra Y chromosome to certain types of behavior. Interesting to the professional and to the general reader alike.

Schizophrenia Bulletin. Natl. Inst. of Mental Health, 1969–74.
Prepared jointly by the Center for Studies of Schizophrenia and the National Clearinghouse for Mental Health Information. "Its purpose is to facilitate the dissemination and exchange of information about schizophrenia and to provide abstracts of the recent literature." The Bulletins succeed admirably in these purposes; each issue contains essay material, annotated bibliographies of recently published works, and unannotated listings. Highly recommended, and not merely for the medical library or the practitioner. All are illustrated; the listing below has been carried through November, 1974.

2. Fall, 1970. 104 p.		017-024-00093-1
3. Winter, 1970. 88 p.		017-024-00133-3
4. Fall, 1971. 102 p.		017-024-00144-9
6. Fall, 1972. 120 p.		017-024-00246-1
8. Spring, 1974. [1973]. 136 p.		017-024-00312-3

Social and Psychological Aspects of Applied Human Genetics; a Bibliography. J. R. Sorenson. John E. Fogarty Internatl. Center for Advanced Study in the Health Sciences [1973]. 98 p.

017-053-00012-4

". . . a selective compilation of books and articles which focus on the psychological and social issues of applied human genetics." Particular emphasis is laid upon problems, issues, and questions of genetic counseling; the "human mechanism" in which genetics has been applied to date. It is difficult to estimate the number of citations (unannotated), but they must number at least 1,500.

PUBLIC RELATIONS

Public Affairs Handbook 2 vols. Off. of Econ. Opportunity. [1968]. Free from the Off.
——Vol. 1. The Printed Word. [37] p. il.
A handy little guide that tells you how to work with newspapers in organizing a community action group.
——Vol. 2. Sight and Sound: How to Do It Handbook to Help You in Your Use of Tape and Film in Working with Local Radio and Television Stations. 1968. 30 p.

Public Affairs Handbook, 1972. Off. of Economic Opportunity, 1972. 28 p. Purchase from the Off.
How a community action agency can "tell its story," using the various news media.

Voice of America. U.S. Information Agency [1970]. [8] p. il. Free from the Agency.
Programming briefly explained; transmission and audience-orientation likewise.

READING AND READING DISORDERS

Child with a Reading Disorder; Fact Sheet for Parents. Dept. of Health, Educ., and Welfare, 1969. Folder. Free from the Dept.

Important because it emphasizes the fact that reading disability does not totally impair a child's ability to achieve a good deal in areas not related to reading.

Reading Crisis in America. R. L. Holloway. Off. of Educ., 1973. [16] p. il.   017-000-01131-0
The crisis as a "people" problem, and the spawn of underprivilege. Touching pictures of our forgotten young tell us the price they pay for being born underprivileged.

Reading Forum; a Collection of Reference Papers Concerned with Reading Disability. E. O. Calkins, ed. Natl. Inst. of Neurological Diseases and Stroke, NINDS Mono. 11 (1971). 256 p.
017-049-00012-7
Seventeen papers and a directory of remedial reading services.

Relationship between Speech and Reading. I. G. Mattingly and J. F. Kavanagh. Natl. Inst. of Child Health and Human Development, 1973. [72] p. il. Free from the Inst.
Something we take so for granted that it comes as a surprise that its exact mechanism is still largely unknown.

Target for the '70's: You Can Help the Right-to-Read Effort. Off. of Educ., 1974. Folder. Purchase from the Off.
A series of steps the Office of Education offers you, your organization, and your community for assisting in the nation's reading problem. Planning steps; action steps, including some very interesting ideas. Concludes with "activities particularly suited for reading associations." Highly recommended, and its auspices are above reproach!

RECREATION

(Almost) Everything You Ever Wanted to Know about Boating . . . but Were Ashamed to Ask. U.S. Coast Guard, 1972. 24 p. il. Purchase from the Coast Guard.

Questions and answers on everything from personal safety to the various signals to obey if you value your life and your boat. Very amusingly illustrated and excellently executed.

Building Your Safe Campfire; a Guide for Leaders and Youth.
Forest Serv., PA-1017 (1972). [15] p. il.   001-000-02627-5
Booklet can be kept in a small pocket. Importance of learning the simple rules illustrated here lies in the fact that 90 percent of forest fires are caused by man.

Camping in the National Forests, America's Playgrounds. Dept. of Agr., PA 502 [1971]. 16 p. il. Free from the Dept.   001-000-02897-9
Camping is an old American tradition. And our national forests are ideal sites for camping.

Camping in the National Park System. Natl. Park Serv. [1975]. [34] p. il.   024-005-00573-1
Ninety-six areas of the System provide camping facilities; limited camping facilities also in some backcountry areas to accommodate visits by canoeists, hikers, horseback riders, and other outdoor enthusiasts. Alphabetically by state, with very full information in tabular form.

Developing America's Outdoor Recreation Opportunities; Campgrounds. Bur. of Outdoor Recreation, 1972. [22] p. il.
          024-016-00050-1
Very useful booklet for those planning to organize campgrounds. Where and how to get advice and help; and a bibliography. *Not everyman's camping guide!* Repeat: for the organizer.

Guides to Outdoor Recreation Areas and Facilities. Bur. of Outdoor Recreation [1973]. 79 p.   024-016-00064-1
Guide to material published by private, state, and federal organizations.

How Effective Are Your Community Recreation Services? D. M. Fish and others. Bur. of Outdoor Recreation, 1973. [202] p. il.
          024-016-00065-0

Handbook for those engaged in these projects; how to evaluate your projects and their success.

National Forest Vacations. Dept. of Agr., PA 1037 [1973]. 54 p. il. 001-000-02833-2
A booklet that extends a practically irresistible invitation. Not only tells you what can be done in our forest areas, but includes a detailed directory, by state, of these areas and their facilities, costs, and so on. Excellent illustrations. Heartily recommended.

National Scenic and Recreation Trails . . . Bur. of Outdoor Recreation, 1970. [26] p. 024-016-00032-3
A sort of catalog of what such recreation trails offer and where they are; covers the entire country.

Outdoor Recreation; a Legacy for America. Bur. of Outdoor Recreation [1973]. 89 p. il. 024-016-00066-8
How the Government preserves and enlarges that legacy; magnificent illustrations of lovely areas; much statistical data. Very fine. One of the easiest-to-follow books on this subject the compiler has ever seen.

Proceedings, National Symposium on Trails . . . Bur. of Outdoor Recreation [1971]. 132 p. il. 024-016-00042-1
Largely on establishing trails.

Reclamation's Recreational Opportunities. Bur. of Reclamation, 1975. Folder. il. 024-003-00094-9
Handy little directory; recreational information by state.

Recreation Symposium Proceedings . . . Forest Serv., 1971. 211 p. il. Free from the Serv. 001-001-00246-1
Sponsored by the Forest Service, State University of New York College of Forestry, and Pinchot Institute for Environmental Forest Research. A "collection of 26 papers . . . bringing together present knowledge about forest recreation research for recreation use. The Symposium was designed to help meet the need of the planner

and manager in both public and private areas of the forest recreation resources." Every aspect of the subject: including why we have campers and hikers at all. Very fine.

Ski Safely in Your National Forest. Forest Serv., 1971. 6 p. il. Free from the Serv.

Urban Recreation . . . Dept. of Housing and Urban Develop., 1974. 78 p. il. Free from the Dept.
"Report prepared for the Nationwide Outdoor Recreation Plan by the Interdepartmental Work Group on Urban Recreation." Major findings and recommendations of the group. Discussions of recreation in urban settings; evaluating urban recreation; needs and problems; present efforts; future plans. Very fine study.

SCIENCE AND TECHNOLOGY

Directory of Information Resources in the United States: Biological Sciences. Library of Cong., 1972. 577 p.   030-000-00060-9
Based on a register of information sources continuously expanded and updated since 1962. Includes areas of interest, holdings, publications, and information sources for over 2,200 institutions. Subject index.

Directory of Information Resources in the United States: Social Sciences. Library of Cong., 1973. 700 p.   030-000-00065-0

Early Stationary Steam Engines in America; a Study in the Migration of a Technology. C. Pursell. Smithsonian Inst. 152 p. il. Purchase from the Inst.
"The first scholarly history of the transatlantic migration of the steam engine to the American colonies and its subsequent development in the United States."

Eighteenth Century Gunfounding. M. Jackson and C. deBeer. Smithsonian Inst. 200 p. il. Purchase from the Inst.

". . . begins with a discussion of two Dutch masterfounders—Jan and Pieter Verbruggen—in Holland and later at the Royal Brass Foundry in Great Britain during the American War of Independence. 50 contemporary drawings reveal many elements of the art of founding, providing a link between ancient metalworking techniques and later revolutionary developments."

Guide for Care and Use of Laboratory Animals. Natl. Insts. of Health, 1972. 56 p. il.   017-040-00343-9
A handy—and popular—guide among students who work with such small creatures.

Immigrant Scientists in the United States; Study of Characteristics and Attitudes. Natl. Science Found. [1973]. 101 p. il.
038-000-00143-4

Nature of Scientific Discovery. O. Gingerich, ed. Smithsonian Inst., 1974. 400 p. Purchase from the Inst.
Essays derived from the proceedings of the Copernicus Symposium held at the Smithsonian in 1973.

Science Policy; Working Glossary. F. P. Huddle. House of Representatives, 1972. 58 p. Free from the House Document Room.

Science, Public Policy and the Scientist Administrator; an Anthology. Natl. Insts. of Health [1972]. 265 p. il. Free from the Insts.
"Purpose . . . is two-fold . . . to provide the reader with an understanding and at times a critical review of the many . . . complex issues affecting science and public policy. Secondly [to] provide a glimpse into those personalities and forces, both within and without the Government, that bear directly on these issues . . ." Thirty-four essays.

Technology Transfer; a Selected Bibliography; Revised Edition. T. S. Heller and others. Natl. Aeron. and Space Admin., Contractor Rept. 1724 (1971). 175 p. Purchase from the Admin.

A fine introductory note says: ". . . technology is conceived to be technical information and capability, including scientific knowledge, making possible the conception, development, design, production and distribution of goods and services. Transfer here means the movement of science or technology (in either an embodied form or as information only) from one known place to another . . ." Five hundred and sixty-two citations; 65 abstracts of "key" literature.

SEWING

Clothing Repairs. Dept. of Agr., Home and Garden Bull. 107 (1965). 30 p. il.   001-000-00778-5
Salvaging old or damaged garments.

Clothing Speaks; 4-H Member's Guide. R. H. Haines. Fed. Extension Serv., ESC-566 (1970). 55 p. il.   001-005-00005-7
Patterns, sewing hints, and so on, on a learner's level.

How to Tailor a Woman's Suit. Dept. of Agr., Home and Garden Bull. 177 (1968). 24 p. il.   001-000-00836-6
Styles have changed a bit; but thread, needle, scissors, thimble are still in style. This booklet is full of timely hints on home sewing and alteration-making.

Simplified Clothing Construction. Dept. of Agr., Home and Garden Bull. 59 (1967). 32 p. il.   001-000-00847-1
Very good; many detailed instructions and illustrations.

SMALL BUSINESS

Buying and Selling a Small Business. V. A. Bunn. Small Bus. Admin., 1969. 122 p.   045-000-00003-6
With price changes since this was published, some alterations in calculations have to be made. But the sound basic advice is still

there: analyzing the potential market, finding the buyer or seller, figuring price and profits.

EDA Technical Assistance; What It Is; How to Apply. Econ. Develop. Admin. [1974]. 15 p. Free from the Admin.

Export Information Services for U.S. Business Firms. Domestic and Internatl. Bus. Admin. [1974]. 8 p. il. Free from the Admin.

Export Marketing for Smaller Firms. Small Bus. Admin.. 1973. 134 p. il.   045-000-00112-1
Smaller firms often do not think in terms of exporting what they make—an activity that can occasionally be profitable to them. This book tells something of the hows and whys.

Exporting Is Easier Than You Think. Domestic and Internatl. Bus. Admin., 1974. 6 p. Free from the Admin.

Franchise Opportunities Handbook, Sept. 1975. Domestic and Internatl. Bus. Admin., 1973. 188 p.   003-025-00044-6
Detailed listing of companies that franchise.

Key Features of SBA's Principal Lending Programs. Small Bus. Admin. [1972]. 4 p. Free from the Admin.

Loans to Local Development Companies. Small Bus. Admin. [1972]. 11 p. Free from the Admin.

Minority Business Enterprise—A Bibliography, July 1973. [T. M. Haggerty and others, comps.] Minority Bus. Enterprise Off., 1973. 231 p. Free from the Dept. of Commerce.
". . . intended to serve as the basis for what it is hoped will ultimately evolve into a comprehensive and useful research tool for all pertinent references . . . " Divided into five parts: bibliographies; books and monographs; articles, reports, and speeches; directories; and listing of pertinent periodicals. Very fine.

Minority Enterprise; Small Business Investment Company. Small Bus. Admin., 1972. 16 p. Free from the Admin.

1975–76 Directory of United States Trade Shows and Expositions. U.S. Travel Serv., 1975. 59 p. il. Purchase from the Serv.
Five hundred events that will interest the visitor to our shores. (The listing is not intended to be complete.) There is a chronology by month; one by day; and an exhaustive subject listing—listing people to address, where; brief description of the purpose of the fairs; dates and places where they will be held. A mimeographed insert shows recent changes. There is a valuable classified index.

Profit by Your Wholesaler's Services. R. M. Hill. Small Bus. Admin., Small Marketers Aids 140 (1970). 5 p. Free from the Admin.

Questions and Answers on Guaranteed and Direct Loans for Veterans. Veterans Admin., Pamph. 26-4 (1974). 31 p. Free from the Admin.

SBA Business Loans, Lending Objectives, Size Standards, Credit Requirements, Amount and Terms, Collateral Eligibility, How to Apply. Small Bus. Admin. [1973]. 16 p. il. Free from the Admin.
You can't just walk in; you have to have something concrete and practical in mind. This booklet tells you what those practical ideas must be, and how SBA can help you realize them.

SBA Disaster Loans to Restore or Replace Businesses, Homes. Small Bus. Admin. [1971]. 15 p. Free from the Admin.
Try not to let disasters happen; but if one does, SBA is there with practical ideas, and sometimes, financial help.

SBIC Financing for Small Business; Money for Growth: Small Bus. Admin., 1973. 14 p. Free from the Admin.
How you can arrange for a loan from SBA; how you can use it

(if you get it) for venture capital needs and for management help. SBIC stands for Small Business Investment Company.

SBIC: Starting a Small Business Investment Company. Small Bus. Admin., 1974 [1973]. 22 p. Purchase from the Admin.
"Government-backed, flexible financing devices for furnishing equity capital and long-term loan funds for small businesses to operate, grow, and modernize." Every aspect is discussed.

Selected Publications to Aid Domestic Business and Industry. Dept. of Commerce, 1974. 22 p. Free from the Dept.
". . . includes some of the periodicals, reports, and booklets that are available for sale or for reference purposes in the District Office libraries." Free and cost items are cited, under 26 major categories.

Selling to the U.S. Government. Small Bus. Admin. [1973]. 28 p. il. Free from the Admin.

Small Business and the Energy Crisis; Hearings . . . The Senate, 1974. 258 p. il. Free from the Comm.
Before the Subcommittee on Small Business of the Senate's Banking, Housing, and Urban Affairs Committee.

Small Marketers Aids. Small Bus. Admin., 1968–73. Purchase from the Admin.
Some 54 of these handy little hint books are still available, but it has seemed to the compiler that only those issued comparatively recently should be cited here. A full listing is available from the Small Business Administration free. *All titles below are free.*
   71. Checklist for Going into Business. [1972]. [12] p.
      "Here are some questions to help you think through about what you need to know and do [to enter business.] Check each question. If the answer is *yes* [you are all right!] . . . if the answer is *no,* you have some work to do."

131. Retirement Plans for Self-employed Owner Managers. F. J. Costello, Jr., 1968. 8 p.
140. Profit by Your Wholesaler's Services. R. M. Hill. [1970]. 5 p. These are numerous, and can save you time and money.
150. Business Plan for Small Retailers. 1972. [24] p.
". . . designed to help the owner-manager . . . in drawing up business plans."

Starting and Managing Series. Small Bus. Admin., 1968–72.
An invaluable group, particularly at the present time, when so many of the unemployed may be thinking of opening a small shop of their own. The booklets tell you not only where to apply for initial advice, but what problems to anticipate in site location, from competition, cost of advertising, how to appeal most cheaply to the largest clientele, problems of hiring (and the local, county, state, and Federal agencies that may be involved), insurance, and so on. For their length, they are astonishingly informative. Of course, changes in cost since their publication must be considered in reckoning the expenses of founding your own small business. Here, incidentally, the Small Business Administration can be most helpful. The compiler has excluded all titles prior to 1968.

15. Starting and Managing a Swap Shop or Consignment Sale Shop. H. H. Ware. 1968. 78 p. il.   045-000-00061-3
16. Starting and Managing a Small Shoe Service Shop. G. Johnson. 1968. 86 p.   045-000-00062-1
17. Starting and Managing a Small Retail Camera Shop. M. Bragin. 1969.   045-000-00063-0
18. Starting and Managing a Retail Flower Shop. P. R. Krone. 1970. 121 p.   045-000-00064-8
19. Managing a Pet Shop. J. Ross and S. Gores. 1970. 40 p.   045-000-00065-6
20. Starting and Managing a Small Retail Music Store. R. S. Erlandson. 1970. 81 p. il.   045-000-00107-5
21. Starting and Managing a Small Retail Jewelry Store. J. S. MacArthur. 1971. 78 p. il.   045-000-00099-1
22. Starting and Managing an Employment Agency. M. Harper and A. R. Pell. 1971. 118 p. il.   045-000-00109-1

23. Starting and Managing a Small Drive-in Restaurant. F. X. McKenna. 1972. 65 p. il.   045-000-00113-0

Thirty-three Money-saving Ways to Conserve Energy in Your Business. Comm. Dept. [1973]. [8] p. il.   003-000-00413-9

Urban Business Profiles. Econ. Develop. Admin., 1972.
"It is hoped that these reports will serve as a meaningful vehicle to introduce the prospective small urban enterpreneur to selected urban-oriented business. More specifically, a judicious use of the *Profiles* could provide a better understanding of the opportunities, requirements, and problems associated with particular businesses, provide guidleines on types of information required for location-specific feasibility studies, assist urban development groups in their business creation activities." A very helpful group indeed. It is to be hoped it will be continued (perhaps more monosyllabically.)

Bowling Alleys. 22 p.	003-011-00065-8
Building Service Contracting. 28 p.	003-011-00068-2
Children's and Infant's Wear. 14 p.	003-011-00061-5
Contract Construction. 26 p.	003-011-00055-1
Contract Dress Manufacturing. 16 p.	003-011-00067-4

Customs Plastics, Processing Industries, Warm Thermoforming, Cold Stamping, Casting, Foamed Plastics, Fabricating (Thermoforming). 30 p.   003-011-00064-0

Dry Cleaning. 16 p.	003-011-00066-6
Furniture Stores. 20 p.	003-011-00054-2

Industrial Launderers and Linen Supply. 22 p.

003-011-00057-7

Machine Shop Job Work. 23 p.	003-011-00058-5
Mobile Catering. 18 p.	003-011-00060-7
Pet Shops. 24 p.	003-011-00071-2
Photographic Studios. 15 p.	003-011-00069-1
Real Estate Brokerage. 18 p.	003-011-00053-4
Savings and Loan Associations. 24 p.	003-011-00062-3
Supermarkets. 27 p.	003-011-00063-1

Venture Capital; Guide for New Enterprises. A. J. Kelley and others. Agr. and Forestry Comm., the Senate, 1972. 134 p. Free from the Comm.
Prepared by Management Institute, School of Management, Boston College.

SOCIAL SECURITY

The publications of the Social Security Administration are multitudinous, to say the least. They cover in detail every conceivable instance of the application of the laws and regulations that govern the Administration. These *particular* applications are usually available as pamphlets (i.e., *If You're Self-Employed* . . .) *free* from the Administration (more properly from its local offices). Bear in mind that there are probably more recent editions than those cited below.

Basic Readings in Social Security. I. C. Merriam. Social Security Admin., 1970. 181 p.   017-070-00142-4
Partially annotated listing covering literature from the Act of 1935 to the Amendment of 1969.

Brief Explanation of Medicare. Social Security Admin., 1974. [12] p.   017-070-00248-0

Disabled? Find Out about Social Security Disability Benefits. Social Security Admin. [1972]. 10 p. Free from the Admin.

Farmers; How to Report Your Income for Social Security. Social Security Admin. [1972]. 8 p. il.   017-070-00199-8
The compiler cannot find that there is a more recent edition, so presumably the advice is still good.

Help! I'm a Number. Social Security Admin., 1972. 11 p. il. Purchase from the Admin.
What your Social Security number means, now and in the future.

History of the Provisions of Old-Age, Survivors, Disability, and Health Insurance, 1935–1972. Social Security Admin., 1973. 10 p. Free from the Admin.
Not widely known, as it deserves to be. This is a phase of American social history, here told with tables of dates and benefits.

How to Claim Medical Insurance Benefits. Social Security Admin. [1972]. 4 p. Free from the Admin.

How Medicare Helps When You Enter a Hospital. Social Security Admin., 1973. [4] p. Purchase from the Admin.

If You Become Disabled. Social Security Admin. [1975]. 25 p.
017-070-00257-9

Medicaid, Medicare; Which Is Which? Social and Rehab. Serv., 1971. [29] p. 017-064-00007-0
Booklet of basic definitions in a field not entirely clear until you read this booklet.

Medicare; Health Insurance for the Aged. Social Security Admin. [1973]. 017-070-00242-1
With proper understanding of what Medicare (and other sources) offer, the plight of the elderly can be alleviated.

Pocket Guide to Supplemental Security Income. Social Security Admin. 1973. 10 p. Free from the Admin.

Size and Shape of the Medical Care Dollar; Chart Book, 1972. Social Security Admin. [1972]. 36 p. il. 017-070-00222-6
Changes in the costs of health services and supplies, residential care, medical fees, consultations.

Social Security; What It Means to You. Social Security Admin. [1972]. 42 p. il. Free from the Admin.
Payments; costs; family coverage; retirement; disability; death; age. Detailed and clear explanation.

What Your Medicare Insurance Pays. Social Security Admin., 1973. [4] p. Purchase from the Admin.

Your Medicare Handbook; Health Insurance under Social Security, Hospital Insurance. Social Security Admin., SSI 50 (1974). 31 p.   017-070-00228-5
What you have coming to you from various sources, and how to go about securing it.

Your Social Security. Social Security Admin., 1975. 28 p. Free from Consumer Product Information, Pueblo, Colo.

SOIL CONSERVATION

Assistance Available from the Soil Conservation Service. Dept. of Agr., Inform. Bull. 345 (1970). [30] p. il.   001-000-3319-1
Technical assistance to industry, concerned groups, cities—and to even larger entities.

Control of Erosion and Sediment Deposition from Construction of Highways and Land Development. R. E. Thronson. Water Programs Off., 1971. 50 p. il.   055-001-00164-9
"Soils, their attendant pesticides and nutrients, become a liability to water resources management and to the water-using society, and a significant loss to the landowner when stolen from the lands by uncontrolled runoff." Booklet is a very good exposition of this theme, and is studded with thoroughly convincing photographs.

Controlling Erosion on Construction Sites. Dept. of Agr., Agr. Inform. Bull. 347 (1970). 32 p. il.   001-000-01158-8
Each year more than a million acres of land become the sites for new construction.

Soil Erosion; Work of Uncontrolled Water. R. D. Hockensmith and J. G. Steele. Dept. of Agr., Agr. Inform. Bull. 260 (1971). 16 p. il.   001-000-01550-8

Windbreaks for Conservation. A. E. Ferber. Dept. of Agr., Agr. Inform. Bull. 339 (1969). 30 p. il. Free from the Dept.

001-000-00671-1

SOLAR HEATING

There is a good deal available on solar heating. The compiler has chosen the one title below as most comprehensive.

Solar Home Heating and Cooling Demonstration Act, 1974; Hearings . . . The Senate, 1974. 343 p. il. Free from the Comm.
Hearings before the Special Subcommittee on National Science Foundation, of the Senate's Committee on Labor and Public Welfare. The text of the Act is followed by testimony of experts. Included in their discussions are plans, cross sections, and many tables. The compiler has chosen this *one* title as being very comprehensive.

SOLID WASTE DISPOSAL

Let's Dump the Dump; the ABC's of Solid Waste Management. Environ. Protect. Agency [1972]. [16] p. il. Free from the Agency. Another of the valuable picture-book treatments of an important subject. In this case, the pictures are semicomic drawings.

Manual of Septic Tank Practice. Public Health Serv., 1969. 92 p. il. 017-001-00177-5
Very good; *but* for large establishments.

Policies for Solid Waste Management. Bur. of Solid Waste Management., 1970. 64 p. 017-014-00006-4
Maintains that solid wastes differ from air and water pollutants and must be managed differently. Investigates, evaluates, and makes recommendations for the future. Ecology students will find this booklet very useful.

Soils and Septic Tanks. W. H. Bender. Dept. of Agr., Agr. Inform. Bull. 349 (1971). 12 p. il   001-000-01023-9
How soil must be taken into account.

Solving the Abandoned Car Problem in Small Communities. W. T. Dehn. Environ. Protect. Agency, 1974. 23 p. il.   055-002-00119-0

SURVEYING

Elements of Surveying. Dept. of the Army, Tech. Manual 5-232 (1971). 304 p. il.   008-020-00388-3
Instruments, equipment; their use; measuring; leveling; traversing; triangulation; land surveys.

Surveying Our Public Lands. Bur. of Land Management, 1969. 16 p. il.   024-011-00007-1
"The story of public land surveys in the United States."

TAXES AND TAXATION

Armed Forces Federal Income Tax for 1975 Income Tax Returns; 1976 ed. Dept. of the Navy, 1976. Issued annually.

             008-044-00025-2
Exemptions you may claim if you are in the Armed Forces— enough to delight any fighting man. Note that this is *not* an Internal Revenue Service publication.

INTERNAL REVENUE SERVICE
TAX INFORMATION PUBLICATONS

These publications are issued annually.

501. Your Exemptions and Exemptions for Dependents.
             048-004-00814-9

531. Reporting Your Tips for Federal Tax Purposes.

048-004-00853-0

532. Filing and Dependency Information for Students and Parents. 048-004-00825-4

533. Information on Self-Employment Tax. 048-004-00854-8

534. Tax Information on Depreciation. 048-004-00855-6

535. Tax Information on Business Expenses. 048-004-00856-4

536. Losses From Operating a Business. 048-004-00857-2

537. Installment and Deferred Payment Sales. 048-004-00858-1

538. Tax Information on Accounting Periods and Methods.

048-004-00859-9

539. Withholding Taxes from Your Employees Wages.

048-004-00860-2

540. Tax Information on Repairs, Replacements and Improvements. 1975. 048-004-00861-1

541. Tax Information on Partnership Income and Losses.

048-004-00862-9

542. Corporations and the Federal Income Tax.

048-004-00863-7

543. Sale or Other Disposition of a Business Interest.

048-004-00864-5

544. Sales on Other Dispositions of Assets. 048-004-00865-3

545. Income Tax Deductions for Interest Expense.

048-004-00826-2

546. Income Tax Deductions for Taxes. 1975. 048-004-00866-1

547. Tax Information on Disasters, Casualty Losses and Thefts. 1975. 048-004-00867-0

548. Tax Information on Deductions for Bad Debts. 1975.

048-004-00868-8

549. Condemnations of Private Property for Public Use.

048-004-00869-6

550. Tax Information on Investment Income and Expenses.

048-004-00870-0

552. Recordkeeping Requirements and a Guide to Tax Publications. 048-004-00827-1

553. Highlights of 1975 Changes in the Tax Law.

048-004-00828-9

585. Voluntary Tax Methods to Help Finance Political Campaigns.
048-004-00888-2
586. The Collection Process. 1975. 048-004-00809-2
    586/span. Spanish ed. 048-004-01281-2
587. Tax Information on Operating a Business in Your Home.
048-004-00889-1
588. Tax Information on Condominiums and Co-operative Apartments. 048-004-00890-4
589. Tax Information on Subchapter Corporations.
048-004-00891-2
590. Tax Information on Individual Retirement Savings Programs.
1975. 048-004-00811-4
591. Tax Information on Credit for Home Purchase. 1975.
048-004-00808-4
592. The Federal Gift Tax. 1975. 048-004-00813-1

Information on Preparing Your Tax Return. . . . Internal Rev. Serv. Issued annually. 32 p. 048-004-00852-1

Tax Guide for Small Business; Individuals, Partnerships, Corporations; Income, Excise, and Unemployment Taxes for Use in Preparing Your 1973 Returns. Internal Revenue Serv. Purchase from the Serv.
Issued annually.

Your Income Tax, for Individuals, for Use in Preparing Your Returns. Internal Revenue Serv. Purchase from the Serv.
Issued annually.

TELEVISION

Surgeon General's Report by the Scientific Advisory Committee on Television and Social Behavior; Hearings . . . The Senate, 1972. 2 vols. Free from the Comm.
Vol. 1 is 306 p.; Vol. 2 is [307-526]p. A monumental study of the social effects of television. Letters, documents, testimony by ex-

perts. Vol. 2 consists of three absorbing studies: "Violence Index; a Rating of Various Aspects of Dramatic Violence on Prime-Time and Network Television, 1967 Through 1970"(G. Gerbner); "Economics of Network Children's Television Programming" (A. Pearce); "The Violence Profile; Some Indicators of the Trends in and the Symbolic Structure of Network Television Drama, 1967–71" (G. Gerbner). Note that Vol. 2 is Appendix A.

Television and Growing Up; the Impact of Televised Violence; a Report to the Surgeon General . . . from the Surgeon General's Scientific Advisory Committee on Television and Social Behavior. Public Health Serv., 1971 [1972]. 279 p. il.   017-024-00186-4
"All the available statistics confirm the pervasive role television plays in the United States, if not throughout the world."

Violence on Television; Hearings . . . The Senate, 1974. 194 p. il. Purchase from the Comm.
Hearings before the Subcommittee on Communications, Committee on Commerce. The background of the investigation is briefly noted: it goes back to 1972, and is based upon the conclusion of the Surgeon General's Committee that "the causal relationship between televised violence and antisocial behavior is sufficient to warrant appropriate and immediate remedial measures." (The Surgeon General's staff then prepared and published *Television and Growing Up* [which see]). The Committee then discusses follow-up work. Government officials, university personnel, television administrators, and industry spokesmen are heard from.

TEXTILES

Textile Conservation. J.E. Leene, ed. Smithsonian Inst. 266 p. il. Purchase from the Inst.
"Aimed primarily at the restorers of textiles, curators and scientists, the book contains twenty chapters by leading European and American authorities. Subjects include basic information on the characteristics of textiles and dyestuffs, the principles of cleaning,

and the practice of conservation and restoration of textiles, lace, beadwork, featherwork and leather."

TIME

Standard Time in the United States; History of Standard and Daylight Saving Time in the United States and Analysis of Related Laws. Dept. of Transportation, 1970. 27 p. il.

050-000-00024-9

Standard Time Zone Chart of the World . . . Mercator Projection. Naval Oceanographic Off., Pub. 5192 (1970).   008-042-00018-7 Colored chart 36" x 54". Scale is 1:39,000,000 at the Equator.

TRANSPORTATION

Bibliographic List. Dept. of Transportation, 1969–71. Purchase from the Dept.

These are prepared by the Library Services Division of the Office of Administration Operations within the Department itself. All are partially annotated. Through 1971, seven titles had been issued.

1. Transportation for the Handicapped. 1969. 26 p.
2. Aircraft Noise and Sonic Boom. 1969. 41 p.
3. Department of Transportation; Selected Readings. A. O'Brien, comp. 1970. 15 p.
   Partially annotated; 77 references.
4. Airport Problems; Access and Air Traffic Congestion; Selected Readings. M. R. Haywood, comp. 1971. 34 p.
5. Hijacking; Selected Readings. 1971. 53 p.
6. Urban Mass Transportation. D. E. Willis, comp. 140 p.
7. Aircraft and Air Pollution; Selected Readings. D. J. Poehlman, comp. 1971. 61 p.

Economic and Social Effects of Highways; Summary and Analysis. Fed. Highway Admin., 1972. 104 p. il.   050-001-00036-9

"Highlights the matters of current concern, such as land development patterns at interchanges, effects of highways in aiding an
underdeveloped area, residential experience with the highways . . .
and trends in rates of home mortgage foreclosures . . ." Also includes directory material. Made up from some 200 reports.

Highway Joint Development and Multiple Use. Bur. of Public
Roads [1970]. 126 p. il.   050-002-00080-2
Status report on multiple use of highway right of way for projects
such as parking facilities, school areas, business sections, shopping
centers, and so on.

Interstate System Route Log & Finder List. Federal Highway
Admin. [1971]. 40 p. il.   050-001-00019-5
Guide to the 42,500 mile network of rural and urban freeways
known as the National System of Interstate Defense Highways.

**1972 National Transportation Report; Present State; Future Alterna-
tives.** Dept. of Transportation, 1972. 437 p. il.

050-000-00058-3
Comprehensive report on the nation's transportation system, with
outlook and guidelines for the future. Packed with charts and
statistics.

1974 Driver License; Administrative Regulations and Fees. Federal
Highway Admin., 1974. Purchase from the Admin.
Will be replaced by the time this edition of this *Guide* appears.
But be sure to get it, if you drive. It tabulates the regulations,
the qualifications needed to obtain licenses in the fifty states and
District of Columbia; and driver license content and driver im-
provement provisions. (Valuable information, but *exceedingly* small
print.)

Passenger Car License Plates, 1975. Fed. Highway Admin. [1975].
[4] p. il.   050-001-00095-4
A later issue will probably be available by the time this *Guide*

appears. However, you will be sent the latest edition if you request the title. Illustrations in color show every state license, and the text gives every bit of conceivable information.

Smithsonian Collection of Automobiles and Motorcycles. Smithsonian Inst. 164 p. il. Purchase from the Inst.
"Here are descriptions and illustrations of the more than 40 automobiles, trucks, and self-powered cycles dating from 1869 that make up the museum's outstanding collection."

Social and Economic Effects of Highways. Fed. Highway Admin., 1974. 180 p. Free from the Admin.   050-001-00075-0
Includes a 1975 supplement of 25 pages. ". . . shows some of the problems as well as the progress of social and economic studies dealing with effects of highways on individuals, communities, and regions . . ." Includes a series of papers by consultants on the social and economic effects of highways. Also draws on experience of other areas, and on no less than 200 or more highway impact studies. Tentative conclusions for meeting some of the problems are given. Very good.

Transportation and New Energy Policies; Hearings . . . The Senate, 1974. 671 p. il. Free from the Comm.
Hearings before the Subcommittee on Transportation of the Senate's Public Works Committee.

Transportation Planning and Priorities for the Seventies; Hearings . . . 2 parts. The Senate, 1974. Free from the Comm.
Before the Subcommittee on Transportation of the Senate's Public Works Committee.
    Part 1. 126 p. il.
    Part 2. 177 p. il.

Urban Freeway Surveillance and Control; the State of the Art. P. F. Everall. Federal Highway Admin., 1973. 177 p. il.
                                                    050-001-00058-0
For a very small group, admittedly (those concerned with traffic

flow), but several chapters lend this book more general interest. Freeway problems and their causes are discussed; and some suggestions are made for relieving a growing problem.

Urban Transportation Needs; a Series of 8 Lectures . . . Dept. of Transportation [1972]. 56 p. il. Free from the Dept.
Lectures given at the Center for New York City Affairs, New School for Social Research, by the Department of Transportation. They cover economic problems; environmental and urban issues; safety and cargo security; the consumer in transportation; urban transportation and the law; political and institutional factors; and new and renewed systems.

Wheels and Wheeling; the Smithsonian Cycle Collection. S. H. Oliver and D. H. Berkebile. Smithsonian Inst. 104 p. il. Purchase from the Inst.
"The bicycle is now accepted as a permanent and important factor in American transportation. It was not always so, and this amusing and informative volume traces the bicycle's development and the social scene surrounding its progress."

TRAVEL

Festival, U.S.A., 1976. U.S. Travel Serv., 1976. 66 p.
003-012-00027-1
Detailed listing of United States fairs, exhibitions, etc., by date and state.

Visa Requirements for Foreign Governments. Dept. of State [1975]. 8 p.   044-000-01561-7

You and Your Passport. Dept. of State [1974]. 16 p. il.
044-000-01480-7

Youth Travel Abroad; What to Know Before You Go. Dept. of State, Genl. Foreign Policy Ser. 263 [1974]. 20 p. il.
044-000-01571-4

CUSTOMS

Customs Highlights for Government Personnel (Civilian and Military). Bur. of Customs, 1973. Folder. il.   048-002-00034-8

Importing a Car; U.S. Customs. Bur. of Customs [1972]. [9] p. il.   048-002-00032-3

Know Before You Go; Customs Hints for Returning U.S. Residents. Bur. of Customs, 1974. 30 p. il.   048-002-00039-1

Pets; Wildlife; Customs. Bur. of Customs [1973]. 7 p. il. Free from the Bur.

Travellers: So You Want to Import a Pet. Bur. of Customs [1970]. [8] p. il. Free from the Bur.
The rules you have to abide by.

United States Customs Hints for Visitors (Nonresidents). Bur. of Customs [1972]. [3] p. il.   048-02-00038-2

U.S. Customs Trademark Information. Bur. of Customs, 1974. Folder. Purchase from the U.S. Customs Serv.

POCKET GUIDES

Armed Forces Information and Education [Office] Pocket Guides. 1969–73.
Only six remain of this excellent and once extensive group of guides meant to tell something of foreign countries to our armed forces stationed abroad.

Great Britain. 1973. 70 p. il.   008-001-00095-2
Japan. 1970. 116 p. il.   008-001-00005-7
Korea. 1970. 106 p. il.   008-001-00006-5

Low Countries (Netherlands, Belgium, Luxembourg). 1970. 127
p. il.   008-001-00007-3
Philippines. 1969. 84 p. il.   008-001-00009-0
Vietnam. 1971. 90 p. il.   008-001-00011-1

UNITED STATES: THE BUDGET

Budget of the United States Government; Fiscal Year 1976. Off.
of Management and Budget, 1976. 384 p.   041-001-00094-1
". . . contains the information that most users of the Budget would
normally need, including the Budget Message of the President.
The book presents an overview of the President's budget proposals, which includes explanations of spending programs and estimated receipts. The document also contains a description of the
budget system and various summary tables . . ." Nine detailed
parts.

——**Appendix.** [1975]. 1092 p.   041-001-00095-0
". . . contains more detailed information than any of the other
budget documents. It includes for each agency the proposed text
of appropriation language, budget schedules for each account, explanations of the work to be performed and the funds needed,
proposed general provisions applicable to the appropriations of
entire agencies . . . and schedules of permanent positions. Supplemental proposals for the current year and new legislative proposals are identified separately . . ." For ordinary readers, far too
detailed.

——**United States Budget in Brief . . . 1976.** 64 p. 041-001-00096-8
". . . provides a more concise, less technical overview of the 1976
Budget than do the other volumes. Summary and historical tables
on the Federal budget and debt are also provided, together with
graphic displays."

——**Special Analyses. . . .** [1975]. 281 p.   041-001-00097-6
". . . contains 17 special analyses that are designed to highlight
specified program areas or provide other significant presentations of

Federal budget data." This document "contains analytical information about: Government finances and operations as a whole and how they affect the economy; Government-wide program and financial information for Federal education, manpower, health, income security, civil rights, and crime reduction programs; trends and developments in the areas of Federal aid to State and local governments, research and development, and environmental protection."

UNITED STATES: DEPARTMENTS AND AGENCIES

Below are listed titles descriptive of governmental departments and agencies—their functions and so on. For works descriptive of the government as an *entire,* active entity that enters every part of your life, see "United States: Government," below.

Organization of Federal Executive Departments and Agencies. The Senate, 1973. Chart.   052-070-02844-1
Chart is 36" x 44", prepared by the Committee on Government Operations, the Senate. An indispensable *vade mecum,* showing the interrelationships of something like 1,000 agencies, Departments, Bureaus, Offices, etc. Unreservedly recommended.

United States Government Manual, 1975–76. Federal Register Off. [1975]. 831 p.   022-003-00910-8
One of the most useful and popular government publications, this is the official handbook of the three branches of the Federal Government. Describes the purpose of Government programs, emphasizing their activities rather than their structures. Lists top personnel. Includes a new "Guide to Government Information," and is excellently indexed, with useful appendices.

DEPARTMENT OF AGRICULTURE

Your United States Department of Agriculture; How It Serves People on the Farm and in the Community, Nation, World. Dept. of Agr., PA 824 [1974]. 14 p. Free from the Dept.

The Department was created in 1862, and has been at its good work ever since. This book gives some idea of its works and workings. Included is a chart of organization.

DEPARTMENT OF COMMERCE

Fourteen Ways the U.S. Department of Commerce Can Help You Make Your Business More Profitable. Bur. of Internatl. Commerce. [1974]. 11 p. il. Free from the Dept. of Commerce.

National Bureau of Standards. Natl. Bur. of Standards, Spec. Publ. 367 [1972]. 64 p. il.   003-003-01053-7

NOAA Story. Natl. Oceanic and Atmospheric Admin. [1973]. 67 p. il. Free from the Admin.   003-017-00084-2
The functions and activities of one of our most interesting agencies.

Operations of the Weather Bureau. Weather Bur., 1969. 226 p. il. Free from the Natl. Weather Serv.
Description of activities in detail. Of the functions of the Bureau, the meteorological and hydrological operations are said to be unique. An annual edition is planned.

United States Department of Commerce; Serving a Growing Economy and a Growing People. Dept. of Commerce, 1974. 26 p. il. Free from the Dept.
Contains an organizational chart showing the functions of each agency within the Department.

DEPARTMENT OF DEFENSE

Armed Forces Report, 1973; Serving the Nation. Dept. of Defense, 1973. [32] p. il. Free from the Dept.
The kind of report that belongs, in particular, in school libraries because it tells a good deal of what each of the Armed Forces does (and particularly how they discharge their functions *other*

than military in their service to the people). Illustrations are very fine.

DEPARTMENT OF HEALTH, EDUCATION, AND WELFARE

Common Thread of Service: Historical Guide to HEW. Dept. of Health, Educ., and Welfare [1972]. 52 p. il.   017-000-00113-2

Grants; Policy Statement. Pub. Health Serv., 1974. 74 p.

017-020-00055-2

The "basic framework within which grantee institutions and Public Health Service agencies are expected to operate . . ." How to apply; costs; changing your project; how to write a report, etc.

HEW . . . People Serving People. Dept. of Health, Educ., and Welfare [1970]. 41 p. il. Free from the Dept.

A "profile" of the Department's many agencies and activities.

National Institute of Education; Brief Outline of Its History, Status, and Tentative Plans. Natl. Inst. of Educ., 1973. 27 p. Free from the Inst.

National Institutes of Health; Profile. R. J. Maselka. Natl. Insts. of Health [1973]. [25] p. il. Free from the Insts.

Compilation of fourteen articles in the Buffalo (N.Y.) *Evening News,* Feb. 19, 1972, to Aug. 8, 1973.

Profile of the United States Public Health Service, 1798–1948. B. Furman [and R. C. Williams]. Public Health Serv., 1973. 487 p. il.   017-052-00140-0

The Service dates back to an Act for the Relief of Sick and Disabled Seamen, July 16, 1798. Profusely illustrated, with most interesting text.

This Is the Office of Education. Off. of Educ., 1970. [12] p. Free from the Off.

DEPARTMENT OF HOUSING AND
URBAN DEVELOPMENT

How About HUD? Dept. of Housing and Urban Develop., 1971. Folder. Free from the Dept.

DEPARTMENT OF THE INTERIOR

Bureau of Outdoor Recreation; Focal Point for Your Outdoor America. Bur. of Outdoor Recreation [1975]. 20 p. il.
024-016-00075-7

United States Department of the Interior, America's Guardian of Natural Resources. Dept. of the Interior, 1972. 35 p. il.
024-000-00646-8
A description—with excellent illustrations—of the various bureaus of the Department and what they do. Illustrations, by the way, are not of the Department but of America's natural beauties.

DEPARTMENT OF JUSTICE

FBI Laboratory, 1972; a Brief Outline of the History, the Services, and the Operating Techniques of the World's Greatest Scientific Crime Laboratory. Fed. Bur. of Investigation, 1972. [35] p. il. Free from the Bur.
The laboratories and how they work. Particularly interesting are the stories from the lab's files on criminal cases—several of which are related. The lab has many times proved guilt—and many times innocence.

Know Your FBI. Fed. Bur. of Investigation [1970]. 24 p. il. Free from the Bur.

99 Facts about the FBI. Fed. Bur. of Investigation [1972]. 26 p. il. Free from the Bur.

Story of the Federal Bureau of Investigation. Fed. Bur. of Investigation [1974]. 21 p. il. Free from the Bur.
"The purpose of this report is to acquaint the youth of America with the work of the FBI." The story is told, and illustrated, fascinatingly. Particularly interesting are the stories (all too briefly told) of how the Bureau solved some of its hardest and most famous cases.

United States Department of Justice; Functions and Organization. Dept. of Justice, 1970. [51] p. il. Free from the Dept.

DEPARTMENT OF LABOR

Origin of the U.S. Department of Labor. J. Grossman. Dept. of Labor, 1973. 7 p. il. Free from the Dept.
A reprint from the *Monthly Labor Review* of March 4, 1973. The Department was signed into existence on March 4, 1913.

DEPARTMENT OF STATE

Biographical Register (Department of State, U.S. Mission to the United Nations, Agency for International Development, Action [Peace Corps], U.S. Arms Control and Disarmament Agency, U.S. Information Agency, Foreign Agricultural Service, Overseas Private Investment Corporation), 1972. Dept. of State. Dept. and Foreign Serv. Ser. 126 (1972). 434 p.   044-000-01490-4
Revised as of June 30, 1973. Thousands of brief biographical notices on State Department and other Federal employees in the field of foreign affairs.

Your Department of State. Dept. of State. Dept. and Foreign Serv. Ser. 124 (1970). 16 p. il.   044-000-01260-0
"The official channel through which the American people conduct their relations with the other governments and peoples of the world." How the Department carries on its work; some staggering statistics are cited.

DEPARTMENT OF TRANSPORTATION

U.S. Department of Transportation—Facts and Functions. Dept. of Transportation. 1971. [37] p. il. Purchase from the Dept.
Each of the agencies is described. Illustrations show we are a nation perpetually on the go.

DEPARTMENT OF THE TREASURY

Secret Service Story. Dept. of the Treasury, [n.d.]. [8] p. il. Purchase from the Dept.
The Service was created in 1865, as a result of rather rampant forgery. (It was difficult at that time to detect one of the 4,000 varieties of counterfeit notes from the 7,000 varieties of genuine notes!) The functions of the Service have increased since that time, and its newer duties are briefly described.

What the Treasury Does. Dept. of the Treasury [1970]. 8 p. il. Free from the Dept.

UNITED STATES POSTAL SERVICE

Consumer's Guide to Postal Services and Products. U.S. Postal Serv., Pub. 201 (1974). 16 p. il. Free from the Serv.
The new United States Postal Service dates to 1971. This fine brochure tells something of its problems, its vast work, and what it can do (and does) do for you.

Directory of Post Offices (with ZIP Codes). U.S. Postal Serv. 1974.
039-000-00247-7

Information. U.S. Postal Serv., 1973. 35 p. Free from the Serv.
A brief history; includes a list of Postmasters General, beginning

with Benjamin Franklin. Discusses the 1969 reform activities from which emerged the U.S. Postal Service. Finally, a history of the accomplishments of this latest Service.

Mailer's Guide; April, 1974. U.S. Postal Serv. [1974]. 47 p. Purchase from the Serv.
The Service employs nearly 700,000 persons. This is a guide to what they offer you—every conceivable bit of information about mailing rates, types of classes, packing, etc. Fine booklet.

Mr. Zip; Who He Is, What He Does. Post Office Dept. [1969]. Folder. il. Free from the Postal Serv.

National Zip Code Directory, 1975–76. U.S. Postal Serv. [1973]. 1807 p.   039-000-00252-3
Probably every library, and every other place that can use this, already has it; but how does one leave it out of a "popular guide?"

Neither Snow, nor Rain . . . Story of the United States Mails. C. H. Scheele and C. Minikin. Smithsonian Inst., 1970. 99 p. li.
                                                                                047-000-00091-2
Told with excellent drawings and photographs.

Packaging for Mailing. U.S. Postal Serv., 1973. [16] p. il. Free from the Serv.

Short History of the Mail Service. C. H. Scheele. Smithsonian Inst. 229 p. il. Purchase from the Inst.
" . . provides Old World background for a comprehensive description of the United States mail service from colonial times to the present."

What Mailers Should Do to Get the Best Service: Preparation; Timing; Coordination. U.S. Postal Serv., Pub. 153 (1970). 12 p. il. Free from the Serv.
". . . mailers can help themselves to better service by improving their own mailing practices." Here are some hints.

Your New United States Postal Service. U.S. Postal Serv., n.d. Folder. Free from the Serv.

We send out annually 82,000,000,000 pieces of mail—almost as much as all of the rest of the world combined. This booklet outlines new ideas and programs—new ways for serving you and ways of helping pay for all this service.

VETERANS ADMINISTRATION

VA: What It is, Was, and Does: VA History in Brief. Veterans Admin., VA Pamph. 06-72-1 (1972). [16] p. Free from the Admin.

UNITED STATES: THE FLAG

How to Respect and Display Our Flag. Marine Corps [1968]. 32 p. il. Free from the Corps.

Includes an illustrated history of the flag—from the Revolution, and in color.

Our Flag. House of Representatives . . . [1970]. 32 p. il. Purchase from the House Document Room.

91st Congress, 1st Session; House Doc. 209.

Star Spangled Banner. Smithsonian Inst., 1964. 16 p. il. Purchase from the Inst.

Handsomely illustrated story of our flag.

This Is Our Flag; Be Proud of It. Post Office Dept., 1970. Colored poster.   039-000-00141-1

United States Flag for Burial or Memorial Purposes. Veterans Admin., 1970. 9 p. Free from the Admin.

Circumstances that qualify; presentation of the flag; agencies that issue it; methods of draping; replacement.

UNITED STATES: FOREIGN POLICY AND INTERNATIONAL RELATIONS

This section deals with our policies toward other nations and not within nations themselves. For those, see "International Relations," above.

Chiefs of Mission as of July 1, 1975. Dept. of State, 1975. 9 p. Free from the Dept.
The personnel as of this date—not a historical listing.

Foreign Consular Offices in the United States, 1973. Dept. of State. Dept. and Foreign Serv. Ser. 128 (1973). 100 p.   044-000-01589-7
An annual; by the time this edition of this *Guide* appears, there will be an updated edition. This will be sent automatically, since the series and series number remain constant.

Future Directions of U.S. Policy towards Southern Rhodesia; Hearings . . . House of Representatives, 1973. 200 p.

052-070-01884-4

Before the Subcommittee on Africa of the Subcommittee on International Organizations and Movements (Committee on Foreign Affairs). Reprints remarkable documents covering economic conditions in Southern Rhodesia, and cites our efforts, including sanctions, to better the situation.

Multinational Corporations and United States Foreign Policy; Hearings . . . The Senate, 1973–74. 10 parts.
This profound—and lengthy—study is an exhaustive study of the potentially dangerous situation that may arise when a comparatively limited number of giant corporations begin to become acquisitive around the world. The very heartening thing about these hearings is the complete freedom with which every shade of opinion is expressed; and many economists are most certainly agreed that

multinational corporations are not necessarily a bad idea. The present study, in so far as it can be almost casually annotated, examines the possible impact of these supergiant corporations on the foreign policy of the United States (and, by implication, on the foreign policies of almost any other country in the world). Parts 1 and 2 are out of print.

3. Overseas Private Investment Corporation (OPIC). 1973 [1974]. 651 p. il.   052-070-02169-1
4. Executive Session. 1974. 214 p. il.   052-070-02357-1
5. Multinational Petroleum Companies and Foreign Policy. 1974. 296 p.   052-070-02434-8
6. Appendix to Part 5. 1974. 347 p.   052-070-02497-6
7. Multinational Petroleum Companies and Foreign Policy. 1974. 594 p. il.   052-070-02609-0
8. Appendix to Part 7. 1975. 773 p.   052-070-02870-0
9. Multinational Petroleum Companies and Foreign Policy. 1974 [1975]. 281 p.   052-070-02985-4
10. Investments by Multinational Companies in the Communistic Bloc Countries. 1975. 405 p.   052-070-02986-2

Persian Gulf, 1974: Money, Politics, Arms, and Power; Hearings . . . House of Representatives, 1974 [1975]. 267 p.
052-070-02769-0
Before the Subcommittee on the Near East and South Asia, of the House's Committee on Foreign Affairs. A very detailed review of our involvement in this area that became a "major policy concern" for the United States in 1974.

Relief and Rehabilitation of War Victims in Indochina; Hearings . . . The Senate, 1973. 2 pts. Free from the Comm.
Hearings were before the Subcommittee to Investigate Problems Connected with Refugees and Escapees, of the Committee on the Judiciary. Findings are based upon testimony of individuals who visited the areas, or of groups active in relief work.
Part 1. Crisis in Cambodia. 143 p.
Part 2. Orphans and Child Welfare. 107 p.

Two Weeks . . . Dept. of State, Genl. Foreign Policy Ser. 236 (1969). 35 p. il.   044-000-00225-6

Charmingly illustrated account of President Nixon's world-ranging activities in just two weeks in the summer of 1969. He talked in Washington to men on the moon, welcomed them home to earth in the Pacific; visited Romania; completed a flight around the world. (Two billion people are estimated to have heard that moon-talk.)

United States Chiefs of Mission, 1778–1973. R. Dougall and M. P. Chapman. State Dept., Dept. and For. Service Ser. 147 (1973). 229 p.   044-000-01492-1

Our foreign representatives from the Revolution to March 31, 1973.

United States–Republic of China Relations; Hearings . . . House of Representatives, 1971. 84 p. Free from the Comm.

The testimony of five witnesses before the Foreign Affairs Committee; text of the Mutual Defense Treaty between U.S. and the Republic of China; a number of pertinent official statements.

U.S. Foreign Policy for the 1970's; a Comparative Analysis of the President's Foreign Policy Report to Congress. House of Representatives, 1972. 96 p. Free from the House Document Room.

Prepared for the Committee on Foreign Affairs by the Congressional research staff of the Library of Congress. The practice of the President's making this report dates to 1970. The present work compares the 1972 with the 1970 and 1971 reports, as well as with other documents and data. Invaluable. (The Senate also issued this document in 1972; available from the Senate Document Room.)

U.S. Foreign Policy for the 1970's; a New Strategy for Peace. R. M. Nixon. Off. of the President, 1970. 160 p.   040-000-00183-2

Prior to this speech, it had been the custom for the President to address the Congress on "special aspects" of foreign affairs. This title represents something new—a "comprehensive report" to the Congress on the foreign policy of the Administration as a whole.

Volunteers in ACTION, Peace Corps, VISTA. ACTION, Action Pamph. 4000-8 [1973]. 46 p. il. Free from ACTION.
Beautifully designed and illustrated booklet that describes the activities of the Peace Corps, VISTA, UYA, SCORE, AGE, RSVP, Foster Grandparents, and Senior Companion programs.

UNITED STATES: GEOGRAPHY

American Samoa. Dept. of the Interior [1973]. [7] p. il. Free from the Dept.

America's Islands. Natl. Ocean Survey, 1974. 31 p. il. Free from the Survey.
Classification of islands from Hawaii to the Florida Keys; islands for recreation; island preservation. Appendixes list: Hawaiian Islands; fifty largest islands adjacent to contiguous U.S.; fifty largest Alaskan islands; charts and information. For any age group.

Dictionary of Alaska Place Names. D. J. Orth. Geol. Survey, Prof. Paper 567 (1967). 1084 p. il.   024-001-00702-9
Colored maps. Wherever possible, the origin of the names (and there are thousands!) is cited, along with exact latitude and longitude.

Elevations and Distances in the United States. Geol. Survey, [1974]. 22 p. il.   024-001-00349-0
Very handy statistical booklet; indicates distances within the United States, and where highest (and lowest) spots occur in each state.

Guam. Dept. of the Interior [1973]. [7] p. il. Free from the Dept.

Islands of America. Bur. of Reclamation, 1970. 95 p. il.
                     024-016-00031-5
Great deal of interesting data, and magnificent photographs.

Territorial Areas Administered by the United States. Dept. of the Interior 1973. 22 p. Purchase from the Dept.
Caribbean and Pacific areas; includes reduced maps.

Trust Territories. Dept. of the Interior [1973]. Folder. il. Free from the Dept.   024-007-00027-8
What a Trust Territory is. A rough map indicates the extent of the Pacific group, which occurs over an area in the Pacific Ocean roughly equivalent to the land mass of the United States.

U.S. County Outline Map, 1970. Bur. of the Census, 1971.
                                                                                     003-001-01896-9
Boundaries of counties and county equivalents as of Jan. 1, 1970. Map 28" x 41".

Virgin Islands. Dept. of the Interior [1973]. [5] p. il. Free from the Dept.

UNITED STATES: GOVERNMENT

Titles that deal with the actual *workings* of our government are cited here—also some that are not entirely devoted to descriptions of departments and agencies.

Executive Privilege; Secrecy in Government; Freedom of Information; Hearings . . . The Senate, 1973. 3 vols.
Hearings before the Subcommittee on Intergovernmental Relations of the Senate's Committee on Government Relations. Not for the average reader. An exhaustive study, including the testimony of experts in every field of the subject. Vol. 2 is out of print.
    Vol. 1. 537 p. il.   052-070-01997-2
    Vol. 3. 620 p. This volume is an appendix.   052-070-02165-9

Federalism in 1974; the Tension of Interdependence. Advisory Commission on Intergovernmental Relations, 1974. 25 p.
                                                                                     052-004-00061-6
"The Commission is the 'only official monitor of the workings of our Federal system . . .'" This is a summary of the 1974 governmental year. A fine work, particularly interesting because diverse views

are expressed frankly. (There was plainly no censorship.) The report is encouraging because it shows how the country survived a major crisis; it represents the Commission's "best consensus" on our economy, energy, federal mandating, changes in federal aid, and governmental accountability (these are the main division of the report).

International Economic Report of the President, Together with the Annual Report of the Council on International Economic Policy. [President of the United States], 1975. 166 p.   041-015-00072-1
Detailed statistical study, the third Economic Report. In three parts: progress toward achieving the nation's international economic goals; current international economic issues; Appendix—the report to the President on activities and conclusions of the International Economic policy during 1974.

THE CONGRESS

Congressional District Atlas (Districts of the 93rd Congress). Bur. of the Census [1973]. [357] p. il.   003-024-00106-3
Shows the boundaries of all Congressional districts.
——Supplement for Districts of the 94th Congress [64] p. 1975.
003-024-01052-2

Congressional Pictorial Directory. 94th Congress, Jan., 1975. The Congress, 1975. 202 p. il.   052-070-01658-2
Biographical data, and photographs of members.

History and Operations of the House Majority Whip Organization. House of Representatives, 1973. 16 p. il. Free from the House Document Room.
This is House Document 93-126. It tells, briefly, how "order in the House" developed and is maintained.

Official Congressional Directory . . . for the Use of the United States Congress. [1976]. The Congress. Issued annually.
052-070-03117-4

Complete listing, including biographical material, of both Houses; all the chief personnel of Departments and national agencies; with addresses. International agencies; consular officials and offices; press galleries; maps of Congressional districts.

JUDICIAL SYSTEM

Supreme Court of the United States. House of Representatives, 1973. 20 p. il. Free from the House Document Room.
House Document 93-23 (and to be ordered as such) describes the history, the make-up, the functions, of the Court. There is a complete list of all Justices who have ever served.

United States Courts; Their Jurisdiction and Work. J. F. Spaniol, Jr. House of Representatives, 1973. 17 p.   052-070-02832-7
Prepared for the Committee on the Judiciary. Brief discussion of the federal court system from the Supreme Court down.

THE PRESIDENCY

If Elected; Unsuccessful Candidates for the Presidency, 1796–1968. L. B. Miller and others. Natl. Portrait Gallery, 1972. 512 p. il.
047-006-00008-2
Promises, with engaging (and otherwise) illustrations of practically every American who has ever run for our highest office.

Inaugural Addresses of the Presidents of the United States from George Washington, 1789, to R. M. Nixon, 1973. House of Representatives, House Doc. 93-208 (1974). 283 p. il.   052-071-00392-4

Nomination and Election of the President and Vice-President of the United States, Including the Manner of Selecting Delegates to National Political Conventions. R. D. Hupman and F. R. Vale, comps. The Senate, 1972. 273 p. il.   052-002-00010-9
Based on laws in effect January 1, 1972, including laws relating to

minor and new parties, independent candidates, and corrupt practices.
——Supplement. 1972. 107 p.   052-002-00011-7

UNITED STATES: HISTORY

Admiral William Veazie Pratt, U.S. Navy. G. R. Wheeler. Naval Operations Off., 1974. 456 p. il.   008-046-00069-7
"The period of William Veazie Pratt's naval career coincided with an era of extraordinary historical importance." Admiral Pratt's dates were 1869–1957. He was graduated from the Naval Academy in 1889 and became Chief of Naval Operations in 1930.

American Military History. M. Matloff, gen. ed. Dept. of the Army, Off. of the Chief of Military History, 1969; repr. and partially rev., 1973. 713 p. il.   008-029-00089-0
"Except for Chapters 27 and 28, which have been considerably revised, this edition is essentially a reprint of the 1969 edition." There are fifteen contributors; they tell, and tell superbly, the story of our Army from the Revolution to Vietnam. There is a chapter on European beginnings and Colonial America, and the introductory chapter discusses the theory of military history. The work is history in the finest senses of the word.

American Revolution; a Selected Reading List. Library of Cong., 1968. 38 p.   030-000-00019-6

Battleship in the United States Navy. Naval Operations Off., 1970. [65] p. il.   008-046-00012-3
America (the 1780s) was the first battleship built in North America. The story from there.

Battle Streamers of the United States Navy. Naval Operations Off., 1972. 24 p. il.   008-047-00144-8
There is a great deal of naval history behind each of these streamers. Illustrations are in color.

Brief History of the 12th Marines. C. R. Smith. Historical Div. Headquarters, U.S. Marine Corps, 1972. 84 p. il. Marine Corps Historical Reference Pamphlet 8. Free from the Corps.
"Concise narrative of the regiment from its initial action close to half a century ago through its participation in the Vietnam conflict. Official records of the Marine Corps and appropriate historical works were utilized in compiling this short history." Excellent; maps and photographs are superb.

Brief History of the United States Marine Corps. N. W. Hicks. Marine Corps, 1964. 57 p. Free from the Corps.

Chiefs of Naval Operations and Admiral's House; Seapower . . . Guardian of Freedom. Naval Operations Off. [1969]. [48] p. il.
008-046-00010-7
Story of the several Chiefs; the role of the Navy in preserving peace.

Chronology of the United States Marine Corps. Marine Corps, 1965–66. 2 vols. Free from the Corps.
The volumes are strictly chronologies, with rather dry explicatory text. This does not lessen their value.
  1. (1965). 1775–1934. W. M. Miller and J. H. Johnstone. 129 p. il.
  2. (1966). 1935–1946. C. A. Tyson. 139 p. il.

Creating Independence, 1763–89; Background Reading for Young People; Selected, Annotated Bibliography. M. N. Coughlin, comp. Library of Cong., 1972. 62 p. il.
030-001-00046-0

Dictionary of American Naval Fighting Ships. Dept. of the Navy, Off. of Chief of Naval Operations, Naval Historical Div., 1959–71. 5 vols.
A gold mine of information and a fascinating mine at that. It includes "basic information on every naval ship that has served its part." (That is, as far back as the American Revolution.) Arrangement is strictly alphabetic, so that John Paul Jones is listed under the J's.

1. 1959; repr. 1970. *Letters A-B.* 351 p. il.   008-046-00041-7
4. 1969. *Letters L-M.* 745 p.il.   008-046-00009-3
5. 1971. *Letters N-Q.* 639 p. il.   008-046-00051-4

Directory, U.S. Army Museums. Off. of the Chief of Military History, 1968 [1969]. 95 p. il. Free from the Off.
In loose-leaf form. Fifty-nine museums are described.

Draft: Past, Present, Future; General Description of the Selective Service System. Selective Serv. System [1972]. 11 p. il. Free from the System.
A brief history.

Harmon Lectures. Air Force Acad., Denver, Colo., 1959–74. Purchase from the Academy.
The Department of History of the Air Force is the sponsor of this series of lectures. Their purpose is twofold: "to further the newly awakened interest in military history which has been evidenced throughout the United States, and to stimulate our Cadets toward developing a lifelong interest in this . . . professional history." Although he is not certain the lectures are all still available, the compiler ranks them so highly that he has again listed the whole group, even where they exceed the time limits of this edition. The group is available free to colleges and universities. Every title is by an expert; and the group as a whole is recommended without reservation.

1. Why Military History? W. F. Craven 1959.
2. The Military Leadership of the North and South. T. H. Williams. 1960.
3. Pacific Command. L. Morton. 1961.
4. Operation Pointblank: a tale of Bombers and Fighters. W. R. Emerson. 1962. [46] p.
5. John J. Pershing and the Anatomy of Leadership. F. E. Vandiver. 1963. 21 p. il.
   A sympathetic portrait of a soldier's soldier.
6. Mr. Roosevelt's Three Wars: FDR as War Leader. M. Matloff.
   A famous military historian assesses FDR in World Wars I

and II (and comments on how FDR saw himself); then he asks about the "third war"—that for peace.

7. Problems of Coalition Warfare; the Military Alliance against North Africa. G. A. Craig. 1965.

8. Innovations and Reform in Warfare. P. Paret. 1966.

9. Strategy and Policy in Twentieth-Century Warfare. M. Howard. 1967. 13 p.

10. George C. Marshall: Global Commander. F. C. Pogue. 1968. [23] p.
   Assessment of a very great general by a friend of many years.

11. War of Ideas: the United States Navy, 1870–90. E. E. Morison. 1969. 15 p. il.
   Years in "which in fact the Navy did not look so good . . ." (and the story of how it was made to look better).

12. Historical Development of Contemporary Strategy. T. Ropp. 1970. [20] p. il.

13. Military in the Service of the State. Sir J. W. Hackett. 1970 [1971]. 22 p. il.
   The lecturer agrees that the highest service of the military lies, probably, in the "moral sphere."

14. The Many Faces of George S. Patton, Jr. M. Blumenson. 1972. 27 p. il.

15. The End of Militarism. R. W. Weighley. 1973. 15 p.

Japan Expedition, 1852–1854; the Personal Journal of Commodore Matthew C. Perry. Roger Pineau, ed. Smithsonian Inst. 241 p. il. Purchase from the Inst.
"Commodore Perry's record of the voyage that opened an isolated Japan to commerce with the Western World. Perry's diaries, kept throughout the trip, were eventually illustrated and bound into three volumes. It is from these that this account has been transcribed and edited."

Historic Preservation in San Francisco's Inner Mission, and Take a Walk through Mission History. J. L. Waldhorn. Dept. of Housing and Urban Devel., 1974. [56] p. il.   023-000-00280-9
Copiously illustrated, including wonderful drawings of nineteenth-

century homes and buildings. Three walking tours are suggested. This is city history as you like it.

Historic Ship Exhibits in the United States. Naval Operations Off., 1969. [70] p. il. 008-046-00024-7
Fifty museums are cited briefly, as well as memorials and installations; for example, Pearl Harbor. Fine photographs.

Last Salute: Civil and Military Funerals, 1921–69. B. C. Mossman and M. W. Stark. Dept. of the Army, 1971. 429 p. il.
008-029-00086-5
Accounts of funerals held for civil and military officials, active or retired, and for the unknown servicemen in three wars between 1921 and 1969.

Lewis and Clark; a Brief Account of Their Expedition. Bur. of Land Management, 1973. 12 p. il. 024-011-00003-8
Excellent brief account; useful especially to students in high school.

Medal of Honor Recipients, 1863–1973; "In the Name of the Congress of the United States." The Senate, 1973. 1,231 p. il.
052-070-02039-3
Prepared for the Veterans' Affairs Committee by the Congressional Reference Service and others. The history of the Medal (it was authorized in 1862); a complete listing of recipients, by war, conflict, incident—and interims. Brief biographical data on each recipient, and a full account of the incident of valor and/or self-sacrifice that led to award of the Medal. A listing, by state, of recipients; calendar of legislation; then some of the actual legislation. There is a detailed, selective, bibliography, the work of E. V. and D. C. McAndrews; and a very fine piece of work it is.

Monitors of the U.S. Navy, 1861–1937. R. W. Webber. Naval Operations Off. [1969]. 48 p. il. 008-046-00015-8

Naval Documents of the American Revolution. Naval Historical Div., 1964–70. 5 vols.

This work represents "an exhaustive search . . . of archives and collections (public and private) in this country and abroad" to supplement the editors' own transcripts, photographs, etc., or letters, documents, and so on. A gigantic historical task.

1. Atlantic Theatre, Dec. 1, 1775–Sept. 2, 1775; European Theatre, Dec. 6, 1774–Aug. 9, 1775. 1964. 1,451 p. il.

008-046-00035-2

2. Atlantic Theatre, Sept. 3, 1775–Oct. 31, 1775; European Theatre, Aug. 11, 1775–Oct. 31, 1775; Atlantic Theatre, Nov. 1, 1775–Dec. 7, 1775. 1966. 1,463 p. il.   008-046-00036-1

4. American Theatre, Feb. 19–April, 1776; European Theatre, Feb. 1–May 25, 1776; American Theatre, April 18–May 8, 1776. W. B. Clark, ed. 1969. 1,580 p. il.   008-046-00038-7

5. American Theatre, May 9, 1776–July 3, 1776. W. J. Morgan, ed. 1970. 1,486 p. il.   008-046-00046-8

Periodical Literature on the American Revolution; Historical Research and Changing Interpretations, 1895–1970; a Selective Bibliography. Library of Cong., 1971. 93 p.   030-001-00040-1

Privateers in Charleston, 1793–1796. M. H. Jackson. Smithsonian Inst., 1969. 160 p. il. Purchase from the Inst.
". . . provides many fascinating details and little known facts about the seafaring and commercial life of the young United States during the period of the French war against England, Holland, and Spain. The port of Charleston, South Carolina, became a convenient and supportive haven for the privateers she commissioned."

Protecting Sherman's Lifeline; Battles of Brice's Cross Roads and Tupelo, 1864. E. C. Beares. Natl. Park Serv., 1971 [1972]. [40] p. il.   024-005-00285-5
Detailed account no Georgian wants to read. Plans and maps are very good.

Seacoast Fortifications of the United States; an Introductory History. E. R. Lewis. Smithsonian Inst. 160 p. il. Purchase from the Inst.

" . . survey of seacoast fortification by the United States between the first program of harbor defense, 1794, and the final constructions of World War II . . ."

Uniforms of the United States Navy, 1776–1898. Naval Operations Off., 1966. 13 leaves. 008-046-00032-8
Our Navy has gained in efficiency—but how much it has lost in color! These prints are framable, and would decorate any boy's room very well.

United States Air Force History; an Annotated Bibliography. Dept. of the Air Force, 1971. 106 p. 008-070-00307-4

United States Marine Corps Ranks and Grades, 1775–1969. B. C. Nalty and others. Marine Corps, 1970. 62 p. il. Free from the Corps.
Fine old illustrations, including one of a second lieutenant in the regular uniform prescribed by the 1859 regulations and a drawing of an officer's uniform in 1847.

United States Naval Aviation, 1910–70. A. O. van Wyen and L. M. Pearson. Dept. of the Navy, 1970. 440 p. il. 008-041-00059-8
Essentially a month-by-month chronicle.

United States Naval History; Bibliography. Off. of Naval Operations, 1973. Purchase from the Off.

UNITED STATES: POPULATION

Census Portraits. Bur. of the Census, Ser. CP-73 (1974). 52 numbers. Purchase from the Bur.

1. Alabama	6. Colorado
2. Alaska	7. Connecticut
3. Arizona	8. Delaware
4. Arkansas	10. Florida
5. California	11. Georgia

12. Hawaii	33. New York
13. Idaho	34. North Carolina
14. Illinois	35. North Dakota
15. Indiana	36. Ohio
16. Iowa	37. Oklahoma
17. Kansas	38. Oregon
18. Kentucky	40. Rhode Island
19. Louisiana	42. South Dakota
20. Maine	43. Tennessee
21. Maryland	44. Texas
22. Massachusetts	45. Utah
24. Minnesota	46. Vermont
25. Mississippi	47. Virginia
26. Missouri	48. Washington
27. Montana	49. West Virginia
29. Nevada	50. Wisconsin
30. New Hampshire	51. Wyoming
31. New Jersey	52. Puerto Rico
32. New Mexico	

Population and the American Future; the Report . . . Commission on Population Growth and the American Future, 1972. 186 p. il.

052-058-00002-3

Superb study of every aspect of the "population problem." Based on the cooperation of scores of scientists and sociologists, as well as of hundreds of published studies. Discusses population growth; distribution; population and the economy; resources and environment; social factors (age structure, family, minorities, etc.); population and public policy; education; status of women and children; human reproduction; stabilizing the population; immigration. Makes recommendations in a great many areas.

Population Challenge . . . What It Means for America; Conservation Yearbook 2. Dept. of the Interior. 80 p. il.   024-000-00444-9

Beautifully illustrated description of our resources, and our coming problems, and how the Department is making plans to solve them.

Population Distribution, Urban and Rural, in the United States.
Bur. of the Census, 1970.   003-024-00224-8
Colored map.

We the Americans. Bur. of the Census. 1972–75. 15 parts.
Captivating group. Not only is the format of each of the 15 parts
most attractive (there is, for example, frequent use of color), but
the contents are informative and very revealing.

1. Who We Are. [1972]. 16 p. il.   003-024-00006-7
   Our numbers, our ethnic groups; something of our past.
2. We the Black Americans. [1972]. 13 p. il.   003-024-00018-1
   There were 22,580,289 blacks on April 1, 1970—more than
   all the population of Canada!
3. Our Homes. 1972. [17] p. il.   003-024-00043-1
   There were 69,000,000 homes in 1970.
4. We the American Women. 1973. [12] p. il.   003-024-00122-5
   Women constitute a respectable percentage of the work force,
   and are, in addition, expected to keep those 69,000,000 homes
   clean.
5. Our Incomes. 1975. 16 p. il.   003-024-00126-8
6. Nosotros . . . los Mexicanos Americanos . . . los Puerto-
   riqueños . . . los Cubanos Americanos . . . los Americanos de
   la America Central . . . los Americanos de la America del
   Sur. 1973. 19 p. il.   003-024-00197-7
   Their story told in English and Spanish.
7. Our Cities and Suburbs. 1973. 14 p. il.   003-024-00189-6
   We are becoming an increasingly urban people.
9. The Work We Do. 1973. [15] p.il.   003-024-00199-3
   You name it, we do it; and *well.*
10. The American Elderly. 1973. [14] p. il.   003-024-00200-1
11. The Young Marrieds. 1973. [15] p. il.   003-024-00190-0
12. The First Americans. 1973. [19] p. il.   003-024-00204-3
    We preceded the *Mayflower* and Jamestown. (The compiler
    means the Indians and the descendants of Pocahontas.)
13. The Asian Americans. 1973. 14 p. il.   003-024-00205-1
14. The Youth of America. 1973. 15 p. il.   003-024-00201-9
15. The American Foreign Born. 1973. 15 p. il.   003-024-00206-0

UNITED STATES: STATISTICS

Century of Public School Statistics. Off. of Educ., 1974. Folder.
017-080-01247-2
Summary covers 1869–70 to 1969–70. Two summaries, in fact, one demographic, the other fiscal.

Employment and Earnings; States and Areas, 1939–72. Bur. of Labor Statistics, Bull. 1370-10 [1972]. 682 p. il. 029-001-01301-9
Earnings of employees of different industries by 221 major geographic areas. Illustrated by graphs and charts. A valuable adjunct to any history of American labor and economy.

Pocket Data Book, USA, 1973. Bur. of the Census, 1973. 352 p. il.
003-024-00109-8
Prepared under the direction of W. Lerner. Tables, charts, diagrams, cover everything from population to foreign commerce. In 28 categories, and invaluable.

Productivity and the Economy . . . Revised 1973 Edition. Bur. of Labor Statistics, Bull. 1779 (1973). 65 p. il. 029-001-01070-2
". . . designed to show what productivity is and how it operates . . . divided into three parts. The first shows how productivity has developed over time; the second presents changing factors that are influenced by productivity; and the third traces trends in the various factors that influence productivity." It is difficult to overrate the value of the charts that accompany the text in this work.

Standard Metropolitan Statistical Areas and Central Cities; Changes in Employment for Manufacturing, Retail Trade, Wholesale Trade, and Selected Services between 1958–1967; Changes in Population between 1960–1970. Bur. of the Census, Employment and Population Changes, Spec. Econ. Rept. ES 20-72-1 (1972). 65 p.
003-024-00020-2
"This report brings together information from the 1960 and 1970

censuses of population and the 1958 and 1967 censuses of manu-
facturers, retail trade, and wholesale trade" in order to assess the
continuing "importance of the central cities as centers of population
and employment."

Statistical Abstract of the United States, 1972. Bur. of the Census
[1974]. 1017 p. il.   003-024-00422-4
"Standard summary of statistics on the social, political, and economic organization of the United States." Population; vital statistics;
immigration and naturalization; education; law; geography; income;
distribution and services, etc. Formidable and indispensible.

——Supplement: **USA Statistics in Brief, 1974.** [1974]. [10] p.
                                        003-024-00744-4

UNITED STATES: WATERGATE INVESTIGATION

Brief on Behalf of the President of the United States; Hearings . . .
House of Representatives, 1974. 123 p.   052-070-02532-8
Before the House Committee on the Judiciary.

**Comparison of White House and Judiciary Committee Transcripts
of Eight Recorded Presidential Conversations; Hearings . . .** House
of Representatives, 1974. 63 p.   052-070-02444-5
Before the Committee on the Judiciary.

Debate on Articles of Impeachment; Hearings . . . House of Representatives, 1974. 562 p.   052-070-02585-9
Before the House Committee on the Judiciary.

Errata; Hearings . . . House of Representatives, 1974. 21 p.
                                                052-070-02598-1
These are not of course Hearings. They are corrections to the fol-
lowing: Transcripts of *Eight Recorded Presidential Conversations;
Statement of Information,* Books 2, 7, 9, and 10, Appendix 1;

Testimony of Witnesses, Book 3—all of which are listed in this section.

Final Report of the Select Committee on Presidential Campaign Activities. The Senate, 1974. 1,250 p. Purchase from the Comm. "Culmination of 1½ years' work of the Senate Select Committee on Presidential Campaign Activities. . . . The Chairman says: "It is a matter of special satisfaction and pride to me that our Committee assumed its responsibility initially in a bipartisan manner, and despite all the pressures inherent in such a highly politically charged investigation, ended its work in a bipartisan manner." The Report is the unanimous report of the full committee. Reports of witnesses, examination of documents (many of which are reproduced). Particularly interesting in the study of Watergate, it relates in detail how the Select Committee went about its work—from mountainous paper work to the employment of computers for special purposes. The individual views of some Committee members are given in full. A document very difficult to annotate adequately in any meaningful way. But it shows our Congress at its best.

Impeachment Inquiry; Hearings . . . House of Representatives, 1975. 3 books.
Before the Committee on the Judiciary. Separate books are these:
 1. 702 p.   052-070-02720-7
 2. [703-1454] p.   052-070-02721-5
 3. [1455-2258] p.   052-070-02722-3

Impeachment; Miscellaneous Documents. The Senate, 1974. 292 p.
Free from the Committee
Prepared for the Committee on Rules and Administration. This is a discussion of procedures and laws of impeachment, citing, among other things, cases that have been tried in the past. One interesting question is that of the effect of an incomplete hearing on a new Congress.

Impeachment of Richard M. Nixon, President of the United States;

Report of the Committee on the Judiciary . . . House of Representatives, 1974–75. 11 books; 4 appendices.

House Watergate Papers

Book I. Events Prior to the Watergate Break-in, Dec. 2. 1971–June 17, 1972. 1974. 271 p.   052-070-02409-7

Book II. Events Following the Watergate Break-in, June 17, 1972–Feb. 9, 1973. 1974. 680 p. il.   052-070-02410-1

Book III: Parts 1 and 2. Events Following the Watergate Break-in, June 20, 1972–March 22, 1973. 1974. 1,281 p. il.

052-070-02411-9

Book V: Parts 1 and 2. Department of Justice/ITT Litigation—Richard Kleindienst Nomination Hearings. 1974. 980 p. il.

052-070-02413-5

Book VI: Parts 1 and 2. Political Contributions by Milk Producers Cooperatives: the 1971 Milk Price Support Decision. 1974. 984 p. il.   052-010-02414-3

Book VII: Parts 1, 2, 3, and 4. White House Surveillance Activities and Campaign Activities. 1974. 2,090 p. il.

052-070-02415-1

Book VIII. Internal Revenue Service. 1974. 440 p. il.

052-070-02416-0

Book IX: Parts 1 and 2. Watergate Special Prosecutors; Judiciary Committee's Impeachment Inquiry. 1974. 1,069 p. il.

052-070-02417-8

Book X. Tax Deduction for Gift of Papers. 1974. 552 p. il.
052-070-02433-0

Book XI. Bombing of Cambodia. 1974. 599 p. il. 052-070-02458-5

Book XII. Impoundment of Funds; Government Expenditures on President Nixon's Private Properties at San Clemente and Key Biscayne. 187 p. il.   052-070-02459-3

Appendix 1. Presidential Statements on the Watergate Break-in and Its Investigation. 1974. 110 p.   052-070-02456-9

Appendix 2. Papers in Criminal Cases Initiated by the Watergate Special Prosecution Force. 1974. 381 p.   052-070-02461-5

Appendix 3. White House Edited Transcripts (April 4, 1972, March 22, 1973, June 23, 1972; John Ehrlichman's Handwritten

Notes; Affadavit of Bruce A. Kehrli).   052-070-02587-5
Appendix 4. Political Matters Memoranda. August 13, 1971–
September 18, 1972. 1972 [1974]. 151 p.   052-070-02588-3

Impeachment; Selected Materials. Comm. on the Judiciary, House
of Representatives, 1973. 718 p.   052-071-00381-9

Minority Memorandum on Facts and Law; Hearings. House of
Representatives, 1974. 163 p.   052-070-02470-4

**Presidential Campaign Activities of 1972; Hearings . . . [Watergate
and Related Activities.]** Senate, 1973–74. 14 books in 3 phases;
Appendix (2 books).
Before the Select Committee on Campaign Activities. Issued in three
phases and two Appendixes. Phase 1 (9 books) deals with the
Watergate investigation. Phase 2 (3 books) deals with campaign
activities. Phase 3 (2 books) deals with campaign financing. The
Appendixes contain legal documents relating to the Select Committee hearings.

  Phase 1: Watergate Investigation. 9 books.
    1. May 17–24, 1973. 1973. 456 p.   052-070-01843-7
    2. June 5–14, 1973. 1974. [457-910] p.   052-070-01962-0
    3. June 25 and 26, 1973. 1974. [911-1345] p.
                                                   052-070-01963-8
    4. June 27–July 10, 1973. 1974. [1347-1813] p.
                                                   052-070-01964-6
    5. July 11–17, 1974. [1815-2217] p.   052-070-01965-4
    6. July 18–25, 1973. 1974. [2219-2655] p.   052-070-01966-2
    7. July 26–30, 1973. 1974. [2657-3015] p.   052-070-01967-1
    8. July 31–Aug. 2, 1973. 1974. [3017-3401] p.
                                                   052-070-01968-9
    9. Aug. 3–Sept. 25, 1973. 1973 [1974]. [3403-3898] p.
                                                   052-070-02122-5
  Phase 2: Campaign Practices. 3 books.
    10. Sept. 26 and Oct. 3, 1973. 1973 [1974]. [3899-4374] p.
                                                   052-070-02144-6

11. Oct. 4–31, 1973. 1973 [1974]. [4375-4895] p.

052-070-02199-3

12. Nov. 1 and 6, 1973. 1973 [1974]. [4897-5272] p.

052-070-02200-1

Phase 3: Campaign Financing. 2 books.

13. Nov. 7–15, 1973. 1974 [5273-5858] p.   052-070-02231-1

14. 1974. 524 p.   052-070-02350-3

Appendix to the Hearings: Legal Documents Relating to the Select Committee Hearings . . . 2 parts.

1. 1974. 1,248 p.   052-070-02407-1

2. 1974. 948 p.   052-070-02408-9

Statement of Information; Background Memorandum; Hearings . . . House of Representatives, 1974. 6 p.   052-070-02460-7

"White House Staff and President Nixon's Campaign Organizations." Before the House's Committee on the Judiciary.

Statement of Information Submitted on Behalf of President Nixon; Hearings . . . House of Representatives, 1974. 4 books.

Before the House Committee on the Judiciary.

1. Events Following the Watergate Break-in, June 19, 1972–March 1, 1974. 1974. 242 p. il.   052-070-02420-8

2. Department of Justice–ITT Litigation. 1974. 208 p. il.

052-070-02421-6

3. Political Contributions by Milk Producers Cooperatives: the 1971 Milk Price Support Decision. 1974. 217 p. il.

052-070-02422-4

4. White House Surveillance Activities. 1974. 225 p. il.

052-070-02423-2

Summary of Information; Hearings. House of Representatives, 1974. 184 p.   052-070-02469-1

Before the Committee on the Judiciary.

Testimony of Witnesses; Hearings . . . House of Representatives, 1974. 3 books.

Before the Committee on the Judiciary.
1. Alexander Butterfield, Paul O'Brien, and Fred C. LaRue.
   275 p.   052-070-02433-0
2. William O. Bittman, John N. Mitchell, and John W. Dean, III.
   355 p. il.   052-070-02436-4
3. Henry E. Petersen, Charles W. Colson, and Herbert W. Kalm-
   bach. 746 p. il.   052-070-02437-2

Transcripts of Eight Recorded Presidential Conversations; Hearings . . . House of Representatives, 1974. 218 p.   052-070-02400-3

VETERANS AND VETERANS RIGHTS

As You Were; Vietnam Era Veterans in Federal Employment.
Civil Serv. Comm., Pamph. BRE-34 [1972]. [46] p. il. Free from
the Comm.
The training offered a group long regarded as forgotten; the opportunities open.

Educational Benefits Available for Returning Vietnam Era Veterans;
Hearings . . . Part 1. The Senate, 1972. 557 p.   052-070-01702-3
Before the Subcommittee on Readjustment, Education, and Employment, Committee on Veterans' Affairs. This is not easy reading, and will appeal primarily to libraries, which may want to
have on hand the various legislative bills and reports pertinent
to them.

Source Material on the Vietnam Era Veteran. The Senate, 1974.
935 p.   052-070-02222-1
A nine-chapter discussion that touches on every aspect of the
tragic problem of the returning Vietnam veteran. Over 150 articles
and other sources are reproduced. The chapters are as follows:
Society and the Vietnam Era Veteran; Disabled Vietnam Era
Veterans; Minority Veterans; Drug Abuse and the Vietnam Era
Veteran; Educational Benefits and Readjustment; Medical Care of
Vietnam Veterans; General Information and Views Concerning the
Vietnam Era Veteran; Employment and Unemployment; and Men-
tal Health and Psychological Readjustment.

VIETNAM WAR 345

Study of the Problems Facing Vietnam Era Veterans on Their Readjustment to Civilian Life. The Senate, 1972. 269 p. Purchase from the Veterans Affairs Comm.
"The full report of a study conducted for the Veterans Administration by Louis Harris Associates, Inc." The first professional survey sponsored by the VA. Extremely statistical, but filled with valuable conclusions.

Vietnam Veteran in Contemporary Society; Collected Materials Pertaining to Young Veterans. Veterans Admin., IB 11-22 (1972). [394] p. il.   051-000-00057-9
Extraordinarily perceptive study by experts. Divided into four parts: Introduction; Youth in the United States Today; Vietnam Experience; and New Veteran, a General Readjustment. Every aspect of the problem of returning veterans is gone into in detail. A book for every library, and for every veteran.

VIETNAM WAR

Base Development in South Vietnam, 1965–1970. C. H. Dunn. Army Dept., 1972. il.   008-020-00427-8
Second in the Vietnam Studies; describes the tasks, accomplishments, and problems of Army engineers in the construction of ports, storage areas, ammunition dumps, housing, bridges, roads, and other conventional facilities for such terrain as Vietnam.

Background Information Relating to Southeast Asia and Vietnam. The Senate, Foreign Relations Comm., 1970. 455 p.
052-070-00837-7

Causes, Origins, and Lessons of the Vietnam War; Hearings . . . The Senate, 1973. 340 p. il.   052-070-01713-9
Before the Committee on Foreign Relations. Statements by university personnel, reporters, Government officials. Appendix includes documents relating to OSS activities in French Indochina; "Detachment 404" mission to Saigon; Secret Intelligence Branch (SI) reports and documents relating to the Viet Minh; Strategic Service Unit reports from French Indochina.

Communications-Electronics, 1962–70. T. M. Rienzi. Dept. of the Army, 1972. 184 p. il.   008-020-00425-1
First in the Vietnam Studies group; describes some of the most important experiences, problems, and achievements in the field of communications-electronics in Vietnam. A great deal of know-how and ingenuity were needed!

Congress and the Termination of the Vietnam War . . . The Senate, 1973. 17 p. Purchase from the Comm.
Prepared by the Library of Congress for use by the Committee on Foreign Relations. Of considerable interest; the conclusion is that the Congress could have ended the war and taken other important steps.

European Reactions to U.S. Policies in Vietnam; Hearings . . . House of Representatives, 1973. 65 p. Free from the Comm.
Before the Subcommittee on Europe, House Foreign Affairs Committee.

Marines in Vietnam, 1954–1973; Anthology and Annotated Bibliography. Marine Corps, Historical and Museums Div., Headquarters, 1974. 277 p. il.   008-055-00070-0
Articles from the *Proceedings* of the U.S. Naval Institute, *Naval Review,* and *Marine Corps Gazette.* Purpose is to serve as an "interim reference for use within the Marine Corps and for answering inquiries from other Government agencies . . ." Thirteen articles that "provide a general overview of Marine involvement in the Vietnam War." A first-class history.

Small Unit Action in Vietnam, Summer 1966. F. J. West, Jr. Marine Corps, 1967. 123 p. il. Free from the Corps.
More detailed than most of the Historical Reference Pamphlets. The account of the Corps's action is accompanied by fine photographs made on the scene at the time.

U.S. Involvement in the Overthrow of Diem, 1963; a Staff Study. The Senate, 1972. 73 p. Free from the Senate Document Room.

Based on the Pentagon Papers, and prepared for use of the Senate's Committee on Foreign Relations by A. L. Hollick. Sen. J. W. Fulbright's Preface makes the point that "the facts of U.S. policy toward the Diem regime were limited to such a tight circle of U.S. officials that significant debate over the desirability of support of Diem, much less of an Indo-China presence, was precluded." It is this sort of partisan frankness that makes Congressional sources surprisingly exciting reading.

U.S. Marine Corps: Civic Action Effort in Vietnam, March 1965–March 1966. R. H. Stolfi. Marine Corps, 1968. 96 p. il. Free from the Corps.
". . . part of a continuing program to keep Marines informed of the ways of combat and civic action in Vietnam." Certainly not limited in appeal to members of the Armed Forces. Excellent colored map.

Vietnam; May 1972; a Staff Report . . . J. G. Lowenstein and R. M. Moose. The Senate, 1972. 32 p. Free from the Comm.
The report was prepared for use by the Committee on Foreign Relations. (For security reasons some passages have been deleted.) Based on interviews of Representatives who visited several areas in South Vietnam. Their impressions are frankly reported.

VITAL STATISTICS

Health Characteristics of Low Income Persons. M. L. Bauer. Natl Center for Health Statistics, Vital and Health Statistics, Ser. 10 (data from Natl. Health Survey), No. 14 (1972). 51 p. il.

017-022-00227-2

An exceedingly difficult title to cite (as can be seen above). It is "an analysis of health characteristics of persons with family income under $5,000; and comparison of aid recipients with nonrecipients." It is difficult to make the reader see the readability of this material, if not its value; but it shows many Governmental agencies at their best.

Height and Weight of Children; Socioeconomic Status, United States. Natl. Center for Health Stat., Vital and Health Statistics, Ser. 11 (data from Natl. Health Survey), No. 119 (1972). 87 p. il.
017-022-00232-9
Effects of socioeconomic factors on the growth of children of ages 6-11. A direct correlation between background and height was observed. Illustrated with many tables.

Leading Causes of Death in Selected Areas of the World . . . The Senate, 1972. 80 p. il. Free from the Comm.
Prepared for the Special Commission on International Health, Education, and Labor Programs, Labor and Public Welfare Committee, the Senate.

One Hundred Years of Marriage and Divorce Statistics, United States, 1867–1967. A. W. Plateris. Natl. Center for Health Statistics, Vital and Health Statistics, Ser. 21-24 (1974). 61 p. il.
017-022-00303-1

Where to Write for Birth and Death Records, United States and Outlying Areas. Public Health Serv., 1970. 9 p.   017-022-00372-4

VOCATIONAL REHABILITATION

Introduction to the Vocational Rehabilitation Process. J. F. McGowan and T. L. Porter. Rehab. Serv. Admin., Rehab. Serv Admin. Ser. 68-32 (1968). 201 p. il.   017-061-00021-6
Provides "a source of basic training material which can be used by State agency personnel for the orientation of new counselors; for beginning courses in rehabilitation counselor training programs; and for inservice training of experienced rehabilitation counseling personnel."

National Directory of Rehabilitation Facilities, 1972. Social and Rehab. Serv., 1972. Purchase from the Serv.

WASHINGTON, D.C.

Brief Guide to the National Gallery of Art of the United States of America, Washington, D.C. Natl. Gallery of Art [1969]. 30 p. il. Free from the Gallery.
A gallery of this magnificence cannot be "briefly" surveyed.

Capitol; a Pictorial History. House of Representatives, House Doc. 93-139 [1973]. 112 p. il. Purchase from the House Document Room.

Elements of the Comprehensive Plan for the National Capital [General Land Use Objectives]. Natl. Capital Planning Comm. [1970]. 44 p. il. Free from the Comm.
The length is deceptive: included are many separate photographs and several supersuperb maps. Mass transportation plans; major throughway plans. Carries you to 1985.

Georgetown Historic Waterfront, Washington, D.C.; Review of Canal and Riverside Architecture. C. W. Werner. Natl. Park Serv., 1968. 92 p. il.   024-005-00206-5

Guidebook to Diplomatic Reception Rooms: Suite of Large Reception Rooms; John Quincy Adams State Drawing Room; Thomas Jefferson State Reception Room; Benjamin Franklin State Dining Room; Suite of Small Reception Rooms; James Monroe Reception Room; James Madison Dining Room; Martin Van Buren Dining Room. Dept. of State, 1971. 88 p. il. Free from the Dept.
The rooms are in the old State Department Building.

Historical Highlights of the Treasury Building, Washington, D.C. Dept. of the Treasury [1969]. 11 p. il. Free from the Dept.

Information for Readers in the Library of Congress. Library of Cong., 1972. 12 p. il. Free from the Library.
How to use one of the world's largest libraries.

John E. Fogarty International Center for Advanced Study in the Health Sciences. Natl. Insts. of Health [1971]. [15] p. il. Free from the Insts.

A search through some of the finest treatises in this edition of this *Guide* will reveal the quality of the Center's work; what is not so easy to visualize is its physical beauty in the Maryland hills.

National Collection of Fine Arts; National Portrait Gallery; Museums of the Smithsonian Institution. Natl. Collection of Fine Arts [1969]. 16 p. il. Free from the Collection.

National Historic Landmark; Department of the Treasury. Dept. of the Treasury [1972]. 38 p. il.   048-000-00201-3

National Library of Medicine. Natl. Library of Med. [1972]. 16 p. il. Free from the Library.

Official White House China; 1789 to the Present. M. B. Klapthor. Smithsonian Inst., 1974. 304 p. il. Purchase from the Inst.

"This handsomely illustrated volume is the first authoritative study of presidential china—both porcelain and earthenware—from the administration of George Washington to that of John F. Kennedy."

Outdoor Sculpture of Washington, D.C.; a Comprehensive Historical Guide. J. M. Goode. Smithsonian Inst., 1974. 528 p. il. Purchase from the Inst.

A paperback (there is also a cloth edition). "More than 500 photographs illustrate this comprehensive survey . . ."

Pentagon. Dept. of the Army, USASCAF Pamph. 2 (1968). [16]. p. il.   008-020-00282-8

One of the world's most immense structures is described, and a clarification of its basic simplicity is attempted. Actually, once one has stopped gaping at the vastness of its interior, the Pentagon is not at all difficult to get about in.

Washington in the New Era, 1870–1970. L. W. Brown and E. M. Lewis. Natl. Portrait Gallery, 1972. 40 p. il.   047-006-00007-4

History of the growth and development of the black population in our national Capital.

Welcome to Washington. Natl. Park Serv. [1970]. 12 p. il. Free from the Serv.
Micro-introduction to a marvelous city. The major sights and landmarks.

SMITHSONIAN INSTITUTION

Increase and Diffusion; a Brief Introduction to the Smithsonian Institution, Washington, D.C. Smithsonian Inst., 1970. 87 p. il. Free from the Inst.
However great the sacrifice, at some time before you die, see the Smithsonian! One of the world's wonders. Here its story, and its greatness, are told—with the usual Smithsonian modesty. (The Institution has irreverently been called "the nation's attic.")

Papers of Joseph Henry. Vol. 1: The Albany Years, December, 1797–October, 1832. N. Reingold, ed. Smithsonian Inst. 535 p. il. Purchase from the Inst.
"Inaugurating a series of 15 volumes, this important publication documents the formative years of the first Secretary of the Smithsonian Institution. Joseph Henry was one of the founders of the American scientific community . . ."

Biographical Sketch of James Smithson. S. P. Langley. Smithsonian Inst., repr. 1964. 20 p. il. Purchase from the Inst.
Smithson, an illegitimate son of the Duke of Northumberland, left the sum of money—a good one in his day—that made possible the ultimate foundation of one of the greatest museums and research centers in the world.

Smithsonian Institution; an Establishment for the Increase and Diffusion of Knowledge among Men. W. Karp. Smithsonian Inst. 124 p. il. Purchase from the Inst.
"Story of the Smithsonian and the wide diversity of its activities.

Color pictures enhance the narration of the legacy; developments in natural history; flight and space; the arts; the society of scholars."

Smithsonian Institution, Washington, D.C. Smithsonian Inst. [1970]. Folder. Free from the Inst.
A very brief guide to the exhibits, and some of the activities, of a very great organization.

WATER RESOURCES AND SUPPLY

Amazon—Measuring a Mighty River. Geol. Survey [1973]. 18 p. il.
024-001-02038-6
Folder showing the potential of the world's mightiest river, and plans and hopes for developing this potential. Booklet is highly recommended to students (in almost any grade).

Clean Water; Report to Congress—1974. Environ. Protection Agency, 1974. 61 + 22 p.   055-001-00902-0
Second of the reports. "Covering measures taken to implement the objectives of the [Federal Water Pollution Control] Act." 1973 is covered; work accomplished is discussed. Particularly interesting for the chapter on research and development.

Design of Small Dams. 2d ed. Bur. of Reclamation, 1974. 816 p. il.   024-003-00089-2
"Addressed to the designer. . . . does not include in its scope the field of construction practices or methods. However, as the integrity of the design requires adherence to limiting specifications for materials and to the practice of good workmanship in construction, appendixes are included on Construction of Embankments, Concrete Construction, and Sample Specifications." Admittedly for a very small group, but interesting for the insights it affords even the layman into the problems of designing structures so important in our economy.

A Drop to Drink . . . a Report on the Quality of Our Drinking Water. Environ. Protect. Agency, 1975. 12 p. il.   055-000-00147-2
An adult drinks from one and a half to five or more quarts per day; learn how it comes to you purified.

Economics of Clean Water—1973. Environ. Protection Agency, 1973 [1975]. 120 p. il. Purchase from the Agency.
Sixth of the reports. "Scope is broader than previous reports. For the first time, economic factors—essential to a broad assessment of control programs and policies—are examined. Particular attention is afforded those factors that may constrain implementation of control programs. Also examined for the first time are two major sources of nonpoint pollution—agricultural soil loss and nitrogen fertilizer." Discusses: nature and trends in water pollutants; municipal costs; industrial costs; benefits from water quality enhancement; constraints. This report is of wide general interest.

Glossary of Water Resource Terms. O. A. Titelbaum. Water Program Off. [1970]. 39 p. Free from the Off.

Hydrologic Cycle. Environmental Science Services Admin. [1970]. [8] p. il. Free from the Admin.   003-014-00025-8

Illinois River. Forest Serv. [1971]. [12] p. il. Free from the Serv.

Lake Erie; Bibliography. Dept. of the Interior, Water Resources Scientific Inform. Center, WRSIC 72-209 [1972]. 240 p. Free from the Dept.

Lake Huron; Bibliography. Dept. of the Interior, Water Resources Scientific Inform. Center, WRSIC 72-210 [1972]. 95 p. Free from the Dept.

Lake Michigan; Bibliography. Dept. of the Interior, Water Resources Scientific Inform. Center, WRSIC 72-211 [1972]. 264 p. Free from the Dept.

Lake Superior; Bibliography. Dept of the Interior, Water Resources Scientific Inform. Center, WRSIC 72-213 [1972]. 127 p. Free from the Dept.

Large Rivers of the United States. K. T. Iseri and W. B. Langbein. Geol. Survey, Cir. 686 [1974]. 10 p. il. Free from the Survey.
Figures and data on 28 rivers—from the Mississippi (3,710 miles long, with a drainage area of 1,247,266 square miles) to much lesser streams. The Hudson is 306 miles long, and drains 13,370 square miles.

Maintaining Subsurface Drains. Dept. of Agr., Leaf. 557 [1972]. 8 p. il.   001-000-02666-6
Common trouble spots. Maintenance of inlets, outlets, etc.

New Water. Dept. of the Interior, 1970. 36 p. il.   024-000-00019-2
The Department's work in converting salt water to fresh "to save our natural water heritage."

Potomac; Its Water Resources. Geol. Survey [1968]. 24 p. il. Free from the Survey.
We don't think of the Potomac as having problems; but it has them.

Rain—a Water Resource. Geol. Survey [1973]. 7 p. il.
                                                    024-001-02452-7
Excellent for the student of early (and later) grades; a beautiful drawing shows the hydrologic cycle.

Replenishing Underground Water Supplies on the Farm. D. C. Muckel and W. C. Bianchi. Dept. of Agr., Leaflet 452 [1972]. 8 p. il.   001-000-02474-4

River Basins of the United States. Geol. Survey, 1970–72.
So far, five of this promising group have been published.
    1. Colorado. [1972]. [6] p.   024-001-02115-3

2. Columbia. [1972]. [6] p.   024-001-02203-6
3. Delaware. [1972]. [6] p.   024-001-02202-8
4. Hudson. [1972]. [6] p.   024-001-02114-5
5. Potomac. [1970]. [8] p.   024-001-02034-3

Story of the Colorado–Big Thompson Project. Bur. of Reclamation, 1968. 54 p. il.   024-003-00001-9
"One of the most exciting water-development enterprises in American history." Chronology of the area, 1803–1959; and a fine colored map.

Story of the Hoover Dam. Bur. of Reclamation, 1966. 77 p. il.
024-003-00065-5
The dam is one of the greatest engineering feats of all time. It is discussed here; and there is a chronology of the area from 1540 to 1964.

Treating Farmstead and Rural Home Water Systems. Dept. of Agr., Farmers' Bull. 2248 (1972). [16] p. il.   001-000-01421-8
How to keep your supply uncontaminated.

Urban Water Planning; Bibliography. G. F. Mangan and H. A. Swenson. Dept. of the Interior, Water Resources Scientific Inform. Center, WRSIC 72-215 [1972]. 373 p. Free from the Dept.

Water Fluoridation; the Search and the Victory. F. J. McClure. Natl. Inst. of Dental Research, 1970. 302 p. il.   017-047-00001-9
A history of the subject, with surprising facts. The 16,000 inhabitants of Pozzuoli, situated near Naples, had a heavy chance of having black teeth (observed in 1901). Causes of mottled enamel, effect of fluoride in water; extremely interesting facts and history.

Water and Industry in the United States. Geol. Survey [1972]. 19 p. il.   024-001-00245-1
How industry uses all our waters, with suggestions for wiser precautions in their use. Another good title for older students.

Water Laws and Concepts. H. E. Thomas. Geol. Survey, Cir. 629 (1970). 18 p. Free from the Survey.
The history of how man has tried to control use of water, with emphasis on American history. Most interesting chapter in our history, and probably little known to the general public.

Water Supply Sources for the Farmstead and Rural Home. Dept. of Agr., Farmers' Bull. 2237 (1971). 18 p. il.   001-000-01527-3
Requirements; ground and surface water sources.

Water in the Urban Environment; Erosion and Sediment. [W. J. Schneider]. Geol. Survey, 1974. [21] p. il.   024-001-02094-7
"The dual role that water plays as both a resource and a hazard. . . . problems of erosion and sediment and possible actions that could remedy the situation."

Wild and Scenic Rivers. Bur. of Outdoor Recreation, 1975. [16] p. il.   024-016-00073-1
Explanation of the national wild and scenic river system.

What Is Water? Geol. Survey. [1972]. [8] p. il.   024-001-02193-5

WEEDS

Canada Thistle and Its Control. J. M. Hodgson. Dept. of Agr., Leaflet 523 (1971). 8 p. il.   001-000-00228-7

Poison Ivy, Poison Oak, and Poison Sumac; Identification, Precautions, Eradication. D. M. Crooks and D. L. Klingman. Dept. of Agr., Farmers' Bull. 1972 (1971). [16] p. il.   001-000-01028-0
Excellent for those who haven't been shown what *Toxicodendron* looks like.

Three Leaves Mean Poison Ivy. Dept. of Agr., PA-839 (1971). Folder. il.   001-000-02523-6

WILDLIFE

Behavior and Ecology of the Asiatic Elephant in Southeastern Ceylon. G. M. McKay. Smithsonian Inst., Smithsonian Contributions to Zoology 125 (1973). 113 p. il.   047-000-00216-8
The only one of this Smithsonian series cited in this *Guide,* since the others are highly specific and technical.

Bison of Yellowstone National Park. M. M. Meagher. Natl. Park Serv., Sci. Mono. Ser. 1 (1973). 161 p. il.   024-005-00524-2
A charming, and greatly informative, book for young and old. Tells an almost unbelievable story of survival.

Directory of National Wildlife Refuges. Bur. of Sport Fisheries and Wildlife, Refuge Leaflet 411 [1972]. 16 p. Free from the Bur.
Listing of the areas; some particulars about each, including the primary wildlife species to be found.

Ecological Studies of the Timber Wolf in Northeastern Minnesota. L. D. Mech and L. D. Frenzel, Jr., eds. Forest Serv., Research Paper NC-52 (1971). 62 p. il. Free from the Serv.

Everglades & Wildlife; Basic Text and Concept. J. C. George. Natl. Park Serv., 1972. [106] p. il.   024-005-00497-1
Gem of a book. Illustrations, chiefly in color, by Betty Fraser— and they are superb. Flora and fauna of a fascinating area discussed in one of the Government's most beautiful books in a long time.

Human Behavior Aspects of Fish and Wildlife Conservation; Annotated Bibliography. D. R. Potter and others, comps. Forest Serv., Genl. Tech. Rept. PNW-4 (1973). 288 p. Free from the Pacific Northwest Forest and Range Experiment Station, Portland, Oreg.

Making Land Produce Useful Wildlife. W. L. Anderson. Dept. of
Agr., Farmers' Bull. 2035 (1969). 29 p. il.   001-000-00021-7
"Our farms and ranches can provide hunting, fishing, trapping,
and the esthetic values inherent in a well balanced landscape . . ."
This Bulletin tells you how to go about it.

Mammals of [National Wildlife Refuges]. Bur. of Sport Fisheries and Wildlife, 1968–72. Free from the Bur.
These are all **Refuge Leaflets**; and they consist of checklists of
mammals which have been observed in the wildlife refuges cited
below. They are not, usually, illustrated. But mammal enthusiasts
assure me they are of great value.
  301. Malheur National Wildlife Refuge. [1969]. 4 p.
  302. National Bison Range. [1969]. 4 p.
  308. Salt Plains National Wildlife Refuge. 1968. 3 p.
  312. Santa Ana National Wildlife Refuge. [1972]. [11] p.
  315. Red Rock Lakes National Wildlife Refuge. 1968. 4 p.
  323. Sacramento Valley National Wildlife Refuges. [1968]. 3 p.
  324. Mingo National Wildlife Refuge. 1968. 4 p.
  325. Kirwin National Wildlife Refuge. 1968. 4 p.
  326. Upper Mississippi River Wildlife and Forest Refuge. 1968.
       4 p.
  327. Squaw Creek National Wildlife Refuge. 1968. 4 p.
  328. Des Lacs National Wildlife Refuge. 1969. 4 p.
  329. Willamette Valley National Wildlife Refuge. [1969]. [4] p.

More Wildlife through Soil and Water Conservation. W. L. Anderson and L. V. Compton. Dept. of Agr., Agr. Inform. Bull. 175
(1971). [14] p. il.   001-000-01425-1
Lovely photographs, with text telling you what to do to preserve
wildlife and water.

Predatory Animals; Hearings . . . House of Representatives, 1973.
397 p. Free from the Comm.
The second part of hearings before the Subcommittee on Fisheries
and Wildlife Conservation and the Environment, of the House
Committee on Merchant Marine and Fisheries. "Predatory" here is

used in a very broad sense, to include animals that prey on our food supply as well as those that go after other animals. Kinds and numbers of such animals; the damage they do; and the danger they face. How we discourage and control them. The testimony cited is by wildlife experts.

White-tailed Deer in the Midwest. Forest Serv., Research Paper NC-39 (1970) [1972]. 34 p. il. Free from the Serv.
"Discusses the present status and future prospects of the non-yarding white-tailed deer population, including range appraisal, habitat, harvest regulation, and population control."

World Wildlife Conference Efforts to Save Endangered Species. Dept. of State, Genl. Foreign Policy Ser. 279 (1973). 30 p.
044-000-01486-6
Report of the Conference. Interesting to us for the lists of endangered animals, birds, reptiles, fishes, shellfishes.

Yellowstone Wildlife. Natl. Park Serv. [1972]. [32] p. il.
024-005-00474-2
Explains "web of life" in this national park; with sections on the wildlife that abounds there, and how to photograph them. Maps and color photographs.

WOMEN

Careers for Women in the 70's. Women's Bur., 1973. 14 p.
029-016-00112-7

Calling All Women in Federal Service; Know Your Rights and Opportunities. Women's Bur., Leaflet 53 [1972]. 11 p. il.
029-016-00009-7

Discover the World; Women in the Air Force. Dept. of the Air Force [1971]. 12 p. il. Free from the Dept.
The opportunities open; how they may broaden the enlistee's view.

Employment Problems of Women; a Classic Example of Discrimination. M. L. Lee and V. J. Jackson. Equal Employment Opportunity Comm., Research Rept. 37 (1972). 30 p. + 16 p. of tables. Free from the Comm.

More than 30,000,000 women work today (out of a work force of some 85,000,000; by 1980 the figure will rise to 37,000,000). At the beginning of the century only 5,000,000 women worked (17 percent of the work force). Nevertheless, despite the spectacular increase in the number of working women, discrimination continues, especially in certain areas. A most interesting study.

Equal Pay. Wages and Hours Div. (Labor Dept.), 1973. 16 p. il. Free from the Div.   029-016-00017-8

Expanding Opportunities; Women in Federal Government. Civil Serv. Comm. [1973]. 16 p. il. Free from the Serv.

Federal Women's Point of View. Civil Serv. Comm., 1972. 12 p. il.
006-000-00627-2
Charming pictorial account of those "good old days" when woman's place was in the home—or the sweatshop, or the fields; and the story of how she raised herself (with some male help). Fascinating chronicle of exploitation: in 1800 the Federal Government hired lady clerks at $600 a year; men made $1,200-1,800. In 1870, higher clerkships in federal agencies were opened to women "at discretion." In 1883, the Civil Service Commission allowed women to compete with men—and the first applicant was a woman, who got the highest score, and the *second* appointment! Traces woman's progress in a mere 171 years.

Great Field for a Woman, Air National Guard; Guard Belongs. Natl. Guard [1973]. [12] p. il. Free from the Guard.

Guide to Federal Laws Prohibiting Sex Discrimination. Civil Rights Comm., Clearinghouse Pub. 46 (1974). 113 p.   005-000-00105-6

Review and Synthesis of Research on Women in the Field of Work. M. B. Kievit. Off. of Educ., Center for Vocational and Technical

Educ., Ohio State Univ., Columbus, Ohio, Inform. Ser. 56 (1972).
96 p.   017-080-00918-8
Notable bibliography, dealing with the dual roles of women—as
workers and housewives.

Women's Bathing and Swimming Costumes in the United States.
C. B. Kidwell. Natl. Museum, Bull. 250 (1968) [1969]. 32 p. il.
Particularly charming for its fine photographs and reproductions of
old drawings.

Women, Uncle Sam Wants You. G. Stevenson. Labor Statistics Bur.,
1973. 9 p. Free from the Bur.
Brief guide to some of the positions open to women and how one
goes about securing one.

WORLD WAR II

**Amphibians Came to Conquer; the Story of Admiral Richmond
Kelly Turner.** G. C. Dyer. Naval Operations Off. [1972]. 2 vols.
                                                008-046-00049-2
The two volumes deal with the work of the amphibians "moving from Pacific island to Pacific atoll" and so on to clear the
"stepping stones to Tokyo."
  1. 596 p. il.
  2. [597-1,278] p. il.

Army Lineage Series. Dept. of the Army, 1969.
The purpose of this series is to gather compactly the official
lineage and honors of all major units of the active Army, Army
Reserve, and thus preserve their history and tradition.

Armor-Cavalry. Part I: Regular Army and Army Reserve. M. L.
Stubbs and S. R. Connor. 1969. 477 p.   008-029-00063-6
Opens with a narrative history of the Armor Branch (Armor and
Cavalry units), contains the lineage, honors, coats of arms, and
distinctive insignia of armor and cavalry units of the active Army
and the Army Reserve. There are more in this series.

First Army in Europe [1943–45]. E. Colby. The Senate, Senate Doc. 91-25 (1969). 189 p. il. Free from the Senate Document Room.

"Attempt in one volume to give the overall picture of the 1st Army's part in defeating the Nazis." A condensation of a very detailed source.

History of the U.S. Marine Corps Operations in World War II. Marine Corps, 1958–69.

Four of the five titles in this fine group are now out of print. The groups represented historical research and writing at their best, and the remaining title is highly recommended.

    5. Victory and Occupation. B. M. Frank and H. I. Shaw, Jr. 1968 [1969]. 945 p. il.   088-055-00041-6

    ". . . Marine Corps activities in the Okinawa invasion and the occupations of Japan and North China, as well as the little-known study of Marine prisoners of war. The book relates the Corps' postwar demobilization and reorganization programs as well."

Iwo Jima; Uncommon Valor [Was Common Virtue]. Marine Corps [1970]. [24] p. il. Free from the Corps.

On the Treadmill to Pearl Harbor; the Memoirs of Admiral James O. Richardson . . . as Told to Vice Admiral George C. Dyer. Dept. of the Navy, Naval Historical Div., 1973. 558 p. il.

Admiral Richardson began his service in 1898, so that some of his illustrations (and personal memories) are of great historical interest. The very great value of his memoirs lies in their factual presentation of a career that spanned over 45 years, ending with a "disagreement" with President F. D. Roosevelt, and the Admiral's separation from his position as Commander-in-Chief of the U.S. Fleet in 1941. The Admiral's unsuccessful efforts, subsequent to May, 1940, to keep the main strength of the fleet from being regularly based at Pearl Harbor are recorded in detail.

Pearl Harbor; Why; How; First Salvage and Final Appraisal. H. N.

Wallin. Naval Historical Off., 1968. 377 p. il.   008-046-00020-4
"Pearl Harbor will long stand out in men's minds as an example of
the results of basic unpreparedness of a peace-loving nation. . . .
The Navy has long needed a succinct account of the salvage operations at Pearl Harbor that miraculously resurrected what appeared to be a forever shattered fleet." Here is the account, bril-
liantly told and illustrated.

**Putt-Putt Air Force; the Story of the Civilian Pilot Training Pro-
gram and the War Training Service (1939–1944).** P. Strickland.
Fed. Aviation Admin., 1970 [1971.] 116 p. il. Free from the Admin.
The heroic groups that did so much to give us the very necessary
force to launch our first effective attacks in World War II, and to
keep them up.

76 Hours . . . Tarawa. Marine Corps, 1968. [22] p. il. Free from
the Corps.
A Japanese admiral boasted that it would take one million Americans and one hundred years to take Tarawa. It took the Marines
seventy-six hours.

U.S. Marine Corps Special Units of World War II. C. L. Upde-
graph. Marine Corps Hist. and Refer. Sect., 1972. 105 p. il. Free
from the Corps.

United States Army in World War II. S. Conn. ed., Office of the
Chief of Military History, 1956–74.

This prodigious work is nearing completion. Of the originally
planned 80 volumes, 75 have appeared. It is impossible, in any
brief commentary, to pay to the work anything like the profound
respect it deserves—certainly the entire set ranks among the finest
histories ever written. (Among other things, they are universally
well written.) They were compiled from every sort of record—from
the account of the soldier in the field to the most carefully worded
commands on the highest levels. Maps are superb and plentiful.
Occasionally, in the very nature of the material dealt with, there is

an interruption of the marvelous narrative writing (if such words may properly be used in speaking of something so essentially terrible as a war history); but these interruptions are rare. The total group has remained under the editorship of Dr. Stetson Conn. It stands as a monument not only of the highest editorship, but also of impeccable wisdom and rightness in selection and accuracy. Dr. Conn and his assistants must have had to sift millions of sources, yet the result is a model of clarity and avoidance of repetition. The editor in chief has divided the titles into eleven major divisions, one of which has a number of subparts. They are explained fully in Dr. Conn's original *Index* (cited below), and in the Chief of Military Office's "List of Publications" (of which the latest the compiler has seen is 1974).

Broadly, the volumes contain three types of history: narrative; analytical (dealing with the problems of strategy and policy); and that concerned with problems of matériel supply and their solution. But this statement must be accepted with a great many reservations; obviously, every part of the entire series employs every type of history. The compiler has limited himself to recent titles.

——Construction in the United States. L. Fine and J. A. Remington. 1972. 747 p. il.   008-029-00081-4
". . . describes the prewar and wartime tasks of military construction as performed first by the Quartermaster Corps and then, during the war, by the Corps of Engineers, including projects as varied as huge new munitions factories, Army training camps, the Pentagon, and construction for 'Manhattan,' the atomic bomb project."

——Last Offensive. C. B. MacDonald. 1973. 532 p. il.
                                                            008-029-00087-3
Focus of this volume is the role of the American Armies—First, Third, Seventh, Ninth, and (to a lesser extent), the Fifteenth, which comprised the largest and most powerful military force the United States had ever put into action. The roles of the Allied Armies, First Canadian, First French, and Second British are recounted in enough detail to put the position of the larger

American forces in perspective. This is the final work in the European subseries of the entire group.

WRITING AND EDITING

Clarity in Technical Reporting. S. Katzoff. Natl. Aeron. and Space Admin., SP-7010 (1964). 25 p.   033-000-00513-0
"Common sense suggestions for improving written technical reports. In particular, the booklet discusses basic attitudes, some elements of composition, the organization and contents of the report, and the editorial." It is important to emphasize that this NASA booklet is by no means limited to highly technical writing; it has very wide use from high school up. Many of us who have had to prepare papers (even papers on history) know that very little practical information is available to help us do so. That is the major value of this booklet.

Dictating Is an Easier Way. Veterans Admin., Handbook H-07-11 (1970). 21 p. il. Free from the Admin.
Easier way, that is, of making your points rapidly—say, 250 words per minute instead of 25. Excellent handbook, both for you and your secretary.

Word Division; Supplement to the Government Printing Office Style Manual. Govt. Printing Off., 1968. 190 p.   021-000-00006-0
Gives proper divisions of thousands of words.

YOUTH

Better Ways to Help Youth; 3 Youth Services Systems. D. Weser and others. Youth Develop. and Delinquency Prevention Admin. [1973]. 52 p.   017-065-00004-1
". . . describes three ways American communities are helping to meet the needs of troubled youngsters. . . . Not a how-to-do-it-book." But don't underrate this booklet as a practical guide; three

experienced workers express their views and tell how their communities are trying to deal with a serious problem.

Breakthrough for Disadvantaged Youth. Manpower Admin., 1969. 256 p.   029-000-00008-5
Based upon the very wide experience of the Administration charged with coming up with new ideas for helping the disadvantaged help themselves. Probably chiefly interesting to those directly engaged in such work. However, this sort of report deserves wide publicity, not only because of the activities it describes, but because it offers solutions to some problems.

Facts about: Adolescence. Natl. Inst. of Mental Health [1972]. 14 p. il.   017-024-00260-7

4-H Gets It All Together. Dept. of Agr., 1973. [36] p. il. Purchase from the Dept.
How the 4-H program works; and how it helps rural youth.

Reaching Out with a New Breed of Worker. Youth Develop. Off. [1973]. [31] p. il.   017-066-00013-7
The concept of the National Center for Youth Outreach Workers, "reaching and contacting youth with problems—beyond the confines of an agency, set hours, and limited knowledge of the individual youth."

Report of the President's Commission on Campus Unrest. The President, 1970. 537 p. il.   040-000-00194-8
Report based on three months' study by a distinguished group of scholars. As the Commission notes: "Campus unrest is a fact of life. It is not peculiar to America. It will go on. Exaggeration of its scope and seriousness and hysterical reactions to it will not make it disappear. They will only aggravate it. When campus unrest takes the form of violent and disruptive protest, it must be met with firm and just response. We make recommendations on what those responses should be." A convincing report, followed by an impressive bibliography.

Youth Involvement. J. R. Weber and C. Custer. Social and Rehab. Serv., 1970. 30 p.   017-060-00094-5
"Youth involvement is the *active* participation of young people in decision-making regarding programs and policies that affect them, and an equally *active* role in implementing these . . ."

Youth and the Meaning of Work. Manpower Admin., Res. Mono. 32 (1974). 34 p. il.   029-000-00199-5
Report of the results of a study of 1,860 male and female graduating seniors (Class of '72) from five different colleges and universities. "An attempt to identify a number of background and demographic variables which contribute to both differences and similarities in the attitudes, values, and expectations of college seniors." (A much fuller report: *Study Report; Youth and the Meaning of Work,* is obtainable from National Technical Information Service, 5825 Port Royal Road, Springfield, Va. 22151. Ask for PB 217360 and cite title.)

Youth Reports. Children's Bur., 1969–71. 3 parts.
A significant group of titles, based on a study of the attitudes of urban and suburban high school students enrolled in college preparatory courses. A series of "youth opinions" which does not seem to have been continued.
   1. Teenagers Discuss the Generation Gap. E. Herzog and others. 1969 [1970]. 36 p. il. Free from the Bur.   017-091-00153-7
   3. Youth Reporters Discuss Legal Age Restrictions. C. E. Sudia and J. H. Rea. 1971. 49 p.   017-091-00172-3

Youth Travel Abroad; What to Know Before You Go. Dept. of State, Genl. Foreign Policy Ser. 263 (1974). 20 p. il.   044-000-01571-4
Passport; programs and how to judge their value; charters; avoiding hassles; finding help when you need it; visas and passports required; sources of further information. Put this one in your travel case.

DEPARTMENTS AND AGENCIES FROM WHICH MATERIAL MAY BE OBTAINED FREE OR MUST BE PURCHASED DIRECTLY

ACTION, Washington, D.C. 20525

Aging, Administration on, Department of Health, Education, and Welfare, Washington, D.C. 20201

Agricultural Research Service, Department of Agriculture, Washington, D.C. 20250

Agriculture, Department of, Washington, D.C. 20250

Air Force, Department of the, the Pentagon, Washington, D.C. 20310

Census, Bureau of the, Department of Commerce, Washington, D.C. 20233

Chief of Military History, Department of the Army, Washington, D.C. 20307

Child Development, Office of, Department of Health, Education, and Welfare, Washington, D.C. 20201

Civil Defense, Office of, Department of the Army, the Pentagon, Washington, D.C. 20310

Civil Rights, Commission on, Department of Labor, Washington, D.C. 20425

Coast and Geodetic Survey, N.O.A.A., Department of Commerce, Rockville, Md. 20852

Coast Guard, Department of Transportation, Washington, D.C. 20590

Commerce, Department of, Washington, D.C. 20230

Copyright Office, Library of Congress, Washington, D.C. 20540

Customs, Bureau of, Treasury Department, Washington, D.C. 20279

Defense, Department of, Washington, D.C. 20301

Defense Civil Preparedness Agency, the Pentagon, Washington, D.C. 20301

Defense Mapping Agency, Hydrographic Center Depot, 5801 Tabor Ave., Philadelphia, Pa. 19120

Disease Control, Center for, Department of Health, Education, and Welfare, 1600 Clifton Rd. N.E., Atlanta, Ga. 30333

Domestic and International Business Administration, Department of Commerce, Washington, D.C. 20230

Dover Publications, 100 Varick St., New York, N.Y. 10014

Drug Enforcement Administration, Department of Justice, Washington, D.C. 20537

Economic Development Administration, Department of Commerce, Washington, D.C. 20230

Economic Opportunity, Office of, Washington, D.C. 20506

Economic Research Service, Department of Agriculture, Washington, D.C. 20520

Education, Office of, Department of Health, Education, and Welfare, Washington, D.C. 20202

Employment Standards Administration, Department of Labor, Washington, D.C. 20210

Energy Research and Development Administration, Office of Public Affairs, Washington, D.C. 20505.

Environmental Data Service, N.O.A.A., Department of Commerce, Rockville, Md. 20852

Environmental Protection Agency, Washington, D.C. 20460

Environmental Technical Applications Service, Department of the Air Force, the Pentagon, Washington, D.C. 20330

Executive Office of the President, P.O. Box 1100, Washington, D.C. 20008

Farmer Cooperative Service, Department of Agriculture, Washington, D.C. 20520

Federal Aviation Administration, Department of Transportation, Washington, D.C. 20591

Federal Bureau of Investigation, Washington, D.C. 20535

Federal Energy Administration, Washington, D.C. 20535

Federal Highway Administration, Department of Transportation, Washington, D.C. 20591

Federal Housing Administration, Department of Housing and Urban Development, Washington, D.C. 20410

Fish and Wildlife Service, Department of the Interior, Washington, D.C. 20240

Food and Drug Administration, Department of Health, Education, and Welfare, Rockville, Md. 20852

Food and Nutrition Service, Department of Agriculture, Washington, D.C. 20250

Forest Service, Department of Agriculture, Washington, D.C. 20250

Forestry, Fisheries, and Wildlife, Division of, Tennessee Valley Authority, Norris, Tenn. 37828

Freer Gallery of Art, Smithsonian Institution, Washington, D.C. 20560

General Accounting Office, Washington, D.C. 20548

Geological Survey, Department of the Interior, Reston, Va. 22092

Health, Education, and Welfare, Department of, Washington, D.C. 20201

Health Manpower Education, Bureau of, National Institutes of Health, Bethesda, Md. 20014

House Civil Rights Committee, House of Representatives, the Capitol, Washington, D.C. 20515

House committees and subcommittees, House of Representatives, the Capitol, Washington, D.C. 20515

House Document Room, House of Representatives, the Capitol, Washington, D.C. 20515

House of Representatives, the Capitol, Washington, D.C. 20515

Housing and Urban Development, Department of, Washington, D.C. 20410

Indian Affairs, Bureau of, Department of the Interior, Washington, D.C. 20240

Indian Arts and Crafts Board, Department of the Interior, Washington, D.C. 20240

Internal Revenue Service, Washington, D.C. 20224

International Commerce, Bureau of, Domestic and International Business Administration, Department of Commerce, Washington, D.C. 20230

Joint Economic Committee, Room G, Dirksen Senate Bldg., Washington, D.C. 20510

Joint Publication Research Service, 1000 N. Glebe Rd., Arlington, Va. 22201

Justice, Department of, Washington, D.C. 20530

Labor, Department of, Washington, D.C. 20210

Labor Statistics, Bureau of, Department of Labor, Washington, D.C. 20210

Lake Survey Center, 650 Federal Bldg., Detroit, Mich. 48226

Land Management, Bureau of, Department of the Interior, Washington, D.C. 20240

Law Enforcement Assistance Administration, Department of Justice, Washington, D.C. 20530

Library of Congress, Washington, D.C. 20340

Manpower Administration, Department of Labor, Washington, D.C. 20210

Map Information Office, Geological Survey, Department of the Interior, Reston, Va. 22092

Maternal and Child Health Service, Department of Health, Education, and Welfare, Rockville, Md. 30852

Medical Service Administration, Department of Health, Education, and Welfare, Washington, D.C. 20201

Medicine and Surgery, Bureau of, Department of the Navy, Washington, D.C. 20372

Mines, Bureau of, Department of the Interior, Washington, D.C. 20240

Minority Business Enterprise Office, Department of the Navy, Washington, D.C. 20372

Narcotics and Dangerous Drugs, Bureau of, Drug Enforcement Administration, Department of Justice, Washington, D.C. 20537

National Advisory Commission on Criminal Justice Standards and Goals, Department of Justice, Washington, D.C. 20530

National Aeronautics and Space Administration, Washington, D.C. 20546

National Archives and Records Service, General Services Administration, Washington, D.C. 20408

National Bureau of Standards, Department of Commerce, Washington, D.C. 20234

National Cancer Institute, Bethesda, Md. 20014

National Clearinghouse for Drug Abuse Information, 11400 Rockville Pike, Rockville, Md. 20852

National Collection of Fine Arts, Smithsonian Institution, Washington, D.C. 20560

National Gallery of Art, Smithsonian Institution, Washington, D.C. 20560

National Guard, Department of the Army, Washington, D.C. 20310

National Highway Traffic Safety Administration, Department of Transportation, Washington, D.C. 20590

National Institute of Alcohol Abuse and Alcoholism, National Institutes of Health, Public Health Service, Bethesda, Md. 20014

National Institute of Child Health and Human Development, Department of Health, Education, and Welfare, Bethesda, Md. 20014

National Institute of Mental Health, Department of Health, Education, and Welfare, Bethesda, Md. 20014

National Institute of Neurological Diseases and Stroke, Department of Health, Education, and Welfare. Bethesda, Md. 20014

National Institute of Occupational Safety and Health, Department of Health, Education, and Welfare, 1600 Clifton Rd. N.E., Atlanta, Ga. 30333

National Institutes of Health, Department of Health, Education, and Welfare, Bethesda, Md. 20014

National Library of Medicine, Department of Health, Education, and Welfare, Bethesda, Md. 20014

National Marine Fisheries Service, Department of Commerce, Rockville, Md. 20852

National Museum, Smithsonian Institution, Washington, D.C. 20560

National Oceanic and Atmospheric Administration, Department of Commerce, Rockville, Md. 20852

National Ocean Survey, N.O.A.A., Department of Commerce, Rockville, Md. 20852

National Park Service, Department of the Interior, Washington, D.C. 20240

National Weather Service, Department of Commerce, Rockville, Md. 20852

Naval Personnel, Bureau of, Department of the Navy, Washington, D.C. 20370

Nuclear Regulatory Commission, Washington, D.C. 20555

Organization of American States, Washington, D.C. 20006

Senate committees, the U.S. Senate, the Capitol, Washington, D.C. 20510

Senate Document Room, the U.S. Senate, Washington, D.C. 20380

Small Business Administration, Washington, D.C. 20416

Smithsonian Institution, Washington, D.C. 20560

Social and Rehabilitation Service, Department of Health, Education, and Welfare, Washington, D.C. 20201

Social Security Administration, 6401 Security Blvd., Baltimore, Md. 21235

Soil Conservation Service, Department of Agriculture, Washington, D.C. 20250

Sport Fisheries and Wildlife, Bureau of, Department of the Interior, Washington, D.C. 20240

State, Department of, Washington, D.C. 20520

Tennessee Valley Authority, Washington, D.C. 20444

Transportation, Department of, Washington, D.C. 20590

Treasury, Department of the, Washington, D.C. 20220

United States Customs Service, Washington, D.C. 20229

United States Information Service, Washington, D.C. 20547

United States Marine Corps, Department of the Navy, Washington, D.C. 20380

United States Postal Service, Washington, D.C. 20260

Veterans Administration, Washington, D.C. 20420

Water Program Operations, Office of, Environmental Protection Agency, Washington, D.C. 20460

Appendix B

GOVERNMENT PRINTING OFFICE BOOKSTORES

Birmingham Room 102A, 2121 Bldg., 2121 Eighth Ave., N., Birmingham, Ala. 35203

Los Angeles Room 1015, Federal Office Bldg., 300 North Los Angeles St., Los Angeles, Calif. 90012

San Francisco Room 1023, Federal Office Bldg., 450 Golden Gate Ave., San Francisco, Calif. 94102

Denver Room 1421, Federal Bldg., 1961 Stout St., Denver, Colo. 80202

Pueblo PDDC, Pueblo Industrial Park, Pueblo, Colo. 81001

Department of Commerce 14th and E Streets, Room 1098, Washington, D.C. 20230

Department of State First Floor, 21st and C St., N.W., Washington, D.C. 20520

Forrestal Bookstore James H. Forrestal Bldg., 1000 Independence Ave., Room 1-J001, Washington, D.C. 20407

Government Printing Office 710 North Capitol St., Washington, D.C. 20402

Pentagon Main Concourse, South End, Washington, D.C. 20310

U.S.I.A. 1776 Pennsylvania Ave., N.W., Washington, D.C. 20547

FLORIDA

Jacksonville   Room 158, Federal Bldg., 400 West Bay St., Jacksonville, Fla. 32202

GEORGIA

Atlanta   Room 100, Federal Bldg., 275 Peachtree St., N.E., Atlanta, Ga. 30303

ILLINOIS

Chicago   Room 1463, 14th Floor, Everett McKinley Dirksen Bldg., 219 South Dearborn St., Chicago, Ill. 60604

MASSACHUSETTS

Boston   Room G25, John F. Kennedy Federal Bldg., Sudbury St., Boston, Mass. 02203

MICHIGAN

Detroit   Room 229, Federal Bldg., 231 West Lafayette Blvd., Detroit, Mich. 48226

MISSOURI

Kansas City   Room 144, Federal Office Bldg., 601 East 12th St., Kansas City, Mo. 64106

NEW YORK

New York   Room 110, 26 Federal Plaza, New York, N.Y. 10007

OHIO

Canton   Federal Office Bldg., 201 Cleveland Ave., S.W. Canton, Ohio 44702

Cleveland   First Floor, Federal Office Bldg., 1240 East Ninth St., Cleveland, Ohio 44114

PENNSYLVANIA

Philadelphia   Room 1214, Federal Office Bldg., 600 Arch St., Philadelphia, Pa. 19106

TEXAS

Dallas Room 1C46, Federal Bldg., U.S. Courthouse, 1100 Commerce St., Dallas, Texas 75202

WASHINGTON

Seattle Room 194, Federal Office Bldg., 915 Second Ave., Seattle, Wash. 98104

WISCONSIN

Milwaukee Room 190, Federal Bldg., 519 East Wisconsin Ave., Milwaukee, Wis. 53202

Appendix C

DEPOSITORY LIBRARIES

Certain libraries are designated depositories for Government publications. Through them Federal Government documents are made available to residents of every state, the District of Columbia, the Canal Zone, Guam, Puerto Rico, and the Virgin Islands.

It is sometimes impossible to purchase desired publications from the Superintendent of Documents. The depositories, however, keep such publications permanently available. Not every Government publication can be consulted at all depository libraries. Designated regional depositories are required to retain one copy of all Government publications made available to depository libraries in printed or microfacsimile form. All other libraries are allowed to select the publications best suited to the interests of their particular clientele.

ALABAMA

Alexander City	Alexander City State Junior College, Thomas D. Russell Library
Auburn	Auburn University, Ralph Brown, Draughon Library
Birmingham	Birmingham Public Library
	Birmingham-Southern College Library
	Jefferson State Junior College, James B. Allen Library
	Samford University, Harwell G. Davis Library
Enterprise	Enterprise State Junior College Library
Florence	University of North Alabama, Collier Library
Gadsden	Gadsden Public Library
Huntsville	University of Alabama, Huntsville Campus Library
Jacksonville	Jacksonville State University, Romana Wood Library

Maxwell A.F. Base	Air University Library
Mobile	Mobile Public Library
	Spring Hill College, Thomas Byrne Memorial Library
	University of South Alabama Library
Montgomery	Alabama State Department of Archives and History Library
	Alabama Supreme Court Library
	Auburn University at Montgomery Library
Normal	Alabama Agricultural and Mechanical College, Drake Memorial Library
St. Bernard	St. Bernard College Library
Troy	Troy State University, Lurleen B. Wallace Educational Resources Center
Tuskegee Institute	Tuskegee Institute, Hollis Burke Frissell Library
University	University of Alabama, School of Law Library
	University of Alabama Library—*Regional*

ALASKA

Anchorage	Alaska Methodist University Library
	Supreme Court of Alaska Library
College	University of Alaska, Elmer E. Rasmuson Library
Juneau	Alaska State Library
Ketchikan	Ketchikan Community College Library

ARIZONA

Coolidge	Central Arizona College, Instruction Materials Center
Flagstaff	Northern Arizona University Library
Phoenix	Department of Library and Archives—*Regional*
	Phoenix Public Library
Tempe	Arizona State University, Matthews Library
Thatcher	Eastern Arizona College Library
Tucson	Tucson Public Library
	University of Arizona Library—*Regional*
Yuma	Yuma City-County Library

ARKANSAS

Arkadelphia	Ouachita Baptist University, Riley Library
Batesville	Arkansas College Library
Clarksville	College of the Ozarks Library
Conway	Hendrix College, O. C. Bailey Library
Fayetteville	University of Arkansas Library
Little Rock	Arkansas Supreme Court Library
	Little Rock Public Library
	University of Arkansas at Little Rock Library
Magnolia	Southern State College, J. M. Peace Library
Monticello	University of Arkansas at Monticello Library
Russellville	Arkansas Polytechnic College, Tomlinson Library
Searcy	Harding College, Beaumont Memorial Library
State College	Arkansas State University, Dean B. Ellis Library
Walnut Ridge	Southern Baptist College, Felix Goodson Library

CALIFORNIA

Anaheim	Anaheim Public Library
Arcadia	Arcadia Public Library
Arcata	Humboldt State College Library
Bakersfield	California State College, Bakersfield Library
	Kern County Library
Berkeley	University of California, General Library
	University of California, Law Library, Earl Warren Legal Center
Carson	Carson Regional Library
Chico	Chico State University Library
Claremont	Pomona College Documents Collection, Honnold Library
Compton	Compton Library
Culver City	Culver City Library
Davis	University of California at Davis Library
	University of California at Davis, School of Law Library
Dominguez Hills	California State College, Dominguez Hills, Educational Resources Center

Downey	Downey City Library
Fresno	Fresno County Free Library
	California State University Library
Fullerton	California State College at Fullerton Library
Garden Grove	Garden Grove Regional Library
Gardena	Gardena Public Library
Hayward	California State College at Hayward Library
Huntington Park	Huntington Park Library, San Antonio Region
Inglewood	Inglewood Public Library
Irvine	University of California at Irvine Library
La Jolla	University of California, San Diego, University Library
Lakewood	Angelo Iacoboni Public Library
Lancaster	Lancaster Regional Library
Long Beach	California State College at Long Beach Library
	Long Beach Public Library
Los Angeles	California State College at Los Angeles, John F. Kennedy Memorial Library
	Los Angeles County Law Library
	Los Angeles Public Library
	Loyola University of Los Angeles Library
	Occidental College, Mary Norton Clapp Library
	Pepperdine University Library
	University of California at Los Angeles Library
	University of California at Los Angeles, Law Library
	University of Southern California Library
Menlo Park	Department of the Interior, Geological Survey Library
Montebello	Montebello Library
Monterey	Naval Postgraduate School Library
Monterey Park	Bruggemeyer Memorial Library
Northridge	California State University at Northridge Library
Norwalk	Los Cerritos Regional Library
Oakland	Mills College Library
	Oakland Public Library

Ontario	Ontario City Library
Pasadena	California Institute of Technology, Millikan Memorial Library
	Pasadena Public Library
Pleasant Hill	Contra Costa County Library
Redding	Shasta County Library
Redlands	University of Redlands, Armacost Library
Redwood City	Redwood City Public Library
Reseda	West Valley Regional Branch Library
Richmond	Richmond Public Library
Riverside	Riverside Public Library
	University of California at Riverside Library
Sacramento	California State Library—*Regional*
	Sacramento City-County Library
	Sacramento County Law Library
	Sacramento State College Library
San Bernardino	San Bernardino County Free Library
San Diego	San Diego County Law Library
	San Diego County Library
	San Diego Public Library
	San Diego State University, Love Library
	University of San Diego Law Library
San Francisco	Mechanics' Institute Library
	San Francisco Public Library
	San Francisco State College, Social Science and Business Library
	Supreme Court of California Library
	U.S. Court of Appeals for Ninth Circuit Library
	University of San Francisco, Richard A. Gleeson Library
San Jose	San Jose State College Library
San Leandro	San Leandro Community Library Center
San Luis Obispo	California State Polytechnic University Library
San Rafael	Marin County Free Library
	Orange County Law Library
Santa Ana	Santa Ana Public Library

Santa Barbara	University of California at Santa Barbara Library
Santa Clara	University of Santa Clara, Orradre Library
Santa Cruz	University of California at Santa Cruz Library
Santa Rosa	Santa Rosa-Sonoma County Public Library
Stanford	Stanford University Libraries
Stockton	Public Library of Stockton and San Joaquin County
Thousand Oaks	California Lutheran College Library
Torrance	Torrance Civic Center Library
Turlock	Stanislaus State College Library
Valencia	Valencia Regional Library
Van Nuys	Los Angeles Valley College Library
Ventura	Ventura County Library Services Agency Library
Visalia	Tulare County Free Library
Walnut	Mount San Antonio College Library
West Covina	West Covina Library
Whittier	Whittier College, Wardman Library

CANAL ZONE

Balboa Heights	Canal Zone Library-Museum

COLORADO

Alamosa	Adams State College Learning Resources Center
Boulder	University of Colorado Libraries—*Regional*
Colorado Springs	Colorado College, Charles Leaming Tutt Library
	University of Colorado, Colorado Springs Library
Denver	Colorado State Library
	Denver Public Library—*Regional*
	Department of Interior, Bureau of Reclamation Library
	Regis College, Dayton Memorial Library
	U.S. Court of Appeals, Tenth Circuit Library
	University of Denver, Penrose Library
Fort Collins	Colorado State University Library
Golden	Colorado School of Mines, Arthur Lakes Library
	Jefferson County Public Library, Bonfils-Stanton Regional Library
Grand Junction	Mesa County Public Library

Greeley	University of Northern Colorado Library
Gunnison	Western State College, Leslie J. Savage Library
La Junta	Otero Junior College, Wheeler Library
Pueblo	Pueblo Regional Library
	Southern Colorado State College Library
U.S. Air Force Academy	Academy Library

CONNECTICUT

Bridgeport	Bridgeport Public Library
Danbury	Western Connecticut State College, Ruth A. Haas Library
Danielson	Quinebaug Valley Community College
Enfield	Enfield Public Library
Hartford	Connecticut State Library—*Regional*
	Hartford Public Library
	Trinity College Library
Middletown	Wesleyan University Library
Mystic	Marine Historical Association, Inc., Mystic Seaport Library
New Britain	Central Connecticut State College, Elihu Burritt Library
New Haven	Southern Connecticut State College Library
	Yale University Library
New London	Connecticut College Library
	U.S. Coast Guard Academy Library
Pomfret	Pomfret School Library
Stamford	Stamford Public Library
Storrs	University of Connecticut, Wilbur Cross Library
Waterbury	Silas Bronson Library
West Haven	University of New Haven Library

DELAWARE

Dover	Delaware State College, William C. Jason Library
	State Department of Community Affairs and Economic Development, Division of Libraries
	State Law Library in Kent County

Georgetown	Delaware Technical and Community College, Southern Branch Library
Newark	University of Delaware, Morris Library
Wilmington	New Castle County Law Library
	Wilmington Institute and New Castle County Library

DISTRICT OF COLUMBIA

Washington	Advisory Commission on Intergovernmental Relations Library
	Civil Aeronautics Board Library
	Civil Service Commission Library
	Department of Commerce Library
	Department of Health, Education, and Welfare Library
	Department of Housing and Urban Development Library
	Department of the Interior Central Library
	Department of the Interior, Geological Survey Library
	Department of Justice Main Library
	Department of State Library
	Department of State, Office of Legal Advisor, Law Library
	Department of Transportation, National Highway Traffic Safety Administration Library
	District of Columbia Public Library
	Federal City College Library
	Federal Deposit Insurance Corporation Library
	Federal Election Commission Library
	General Accounting Office Library
	General Services Administration Library
	Georgetown University Library
	Indian Claims Commission Library
	National Agricultural Library
	National War College Library
	Navy Department Library

Navy Department, Office of Judge Advocate General Library

Office of the Adjutant General, Department of Army Library

Office of Management and Budget Library

Postal Service Library

Treasury Department Library

Veterans Administration, Central Office Library

FLORIDA

Boca Raton	Florida Atlantic University Library
Clearwater	Clearwater Public Library
Coral Gables	University of Miami Library
Daytona Beach	Volusia County Public Libraries
De Land	Stetson University, duPont-Ball Library
Fort Lauderdale	Fort Lauderdale Public Library
	Nova University Library
Fort Pierce	Indian River Community College
Gainesville	University of Florida Libraries—*Regional*
Jacksonville	Haydon Burns Library
	Jacksonville University, Swisher Library
	University of North Florida Library
Lakeland	Lakeland Public Library
Leesburg	Lake-Sumter Community College Library
Melbourne	Florida Institute of Technology Library
Miami	Florida International University Library
	Miami Public Library
Opa Locka	Biscayne College Library
Orlando	Florida Technological University Library
Palatka	St. Johns River Junior College Library
Pensacola	University of West Florida, John C. Pace Library
Port Charlotte	Charlotte County Library System
St. Petersburg	St. Petersburg Public Library
	Stetson University, College of Law Library
Sarasota	Sarasota Public Library
Tallahassee	Florida Agricultural and Mechanical University, Coleman Memorial Library

	Florida State Library
	Florida State University, R. M. Stozier Library
	Florida Supreme Court Library
Tampa	Tampa Public Library
	University of South Florida Library
	University of Tampa, Merle Kelce Library
Winter Park	Rollins College, Mills Memorial Library

GEORGIA

Albany	Albany Public Library
Americus	Georgia Southwestern College, James Earl Carter Library
Athens	University of Georgia Libraries
Atlanta	Atlanta Public Library
	Atlanta University, Trevor Arnett Library
	Emory University, Robert W. Woodruff Library
	Emory University, School of Law Library
	Georgia Institute of Technology, Prince Gilbert Memorial Library
	Georgia State Library
	Georgia State University Library
Augusta	Augusta College Library
Brunswick	Brunswick Public Library
Carrollton	West Georgia College, Sanford Library
Columbus	Columbus College, Simon Schob Memorial Library
Dahlonega	North Georgia College Library
Decatur	Dekalb Community College-South Campus, Learning Resources Center
Gainesville	Chestatee Regional Library
Macon	Mercer University Library
Marietta	Kennesaw Junior College Library
Milledgeville	Georgia College at Milledgeville, Ina Dillard Russell Library
Mount Berry	Berry College, Memorial Library
Savannah	Savannah Public and Chatham-Effingham Liberty Regional Library
Statesboro	Georgia Southern College, Rosenwald Library

Valdosta | Valdosta State College, Richard Holmes Powell Library

GUAM

Agana | Nieves M. Flores Memorial Library

HAWAII

Hilo | University of Hawaii, Hilo Campus Library
Honolulu | Chaminade College of Honolulu Library
| Hawaii Medical Library, Inc.
| Hawaii State Library
| Municipal Reference Library of the City and County of Honolulu
| Supreme Court Law Library
| University of Hawaii Library
Laie | Church College of Hawaii, Woolley Library
Lihue | Kauai Public Library
Pearl City | Leeward Community College Library
Wailuku | Maui Public Library

IDAHO

Boise | Boise Public Library and Information Center
| Boise State College Library
| Idaho State Law Library
| Idaho State Library
Caldwell | College of Idaho, Terteling Library
Moscow | University of Idaho Library—*Regional*
Pocatello | Idaho State University Library
Rexburg | Ricks College, David O. McKay Library
Twin Falls | College of Southern Idaho Library

ILLINOIS

Bloomington | Illinois Wesleyan University Libraries
Carbondale | Southern Illinois University Library
Carlinville | Blackburn College Library
Carterville | Shawnee Library System
Champaign | University of Illinois Law Library, College of Law

Charleston	Eastern Illinois University, Booth Library
Chicago	Chicago Public Library
	Chicago State University Library
	De Paul University, Lincoln Park Campus Library
	Field Museum of Natural History Library
	John Crerar Library
	Loyola University of Chicago, E. M. Cudahy Memorial Library
	Newberry Library
	Northeastern Illinois University Library
	University of Chicago Law Library
	University of Chicago Library
	University of Illinois, Chicago Circle Campus Library
Decatur	Decatur Public Library
De Kalb	Northern Illinois University, Swen Franklin Parson Library
Edwardsville	Southern Illinois University, Lovejoy Memorial Library
Elsah	Principia College, Marshall Brooks Library
Evanston	Northwestern University Library
Freeport	Freeport Public Library
Galesburg	Galesburg Public Library
Jacksonville	MacMurry College, Henry Pfeiffer Library
Kankakee	Olivet Nazarene College, Memorial Library
Lake Forest	Lake Forest College, Donnelley Library
Lebanon	McKendree College, Holman Library
Lisle	Illinois Benedictine College, Theodore F. Lownik Library
Lockport	Lewis University of Science and Technology Library
Macomb	Western Illinois University Memorial Library
Moline	Black Hawk College, Learning Resources Center
Monmouth	Monmouth College Library
Mount Carmel	Wabash Valley College Library, Media Center
Normal	Illinois State University, Milner Library
Oak Park	Oak Park Public Library

Palos Hills	Moraine Valley Community College Library
Park Forest South	Governors State University Library
Peoria	Bradley University, Cullom Davis Library
	Peoria Public Library
River Forest	Rosary College Library
Rockford	Rockford Public Library
Springfield	Illinois State Library—*Regional*
Urbana	University of Illinois Library
Wheaton	Wheaton College Library
Woodstock	Woodstock Public Library

INDIANA

Anderson	Anderson College, Charles E. Wilson Library
Bloomington	Indiana University Library
Crawfordsville	Wabash College, Lilly Library
Evansville	Evansville and Vanderburgh County Public Library
	Indiana State University, Evansville Campus Library
Fort Wayne	Indiana-Purdue Universities, Regional Campus Library
	Public Library of Fort Wayne and Allen County
Gary	Gary Public Library
	Indiana University, Northwest Campus Library
Greencastle	De Pauw University, Roy O. West Library
Hammond	Hammond Public Library
Hanover	Hanover College Library
Huntington	Huntington College Library
Indianapolis	Butler University, Irwin Library
	Indianapolis Public Library
	Indiana State Library—*Regional*
	Indiana Supreme Court Law Library
	Indiana University, Law Library
Jeffersonville	Indiana University, Southeastern Campus Library
Kokomo	Indiana University, Kokomo Regional Campus Library
Lafayette	Purdue University Library

Muncie	Ball State University Library
-	Muncie Public Library
Notre Dame	University of Notre Dame, Memorial Library
Rensselaer	St. Joseph's College Library
Richmond	Earlham College, Lilly Library
	Morrison-Reeves Library
South Bend	Indiana University at South Bend Library
Terre Haute	Indiana State University, Cunningham Memorial Library
Valparaiso	Valparaiso University, Moellering Memorial Library

IOWA

Ames	Iowa State University of Science and Technology Library
Cedar Falls	University of Northern Iowa Library
Council Bluffs	Free Public Library
	Iowa Western Community College, Hoover Media Library
Davenport	Davenport Public Library
Des Moines	Drake University, Cowles Library
	Drake University Law Library
	Iowa State Traveling Library
	Public Library of Des Moines
Dubuque	Carnegie-Stout Public Library
	Loras College, Wahlert Memorial Library
Fayette	Upper Iowa College, Henderson-Wilder Library
Grinnell	Grinnell College, Burling Library
Iowa City	University of Iowa, Law Library
	University of Iowa Library—*Regional*
Lamoni	Graceland College, Frederick Madison Smith Library
Mount Vernon	Cornell College, Russell D. Cole Library
Orange City	Northwestern College, Ramaker Library
Sioux City	Sioux City Public Library

KANSAS

| Atchison | Benedictine College Library |
| Baldwin City | Baker University Library |

Colby	Colby Community Junior College Library
Emporia	Kansas State Teachers College, William Allen White Library
Hays	Fort Hays Kansas State College, Forsyth Library
Hutchinson	Hutchinson Public Library
Lawrence	University of Kansas Law Library
	University of Kansas, Watson Library
Manhattan	Kansas State University, Farrell Library
Pittsburg	Kansas State College of Pittsburg, Porter Library
Salina	Kansas Wesleyan University, Memorial Library
Topeka	Kansas State Historical Society Library
	Kansas State Library
	Kansas Supreme Court Law Library
	Washburn University of Topeka, Law Library
Wichita	Wichita State University Library

KENTUCKY

Ashland	Ashland Public Library
Barbourville	Union College, Abigail E. Weeks Memorial Library
Bowling Green	Western Kentucky University, Cravens Graduate Center and Library
Covington	Thomas More College Library
Danville	Centre College, Grace Doherty Library
Frankfort	Kentucky Department of Libraries
	Kentucky State University, Blazer Library
	State Law Library
Highland Heights	Northern Kentucky State College Library
Lexington	University of Kentucky, Law Library
	University of Kentucky, Margaret I. King Library —*Regional*
Louisville	Louisville Free Public Library
	University of Louisville, Belknap Campus Library
	University of Louisville Law Library, Belknap Campus
Morehead	Morehead State University, Johnson Camden Library
Murray	Murray State University Library

Owensboro	Kentucky Wesleyan College Library
Pikeville	Pikeville College Library
Richmond	Eastern Kentucky University, John Grant Crabbe Library

LOUISIANA

Baton Rouge	Louisiana State University Law Library
	Louisiana State University Library—*Regional*
	Southern University Library
Eunice	Louisiana State University at Eunice, Le Doux Library
Hammond	Southeastern Louisiana University, Sims Memorial Library
Lafayette	University of Southwestern Louisiana Library
Lake Charles	McNeese State University, Frazar Memorial Library
Monroe	Northeast Louisiana University, Sandel Library
Natchitoches	Northwestern State University, Watson Memorial Library
New Orleans	Isaac Delgado College, Moss Technical Library
	Law Library of Louisiana
	Loyola University Library
	New Orleans Public Library
	Southern University in New Orleans Library
	Tulane University, Howard-Tilton Memorial Library
	University of New Orleans Library
	U.S. Court of Appeals, Fifth Circuit Library
Pineville	Louisiana College, Richard W. Norton Memorial Library
Ruston	Louisiana Technical University Library—*Regional*
Shreveport	Louisiana State University at Shreveport Library
	Shreve Memorial Library
Thibodaux	Francis T. Nicholls State University, Leonidas Polk Library

MAINE

Augusta	Maine Law and Legislative Reference Library
	Maine State Library

Bangor	Bangor Public Library
Brunswick	Bowdoin College, Hawthorne-Longfellow Library
Castine	Maine Maritime Academy, Nutting Memorial Library
Lewiston	Bates College Library
Orono	University of Maine, Raymond H. Fogler Library—*Regional*
Portland	Portland Public Library
	University of Maine Law Library
Springvale	Nasson College Library
Waterville	Colby College Library

MARYLAND

Annapolis	Maryland State Library
	U.S. Naval Academy, Nimitz Library
Baltimore	Enoch Pratt Free Library
	Johns Hopkins University, Milton S. Eisenhower Library
	Morgan State College, Soper Library
	University of Baltimore, Langsdale Library
	University of Maryland, Baltimore County Library
	University of Maryland, School of Law Library
Bel Air	Harford Community College Library
Chestertown	Washington College, Chester M. Miller Library
College Park	University of Maryland, McKeldin Library—*Regional*
Cumberland	Allegany Community College Library
Frostburg	Frostburg State College Library
Germantown	Atomic Energy Commission Library
Patuxent River	Naval Air Station Library
Rockville	Montgomery County Department of Public Libraries
Salisbury	Salisbury State College, Blackwell Library
Towson	Goucher College, Julia Rogers Library
Westminster	Western Maryland College Library

MASSACHUSETTS

Amherst	Amherst College Library

	University of Massachusetts, Goodell Library
Belmont	Belmont Memorial Library
Boston	Boston Athenaeum Library
	Boston College, Bapst Library
	Boston Public Library—*Regional*
	Northeastern University, Dodge Library
	State Library of Massachusetts
Brookline	Public Library of Brookline
Cambridge	Harvard College Library
	Massachusetts Institute of Technology Libraries
Chicopee	Our Lady of the Elms College Library
Lowell	Lowell Technological Institute, Alumni Memorial Library
Lynn	Lynn Public Library
Marlborough	Marlborough Public Library
Medford	Tufts University Library
Milton	Curry College Library
New Bedford	New Bedford Free Public Library
North Dartmouth	Southeastern Massachusetts University Library
North Easton	Stonehill College, Cushing-Martin Library
Springfield	Springfield City Library
Waltham	Brandeis University, Goldfarb Library
Wellesley	Wellesley College Library
Wenham	Gordon College, Winn Library
Williamstown	Williams College Library
Wilmington	Wilmington Memorial Library
Worcester	American Antiquarian Society Library
	University of Massachusetts, Medical Center Library
	Worcester Public Library

MICHIGAN

Albion	Albion College, Stockwell Memorial Library
Allendale	Grand Valley State College Library
Alma	Alma College, Monteith Library
Ann Arbor	Great Lakes Basin Library
	University of Michigan, Harlan Hatcher Library

Benton Harbor	Benton Harbor Public Library
Bloomfield Hills	Cranbrook Institute of Science Library
Dearborn	Henry Ford Centennial Library
	Henry Ford Community College Library
Detroit	Detroit Public Library—*Regional*
	Marygrove College Library
	Mercy College of Detroit Library
	University of Detroit Library
	Wayne County Public Library
	Wayne State University Law Library
	Wayne State University, G. Flint Purdy Library
Dowagiac	Southwestern Michigan College Library
East Lansing	Michigan State University, Law Library
	Michigan State University Library
Escanaba	Michigan State Library, Upper Peninsula Branch
Farmington	Martin Luther King Learning Resources Center, Oakland Community College
Flint	Charles Stewart Mott Library
	Flint Public Library
Grand Rapids	Grand Rapids Public Library
	Calvin College Library
Houghton	Michigan Technological University Library
Jackson	Jackson Public Library
Kalamazoo	Kalamazoo Library System
	Western Michigan University, Dwight B. Waldo Library
Lansing	Michigan State Library—*Regional*
Livonia	Schoolcraft College Library
Marquette	Northern Michigan University, Olsen Library
Monroe	Monroe County Library System
Mt. Clemens	Macomb County Library
Mt. Pleasant	Central Michigan University Library
Muskegon	Hackley Public Library
Olivet	Olivet College Library
Petoskey	North Central Michigan College Library
Port Huron	Saint Clair County Library System
Rochester	Oakland University, Kresge Library

Saginaw	Hoyt Public Library
Traverse City	Northwestern Michigan College, Mark Osterlin Library
University Center	Delta College Library
Warren	Warren Public Library, Arthur J. Miller Branch
Ypsilanti	Eastern Michigan University Library

MINNESOTA

Bemidji	Bemidji State College, A. C. Clark Library
Collegeville	St. John's University, Alcuin Library
Duluth	Duluth Public Library
Mankato	Mankato State College Memorial Library
Minneapolis	Anoka County Library
	Minneapolis Public Library
	Southdale-Hennepin Area Library
	University of Minnesota, Wilson Library—*Regional*
Moorhead	Moorhead State College Library
Morris	University of Minnesota at Morris Library
Northfield	Carleton College Library
	St. Olaf College, Rolvaag Memorial Library
St. Cloud	St. Cloud State College Library
St. Paul	Minnesota Historical Society Library
	Minnesota State Law Library
	St. Paul Public Library
	University of Minnesota, St. Paul Campus Library
Saint Peter	Gustavus Adolphus College Library
Stillwater	Stillwater Public Library
Willmar	Crow River Regional Library
Winona	Winona State College, Maxwell Library

MISSISSIPPI

Cleveland	Delta State University, W. B. Roberts Library
Columbus	Mississippi State College for Women, J. C. Fant Memorial Library
Hattiesburg	University of Southern Mississippi Library
Jackson	Jackson State College Library

	Millsaps College, Millsaps-Wilson Library
	Mississippi Library Commission
	Mississippi State Law Library
Lorman	Alcorn Agricultural and Mechanical College Library
State College	Mississippi State University, Mitchell Memorial Library
University	University of Mississippi Library
	University of Mississippi, School of Law Library

MISSISSIPPI

Cape Girardeau	Southeast Missouri State College, Kent Library
Columbia	University of Missouri Library
Fayette	Central Methodist College Library
Fulton	Westminster College, Reeves Library
Jefferson City	Lincoln University, Inman E. Page Library
	Missouri State Library
	Missouri Supreme Court Library
Joplin	Missouri Southern State College Library
Kansas City	Kansas City Public Library
	Rockhurst College Library
	University of Missouri at Kansas City, General Library
Kirksville	Northeast Missouri State Teachers College, Pickler Memorial Library
Liberty	William Jewell College Library
Rolla	University of Missouri at Rolla Library
St. Charles	Lindenwood College, Margaret Leggat Butler Library
St. Joseph	St. Joseph Public Library
St. Louis	St. Louis County Library
	St. Louis Public Library
	St. Louis University, Law Library
	St. Louis University, Pius XII Memorial Library
	U.S. Court of Appeals, Eighth Circuit Library
	University of Missouri at St. Louis, Thomas Jefferson Library

	Washington University, John M. Olin Library
Springfield	Drury College, Walker Library
	Southwest Missouri State College Library
Warrensburg	Central Missouri State College, Ward Edwards Library

MONTANA

Billings	Eastern Montana College Library
Bozeman	Montana State University Library
Butte	Montana College of Mineral Science and Technology Library
Helena	Carroll College Library
	Montana Historical Society Library
	Montana State Library
Missoula	University of Montana Library—*Regional*

NEBRASKA

Blair	Dana College, Dana-LIFE Library
Crete	Doane College, Whitin Library
Fremont	Midland Lutheran College Library
Kearney	Kearney State College, Calvin T. Ryan Library
Lincoln	Nebraska Publications Clearinghouse, Nebraska Library Commission—*Regional*
	Nebraska State Library
	University of Nebraska, Don L. Love Memorial Library
Omaha	Creighton University, Alumni Library
	Omaha Public Library
	University of Nebraska at Omaha, Gene Eppley Library
Scottsbluff	Scottsbluff Public Library
Wayne	Wayne State College, U.S. Conn Library

NEVADA

Carson City	Nevada State Library
	Nevada Supreme Court Library
Las Vegas	Clark County Library District Library

University of Nevada at Las Vegas, James R. Dickinson Library

Reno | Nevada State Historical Society Library
University of Nevada Library—*Regional*

NEW HAMPSHIRE

Concord | Franklin Pierce Law Center Library
New Hampshire State Library
Durham | University of New Hampshire Library
Franconia | Franconia College Library
Hanover | Dartmouth College, Baker Library
Henniker | New England College Library
Manchester | Manchester City Library
St. Anselm's College, Geise Library
Nashua | Nashua Public Library

NEW JERSEY

Bayonne | Bayonne Free Public Library
Bloomfield | Free Public Library of Bloomfield
Bridgeton | Cumberland County Library
Camden | Rutgers University-Camden Library
Convent Station | College of St. Elizabeth, Mahoney Library
Dover | County College of Morris Library
East Orange | East Orange Public Library
Elizabeth | Free Public Library of Elizabeth
Glassboro | Glassboro State College, Savitz Learning Resource Center
Hackensack | Johnson Free Public Library
Irvington | Free Public Library of Irvington
Jersey City | Free Public Library of Jersey City
Jersey City State College, Forrest A. Irwin Library
Madison | Drew University, Rose Memorial Library
Mahwah | Ramapo College Library
Mount Holly | Burlington County Library
New Brunswick | Free Public Library
Rutgers University Library

Newark	Newark Public Library—*Regional*
	Rutgers-the State University, John Cotton Dana Library
Passaic	Passaic Public Library
Plainfield	Plainfield Public Library
Pomona	Stockton State College Library
Princeton	Princeton University Library
Rutherford	Fairleigh Dickinson University, Messler Library
Shrewsbury	Monmouth County Library
South Orange	Seton Hall University Library
Teaneck	Fairleigh Dickinson University, Teaneck Campus Library
Toms River	Ocean County College Learning Resources Center
Trenton	New Jersey State Library, Law and Reference Bureau, Department of Education
	Trenton Free Public Library
Union	Kean College of New Jersey, Nancy Thompson Library
Upper Montclair	Montclair State College, Harry A. Sprague Library
Wayne	Wayne Public Library
West Long Branch	Monmouth College, Guggenheim Memorial Library
Woodbridge	Free Public Library of Woodbridge

NEW MEXICO

Albuquerque	University of New Mexico, Medical Sciences Library
	University of New Mexico, School of Law Library
	University of New Mexico, Zimmerman Library—*Regional*
Hobbs	New Mexico Junior College, Pannell Library
Las Cruces	New Mexico State University Library
Las Vegas	New Mexico Highlands University, Donnelly Library
Portales	Eastern New Mexico University Library

Sante Fe	New Mexico State Library—*Regional*
	Supreme Court Law Library
Silver City	Western New Mexico University, Miller Library

NEW YORK

Albany	New York State Library—*Regional*
	State University of New York at Albany Library
Auburn	Seymour Library
Bayside	Queensborough Community College Library
Binghamton	State University of New York at Binghamton Library
Brockport	State University of New York, Drake Memorial Library
Bronx	Herbert H. Lehman College Library
	New York Public Library, Mott Haven Branch
Bronxville	Sarah Lawrence College Library
Brooklyn	Brooklyn College Library
	Brooklyn Law School, Law Library
	Brooklyn Public Library
	Polytechnic Institute of Brooklyn, Spicer Library
	Pratt Institute Library
	State University of New York, Downstate Medical Center Library
Buffalo	Buffalo and Erie County Public Library
	State University of New York at Buffalo, Lockwood Memorial Library
Canton	St. Lawrence University, Owen D. Young Library
Corning	Corning Community College, Arthur A. Houghton, Jr. Library
Cortland	State University of New York, College at Cortland, Memorial Library
Delhi	State University Agricultural and Technical College Library
Douglaston	Cathedral College Library
East Islip	East Islip Public Library
Elmira	Elmira College, Gannett-Tripp Learning Center

Farmingdale	State University Agricultural and Technical Institute at Farmingdale Library
Flushing	Queens College, Paul Klapper Library
Garden City	Adelphi University, Swirbul Library
	Nassau Library System
Geneseo	State University College, Milne Library
Greenvale	C. W. Post College, B. Davis Schwartz Memorial Library
Hamilton	Colgate University Library
Hempstead	Hofstra University Library
Ithaca	Cornell University Library
	New York State Colleges of Agriculture and Home Economics, Albert R. Mann Library
Jamaica	Queens Borough Public Library
	St. John's University Library
Kings Point	U.S. Merchant Marine Academy Library
Mount Vernon	Mount Vernon Public Library
New Paltz	State University College Library
New York City	City University of New York, City College Library
	College of Insurance, Ecker Library
	Columbia University Libraries
	Cooper Union Library
	Fordham University Library
	New York Law Institute Library
	New York Public Library, Astor Branch
	New York Public Library, Lenox Branch
	New York University, Law Library
	New York University Libraries
	State University of New York, Maritime College Library
Newburgh	Newburgh Free Library
Oakdale	Dowling College Library
Oneonta	State University College, James M. Milne Library
Oswego	State University College, Penfield Library
Plattsburgh	State University College, Benjamin F. Feinberg Library

Potsdam	Clarkson College of Technology, Harriet Call Burnap Memorial Library
	State University College, Frederick W. Crumb Memorial Library
Poughkeepsie	Vassar College Library
Purchase	State University of New York, College at Purchase Library
Rochester	Rochester Public Library
	University of Rochester Library
St. Bonaventure	St. Bonaventure College, Friedsam Memorial Library
Saratoga Springs	Skidmore College Library
Schnectady	Union College, Schaffer Library
Southampton	Southampton College Library
Staten Island (Grymes Hill)	Wagner College, Horrmann Library
Stony Brook	State University of New York at Stony Brook Library
Syracuse	Syracuse University Library
Troy	Troy Public Library
Utica	Utica Public Library
West Point	U.S. Military Academy Library
Yonkers	Yonkers Public Library

NORTH CAROLINA

Asheville	University of North Carolina at Asheville, D. Hiden Ramsey Library
Boiling Springs	Gardner-Webb College, Dover Memorial Library
Boone	Appalachian State University Library
Buies Creek	Campbell College, Carrie Rich Memorial Library
Chapel Hill	University of North Carolina Library—*Regional*
Charlotte	Public Library of Charlotte and Mecklenburg County
	Queens College, Everette Library
	University of North Carolina at Charlotte, Atkins Library

Cullowhee	Western Carolina University, Hunter Library
Davidson	Davidson College, Hugh A. & Jane Grey Memorial Library
Durham	Duke University, William R. Perkins Library
	North Carolina Central University, James E. Shepard Memorial Library
Elon College	Elon College Library
Fayetteville	Fayetteville State University, Chesnutt Library
Greensboro	North Carolina Agricultural and Technical State University, F. D. Bluford Library
	University of North Carolina at Greensboro, Walter Clinton Jackson Library
Greenville	East Carolina University, J. Y. Joyner Library
Laurinburg	St. Andrews Presbyterian College, DeTamble Library
Lexington	Davidson County Public Library System
Mount Olive	Mount Olive College, Moye Library
Murfreesboro	Chowan College, Whitaker Library
Pembroke	Pembroke State University Library
Raleigh	North Carolina State Library
	North Carolina State University, D. H. Hill Library
	North Carolina Supreme Court Library
	Wake County Public Libraries
Rocky Mount	North Carolina Wesleyan College Library
Salisbury	Catawba College Library
Wilmington	University of North Carolina at Wilmington, William M. Randall Library
Wilson	Atlantic Christian College, Clarence L. Hardy Library
Winston-Salem	Forsyth County Public Library System
	Wake Forest University, Z. Smith Reynolds Library

NORTH DAKOTA

Bismarck	North Dakota State Law Library
	State Historical Society of North Dakota
	State Library Commission Library
	Veterans Memorial Public Library

Dickinson	Dickinson State College Library
Fargo	Fargo Public Library
	North Dakota State University Library—*Regional*, in cooperation with University of North Dakota, Chester Fritz Library at Grand Forks
Grand Forks	University of North Dakota, Chester Fritz Library
Minot	Minot State College, Memorial Library
Valley City	State College Library

OHIO

Ada	Ohio Northern University, J. P. Taggart Law Library
Akron	Akron Public Library
	University of Akron Library
Alliance	Mount Union College Library
Ashland	Ashland College Library
Athens	Ohio University Library
Batavia	Clermont General and Technical College Library
Bluffton	Bluffton College, Musselman Library
Bowling Green	Bowling Green State University Library
Canton	Malone College, Everett L. Cattell Library
Chardon	Geauga County Public Library
Cincinnati	Public Library of Cincinnati and Hamilton County
	University of Cincinnati Library
Cleveland	Case Western Reserve University, Freiberger Library
	Cleveland Heights-University Heights Public Library
	Cleveland Public Library
	Cleveland State University Library
	John Carroll University, Grasselli Library
	Municipal Reference Library
Columbus	Capital University Library
	Columbus Public Library
	Ohio State Library—*Regional*
	Ohio State University Library
	Ohio Supreme Court Law Library

Dayton	Dayton and Montgomery County Public Library
	University of Dayton, Albert Emanuel Library
	Wright State University Library
Delaware	Ohio Wesleyan University, L. A. Beeghly Library
Elyria	Elyria Public Library
Findlay	Findlay College, Shafer Library
Gambier	Kenyon College Library
Granville	Denison University Library
Hiram	Hiram College, Teachout-Price Memorial Library
Kent	Kent State University Library
Marietta	Marietta College, Dawes Memorial Library
Middletown	Miami University at Middletown, Gardner-Harvey Library
New Concord	Muskingum College Library
Oberlin	Oberlin College Library
Oxford	Miami University, Alumni Library
Portsmouth	Portsmouth Public Library
Rio Grande	Rio Grande College, Jeanette Albiez Davis Library
Springfield	Warder Public Library
Steubenville	College of Steubenville, Starvaggi Memorial Library
	Public Library of Steubenville and Jefferson County
Tiffin	Heidelberg College, Beeghly Library
Toledo	Toledo-Lucas County Public Library
	University of Toledo Library
Westerville	Otterbein College, Centennial Library
Wooster	College of Wooster, the Andrews Library
Youngstown	Public Library of Youngstown and Mahoning County
	Youngstown State University Library

OKLAHOMA

Ada	East Central State College, Linscheid Library
Alva	Northwestern State College Library
Bartlesville	Bureau of Mines, Petroleum Research Center Library
Bethany	Bethany Nazarene College, R. T. Williams Library

Durant	Southeastern State College Library
Edmond	Central State University Library
Enid	Public Library of Enid and Garfield County
Langston	Langston University, G. Lamar Harrison Library
Muskogee	Muskogee Public Library
Norman	University of Oklahoma Libraries
Oklahoma City	Oklahoma City University Library
	Oklahoma County Library System
	Oklahoma Department of Libraries—*Regional*
Shawnee	Oklahoma Baptist University Library
Stillwater	Oklahoma State University Library
Tahlequah	Northeastern State College, John Vaughan Library
Tulsa	Tulsa City-County Library Commission
	University of Tulsa, McFarlin Library
Weatherford	Southwestern State College Library

OREGON

Ashland	Southern Oregon College Library
Corvallis	Oregon State University Library
Eugene	University of Oregon Library
Forest Grove	Pacific University Library
La Grande	Eastern Oregon College, Walter M. Pierce Library
McMinnville	Linfield College, Northup Library
Monmouth	Oregon College of Education Library
Portland	Department of the Interior, Bonneville Power Administration Library
	Lewis and Clark College, Aubrey R. Watzek Library
	Library Association of Portland
	Portland State University Library—*Regional*
	Reed College Library
Salem	Oregon State Library
	Oregon Supreme Court Library
	Willamette University Library

PENNSYLVANIA

Allentown	Muhlenberg College, Haas Library
Altoona	Altoona Public Library

Bethlehem	Lehigh University, Linderman Library
Blue Bell	Montgomery County Community College, Learning Resources Center
Carlisle	Dickinson College, Boyd Lee Spahr Library
Cheyney	Cheyney State College, Leslie Pinckney Hill Library
Collegeville	Ursinus College, Myrin Library
Doylestown	Bucks County Free Library, Center County Library
East Stroudsburg	East Stroudsburg State College, Kemp Library
Erie	Erie Public Library
Greenville	Thiel College, Langenheim Memorial Library
Harrisburg	State Library of Pennsylvania—*Regional*
Haverford	Haverford College Library
Hazleton	Hazleton Area Public Library
Indiana	Indiana University of Pennsylvania, Rhodes R. Stabley Library
Johnstown	Cambria Public Library
Lancaster	Franklin and Marshall College, Fackenthal Library
Lewisburg	Bucknell University, Ellen Clarke Bertrand Library
Mansfield	Mansfield State College Library
Meadville	Allegheny College, Reis Library
Millersville	Millersville State College, Ganser Library
Monessen	Monessen Public Library
New Castle	New Castle Free Public Library
Newtown	Bucks County Community College Library
Norristown	Montgomery County-Norristown Public Library
Philadelphia	Drexel University Library
	Free Library of Philadelphia
	St. Joseph's College Library
	Temple University, Samuel Paley Library
	University of Pennsylvania, Biddle Law Library
	University of Pennsylvania Library
Pittsburgh	Bureau of Mines, Pittsburgh Research Center Library
	Carnegie Library of Pittsburgh
	Carnegie Library of Pittsburgh, Allegheny Regional Branch

La Roche College, John J. Wright Library

University of Pittsburgh, Hillman Library

Pottsville — Pottsville Free Public Library

Reading — Reading Public Library

Scranton — Scranton Public Library

Shippensburg — Shippensburg State College, Ezra Lehman Memorial Library

Slippery Rock — Slippery Rock State College, Maltby Library

Swarthmore — Swarthmore College Library

University Park — Pennsylvania State University Library

Villanova — Villanova University, School of Law Library

Warren — Warren Library Association, Warren Public Library

Washington — Washington and Jefferson College, Memorial Library

Waynesburg — Waynesburg College Library

West Chester — West Chester State College, Francis Harvey Green Library

Wilkes-Barre — King's College, Corgan Library

Williamsport — Lycoming College Library

York — York Junior College Library

Youngwood — Westmoreland County Community College, Learning Resource Center

PUERTO RICO

Mayaguez — University of Puerto Rico, Mayaguez Campus Library

Ponce — Catholic University of Puerto Rico Library

Rio Piedras — University of Puerto Rico General Library

RHODE ISLAND

Kingston — University of Rhode Island Library

Newport — Naval War College Library

Providence — Brown University, John D. Rockefeller, Jr., Library

Providence College, Phillips Memorial Library

Providence Public Library

Rhode Island College Library

Rhode Island State Library

Warwick	Warwick Public Library
Westerly	Westerly Public Library

SOUTH CAROLINA

Charleston	Baptist College at Charleston Library
	The Citadel Memorial Library
	College of Charleston Library
Clemson	Clemson University Library
Columbia	Benedict College, Starks Library
	Columbia College Library
	South Carolina State Library
	University of South Carolina Undergraduate Library
Conway	University of South Carolina, Coastal Carolina Regional Campus Library
Due West	Erskine College, McCain Library
Florence	Florence County Library
	Francis Marion College, James A. Rogers Library
Greenville	Furman University Library
	Greenville County Library
Greenwood	Lander College Library
Orangeburg	South Carolina State College, Whittaker Library
Rock Hill	Winthrop College Library
Spartanburg	Spartanburg County Public Library

SOUTH DAKOTA

Aberdeen	Northern State College Library
Brookings	South Dakota State University, Lincoln Memorial Library
Pierre	South Dakota State Library
Rapid City	Rapid City Public Library
	South Dakota School of Mines and Technology Library
Sioux Falls	Augustana College, Mikkelsen Library and Learning Resources Center
	Sioux Falls Public Library
Spearfish	Black Hills State College Library

| Vermillion | University of South Dakota, I. D. Weeks Library |
| Yankton | Yankton College, Corliss Lay Library |

TENNESSEE

Bristol	King College Library
Chattanooga	Chattanooga Public Library
Clarksville	Austin Peay State University, Felix G. Woodward Library
Cleveland	Cleveland State Community College Library
Columbia	Columbia State Community College Library
Cookeville	Tennessee Technological University, Jere Whitson Memorial Library
Jackson	Lambuth College, Luther L. Gobbel Library
Jefferson City	Carson-Newman College Library
Johnson City	East Tennessee State University, Sherrod Library
Knoxville	Public Library of Knoxville and Knox County, Lawson McGhee Library
	University of Tennessee Law Library
	University of Tennessee Library
Martin	University of Tennessee at Martin Library
Memphis	Memphis Public Library and Information Center
	Memphis State University, John W. Brister Library
Morristown	Morristown College, Carnegie Library
Murfreesboro	Middle Tennessee State University, Andrew L. Todd Library
Nashville	Fisk University Library
	Joint University Libraries
	Public Library of Nashville and Davidson County
	Tennessee State Library and Archives, State Library Division
	Tennessee State University, Martha M. Brown Memorial Library
Sewanee	University of the South, Jesse Ball duPont Library

TEXAS

| Abilene | Hardin-Simmons University Library |
| Arlington | Arlington Public Library |

	University of Texas at Arlington Library
Austin	Texas State Law Library
	Texas State Library—*Regional*
	University of Texas at Austin Library
	University of Texas, Lyndon B. Johnson School of Public Affairs Library
	University of Texas, School of Law Library
Baytown	Lee College Library
Beaumont	Lamar University Library
Brownwood	Howard Payne College, Walker Memorial Library
Canyon	West Texas State University Library
College Station	Texas Agricultural and Mechanical University Library
Commerce	East Texas State University Library
Corsicana	Navarro Junior College Library
Dallas	Bishop College, Zale Library
	Dallas Baptist College Library
	Dallas Public Library
	Southern Methodist University, Fondren Library
	University of Texas at Dallas Library
	University of Texas Health Science Center at Dallas
Denton	North Texas State University Library
Edinburg	Pan American University Library
El Paso	El Paso Public Library
	University of Texas at El Paso Library
Fort Worth	Forth Worth Public Library
	Texas Christian University, Mary Couts Burnett Library
Galveston	Rosenberg Library
Houston	Houston Public Library
	North Harris County College, Learning Resource Center
	Rice University, Fondren Library
	University of Houston Library
Huntsville	Sam Houston State University, Estill Library
Irving	Irving Municipal Library
Kingsville	Texas Arts and Industries University Library

Lake Jackson	Brazosport College Library
Laredo	Laredo Junior College Library
Longview	Nicholson Memorial Public Library
Lubbock	Texas Tech University Library—*Regional*
Marshall	Wiley College, Cole Library
Mesquite	Mesquite Public Library
Nacogdoches	Stephen F. Austin State University Library
Plainview	Wayland Baptist College, Van Howeling Memorial Library
San Angelo	Angelo State University, Porter Henderson Library
San Antonio	St. Mary's University Library
	San Antonio College Library
	San Antonio Public Library, Business and Science Department
	Trinity University Library
	University of Texas at San Antonio Library
San Marcos	Southwest Texas State University Library
Seguin	Texas Lutheran College, Blumberg Memorial Library
Sherman	Austin College, Arthur Hopkins Library
Texarkana	Texarkana Community College, Palmer Memorial Library
Victoria	University of Houston, Victoria Center Library
Waco	Baylor University Library
Wichita Falls	Midwestern University, Moffett Library

UTAH

Cedar City	Southern Utah State College Library
Ephraim	Snow College, Lucy A. Phillips Library
Logan	Utah State University, Merrill Library and Learning Resources Center—*Regional*
Ogden	Weber State College Library
Provo	Brigham Young University Law Library
	Brigham Young University Library
Salt Lake City	University of Utah, Eccles Medical Sciences Library
	University of Utah, Law Library

University of Utah, Marriott Library
Utah State Library Commission, Documents Library
Utah State Supreme Court Law Library

VERMONT

Burlington	University of Vermont, Bailey Library
Castleton	Castleton State College, Calvin Coolidge Library
Johnson	Johnson State College, John Dewey Library
Lyndonville	Lyndon State College, Samuel Reed Hall Library
Middlebury	Middlebury College, Egbert Starr Library
Montpelier	Vermont Department of Libraries
Northfield	Norwich University Library
Putney	Windham College, Dorothy Culbertson Marvin Memorial Library

VIRGIN ISLANDS

Charlotte Amalie (St. Thomas)	College of the Virgin Islands, Ralph M. Paiewonsky Library
	St. Thomas Public Library
Christiansted (St. Croix)	Christiansted Public Library

VIRGINIA

Blacksburg	Virginia Polytechnic Institute, Newman Library
Bridgewater	Bridgewater College, Alexander Mack Memorial Library
Charlottesville	University of Virginia, Alderman Library—*Regional*
	University of Virginia Law Library
Chesapeake	Chesapeake Public Library System
Danville	Danville Community College Library
Emory	Emory and Henry College Library
Fairfax	George Mason College of the University of Virginia, Fenwick Library
Fredericksburg	Mary Washington College, E. Lee Trinkle Library
Hampden-Sydney	Hampden-Sydney College, Eggleston Library

Harrisonburg	Madison College, Madison Memorial Library
Hollins College	Hollins College, Fishburn Library
Lexington	Virginia Military Institute, Preston Library
	Washington and Lee University, Cyrus Hall Mc-Cormick Library
Martinsville	Patrick Henry Community College Library
Norfolk	Armed Forces Staff College Library
	Norfolk Public Library
	Old Dominion University, Hughes Memorial Library
Petersburg	Virginia State College, Johnston Memorial Library
Quantico	Federal Bureau of Investigation Academy Library
	Marine Corps Schools, James Carson Breckinridge Library
Richmond	State Law Library
	U.S. Court of Appeals, Fourth Circuit Library
	University of Richmond, Boatwright Memorial Library
	Virginia Commonwealth University, James Branch Cabell Library
	Virginia State Library
Roanoke	Roanoke Public Library
Salem	Roanoke College Library
Williamsburg	William and Mary College Library
Wise	Clinch Valley College, John Cook Wyllie Library

WASHINGTON

Bellingham	Western Washington State College, Wilson Library
Cheney	Eastern Washington State College Library
Ellensburg	Central Washington State College Library
Everett	Everett Public Library
Olympia	Evergreen State College Library
	Washington State Library—*Regional*
Port Angeles	Port Angeles Public Library
Pullman	Washington State University Library
Seattle	Seattle Public Library
	University of Washington Library

	University of Washington, School of Law Library
Spokane	Spokane Public Library
Tacoma	Tacoma Public Library
	University of Puget Sound, Collins Memorial Library
Vancouver	Fort Vancouver Regional Library
Walla Walla	Whitman College, Penrose Memorial Library

WEST VIRGINIA

Athens	Concord College Library
Bluefield	Bluefield State College Library
Charleston	Kanawha County Public Library
	West Virginia Department of Archives and History Library
Elkins	Davis and Elkins College Library
Fairmont	Fairmont State College Library
Glenville	Glenville State College, Robert F. Kidd Library
Huntington	Marshall University Library
Institute	West Virginia State College Library
Morgantown	West Virginia University Library—*Regional*
Salem	Salem College Library
Shepherdstown	Shepherd College Library
Weirton	Mary H. Weir Public Library

WISCONSIN

Appleton	Lawrence University, Samuel Appleton Library
Beloit	Beloit College Libraries
Eau Claire	University of Wisconsin, Eau Claire, William D. McIntyre Library
Fond du Lac	Fond du Lac Public Library
Green Bay	University of Wisconsin at Green Bay Library
La Crosse	La Crosse Public Library
	University of Wisconsin-La Crosse, Murphy Library
Madison	Department of Public Instruction, Division for Library Services, Reference and Loan Library
	Madison Public Library

	State Historical Society Library—*Regional,* in co-operation with University of Wisconsin, Memorial Library
	University of Wisconsin, Memorial Library
	Wisconsin State Library
Milwaukee	Alverno College Library
	Milwaukee County Law Library
	Milwaukee Public Library—*Regional*
	Mount Mary College Library
	Oklahoma Neighborhood Library
	University of Wisconsin-Milwaukee Library
Oshkosh	University of Wisconsin-Oshkosh, Forrest R. Polk Library
Platteville	University of Wisconsin-Platteville, Elton S. Karrmann Library
Racine	Racine Public Library
River Falls	University of Wisconsin-River Falls, Chalmer Davee Library
Stevens Point	University of Wisconsin-Stevens Point, Learning Resources Center
Superior	Superior Public Library
	University of Wisconsin-Superior, Jim Dan Hill Library
Waukesha	Waukesha Public Library
Wausau	Marathon County Public Library
Whitewater	University of Wisconsin-Whitewater, Harold Andersen Library

WYOMING

Casper	Natrona County Public Library
Cheyenne	Wyoming State Library—*Regional*
Laramie	University of Wyoming, Coe Library
Powell	Northwest Community College Library
Riverton	Central Wyoming College Library
Rock Springs	Western Wyoming College Library
Sheridan	Sheridan College, Mary Brown Kooi Library

INDEX

Numbers in boldface type represent main headings